MYTHS AND LEGENDS
OF **TORRES STRAIT**

MYTHS AND LEGENDS
OF **TORRES STRAIT** collected and translated by MARGARET LAWRIE

TAPLINGER
PUBLISHING
COMPANY
New York

PUBLISHER'S NOTE

The University of Queensland Press gratefully acknowledges the help of the State Government of Queensland, and in particular would like to thank the Department of Aboriginal and Island Affairs for their co-operation and assistance, both to the author and to the publisher. Without their aid, the illustrations and the recording, which are so essential to this book, could not have been included.

First Published in the United States in 1971 by
Taplinger Publishing Co., Inc.
New York, New York

Copyright © 1970 University of Queensland Press,
St. Lucia, Queensland.

International Standard Book Number 0-8008-5464-0
Library of Congress Catalog Card
Number 73-163219

Printed In Australia

Designed by Cyrelle

73-9704

FOR THE PEOPLE OF TORRES STRAIT

ACKNOWLEDGMENTS

I am indebted to many people. Without their help and encouragement this book could hardly have been begun, and it would certainly not have been completed.

The late Mr. J. C. A. Pizzey, first as Minister for Education and Aboriginal and Island Affairs, and then as Premier of Queensland, and the late Sir Fred Schonell, Vice-Chancellor of the University of Queensland, fostered the project from its inception.

Mr. P. J. Killoran, Director of Aboriginal and Island Affairs in Queensland, than whom no one has more knowledge of Torres Strait and Torres Strait Islanders, gave me wise counsel when I needed it. I thank him and his staff—in particular, those members based at Thursday Island—for the co-operation, always freely given, which enabled me to work in that remote region where anyone engaged in research is wholly dependent on departmental facilities for transport, communication, and supply.

I am grateful to Dr. Colin Roderick, Professor of English at the University College of Townsville (now the James Cook University of North Queensland) for guidance during the early stages of the work.

In 1967, the Australian Institute of Aboriginal Studies made a Uher tape recorder and tapes available to me for use in Torres Strait. I thank the Principal, Mr. F. D. McCarthy, for this practical assistance. He and his staff made me very welcome whenever I called at the Institute.

Professor Peter Lawrence, until recently Head of the Department of Anthropology and Sociology at the University of Queensland, has given me a great deal of much appreciated help and guidance in the use of anthropological terms. However, he is an expert and I am an amateur, and if any errors remain the responsibility is entirely mine.

Mr. Selwyn Everist, Queensland Government Botanist, and members of his staff kindly identified plant specimens from Murray Island. The nature of my indebtedness to Mr. B. P. Lambert, Director of National Mapping, is separately acknowledged.

Those who helped with the translations were Wagea Waia and Alfred Aniba of Saibai; Tabepa Mau of Dauan; Namai Pabai and Kada Waireg of Boigu; Maurie Eseli and William Min of Mabuiag; Joe Mairu, Tupo Nona, Ben Nona, and Fr Mara of Badu; Wees Nawia of Kubin; Murray Lui of Coconut Island; Getano Lui of Yam Island; Ned Mosby of Yorke Island; and George Passi of Murray Island. All were endlessly patient teachers, explaining customs and idiomatic expressions—and going on explaining them—until they were satisfied that I understood.

Kala Waia of Saibai, Ephraim Bani of

Mabuiag, Ngailu Bani of Kubin, and Segar Passi of Murray Island illustrated stories from their respective islands, and Segar Passi also provided the numerous water-colour drawings of fauna of the area. The two pencil sketches of *larerkep* were done by George Passi, also of Murray Island. Derek Cumner, missionary-carpenter, drew the sketches of Malo dancers especially for this book.

My husband Ellis understood the necessity for me to be absent from home for long periods; my sons, Greig, David, and Roderick, cheerfully 'batched" for months on end; my daughter Edith typed the whole manuscript: the collection of the myths and legends of Torres Strait was a family involvement.

I would like also to thank my publishers, the University of Queensland Press, in particular the Manager, Mr. Frank Thompson, for his interest and assistance. The job of editing fell to my good friend, Shirley Hockings, whom I thank from the bottom of my heart for transmuting a beginner's effort into a book.

Finally, I express my gratitude to the Queensland Government for their generous financial grant to the publishers. The Premier, Mr. J. Bjelke-Petersen, and the Minister for Aboriginal and Island Affairs, Mr. N. Hewitt, knowing Torres Strait as they do, understand how much it will mean to the Islands people to see their stories illustrated in colour and to have some of their old songs on a record.

CONTENTS

List of Illustrations xiii
List of Maps xv

Note on Preparation of Maps xv
Introduction xvii

STORIES FROM THE WESTERN ISLANDS

Muralag, Gialag, Muri, Nurupai

Pötikain and Ngiangu 5
Waubin 6
Ialbuz 9
Zalagi and the Mari 10
Utua Ninia 11
Dupul and Mumag 12
Aiwali of Muri 13
Waiaba 15

Nagi

Naga 19

Mua

Karakarkula 23
Aukam and Tiai 24
Sik 27
Im 29
The Seven Blind Brothers 30
Wamin Ngurbum 33
Burumnaskai 34
Karum 36
Kuduluk and Kui 37
Burum 38

Muta 39
Raramai 41
Yelub and His Dog 42
Usius 43
Gora and the Buk 44
Goba 45

Badu

Bia 49
Wad and Zigin 53
The Four Beautiful Daughters 55
Dokere 56
Sesere 57
Iawar 61
Biu 62
Kuaka 62
Tubu and the Seven Sisters 63
The Dogai of Zurat 65
Mutuk 68
Wawa 70
Greedy Goba 73
Beug and the Sarup 74
Waii and Sobai 76
Pitai 78

Mabuiag

How Fire Was Brought to Torres
    Strait   83
Sisters Who Quarrelled   85
Kamutnab   85
Wameal   87
Deibui and Teikui   87
The Saga of Kuiam   88
Dogai I   101
Ug   104
Maiwasa   107
The Markai of Tawapagai   108
Amipuru   109
Saurkeke   110
Gigi   113
Waiat   115
Kama   118
Tawaka, the Greedy Man   119
Crocodile Play   120
Waiaba   121
Gi of Dabangai   123

Dauan

Kusa Kap   127
Kabai   132
Gabai   134
Taikoko   138
Kogia   139
The Kiwai Raiders   143

Saibai

The First Man at Saibai   153
Nima and Poipoi   157
The Story of Ait Kadal   161
Wakemab   166
Susui and Dengam   171
Karbai and Pukat   172
Sui   173

Kasakuik   177
Kongasau   178
Wamaladi   180
Metarawai   182
Roa Kabuwam   182
How Baira Got a Wife   185
Agburug   186
Maigi   189
Girbar   190
The Pet Crocodile   192
Biu   194
Aukam   195
Dauan   196
Warupudamaizinga   197
Mibu and the Coconut   198
Amagi   199
Dagmet   200

Boigu

Boigu   207
Kiba   209
Dogai Metakurab   210
Geinau and Jeiai   212
Damak and Daram   214
Waireg   216
Ganalai Dogai   218
Möibu and Bazi   219
The Discovery of the Garden Land
    at Padin   222
Kererum   222
Bukia   224
Wawa   225
Darak and Göidan   227
Podepode and Ngukurpodepode   229
Maui and Usuru   230
Mau and Matang   232
Ausi and Dubua   234
Dugama, Maker of Dugong Magic   236
Babaia and Sagewa   238
Garuge   240

STORIES FROM THE CENTRAL ISLANDS

Masig

Igowa	245
The Diamond Fish	246
Gaibida	247
Umi Markail	248

Iama

Mokan	251
Sigai	252

Kawai—Part I	255
—Part II	256
Uzu, the White Dogai	257
Maida	259
Dugama	260

Waraber

Sagerwazer	269

STORIES FROM THE EASTERN ISLANDS

Ugar

Badi and the Sabei	275
The Snake of Apro	276
Zub and the Lamar	276
The Two Spirit Women of Daoma Kes	278
The Lamar Who Became a Rainbow	279

Erub

Maizab Kaur	283
Rebes and Id	284
Aib	288
Didipapa and Gorarasiasi	289
Imermer and Kikmermer	291

Mer

Gelam	297
Apinini and Sidipuar	300
The Story of Peibri	301
Mukeis	302
Pop and Kod	303
Tagai	304
Nageg and Geigi	306
Markep and Sarkep	312
The Story of Meidu	314

Kaperkaper the Cannibal	316
Kultut	318
The Muiar	319
Paimi a Nawanawa	320
Beizam	321
Terer	322
Kol	324
Gedor of Leiwag	324
Korseim	325
Malo	326
Malo ra Gelar	337
Said	339
Kos and Abob	342
Waiat	344
Deumer	345
Wakai and Kuskus	346
The Origin of Mosquitoes	349
Iruam	350
Adba—Part I	357
—Part II	358
Bila	359
Ganomi and Palai	360
Nilar Makrem	363
Paslag	365
Bai	366

APPENDIX

Norinori	370

LIST OF ILLUSTRATIONS

Wees Nawia of Kubin attired for the modern dance which derives from the myth, "Waubin"   7

Dugong-hunter   16

Saulal time, the season of mating turtle   22

Im (as Banded Wobbegong)   30

Kuduluk ("cuckoo")   37

Mota Charlie, one of the story-tellers   51

The light-coloured dugong of West Torres Strait   58

Sesere (as willy-wagtail)   60

The bird which Kuaka became. The sketch in the corner shows Kuaka standing on the beach at Badu, imploring her brothers, Tagai and Kang, to come back for her   63

Walek, who brought fire to Torres Strait   83

Kaumain staring at his wife, Kamutnab, and her children (Hamelin Boulders)   86

Kuiam in Daudai (New Guinea)   96

Gumu, where Kuiam lived   98

Maurie Eseli, one of the story-tellers   100

The well called I   103

Amipuru   109

Mabuiag warriors   122

Wellington Aragu posing as *dogai* Giz   129

The Kupamal "landed at Sigain Kup, a small cove, armed themselves, and climbed up the rocks at the back of the beach to an enormous boulder which they tried to roll down into the sea"   145

Rock paintings on the under-surface of a boulder above Sigain Kup   145, 146

Outrigger canoe riding at anchor at high tide, outside Saibai Village   148

Low tide off Saibai Village, exposing mud flats   151

Mesea (or Melewal)   152

Budia (as willy-wagtail)   154

Aniba Asa, one of the story-tellers   155

Enosa Waigana, one of the story-tellers   156

Nima and Poipoi with Binibin   159

A warrior of Ait   164

Warriors of Ait obtaining strength from Adibuia, the stone that glowed   164

The partly submerged natural jetty of sand and dead coral running out from Kagar, at the eastern end of Saibai   167

Wakemab crawling out into the sea after being clubbed by two men of Ait   170

Sui (as swamp bird)   175

Kongasau and Adasakalaig   179

Baira and Agburug (as man)   187

Girbar, holding the new varieties of sugarcane, taro, and banana which she brought back to Saibai from the sky   191

The coconut palm which grew in the form of a cross after being struck by lightning   191

Dogai Dagmet   201

Sibika, with his pronged fish-spear and a string of fish   202

Head of harpoon-spear (*wap*), with harpoon (*kuiur*) 204

Poised to jump with his *wap* and harpoon a dugong 205

Geinau (or *deumer*), the Torres Strait pigeon, eating the fruit of the wild plum, *ubar* (or *eneo*) 217

The stone dugong at Samar used in making dugong-magic 237

Bu shells at Waraber arranged round the spot at which skulls collected in former times have since been buried 267

Kaubet (black reef heron) 275

Sir (white reef heron) 275

Sabei, or *bologor* (unicorn fish) 275

Put (decorative armband worn on upper arms) 286

Kadik (bracer, or armguard) 286

Meriam *ares le* (fighting man) 287

A Meriam wearing the head-dress, *dari* 293

The islands of Waier and Dauar photographed from Murray Island 295

Dela Mopwali, one of the story-tellers 296

Deger, or *dangal* (dugong) 299

The island of Dauar, showing the two hills woven by the sisters, Sidipuar and Apinini 300

Marou, one of the story-tellers 301

Peibri sor (stingray) 301

Pilauar (as sea-bird) 302

Serar (as sea-bird) 302

Dau Tom standing behind Tagai's canoe (the long black stone) and Kareg (the red stone) at the edge of the reef at Las 305

Tup (a sardine, of the kind known as Kos) 306

Weres (sardine scoop) 306

Head of a man wearing *larerkep* (ornamental "fish-eyes") 307

Bozar (crested mud goby) 308

Gas (mudskipper) 308

Wirwir (mud-hopper) 308

Paris (Long Tom) 308

Nageg (as triggerfish) 309

Geigi (as Great trevally) 309

Wrapped bananas 311

Zirar (as lizard) 315

Monan (as lizard) 315

Ab (as fish) 315

Wid (as fish) 315

Dibadiba (a small land-bird) 315

Kultut 318

Paimi and Nawanawa (as birds) 320

Melpal umen (eel) 322

Beizam (hammerhead shark) 328

Arti (octopus) 329

Larerkep (ornamental "fish-eyes") 330

Deumer le (Torres Strait pigeon man), a Malo dancer 331

Seuriseuri (starfish) 331

An impression of one of the two masks exhibited at Malo-Bomai initiation ceremonies 335

Wasikor, sacred Malo drum 335

Keparem le (stick man), a Malo dancer 336

Bezar (a small fish) 338

Neis keremkerem kaba (banana plant, of the kind which bears two heads of bananas simultaneously) 339

Kamosar (epaulette shark) 339

At (blue-spotted stingaree) 340

Goar (cowtail or fantail ray) 340

Said (as *womer*, the man-o'-war hawk) 341

Said (as man) 341

Kos (as sardine) 342

Abob (as blowfly) 342

Neud (a green fish) 342

Warib (as garfish) 342

Repair of a stone fish-trap (*sai*) at Murray Island, February 1967 343

Au kosker (as fish) 344

Tole (a small brown sea-bird) 345

Karor ("curlew") 345

The yam, *ketai* (or *kutai*) 346, 347

Old-style canoe 347

Turtle of the kind known as *nam* 347

Kiriskiris ti (a small land-bird)   348
Beuger (booby)   348
Noreb ti (Sun bird)   349
Deo (as sea-bird)   350
The leaf of *wez*, a croton   354
Te pipi and Te sabersaber roasting *ager* in their earth-oven   355

Maiu (golden trevally)   357
Keupai (a fish, the bar-checked Wrasse)   362
Baur (a three-pronged fish spear)   363
Two of the many *puleb* (rudely worked pumice figures) at Leiwag, Murray Island   364
Uzer (canoe paddles)   367

LIST OF MAPS

Torres Strait   xvi
Muralag (Prince of Wales Island), Gialag (Friday Island), Nurupai (Horn Island)   4
Nagi (Mt. Ernest Island), Mua (Banks Island), and Badu (Mulgrave Island)   18
Mabuiag (Jervis Island)   82
Dauan   126
Saibai   150
Route taken by Nima in Binibin   159
Boigu (Talbot Island)   206
Masig (Yorke Island)   244
Iama (Turtlebacked Island or Yam Island)   250
Waraber (Sue Island)   268
Ugar (Stephens Island)   274
Erub (Darnley Island)   282
Mer (Murray Island)   294
Dauar and Waier   294

NOTE ON PREPARATION OF MAPS

The maps of Mabuiag, Dauan, Saibai, Boigu, Waraber, Iama, Masig, Ugar, Mer, and Waier and Dauar have been prepared from original sketches made during my stays at those islands. In every case I had help from an Islander with the outline and principal physical features.

I acknowledge with gratitude the expert help given me by the Director of National Mapping, Mr. B. P. Lambert, which enabled me to obtain an accurate outline of Mua, Badu, and Nagi, and of Erub.

However, the islands of Torres Strait are not big islands, and for most of them maps on a scale large enough to permit the detail necessary for precise location of the physical features and "story" places mentioned in the myths and legends are not available—indeed, the reliability diagram on the most recent maps of Torres Strait (1968), prepared as part of the national mapping programme, marks the greater part of the region as "fair" only. But Torres Strait embodies a people's legends and history, and because the old men who still remember the names of places which have a meaningful part in their Island heritage grow fewer with each succeeding year, it seemed necessary to record those places as best I could—with the help of the Islanders—while there still remained opportunity to do so.

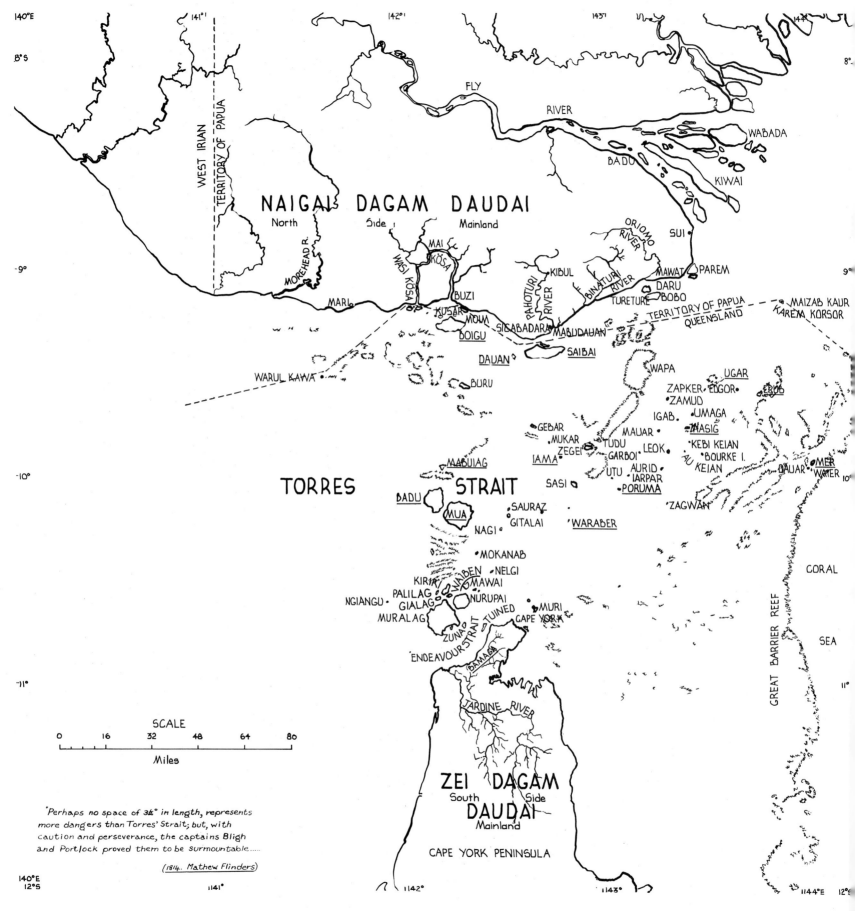

140°E · 141° · 142° · 143° · 144°

8°S · 8°

WEST IRIAN
TERRITORY OF PAPUA

FLY

RIVER

WABADA

BADU

KIWAI

NAIGAI DAGAM DAUDAI
North · Side · Mainland

MOREHEAD R.

ORIOMO RIVER

SUI

MAI
KOSA

WASI KOSA

-9° · 9°

BUZI

MARI

KUSAR

MOM

BOIGU

SIGABADARA

MABUDAUAN

MAWAT · PAREM
DARU
BOBO
TURETURE

KIBUL

PAHOTURI RIVER

BINATURI RIVER

TERRITORY OF PAPUA
QUEENSLAND

MAIZAB KAUR
KAREM KORSOR

DAUAN

SAIBAI

WARUL KAWA

BURU

WAPA

UGAR

ZAPKER · EDGOR
ZAMUD

EROB

IGAB

UMAGA

MASIG

GEBAR

MUKAR
ZEGEI

MAUAR

TUDU
GARBOI

LEOK

KEBI KEIAN
BOURKE I.
AU KEIAN

DAUAR · MER
WAIER

MABUIAG

IAMA

UTU
AURID
IARPAR
PORUMA

SASI

ZAGWAN

-10° · 10°

TORRES · STRAIT

BADU

MUA

SAURAZ
GITALAI

WARABER

NAGI

MOKANAB

NELGI

CORAL

KIRI
PALILAG
GIALAG

WAIBEN
MAWAI

NURUPAI

NGIANGU

MURALAG

TUINED

MURI
CAPE YORK

SEA

ZUNA

ENDEAVOUR STRAIT

BAMAGA

GREAT BARRIER REEF

-11° · 11°

JARDINE RIVER

SCALE

0 · 16 · 32 · 48 · 64 · 80

Miles

ZEI DAGAM
South · Side
DAUDAI
Mainland

*Perhaps no space of 3½° in length, represents
more dangers than Torres' Strait; but, with
caution and perseverance, the captains Bligh
and Portlock proved them to be surmountable.....

(1814. Mathew Flinders)

CAPE YORK PENINSULA

140°E
12°S · 1141° · 1142° · 1143° · 1144°E · 12°S

TORRES STRAIT

The myths and legends contained in this book were recorded and translated at the places which are underlined.

INTRODUCTION

Four years ago, when the people of the Torres Strait Islands told me that they feared their old stories were being forgotten, I promised my help in the task of gathering them together. If I could do this and with the Islanders' help translate them and put them in a book, the old tales would live on and be always available—not only to the Islanders, wherever they might be, but to all others with an interest in them.

For a generation or more, Torres Strait Islanders have been dispersing to mainland Australia. Torres Strait Islanders' children, born since their parents left their island homes, have never seen—and may never see—the islands of their forbears. And increasingly, people in mainland communities would like to know the background of the Torres Strait Islanders who live and work among them.

Ask a Torres Strait Islander where he comes from, and he will name one island. After further questioning you will learn that he calls that island "my homeland" and refers to those who have been born to it as "my countrymen". Look for that island in your atlas, and you are hardly likely to find it. In all probability you will see nothing but a narrow, empty sea passage separating the most northerly tip of Australia from New Guinea—nothing to indicate that the strait is actually a maze of reefs and rocks and islands. This fact is only to be learned by reference to large-scale maps and charts of the region itself. "Perhaps no space of $3\frac{1}{2}°$ in length, presents more dangers than Torres' Strait", wrote Flinders in his Introduction to *A Voyage to Terra Australis*.

Nor will you find it easy to obtain accurate facts and figures about the island in which you have become interested, nor, for that matter, about any of the other islands in Torres Strait, for there are very few books about Torres Strait to be had from a bookshop. There is a fascinating wealth of material upon which to draw, but it is contained for the most part in books which have long been out of print and in Government records. You will have to conduct your own research at libraries in the capital cities if you want to satisfy your curiosity about the Torres Strait Islands and the people who belong to them.

So it is necessary at this point to introduce the general reader to Torres Strait itself and to define the region in which the stories in this book originated. This can be done quickly by quoting a few facts from historical records.

Torres and Prado, in 1606, made the first European passage through Torres Strait, but it is to "our celebrated captain James Cook" that credit goes for "clearing up the doubt which, till then, existed, of the actual separation of Terra Australis from New Guinea" when he "passed through Endeavour's Strait, between Cape York and the Prince of Wales' Islands" in 1770.[1] And to Cook also we owe our first description of the Melanesian people of the island world of Torres' Strait (as it was termed for the first time by Alexander Dalrymple in 1769).[2] For, in Cook's *Journal*, written in his own hand, under the entry made off Possession Island[3] for Wednesday, 22 August 1770, appear these words: ". . . one man who had a bow and a bundle of Arrows, the first we have seen on this coast . . .", and a little further on: ". . . two or three of the Men we saw Yesterday had on pretty large breast plates which we supposed were made of Pearl Oysters Shells, this was a thing as well as the Bow and Arrows we had not seen before . . ."

On his second voyage through Torres Strait in 1792, Bligh took possession of "all the islands seen in the Strait, for his Britannic Majesty George III". Eighty-seven years later, in the Schedule to the Queensland Coast Islands Act of 1879, we have a clear definition of the boundaries of Torres Strait: "Certain Islands in Torres Straits and lying between the Continent of Australia and Island of New Guinea that is to say all Islands included within a line drawn from Sandy Cape northward to the south-eastern limit of Great Barrier Reefs thence following the line of the Great Barrier Reefs to their north-eastern extremity near the latitude of nine and a half degrees south thence in a north-westerly direction embracing East Anchor and Bramble Cays thence from Bramble Cays in a line west by south (south seventy-nine degrees west) true embracing Warrior Reef Saibai and Tuan Islands thence diverging in a north-westerly direction so as to embrace the group known as the Talbot Islands thence to and embracing the Deliverance Islands and onwards in a west by south direction (true) to the meridian of one hundred and thirty-eight degrees of east longitude."[4]

By that time pearl-shelling and bêche-de-mer industries were well established in the area; the London Missionary Society had been at work for eight years (since July 1871); and the Queensland Government had already assumed responsibility for the well-being of the people of the islands in Torres Strait.

The stories in this collection were obtained at thirteen islands, all of which are protected and reserved by the Queensland Government for the

1. Flinders, in the Introduction to *A Voyage to Terra Australis*.
2. *Memoir concerning the Chagos and Adjacent Islands* (London, 1786), p. 4.
3. The manuscript of Cook's *Journal* is in the National Library, Canberra.
   MacGillivray obtained the Island name Bêdanug for Possession Island (*Narrative of the Voyage of H.M.S. Rattlesnake* [1852], II, 315). For Bêdanug we should possibly understand Bedalag, since "l" is often rendered "n" in Island speech, and "a" (as in "ah") as "u" (as in "hut"). *Lag* means island.
4. *Queensland Statutes*, Vol. I (Brisbane, 1911).

Torres Strait Islands people. As a result, the Islanders, despite nearly a century of continuous and increasing contact with European ways and thought, have been able to retain unbroken links with their past. They have never been ousted from the islands to which they belong. These are the people who have made a conscious effort, sustained over a period of four years, to pass on to the general reader, whether he live in Torres Strait or elsewhere, as much as is possible at this late date of that part of their heritage which is embodied in legend and myth.

Between 1965 and 1968 I spent the equivalent of two full years in Torres Strait. The islands at which I stayed were Boigu, Saibai, Dauan, Mabuiag, Badu, and Mua on the Western side of the Strait; Sue, Coconut, Yam, and Yorke Islands in the Central group; and Stephens, Darnley, and Murray Islands in the Eastern division. If we except those in the immediate vicinity of the administrative centre, Thursday Island, they are the only inhabited Torres Strait Islands today. They are home for nearly 4,000 people.[5]

I visited all these islands at least four times, and I also stayed at Bamaga near the tip of Cape York Peninsula, which became the home of many Islanders from Saibai shortly after the end of World War II. The length of my stay at an island at any one time varied from two and a half months, as at Murray Island in 1968, to a day or a night, as at Stephens and Coconut Islands in 1966 and 1967. It was impossible to judge beforehand how long it would take to collect the stories at an island. Some islands proved rich in stories, some poor. Besides, the climate for story-telling varied from island to island. It was necessary for the people and me to get to know each other at each island in turn, and I found that without taking time to obtain at least a working knowledge of two languages—three, if one counts Island pidgin—I could not come within reach of providing an adequate translation. Rather more was involved than arriving at an island, saying, "The people at other islands have told me their stories for inclusion in a book, so that they will not be lost. Will you do the same, please?" and then setting up my tape recorder.

The student and the specialist have long had available to them the stories collected by Haddon, leader of the Cambridge Anthropological Expedition to Torres Strait in 1898. These appear in the published reports of the expedition,[6] together with summaries of the incidents of anthropological significance in each tale.

Regrettably, it was not possible for members of the Cambridge Expedition to concentrate attention on more than two islands, Mer and Mabuiag, because their visit was limited to four months. They were, therefore, unable to attempt collections of stories from every island inhabited at that time. In the final volume of the *Reports* (Cambridge, 1935),

5. The distribution of the population is: Boigu, 320; Saibai, 280; Dauan, 130; Mabuiag, 230; Badu, 650; Mua, 400 (at Kubin, 150; at Gerain, 20; at St. Paul's Mission, 230); Sue Island, 90; Coconut Island, 120; Yam Island, 300; Yorke Island, 160; Stephens Island, 19; Darnley Island, 300; Murray Island, 500. There are between 500 and 559 Saibai Islanders (chiefly) at Bamaga. (These figures were given by the Director of Aboriginal and Island Affairs, June 1969.)

6. *Reports of the Cambridge Anthropological Expedition to Torres Straits* (Cambridge, 1901–1935), Volumes I–VI. Many references to this work follow, so the shortened title *Reports* is used hereafter.

Haddon includes summaries of stories recorded by Landtman[7] and other stories which were sent to him because of his lifelong interest in all matters concerning Torres Strait.

Having had no training in anthropology I can offer no more than translations, and, indeed, I could not have made even this contribution had it not been for the constant help and supervision I received from Islanders. Between us we have attempted to preserve as faithfully as we were able every tale that is remembered and told in Torres Strait today. It is pleasing to report that no important story collected by Haddon has been forgotten during the seventy years that have elapsed since the Cambridge Expedition visited Torres Strait, and, in addition, that it has been possible to add to the number of myths and legends which can be saved for the Islands people.

With the exception of the slight body of tales obtained from Yam and Yorke (Central Islands), and Erub and Ugar (Eastern Islands), where pidgin is spoken by most people, all the stories in this book were first told and recorded in one or other of the two languages of Torres Strait, Mabuiag and Meriam. Those from all the Western Islands were told in Mabuiag, which "has been shown to have relations in structure to the Australian" language;[8] and those from the Eastern island, Mer, were told in Meriam, which is a very complicated Non-Austronesian language belonging to the Kiwai group of languages (of the Fly River mouth and neighbouring coast of Papua).[9] In former times, the language spoken in the Central division was a dialect of Mabuiag.

The stories have seemed to arrange themselves in two main groups, those from the Western Islands, and those from the Eastern Islands. In between are the stories, slight in number, from the Central Islands, which, with one exception—a story, "Sigai", which has a religious significance that links it with Mer, an Eastern Island—are akin to those from the Western Islands. So, the overall organization of the book follows this pattern: first, the big group of stories from the Western Islands; second, the small collection from the Central Islands; and third, those from the Eastern Islands. This arrangement also happens to correspond generally with the broad physical divisions of the islands of Torres Strait, which, moving from west to east, comprise the old, high islands, as well as the two low, mangrove-fringed islands, Saibai and Boigu, of West Torres Strait; the coral cays of Central Torres Strait; and the newer, richer islands of volcanic origin of East Torres Strait.

Within each of the three main sections, the stories have been arranged island by island, the reason for this being that with few exceptions stories are limited in their telling to their island of origin.

From the beginning, I found maps necessary for my own understanding of the stories, so maps have been included for those who are not familiar

7. *The Folk-Tales of the Kiwai Papuans* (Helsingfors, 1917).

8. Ray, the linguist who accompanied the Cambridge Anthropological Expedition (*Reports*, III, 512).

9. Capell (*A Survey of New Guinea Languages*, Sydney University Press, 1969), describes the language of the Eastern Islands of Torres Strait as numeral-dominated, and classifies it as belonging to a sub-type of event-dominated Non-Austronesian languages of New Guinea.

with the region: a general map of the world of the Island people, and a map of each island from which stories originated. All but three were prepared from sketches made while the work of recording and translation was going on; it must be understood that they are approximate only. Without them, however, it would be very difficult to follow action precisely located.

At some islands, artists chose to help in the collection of their myths and legends by illustrating them with water-colours or in pencil or ink; in addition I used the camera freely wherever I went during the recording of the stories. So, in one way or another, all the illustrations in this book were obtained in Torres Strait during the course of the project.

In writing words from each of the Island languages my ear has been my only guide. The vowel sounds I heard seemed similar to those in German, and therefore I adopted the German spelling of vowels whenever I attempted to take down words in Mabuiag or Meriam.

Mention has been made of stories being generally limited in the telling to their islands of origin. I also found that, except in places where the old social structure had completely broken down, further limitations were imposed. In the Western Islands, stories belonged to individual patriclans, whose members alone had the right to learn them.[10] In the Eastern Islands the situation was more complex. Stories could be owned by patriclans, subdivisions of patriclans (patrisubclans or patrilineages), or by individuals.[11] They represented knowledge inherited from the past for the groups and persons owning them, and in each case were restricted to specific group- or individually held territories. Both in the Western Islands and the Eastern Islands, however, only one person in a group was generally acknowledged to know the stories belonging to that group sufficiently well to be able to tell them, and ideally that person was the eldest male in the senior line of descent. At three Western Islands, Saibai, Dauan, and Boigu, before the men told their stories they "called the blood" of their ancestors, in some cases as far back as six or seven generations, each thereby giving proof of his undoubted authority to speak for his people.

When a man told a story in the Western Islands he told it complete. At Murray Island (in the Eastern group), it sometimes happened that a man telling a story said: "There is another part, too. You will have to ask . . . to tell it, because it happened on his land." Trespass is abhorred at this island. Everything is owned, land, reefs, rocks, stones, stars, winds, tracts of sea, and the names of those things are severable and may be separately transferred. A man may speak for what is his, no more. When a girl marries she usually receives dowry land which passes to her son and his heirs and is thus lost to the patrilineage which originally owned it. Therefore, where the action of a story spread over a number of severally owned properties, the story had to be gathered piecemeal, with every one of the several

10. I was told at some Western Islands that in former times young men were taught their patriclan's stories during the period of their initiation.
11. One story, Malo, belonged to all at Murray Island who claimed descent in the male line from the putative first inhabitants of that island. The full details were revealed to the young men when they were initiated into the religion which derived from Malo.

owners contributing the part tied to his land, if it was to be obtained accurately in full. It was tantalizing to be given detail missing from a story and then be enjoined not to use it: "You can't say that. The owner will say it's my lies." With one of the stories, "Terer", the owner—of the land, and the knowledge tied to that land—was absent from Murray Island at the time and I never found him. Thus the story has had to be printed without a detail which I believe was correct anyway. A woman's eldest brother may bestow a name owned by his lineage on one of her children. I came across two instances where stories had been alienated from the names of their central figures at some time in the past. In one, the name survives as the personal name of a man who received it as a gift from the previous owner, but the story has disappeared, presumably either through failure of an owner to provide himself with an heir or failure of an owner to relay it. "Nothing is lost from Murray Island," people said. "It is all here. It belongs to someone." That may once have been so. But today, young men go off to live on the southern mainland and with their going destroy the ability of Murray Island to retain knowledge inherited from the past. When both the owner of the name of a stone (which was once a man) and the owners of the several parts of the story about the man have gone, what is the stone—to them, to their heirs, and to those who stay? I put this question to a Murray Islander. He replied: "The stone still belongs to Murray Island. It has an owner or a caretaker. It is known and precious."

In Torres Strait, until the last member of a clan or a lineage passes away, or an individual owner dies without an heir, stories thus owned are not freed to the rest of the island population. If any of these stories live on, they will do so shorn of their earlier, elaborate, authentic detail. When a whole island is denuded of its people, all its stories may vanish. These have always been lonely islands, where no man had a place except he was born to it. And when all are gone from that place, who knows its past? For whom has it meaning? Nevertheless a few homeless stories survive.

One of these, the first traditional tale to be recorded in Torres Strait, was obtained by MacGillivray[12] at Muralag (Prince of Wales Island) in 1849. It was told to me at another island nearly one hundred and twenty years later by the grandson of a Muralag man, long after the Muralag people as such had ceased to exist.

The fact that ownership of stories is restricted to an island and to groups and individuals within an island accounts in part, I think, for the comparatively few variants obtained. Trespass in the field of another's stories is rare. Besides, there is no feeling of personal involvement in someone else's stories; they are not a part of oneself as one's own stories are; they are of little moment in comparison with one's own. Furthermore, any departure from the version told by the person who has the right to transmit a story

12. *Narrative of the Voyage of H.M.S. Rattlesnake* (1852).

is generally denounced as "lies". These are additional reasons why variants would not easily occur.

I often wished that the Islanders could place their own stories in the publisher's hands direct, with no one else between them and the printed word. Torres Strait is the Islanders' world, and still, today, I think no one really belongs there but the Islanders themselves. They are the fish in the sea, the turtle, the birds; the islands, the reefs, the hills, the rocks and stones; the stars in the sky, which cause thunder and lightning, wind and rain. Torres Strait is its people of the past, the ghosts of its dead, its supernatural beings who are not unlike Island man himself in appearance and behaviour. Torres Strait was created by and from its people—a world that was very largely self-contained.

It is not easy to generalize from these myths and legends, because they vary in content from island to island. Furthermore, the ethnic background of the Mabuiag-speaking islands is different from the background of those islands where Meriam is spoken. So any generalization must be based on the premise that these things are found in Torres Strait, not that these things are found at every island.

I do not know the age of many of the stories, for example those which tell of founders of clans, or first people at islands; but others can be fixed in time at a certain number of generations ago, and so are comparatively recent in origin. All however belong to the old culture, and are told with classic simplicity and precision, as statements of fact; they are essentially word-pictures of men and women, and of what befell them on their island homes.

The Islander was a gardener, a fisherman, a hunter of dugong and turtle, a fighter. Magic and sorcery, dreams, omens, and premonitions permeated his daily living. He was jealous, easily aroused to murderous rage, revengeful and merciless. He was a killer, a hunter of heads. Ritual, ceremony, mourning, decoration of the body, dance and song kept him busy. He was proud, resourceful, and independent. He knew the sea as well as he knew his island and its surrounding reef. If the tales may be taken as evidence, there was little gaiety or fun in the Islander's life.

With his own hands, he fashioned new animal forms from plants and trees, and gave them being by entering them. He went inside existing animals and birds of land and sea, possessed them for a while, and came out—all this without abandoning his human form and personality. He could simply become a fish, or a bird, or an animal.

There is a story from one of the Western Islands of a brother and sister who changed their human form to that of a snake; they were first people (ancestors) of a clan which had the snake as its totem animal. Another story, also from a Western Island, tells of a man who, belonging to the dugong clan in life, spent the first night after his death as a dugong. This man died about 1872, shortly after the London Missionary Society established itself at his island.

There were more classes of supernatural beings in the Western Islands than in the Eastern. One creature, the *dogai*, crops up at every island in the western chain.

The *dogai* was female, sharp-featured and long-eared—she used one ear to sleep on and the other as a cover for her body. She was always looking out for a man to grab as a husband. She appears to have been sub-human in intelligence, but cunning and shrewd. The *dogai* language was a gibberish of the Islanders' tongue.

The first attempt by a Torres Strait Islander to preserve the stories he knew by writing them out was made by Aet Passi at Murray Island in 1898. Five of these are printed in Volume III of the *Cambridge Reports*, together with the interlinear translation attempted by the linguist, Ray, who accompanied the expedition. Aet used corrupt, mission-taught Meriam in writing his stories. The Pasi MS[13] versions are important because their author reached manhood before Murray Island came under Mission influence. They are, therefore, a true voice from the Meriam past. Aet Passi's grandson, George, and I spent many hours on these stories, in an attempt to restore them to pure Meriam and obtain full translations. These are given.

Ned Waria of Mabuiag also wrote out stories in his own language for Ray in 1898.

Since then, a different approach to the preservation of its myths and legends has been made within Torres Strait, through the composition by Islanders of story-songs. These are popular, and are known by everyone at the islands where they were composed.

In this latest attempt by the people of Torres Strait to preserve their myths and legends, this time by first recording them on tape in one or other of the Island languages and then by themselves assisting at their translation into simple English, it has been a privilege and an honour to have a part.

13. So called by Ray. "There is no title to the manuscript, but Pasi concludes with the statement: '*Kaka ditimeda abele jiauali detali abele meb ra nei Ogos* 4, 1898, *a kara nei Passi*', i.e. I began this book write this month of name August 4, 1898, and my name Passi[1]." Ray, *Reports,* III, 228. (The footnote reads: "Elsewhere he spells his name Pasi.") Today, all Aet's descendants spell their surname Passi.

Margaret Lawrie
Evergreen
Westwood
14 September 1969

stories from the

WESTERN ISLANDS

stories from

MURALAG *Prince of Wales Island*

GIALAG *Friday Island*

MURI *Mt. Adolphus Island*

NURUPAI *Horn Island*

—islands now denuded of their original people, but formerly inhabited by Kawalgal (called Kowraregas by MacGillivray, and Kaiwalgal or Kauralgal in the Reports of the Cambridge Expedition).

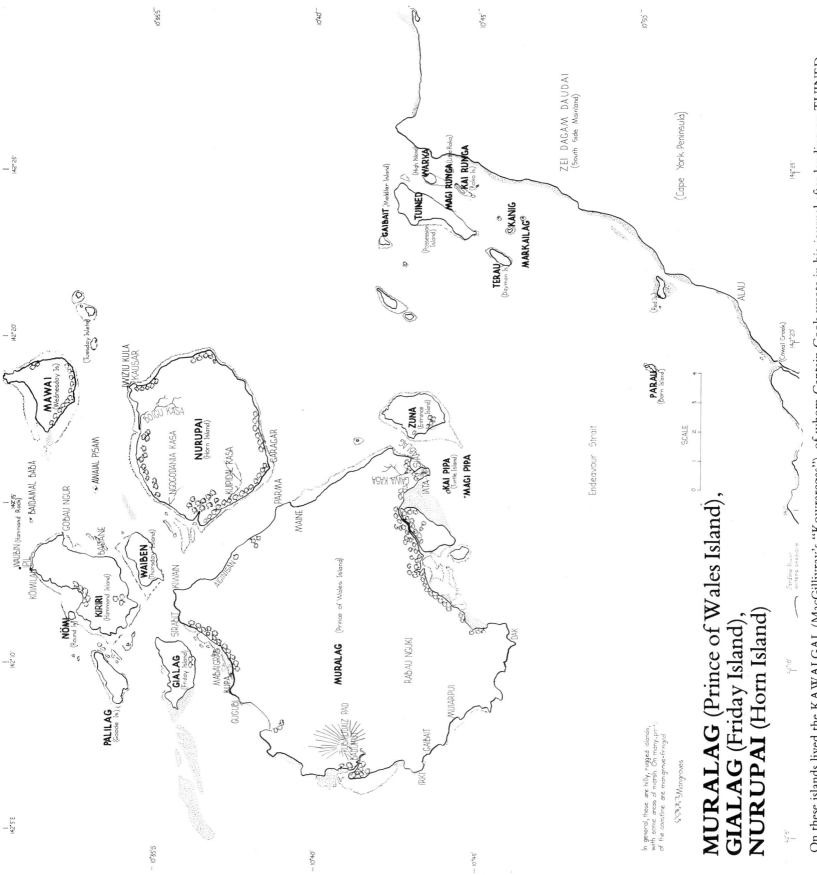

MURALAG (Prince of Wales Island), GIALAG (Friday Island), NURUPAI (Horn Island)

On these islands lived the KAWALGAL (MacGillivray's "Kowraregas"), of whom Captain Cook wrote in his journal after landing on TUINED (Possession Island) on 22 August 1770: "Before and after we Anchor'd we saw a Number of People upon this Island, Arm'd in the same manner as all the others we have seen, Except one man, who had a bow and a bundle of Arrows, the first we have seen upon this Coast . . ." This man

In general, these are hilly, rugged islands, with some areas of marsh. On many parts of the coastline are mangrove-fringed.

:Mangroves

SCALE

0 1 2 3 4

PÖTIKAIN AND NGIANGU [Told by Wees Nawia at Kubin, 2 November 1967]

(The Origin of Booby Island[1])

Pötikain lived by himself at Kupa, a beach on the northern side of Muralag. At very high tides he went to the mouth of the creek nearby to spear *dagai*, a black cat-fish which comes in with such tides; at other tides he fished off the reef with a line.

One morning he walked north from Kupa to the point called Mabaigrab to throw in his line. All day he got not a single bite. He could not understand it. "I have good bait," he said. "Why do the fish not take it?" But he kept on trying because he needed a fish for his evening meal.

Late in the afternoon he heard footsteps approaching from the east, and when, shortly afterwards, he saw Ngiangu, a giant of a man, trudging along in the shallow water close to the beach, he was so terrified that he dropped his line and fell flat on his face. Ngiangu, however, walked straight past him without glancing in his direction.

Pötikain got to his feet and called after him: "Go! Go! Go! Go!"

Presently Ngiangu came to a halt and called back to Pötikain: "May I stay here?"

"Go! Go! Go! Go!" ordered Pötikain.

Ngiangu walked on. Past the point, Gugubi, he called: "May I stay here?"

"Go! Go! Go! Go!" ordered Pötikain.

Ngiangu walked across the reef into the blue sea. "May I stay here?" he asked.

"No," replied Pötikain, "I can see your hair. Go! Go! Go! Go!"

Ngiangu waded out till the water came up to his chin. "May I stay here?" he begged.

"Go! Go! Go! Go!" shouted Pötikain. "I can still see your hair."

Far out to the west Ngiangu called once more: "May I stay here?"

"Yes! Yes! Yes! Yes! You may stay there," said Pötikain, who could no longer see any part of the giant. "Stand firm and stay there for ever. I shall remain at this point."

And at that instant, Ngiangu and Pötikain both turned to stone.

1. Ngiangu is the Islanders' name for Booby Island.

This, the first myth of Torres Strait to be recorded by a European, appears in Mac-Gillivray's *Narrative of the Voyage of H.M.S. Rattlesnake* (1852), II, 30:

The only tradition which I heard of occurs among the Kowraregas, and is worth mentioning for its singularity. The first man created was a giant named Adi, who, while fishing off Hammond Island, was caught by the rising tide and drowned, Hammond Rock springing up immediately after to mark the spot. His wives, who were watching at the time, resolved to drown themselves, and were changed into some dry rocks upon an adjacent reef named after them Ipile, or the wives.

Of it Haddon wrote (*Reports*, V, 18):

I also obtained this tale in 1888 from a Muralug man. Unfortunately I did not copy it down accurately at the time, and so I cannot compare the versions. I was informed that the man's name was Waubin. The small rock, Kaimilaig, off Turtle Head, Numri (Round Island), Palilug (Mecca Reef), and Ipili Reef are his wives. The story itself is *adi* and the man too is *adi*, but it appears to me highly improbable that this was also the man's name.

The version recorded here is a translation of the story told by Wees Nawia, a man of Muralag descent, in the language of West Torres Strait. He supervised the translation.

It is of interest that the men of Kubin—many of whom have Muralag blood—today perform a dance which derives from the hero, Waubin. While they are dancing, each man holds a replica of *baidamal baba* in his right hand, *baidamal baba* being the fighting weapon which, legend has it, was used by Waubin, the huge (*adi*) man who turned into the rock known by his name (called Hammond Rock by Europeans). (*Adi* also means "story". An *adiad* is a giant.)

1. Blue-fish Point (Kiwain). It is directly opposite the Hospital on Thursday Island.

WAUBIN

[Told by Wees Nawia at Kubin, 4 November 1967]

(The Origin of Hammond Rock)

Waubin of Muralag (Prince of Wales Island) fought men and killed them. He fought because he wanted to fight, he killed because he wanted to kill. Fighting and killing were all he ever thought about.

The weapons he used were *kubai* (a throwing stick used with a woomera), *kalak* (a spear), and *baidamal baba*.

Baidamal baba made all men fear and hate Waubin. This weapon, carved from a single piece of wood, was shaped in the middle to fit Waubin's grip. Each end was as deadly as *baidam's* (a shark's) cruel mouth, because its edges were studded with *baidam's* own teeth. With *baidamal baba* Waubin thrust, parried, hacked, and ripped.

From his home beside Rabau Nguki, the big waterhole in the centre of Muralag, Waubin went to all parts of the island looking for men to kill— to Irki, Gaibait, Muiarpui, Dak, Iata, and Aiginisan. And he killed men who came across in their canoes from Adai (Jardine River, on Cape York Peninsula) to visit their friends at Muralag, too.

As the years went by, Waubin collected many wives, for when he killed a man he took the widow back with him to Rabau Nguki.

One day when he set out to fight he found a man named Kiwain, a man as big and strong as himself. But, as always, it proved to be no match, for he soon split the man's skull with *baidamal baba* and the man ran away, leaving behind his wife, whom Waubin took to Rabau Nguki.

Kiwain fled north across the hills until he reached the point of land[1] on Muralag closest to Waiben (Thursday Island). There he died and turned to stone.

The next morning Waubin set out for the eastern side of Muralag, taking some of his wives with him. Before long he met a man named Badane.

Now Badane was a very small man who was armed only with a bamboo knife (*upi*); yet when Waubin struck at him with *baidamal baba* he missed him completely. Badane darted between Waubin's legs and sliced off his right leg at the knee.

Badane then ran to the point where Kiwain had turned to stone the previous day, dived into the sea, and swam to Waiben. From Waiben he swam to Kiriri (Hammond Island), and then he, too, turned to stone.

Wees Nawia of Kubin attired for the modern dance which derives from the myth, "Waubin". In his left hand he holds a replica of *baidamal baba*.

With the help of his wives Waubin reached Rabau Nguki. They staunched the flow of blood from his knee and cared for him.

When the flesh had grown over the stump of his leg, Waubin said to his wives: "My enemies will kill me if I stay in this place. We will leave our home and go to another island." And he led them from Rabau Nguki to Badukut on the western side of Muralag, from Badukut to Gialag (Friday Island), from Gialag to Palilag (Goode Island), from Palilag to Nömi (Round Island), and from Nömi to Köimilai, a point on Kiriri.

Some of his wives he left at Palilag, others at Nömi. They turned to stone.

To those who went with him all the way he said: "Stay where you are! I am going to deep water to fish." And with *baidamal baba* clasped firmly in his right hand, he walked across the reef into the blue sea outside.

He liked east best, so, after planting his left leg firmly in the seabed, he raised *baidamal baba* above his head and threw it as far as he could to the east. It fell into the sea near Gobau Ngur, a rocky headland of Kiriri, and became a reef, its edges sharp and jagged like the teeth of *baidam*'s jaw-bones.

"Stay where you are! Do not move!" Waubin called to his wives. "I am going to stand here for ever. The tide will flow past me from the east and from the west, the wind will strike at my head and my chest. Stay where you are!" Then he and his wives turned to stone.

[Saila Miskin gave the following detail at Thursday Island, 29 July 1969]:

At the time when Waubin was fighting the people of Muralag, a man named Sararai lived on the hill called Kubaiudaizi Pad. He had an only son.

One day Sararai and his son went fishing at a lagoon in the reef outside Badukut. Sararai said: "If we continue to live at our home on Kubaiudaizi Pad, sooner or later we will have to fight Waubin. It would be better for us to stay in this lagoon in peace. From here we shall always be able to look back at our home." Then he and his son lay down in the lagoon and turned to stone.

IALBUZ

[Told at Kubin by Anu Ara, 5 November 1967, and Lizzie Nawia, 8 November 1967]

Long ago there was only one person living on Muralag at Badukut—a man. He fished on the reef, caught crabs in the mangroves, and worked in his garden.

One morning a crab nipped him, removing a lump of flesh from his thigh. He searched until he found the piece of flesh and took it home, where he placed it inside the two halves of a shell called *akul*.[1] He left it there overnight and, the next morning, when he looked inside the *akul*, found that it contained a baby girl. "My daughter," he said.

The father cared for his child well. When she was old enough, he taught her many things—how to find food; how to catch a crab without being nipped by it; and, most important, never to go far from her home. "In this strange land,"[2] he repeatedly warned her, "there are *adiad*[3] everywhere. They will do you an injury if they can."

Despite all that her father had told her, one day while she was searching for crabs she went much further from home than usual. Then she felt thirsty, so she kept on walking until she found a coconut palm. She set her basket down on the ground and climbed up to pull a coconut for drink— and at that moment a female *adiad* came out of the nearby scrub. "Look up at the sun!" said the *adiad*. "You are going to die. You will never see your home again." And with that, the *adiad* beat the trunk of the palm, and it immediately began to grow so tall that the girl was soon hidden from sight in a cloud. The *adiad* then went back into the scrub; but she forgot to take with her the length of *buz*[4] with which she had struck the palm.

When the sun was low in the sky, his daughter had not returned to Badukut, so the father set out to look for her. He followed her tracks until he came to a coconut palm, at the foot of which lay her basket and a length of *buz*. He could hear a strange sound which at first he took to be made by the branches of a tree scraped together by the wind, but which presently he recognized as his daughter's voice coming from far above.

> *Bab (ei)[5] (a)! Ialbuz[6] (ei) (a)*
> *Tukakar (ia) muiatara*
>
> (Father, I am up here, inside a cloud. *Buz* lies on the ground beneath me),

the girl was singing.

1. *Akul*, bivalve shell, found in mangrove swamps, used in former times for cutting purposes.
2. "This strange land", *adidiu lag. Adidiu*, strange, supernatural; *lag*, place, island, (home-) land.
3. *Adiad*, strange beings who are bigger than men.
4. *Buz*, cane-like stem of the twining plant of that name, which was formerly used for "bush" rope.
5. In songs, letters enclosed in parentheses, as (*ei*), (*a*), (*ia*) here, have no meaning, but are merely rhythmic sounds.
6. *Ialbuz*: rope (*buz*); here (*ial*).

9

The man picked up the length of *buz* and beat the trunk of the palm with it. At once the trunk began to shorten, and before long he could see his daughter coming down through the cloud. He called to her, telling her to jump down to him, and soon he was holding her in his arms. "I told you to stay close to home," he said.

The girl told him the story of the *adiad* who had harmed her, and then father and daughter returned to Badukut. The girl has been called Ialbuz ever since.

ZALAGI AND THE MARI [Told by Wees Nawia at Kubin, 8 November 1967]

Zalagi of Iata, on the south side of Muralag, was a good hunter of dugong and turtle, a good fisherman, and a good gardener, but he was a bad husband to his wife, giving her none of the food he obtained and often beating her.

When the woman could no longer endure the harsh treatment meted out to her by her husband, she ran away to her father. He agreed that something would have to be done about it and enlisted the services of a powerful *maidalaig* (sorcerer).

The *maidalaig* set about his business.

First he took a long feather and anointed it with the extract of two scented plants, *matua* and *keri-keri*.[1] Then he stuck the quill in the ground and addressed magic words to it. Finally he asked it to procure a *mari* (ghost) who would punish Zalagi for his shameful behaviour.

When he heard a series of grunts, "M! M! M!", he knew that his request would be granted.

The next time that Zalagi went out on the reef to fish he was followed by a *mari*.

The moment he saw the *mari*, Zalagi took to his heels, hoping to reach the shelter of his home before the *mari* could catch him. But this he could not manage, for no matter how hard he ran, no matter which direction he took, the *mari* was always able to cut him off.

Zalagi raced across Iata to the creek, Gawa Kasa; crossed it; ran on to Sirablag; doubled back on his tracks to Iata. But there the *mari*, who had

1. I could not obtain a specimen of *matua*. *Keri-keri* is a wild ginger.

10

been close behind him all the way, caught him and beat him with a *gurab* (a heavy tree-root).

Zalagi cried out for help. No one answered. He tried to reach his home. The *mari* prevented him from doing so. He ran down to the beach and began to swim out to sea. The *mari* did likewise.

Zalagi swam to the small island of Köi Pipa. There also the *mari* caught him and beat him with his *gurab*. When Zalagi, exhausted, stumbled and fell to the ground, the *mari* sat down beside him and watched him.

As soon as Zalagi could draw breath, he sprang to his feet and rushed back to the sea.

From Köi Pipa he swam to the neighbouring islet, Magi Pipa, but he was never more than an arm's length ahead of the *mari*. Ashore, the *mari* quickly overtook him and this time beat Zalagi until he collapsed on the sand, a broken, witless man.

After a time, Zalagi struggled to his feet and reeled towards the sea. His body moved through the water towards Iata, his place, Iata. He did not even know that the *mari* kept pace with him and beat him all the way.

When Zalagi crawled ashore at Iata, he roused sufficiently to make a last desperate effort to reach his home. He died in the attempt.

The *mari* looked down at Zalagi, saw that he was dead, and said: "M! M! M!"

UTUA NINIA
[Told by Danangai Namai at Kubin, 5 November 1967]

The young boys of Aiginisan used to roam the hills of Muralag daily, searching for the honey of the little black bees.

Whenever they found a tree which had honey inside it, they chopped at it with their stone axes till it fell to the ground, split open the trunk, and gorged to their heart's content.

"*Utua ninia! Utua ninia!* (Honey here! Honey here!)" they sang, as they dipped their fingers in "honeybag".

But, alas, they forgot their duty to the *maidalgal*, the sorcerers who lived by themselves at Maine, not far from Aiginisan.

One day the boys came upon a splendid tree on the hill called Taimerau Pad, so they set to work at once and chopped it down. When they split open the trunk and saw that it contained a great deal of honey, they thrust in their hands to have it. A moment later the two halves of the tree trunk snapped shut.

The boys stared at each other, shocked dumb. They knew they could never free their hands.

Presently, tears streaming from their eyes, they began to move down the hillside, slowly, painfully, dragging the tree behind them. *"Utua ninia! Utua ninia!"* they wailed, *"Utua ninia!"*

Before long two of the boys died. Soon all were dead.

The parents began to worry about their sons, and, as they had still not returned when the sun disappeared, the fathers set out to look for them.

At dawn, swarms of blowflies led them to their children. The men wept.

Afterwards they dug a hole and buried the bodies in it. Then they returned to their wives.

Later, the *maidalgal* told the people of Aiginisan that they had punished the boys for not bringing them a share of the honey that they found.

DUPUL AND MUMAG [Told by Saila Miskin at Thursday Island, 29 July 1969]

This is a story of Gialag (Friday Island).

During the period of his training by the sorcerers,[1] every young man was obliged to spear fish in the morning at low water and then take his fattest fish to the sorcerers at their headquarters, the *kod*. He was permitted to take the rest of the fish to the village and give them to his family.

One morning, two young men, Dupul and Mumag, stayed behind when the others took their fish to the *kod*, and roasted and ate the fat fish that they had speared. Then they took the lean fish to the sorcerers.

After Dupul and Mumag left the *kod*, the sorcerers said: "Those two men brought us lean fish. They ate the fat fish before they came to us. We will have to kill them."

Next morning all the young men went and speared fish at low water as usual. However, when all the rest came in, Dupul and Mumag did not

1. Young men were known as *kernge* while they were receiving their training by the sorcerers. One informant compared the *kod*—the headquarters of the sorcerers—with a high school: "Young men were educated at the *kod*."

12

turn back, but continued to work their way out along the sandbank which runs west from Gialag, spearing fish, taking them to the top of the sandbank and laying them down there, returning to the water and spearing more fish, compelled to behave in this fashion by the sorcerers exercising their magic power.

Eventually Dupul and Mumag reached the end of the sandbank and came to the deep water. They turned to go back to Gialag, only to see that the tide had risen behind them and was running with strength. In a flash they understood that they had been punished by the sorcerers for their failure to take fat fish to the *kod* the previous day. With the tide against them, it was impossible for them to swim home to their island. There was nowhere else for them to go. So they buried themselves in the sand where they stood. Later they turned to stone.

Dupul and Mumag are heard every north-west season when the waves break over the point of the sandbank at which they buried themselves and turned to stone.

Saila Miskin said that the story of these two young men is older than that of Ngiangu and Pötikain. Ngiangu became Booby Island, but when Dupul and Mumag buried themselves at the end of the sandbank which runs west from Gialag (Friday Island), Ngiangu had not yet walked out from Muralag (Prince of Wales Island) and turned to stone.

AIWALI OF MURI [Told by Wees Nawia at Kubin, 1 November 1967]

The people of Muri (Mt. Adolphus Island) lived at Mabi, which is on the west coast of that island.

Daily they worked in their gardens and went out on the reef to fish, seldom venturing far from their homes for fear of the *markai* (ghosts) who lived in the big stone called Umai on the eastern slopes of the big hill—all but the man Aiwali.

Aiwali, who was an excellent fisherman, was not satisfied with the number of fish that he caught off Mabi. He wanted to try his luck on the opposite side of the island, out from the sandbeach called Bag.[1]

The people pleaded with him not to go. They reminded him that he would have to pass close by Umai on his way to Bag; they warned him again and again of the danger to humans from *markai*. It made no difference. His mind was made up.

When he went across to Bag the following morning he caught so many fish that he determined to fish there and at no other spot.

1. Bag is still known as an excellent place to fish.

13

So it came about that Aiwali set out from Mabi each morning with a short spear, walked up the hill, and made his way down the other side past Umai to Bag. Late in the afternoon he strung the fish he had taken during the day and returned by the same route, past Umai, to Mabi.

The *markai* of Umai watched Aiwali from the moment he walked past their home in the morning till the moment he disappeared over the top of the hill in the evening. He was theirs.

Aiwali grew careless about reaching home before dark, but even so he might have gone on living, for one of the *markai* felt friendly towards him.

One afternoon when Aiwali stayed longer than usual on the reef, this friendly *markai* went to the top of the hill and called to him: "Aiwali! Aiwali! Look at the sun. You must go home. It is getting late."

Aiwali glanced in the direction from which the voice had come and saw the *markai*.

"Why does he want me to go home?" thought Aiwali. "It is not very late. There are still many fish to be caught. I am not ready to go home." So he paid no heed to the warning and went on with his work. It was almost dark when he reached Mabi that day.

The people were angry with him. Whereas on previous occasions they had merely scolded him and entreated him not to endanger his life by giving the *markai* an opportunity to catch him, this time they commanded that in future he always return long before nightfall.

Aiwali scarcely heard what they said. "I care nothing about the *markai*. I go to spear fish. I shall continue to return when I have caught all the fish I can see to catch," he vowed to himself.

The next day he went to Bag as usual and speared more fish than ever.

The afternoon wore on. This time the friendly *markai* took a companion with him to the top of the hill. "Aiwali! Aiwali!" they called. "You should go home. The sun is setting." Aiwali speared another fish for reply.

Then the friendly *markai* walked across the reef to Aiwali, grabbed him by the ear and said: "Haven't you got ears to hear? Two of us called and called to you, telling you to go home. It is late. Go home!" Aiwali bent down to pick up a fish. For all the notice he took of the *markai*, the *markai* might not have been there.

At last Aiwali began to string the day's catch. "It is too late now," said the friendly *markai*. "Look at the beach." Aiwali looked at the shore, saw many rows of *markai* standing at the water's edge, and was afraid.

He ran in across the reef, forced his way through the waiting *markai* and sped up the hill. Sometimes the *markai* caught up with him and scratched him and spat on him as they tried to cut off his escape, but each time he put up a desperate struggle and broke away. He tried to hide from them in long grass. It was no use, for they found him at once. In vain the friendly *markai* pleaded with his fellows to spare this human, but they paid him no heed. This man was theirs and they meant to have him.

At length Aiwali reached the top of the hill and began to run down to Mabi. It was then that the *markai* captured him. One of them jabbed a finger in each of Aiwali's ears and jeered: "You wouldn't listen to your *markai* friend! You wouldn't listen to your *markai* friend!"

Close to Mabi the *markai* loosed their hold of Aiwali and vanished, but by that time he was close to death. As the people of Mabi ran to meet Aiwali they saw that he was covered with blood and spittle. When they reached him he was dead.

WAIABA [Told by Ibab Aken of Nurupai at Thursday Island, 29 July 1969]

This is a story of Nurupai (Horn Island).

At Iwiziu Kula, not far from the point on Nurupai called Kausar, there once lived a man named Waiaba.

Waiaba was expert at marking dugong, knowing exactly where to put a *narapat*.[1] He could recognize the spot at which a dugong had left off grazing during the night, and, as that was the spot at which the dugong would resume grazing the following night if the tide were suitable, that was where he placed a *narapat*. He used to examine the reef early in the morning for newly-made tracks and build his *naiat* (hunting platform) later in the day. He was the only man at Nurupai who knew how to build a *naiat*.

Waiaba always shared the dugong he harpooned with the people who lived in the village not far from Iwiziu Kula. Sometimes, quite unintentionally, he gave a smaller portion to this person than to that when he was cutting up. Then those who had received less than others grumbled, believing themselves to have been treated unfairly.

One day, some men who were dissatisfied with the size of their portions of dugong meat became so angry that they decided to kill Waiaba. When he ran away, they chased him round the island above high water mark with their spears. He crossed Boigu Kasa, Ngogodania Kasa, and Kuipidal Kasa, and ran around Garagar, but there the men who were hunting him caught him and killed him.

1. *Narapat*, the pointed stick (*pat*) used to mark the spot in the reef grass (*nar*) where a dugong left off feeding.

Dugong-hunter with harpoon-spear (*wap*) and rope (*amu*) standing on platform (*nat*)   *Artist* Kala Waia

story from

NAGI *Mt. Ernest Island*

NAGI (Mt. Ernest Island), **MUA** (Banks Island), **AND BADU** (Mulgrave Island)

SCALE

miles

MUA

BUZAN NGUR
NAGI

10 miles

NAGA

[Told by Frank Mills at Thursday Island, 24 July 1969]

Naga, head man of Nagi (Mt. Ernest Island), lived in a hole in the ground underneath a big boulder on top of Kai Pad (Mt. Ernest). His people lived at the southern end of the island in the scrub at the foot of Kai Pad. Both Naga and the men whom he led lusted to kill and take heads. These they stored under a tree at Buzan, a sacred place surrounded by giant *bu* shells.[1]

No enemy ever made a surprise attack on Nagi, for by day Naga kept a constant look-out from the top of Kai Pad, and at night, the men left their homes in the scrub and watched from the beach. Mualgal[2] who hoped to land in the dark were appropriately received.

When Naga signalled from the top of Kai Pad that enemy canoes were approaching Nagi, his men went at once to the sacred place at Buzan. There they put on their fighting gear and obtained magical strength for the battle to come. Then they took up their positions as Naga directed.

Naga went down to the beach alone as the canoes ran in. Seeing him, the enemy warriors expected his men to be hidden in the scrub behind him and they advanced towards it. Naga, however, always ordered his men to conceal themselves to right and to left of him. At his whistled command, they converged on the enemy and took them completely by surprise.

Few hostile visitors to Nagi escaped with their lives, for Naga's strategy never failed to rout them utterly. And after every raid, the Nagi men cut off the heads of the enemy dead and took them to the tree at Buzan, where they celebrated their victory.

The Nagi men had no canoes of their own, but Naga could always obtain canoes whenever canoes were needed. He wore a headband with two pelican feathers stuck in it. These feathers, when thrown by him into the sea, magically transformed themselves into canoes which carried the men of Nagi to wherever they wanted to go and fight. When the men returned to Nagi and stepped ashore, the canoes became feathers and Naga replaced them in his headband before he climbed up to his home on Kai Pad.

Naga led his men to Mua (Banks Island) many times in the feather canoes, but, because some of his followers fell to Mua clubs at each visit, the number of fighting men at his command eventually dwindled to an alarming extent. He had, therefore, to abandon the idea of carrying the fight to the enemy and induce the enemy to come to him.

1. *Bu* shell, the Australian Trumpet Shell, *Syrinx aruanus* Linne.
2. Mualgal, the people of Mua (Banks Island).

He had a big drum, and when he beat it the sound travelled to many islands—to Mua, Badu, Mabuiag and Muralag. Hearing it, men at those islands believed that a feast was in progress at Nagi and they would be able to take the men of Nagi by surprise. Too late they learnt that Naga's drum had been beaten to lure them to Nagi. Most of the men who answered the call of Naga's drum had their heads cut off.

The pile of heads under the tree at Buzan grew in size for a long time. After every victory, the men sat round the sacred place and boasted and drank from shared coconuts.

But at last the Mualgal came to understand Naga's tricks, that of luring them to Nagi with his drum, and the surprise attack from each side of him by his men. The next time they sent war-canoes to Nagi, only one canoe ran in towards Naga; the other canoes separated and approached from two sides behind Naga's men, whom Naga, as always, had ordered to hide to his right and his left in the scrub. Few men of Nagi survived this attack by the Mualgal. Naga was one of them.

The Mualgal used the same tactics on another occasion and killed nearly every one of the Nagilgal.[3] Naga escaped and ran up Kai Pad, the Mualgal at his heels. He had nearly reached his home under the big boulder when he was struck down. The Mualgal cut off his head and took it to Mua. His body turned to stone.

3. Nagilgal, the people of Nagi.

[After finishing the story, Frank Mills added this detail]:

About eighty years ago, my father ordered his workmen to bring Naga from the top of Kai Pad and stand him upright on the beach in front of the new village. He is still there today, a solid block of stone, approximately seven feet high and two feet thick, a man with two legs, two arms, belly, chest, and back, but no head, having lost it before he turned to stone.

Where Naga lay on top of Kai Pad a waterhole has formed. It is approximately seven feet long and two feet deep. It has been given the name, *Nagan Nguki*—Naga's water.

stories from

MUA *Banks Island*

Saulal time, the season of mating turtle

KARAKARKULA

[Told by Wees Nawia at Kubin, 31 October 1967]

At Arkai on the island of Mua (Banks Island) there once lived a man named Zangagudan and his two wives, Takamulai and Buziauwar. Every day they either searched for *kutai* and *bua* and *mapet*[1] in the bush or fished on the reef. They used to cook their food in an *amai* (earth–oven).

"Turtle-fast time" (the season of mating turtle) arrived, and one day they saw a turtle-pair (*saulal*) drifting outside in the sea. The two women urged their husband to try and bring in the female turtle, but Zangagudan, who was not a strong man, protested that he could not do it alone. "Then try and find someone to help you," said his wives.

Zangagudan set out from Arkai and walked along the beach. Just beyond Mipa he called out: "Does anyone live here?" There was no reply. He called again: "Does anyone live here?" This time a voice answered from Tuta, not far away, and soon afterwards Karakarkula appeared.

Karakarkula was a giant. He had ferns (*karakar*) growing all over his body. "What do you want?" he asked Zangagudan. So Zangagudan told him about the turtle and asked for his help in catching it and bringing it ashore. "Wait here," said Karakarkula, and then he took a few strides, picked up the turtle and put it on his shoulder, and returned just as quickly as he had gone.

Zangagudan was very happy. "We should cook this turtle straight away," he said. An *amai* was made, Zangagudan cut the flesh from the shell, and Karakarkula drank the blood that collected in the shell while Zangagudan had been cutting up. Then Zangagudan replaced the meat in the shell and set the whole in the *amai* to cook.

Karakarkula felt sleepy. "Do you mind if I have a rest?" he asked Zangagudan. "Not at all," replied Zangagudan. Soon Karakarkula was snoring.

He was still snoring when the turtle was cooked. Zangagudan opened the *amai*, removed the best cuts from the carapace, and hurried back with them past Mipa to his wives at Arkai.

Takamulai and Buziauwar were very happy to see him return with the cooked turtle-meat. "We had better eat it at once," said Zangagudan. "Karakarkula will be very angry when he wakes up and finds I left only dry meat for him. He might come and look for me."

1. *Kutai, bua, mapet,* three varieties of yam. *Mapet* is very stringy.

23

Zangagudan was right. When Karakarkula went to the *amai* and saw the tough shoulder-meat, he was very angry indeed. He ate a little of it, and then he set out for Arkai.

Zangagudan and his wives heard the thunder of the giant's footsteps. "What are we going to do?" asked Takamulai and Buziauwar.

Zangagudan said: "Takamulai, go out into the sea. Buziauwar, walk along the beach and then go up to the sandhill. You'll both be safe from Karakarkula if you do as I say. I myself will not move from this spot, but I shall bury myself in the ground. When Karakarkula reaches Arkai he'll see none of us."

Takamulai walked out into the sea and turned to stone; Buziauwar walked to the sandhill and turned to stone; and Zangagudan buried himself deep in the ground and turned to stone. Karakarkula, finding no one at Arkai, returned to his part of the island and he, too, turned to stone.

[**After finishing the story, Wees Nawia added this detail**]:

Everyone at Kubin knows where these stones which once were people are to be seen.

For a long time no one knew exactly where Zangagudan had hidden himself, but a few years ago when blasting was in progress at Arkai in an effort to obtain a good water-supply for Kubin Village, Zangagudan was finally located. Because of the rock which Zangagudan became when he hid from Karakarkula, the water-supply for Kubin had to be obtained elsewhere on the island.

AUKAM AND TIAI
[**Told by Wees Nawia at Kubin, 31 October 1967**]

This is a Totalai story.

Long ago there were only three people at Totalai: a woman named Aukam, her brother, Poapun, and their uncle (*awade*, mother's brother), a man named Wawa. Aukam lived not far from the western bank of Palga Kasa (a creek), Poapun lived on Totalai Point, and Wawa lived a little to the west of Aukam. Wawa's house was the hollow trunk of a *zanga* tree.

Wawa was a lazy man who did no work. When he woke up in the

morning he used to smell the fish that Aukam was cooking for her breakfast and say: "Greedy Aukam. She gives me nothing to eat. She eats all the fish that she catches herself." He hated his niece for failing to provide him with food, and he made up his mind to punish her for it.

Poapun also expected Aukam to share her fish with him. He had a beautiful spear, a long straight spear with many sharp prongs (*dagulal*), but he loved it so much that he could not bring himself to use it. Sometimes he would take it with him to the reef and occasionally even raise it to throw at a fish, but always, at the last moment, he held back, lest its pointed prongs be blunted through use. Most of the time he kept it suspended from the branch of a tree, and every day he spent much time on his back on the ground, his eyes close to the tips of the prongs. "My beautiful spear. Oh, my beautiful spear," he thought as he gazed at it. And when Aukam passed him on her way home from the reef with a basket full of fish, he used to say: "My sister never gives me any of her fish."

One morning Poapun spent some time on the reef with his spear and, as he was coming in to the beach, caught some small fish under a rock with his bare hands. He snapped off their heads and rubbed the flesh and blood of their bodies round his spear at the junction of shaft and prongs,[1] and then he returned to his home and suspended his spear from the tree.

Presently Aukam came by on her way back to Palga Kasa with the fish she had caught that morning.[2]

Soon afterwards she received a visit from Poapun. "My good brother," she said, "what brings you here? What do you want?" "I speared very few fish this morning, so I came to ask for some of yours," he replied. Aukam strung some of the small fish at the top of her basket and gave them to Poapun, who then took his leave.

He did not go very far, however. He had not failed to observe that Aukam had bigger fish in her basket than those she gave him, so he walked only to the far side of Palga Kasa, hung the string of fish on a mangrove tree and turned back. After dipping himself in the creek he went straight to Aukam, and she, seeing his dripping body, said: "What's wrong? What happened to you?" "The tide is running very strong in the creek, and it swept me away. I lost the fish that you gave me," Poapun told his sister. Aukam gave him a string of big fish this time, and Poapun set out for his place at Totalai. On the way he removed the string of small fish from the mangrove tree. "I have plenty of fish now," he said.

After that, Poapun often imposed on his sister. He ate well without doing any work. And all the time, Wawa continued to complain about Aukam: "You never give me fish. My bad niece, I'll punish you one of these days."

Aukam had a baby boy, Tiai. On those days when she went to her

1. He did this in order to deceive Aukam and give credence to the tale he was about to tell her. She would not fail to notice the condition of his spear as she walked past his place.
2. Aukam fished with a line called *wali*. It was made from fibres of the aerial roots of *dani* (the wild fig-tree).

garden at Palga, she took him with her in a basket and left the basket hanging from a tree while she worked.

Wawa used to see her on her way to Palga, and one day he followed her secretly. As soon as she was out of sight in the garden, he sharpened a stick at both ends. Then he removed the basket from the tree and drove the pointed stick through Tiai's head, in one ear and out the other. Still without making a sound, Wawa hung up the basket and stole back to his home in the *zanga* tree.

Aukam's digging stick broke—a bad omen. Her thoughts flew to Tiai, her son. She ran to the basket, looked inside it, and saw how the child had died. Tears rained from her eyes. Later she saw the tracks of the murderer. "I never thought my uncle would do such a thing," she said.

It was mid-day. "My uncle will be asleep by now. I shall visit him," said Aukam, who knew his ways. She heard him snoring as she approached the *zanga* tree, and he did not waken while she heaped leaves and branches around him and set fire to his home. It was too late to save himself when the heat from the flames roused him from sleep. "Who did this?" he screamed. "I," said Aukam, "your niece. You killed my son, so I now kill you."

Aukam returned to her home beside Palga Kasa and stayed there. She kept Tiai in his basket until all the flesh had disappeared from his bones, and then she wore his bones round her neck. It took her a long time to accept the fact that her son was not on Mua. "Tiai is not on this island," she said then. "He may be at Badu (Mulgrave Island). I had better go to Badu and look for him."

When she arrived at Badu she saw some young men engaged in *tukutuku sagul*.[3] She hid behind a bush and watched them for a while. Presently the spear thrown by one of the players missed the target and landed in the bush behind which she was hiding. The young man went to retrieve it and, seeing Aukam, thought her a *markai* (ghost). "I am no *markai*, but a woman looking for her son, Tiai. Have you seen Tiai?" she said. "Tiai has gone to Gumu,"[4] the young man told her.

Aukam went to Gumu. "Tiai has gone to Buru," she was told. She went to Buru (Turn-again Island), and from Buru to Dauan and Saibai and, finally, Boigu (Talbot Island). At every island she visited she saw young men who were playing at *tukutuku sagul*. At Buru a young man said: "Tiai has gone to Saibai." At Saibai a young man said: "Tiai has gone to Boigu."

So Aukam went to Boigu, which she knew to be the last island: beyond the horizon[5] from Boigu lay the *markai* world, the land of the spirits. And she finally caught up with her son.

He and a number of other young men were throwing spears at a target,

3. *Tukutuku sagul*, a sport in which spears are thrown at a target.
4. Another name for Mabuiag (Jervis Island).
5. *Kibu*, the name of the horizon, which is regarded as both place and boundary.

and Aukam recognized him as soon as she saw him, because he looked different from the other players. She hid behind a bush and watched the game.

Presently Tiai threw his spear at the target and missed completely. The spear came to rest in the bush behind which Aukam was hiding, and when Tiai went to retrieve it he saw Aukam. "Who are you? Are you a *dogai*?" he asked her. "I am a woman, Aukam, who is looking for her son, Tiai," she replied. "I am Tiai," Aukam received for answer.

"I am your mother," Aukam said. "I have come from Mua. These are your bones at my neck. You died at Mua a long time ago." So Tiai learned that he was a ghost, and for a while he stood very still in one place.

The young men with whom Tiai had been playing *tukutuku sagul* saw him engaged in conversation, but they could not see the person to whom he was speaking. They began to grow impatient at the interruption to their sport. Then they saw Tiai wave his spear up and down several times and throw it away.

Tiai walked back to his friends. "Bring me a *zazi* (skirt),"[6] he said. His friends brought the *zazi*, and he tied it round his waist. "Beat a drum for me," he said. One of the men beat the drum for Tiai, and he began to dance, not as men dance, but in the manner of *markai*.

Presently he ran towards Aukam. The ground opened at his feet. "Mother, why do you stand there looking at me? Come to me," he called. The woman took a few steps, and then she and her son disappeared inside the ground.

6. *Zazi*, a skirt worn by women and by dancers, which is made from young coconut leaves, or from teased banana-trunk fibre, or from grass.

At Boigu, "Aukam and Tiai" is not known in detail today. Informants said: "That story belongs to Mua. We only know a little bit about the end." Actually, the account they went on to give of what took place at Boigu is less detailed than that given by Wees Nawia of Kubin (Mua), and they added nothing except this point: Aukam found Tiai at Tuam, "the home of ghosts". (Tuam is situated at the western end of Boigu.)

SIK

[Told by Wees Nawia at Kubin, 1 November 1967]

A woman named Murarat lived by herself at Baua. She wove mats, tended her garden, and dug in the damp sand on the beach for *silel* (shell-fish).[1] She became pregnant and gave birth to a son whom she named Sik.

Sik grew into a handsome boy, and, as soon as he was strong enough to hold a bow and arrows, his mother made them for him and taught him how to use them. She told him to watch the trees and shoot at anything that hopped and flew among the branches. When he killed one of these creatures, he was to bring it to her, and she would cook it.

1. *Silel*, a small, white, bivalve shell, which contains an edible fish.

The first thing that Sik shot was a tiny lizard (*mogai*). He took it to Murarat. "Mother, is it good to eat?" he asked her. "No, my son," she replied, "it is not. Try shooting at creatures that fly about in the trees."

So Sik went into the bush again, and this time he brought back a very small, black bird (*mut*). "Mother," he said, "is this good food?" "My son," said Murarat, "you have shot very good food. I will cook it for you."

After that, Sik went into the bush every day and shot birds. But Murarat worried the whole time he was gone, for fear that he might be stolen by a *dogai* or an *adiad* (a monstrous bush creature). So she made a pronged spear for him and showed him how to throw it, believing that he would be safer spearing fish on the reef than wandering alone in the scrub. She praised him highly when he speared his first fish and told him to obtain that kind of food in future.

Sik had no fear on the reef and walked further and further from home as the days went by. Mururat often told him not to go so far. "You must remember that there are *dogai* and *adiad* everywhere—they want nothing more than a fine youth like you. You must always be on guard against them. Never give them the chance to steal you," she cautioned her son. Sik paid no attention to her words.

One day he did not come home until afternoon. Murarat was by that time almost beside herself with worry. When he appeared, she spoke angrily: "How often have I told you not to go far from this place! I have been looking for you everywhere. One of these days a *dogai* or an *adiad* will surely get you!"

In point of fact a female ghost named Uga—she was a *markai*, not a *dogai* or an *adiad*, but a *markai*—was already waiting to grab Sik. She had caught sight of him several days before when he was spearing a fish and immediately decided that she wanted him for husband.

Sik had no luck at all on the reef one morning, not even seeing a fish, though he walked all the way to Gerain Gizu. He would have gone still further, but that the tide had begun to flow in over the reef, and he had perforce to turn back. After a while he had to come right in and walk close to the edge of the mangroves. A fish jumped under one of the trees; he threw his spear at it, and, as he bent to pick up spear and fish, Uga leapt down from a branch and flung her arms around him. A moment later a waterspout enveloped both Sik and Uga and swept them past Baua to Parbar. Uga rolled Sik in a mat to hide him from the other *markai* who were staying at Parbar at that time.

Murarat became frantic with worry about Sik. Late in the afternoon she gave him up for lost and began to cry. She cried all night long.

There was dancing at Parbar that night. The female *markai*, led by Uga, danced first, and, as soon as they had finished, Uga ran to the mat inside which she had hidden Sik. "Sik! Are you there, Sik?" she whispered. "I am here," replied Sik. Uga hurried back to her companions.

The male *markai* were already dancing. Presently, however, a feather dropped from the head-dress of their leader. "Stop!" he signalled. "There is something wrong—we are, perhaps, being watched by a human. We will dance no more tonight."

Uga, afraid that Sik's presence in their midst would soon be detected by the other *markai*, confided her problem to a female *markai*, her best friend, and showed Sik to her. "What a handsome young man!" said the friend. "My husband," said Uga with pride.

Sik escaped from Parbar the following evening, crawling out of the mat as soon as the *markai* began to dance and then running all the way home to Baua. As he passed Totalai, he called a warning to Poapun,[2] and he also warned Im, who lived just round the point beyond Totalai. "Run for your life," he called to these men, "I'm being chased by *markai*. They're coming after me in a waterspout." That was all he said to Murarat when he reached Baua. He and his mother fled to Gerain Pad (a hill) and hid in a hole in a rock.

Uga discovered Sik's absence shortly after he ran away. When the *markai* dancers complained early of feeling unwell and refused to go on dancing, Uga ran to her husband at once, only to find him gone. So she then told the whole story to her fellow *markai* and begged them to help her bring him back. They set out immediately.

Poapun saw a waterspout and said: "Sik was telling the truth." Im saw it and said: "Sik was telling the truth." Each took to his heels.

The waterspout travelled to Baua and, after circling that place, went straight to the rock in which Sik and Murarat were hiding. Such was the strength of the *markai* power, that it drove through the rock and killed mother and son.

2. Aukam's brother (see "Aukam and Tiai", in this section).

IM   [Told by Wees Nawia of Kubin at Thursday Island, 25 July 1969]

Im was a man who lived all by himself at a spot between Baua and Totalai at the northern end of the island of Mua. He had a very long beard.

Im was not a fighting man. Sometimes he worked in his garden during

Im

the day. At night he played his drum. When he woke up in the morning he went down to the sea and fished.

He did not fish with line and spear like other men. Instead, he tied many wooden fish-hooks to his beard, waded out over the reef, took a deep breath, and went down deep in the water. And there he stayed for long periods at a time, scarcely moving, the strands of his beard streaming up and behind him like so many fishing lines. When a fish took a bait at the end of his beard, Im felt the bite and jerked his head. That was how Im caught fish.

One day Sik ran past his place calling loudly: "Does anyone live here?" Im replied: "Your uncle (*wadwam*)[1] lives here." "Then run for your life. I'm being chased by *markai* in a waterspout," shouted Sik.

Im chose not to flee inland from the *markai*. He walked to a rock on the beach and lay down behind it. Soon afterwards when the *markai* passed by in the waterspout, he turned to stone.[2]

1. There is another Mabuiag kinship term for mother's brother—*awade*.

2. In shape, this stone is exactly like the fish which is called *im* in West Torres Strait. Wees Nawia identified *im* as the Banded Wobbegong (*Orectolobus ornatus* [De Vis])—"Carpet Shark"—which has fringing, weed-like fronds of skin in the region of the mouth.

THE SEVEN BLIND BROTHERS

[Told by Wees Nawia at Kubin, 1 November 1967]

Long ago there were seven blind brothers living at Bupu on the island of Mua. Every day they used to sail their canoe to a reef and spear fish.

Before they set out, each tied on a headband and tucked into it a magic feather (*warka*),[1] after which the magic feathers guided the brothers to their canoe by quivering so long as the brothers kept to the right path and ceasing to quiver if they took a step in the wrong direction. The brothers knew when they had reached their canoe from the abrupt cessation of movement by the feathers. Then they put up their sail and let the wind take them to the reef.

While they were sailing, the magic feathers did not move. When the canoe reached the edge of the reef, however, the feathers began to quiver again—the sign to the brothers that they should take down their sail because shallow water lay ahead and it was time to use poling-sticks. The eldest brother went to the bow of the canoe with his fish-spear and held it ready to throw. He knew when and where to throw it by the particular movement of the feather in his headband.

1. The feather was given additional height by sticking it on to a slender twig of *wali*. The result was that the feather quivered with the slightest movement of the wearer and in the gentlest breeze.

When the canoe was full of fish, the brothers returned to Bupu, guided throughout by the magic feathers. While they were sailing across the passage between the reef and Mua there was no movement of the feathers. When the canoe reached the edge of the island reef, the feathers began to quiver, and they did not leave off until the brothers were safely back at their home.

Though the brothers did not know it, they were watched by a *dogai* every day. She lived on a hill[2] overlooking Bupu and, seeing them sail away in their canoe, became curious as to what they did all day.

At last the *dogai* made up her mind to find out. One afternoon she walked to Bupu and, as soon as she saw the brothers' canoe returning, went out to the edge of the island reef on a drifted log (*betei*). When the brothers began to take down their sail—as they knew they must do from the quivering of the magic feathers in their headbands—the *dogai* wedged the log under the bow, thus preventing the brothers from being able to pole their canoe in across the reef. Very quickly then, she took from the canoe most of the fish that the brothers had caught that day, removed the log, and paddled back to the shore on it.

With the removal of the log, the canoe rode in the water, and the brothers poled in. They thought the tide must have risen suddenly. They were very puzzled, however, when they found there were very few fish to unload. One of the brothers said: "We must have dropped most of the fish outside the canoe as we caught them. Never mind. What we have we'll take home and cook."

Once the *dogai* knew that the brothers fished when they went out in their canoe, she made a practice of meeting them at the edge of the reef on their return and robbing them of their fish. The brothers began to suspect that a thief was stealing from them, but they had no idea who it was.

Then one night the youngest brother lay awake until after his brothers had fallen asleep, took out his father's skull, rubbed it with the scented leaves of *matua*, and asked it to give him a good dream (*mina piki*). "Tell me, if you can, what my brothers and I should do to enable us to see with our eyes. We fill our canoe with fish every day, yet when we return to Bupu the canoe is empty. What happens to the fish we catch?" he begged of it.

While the youngest brother slept, his father came to him in a dream. "Do not go to the reef with your brothers tomorrow," his father said. "After they have gone, go to Arkai. Your magic feather will lead you to turtle tracks on the beach. Follow them to the eggs that were laid. Make a fire and cook two of them, and then smash them against your eyes. After that you will be able to see."

2. Which bears the name, Dogai Pad.

31

So the youngest brother did not go fishing with his brothers the following day, but stayed behind and obeyed the instructions given by his father in the dream. His magic feather guided him to the turtle eggs at Arkai. He dug them up, made a fire, cooked two, and taking an egg in each hand, smashed them against his eyes. He could see. "My good father," he said, "you gave me a beautiful dream. I see Arkai, my home at Bupu, my brothers fishing on the reef—I see everything around me. I am going to take the rest of the turtle eggs home with me."

That afternoon he watched his brothers from the moment they set sail to return to Bupu, so he saw them met at the edge of the island reef by a *dogai*. He saw her put a log under the bow of the canoe, help herself to the fish that his brothers had caught during the day, remove the log and return to the shore on it, and then go to Dogai Pad. The youngest brother felt sad for his brothers who could not see.

When they reached home they said: "We have brought back very few fish, though we caught many." The youngest brother cooked them, and the brothers ate them for their evening meal.

Then the youngest brother said: "Sit down." Quickly he heated the turtle eggs on the hot ground where the cooking fire had burnt, and afterwards went from brother to brother, smashing turtle eggs against their sightless eyes. And now all seven brothers could see. The youngest brother told about his dream, and he told about the *dogai* that had been stealing their fish. After that, the brothers made a plan to catch the *dogai*.

In the morning they tied on their headbands and pretended to let the magic feathers lead them to their canoe. Each took with him *wap* (harpoon-spear), *amu* (rope), and *gabagaba* (club with circular stone head). They sailed to the reef and filled their canoe with fish—very quickly, because now they had eyes to see—and before long put back to Bupu.

They saw the *dogai* paddling out on the drifted log to meet them at the edge of the reef. "That's the one who's been stealing our fish," said the youngest brother.

"Do nothing that will let her know we can see," said the eldest brother. "We've fooled her so far today. But watch her through closed lids the whole time."

While the brothers busied themselves with taking down the sail, the *dogai*, after putting her log under the bow of the canoe, began to remove the brothers' fish. The eldest brother struck her with his *wap*, and the other brothers fell on her with their spears and *gabagaba*.

Before the *dogai* died she said: "What do I care? I tricked you for a long time. I'm going to stay here for ever at the edge of the reef, and you—you and your canoe will turn to stone not far from your home at Bupu."

The *dogai* became a lagoon—Dogai Malu. The brothers poled their canoe ashore and turned to stone along with the canoe. You can see the seven brothers standing side by side just above the high-water mark. Their canoe is not far away.

WAMIN NGURBUM [Told by Wees Nawia at Kubin, 3 November 1967]

Long ago, people used to live on Mua Pad (Mt. Augustus). One of them, a man named Wami, was a *madub*—a very lazy fellow who did little but eat and sleep. He lived by himself and never joined in with the rest of the people, who were always busy, either working in their gardens, clearing, digging, weeding, and planting, or fishing, or hunting. Wami hardly stirred from his home.

He spent many years like that and, indeed, might never have changed his ways, had he not chanced to see a strange object bobbing about in the waves when he woke from sleep one morning and looked out to sea. Curious, he walked down the hill to the beach, to learn that it was a banana sucker that had attracted his attention. Presently, when a wave washed it to his feet, he picked it up. "You are Wami's banana," he told it, and he carried it home.

"My beautiful banana sucker," he crooned to it, "I am going to dig a fine hole in the ground for you. Good banana sucker, grow for me." And Wami planted the treasure that had come to him from the sea.

He scarcely took his eyes from the banana sucker. It was the first thing he looked at when he woke in the morning. He watched it all day long, every day. It was the last thing he saw before he went to sleep at night.

The sucker took root and sent up a pointed head (*ku*). The stem which bore it grew tall and thick and then curved in an arc, so that the swelling head pointed to earth. And as the leaves which sheathed the growing fruit of the head unfolded, Wami could see that his tree would bear beautiful, big bananas.

He spent more time than ever watching it. "*Wamin ngurbum, Wamin ngurbum* (Wami's banana tree, Wami's banana tree)," he gloated. A song came into his head:

Madubal ina inab kuruai iudanu,
Ngai (gar) Wami (a) Wami.

(This curving stem weighed down with ripening bananas
belongs to the *madub.*
I am Wami, Wami. It is mine.)

It was constantly on his lips.

The people living in the village heard him and sent a man to find out
why he was always singing these days. Wami saw him coming and called
to him: "Look at my beautiful banana tree. Its name is *Wamin ngurbum.*"
"May I have a sucker?" asked the man. "You may not," said Wami.

The man returned to the village. "Wami sings because he has a beautiful
banana tree," he told the people. "I asked him to give me a sucker, but he
refused."

A second man asked Wami for a sucker from his banana tree, but he
had no more luck than the first.

Then two men went to Wami, and when they begged for a sucker he
said: "When the bananas are ripe, I shall cut off the bunch. After that I will
give a sucker to the village people. But remember this: everyone is to call
it by my name. This banana is *Wamin ngurbum.*"

[After finishing the story, Wees Nawia added this detail]:

Wami kept his word. The variety of banana grown first on Mua by
Wami, the *madub,* still grows on Mua. Some of the young people mis-
takenly call it *wamen ngurbum,* not understanding that it takes its name from
the *madub,* Wami, who obtained it from the sea.

BURUMNASKAI [Told by Lizzie Nawia at Kubin, 3 November 1967]

Burumnaskai of Mua had many children, all of whom she kept secret for
a long time. She had no husband. Her brother, Kerarai, who lived not far
from her, had neither wife nor children.

One afternoon Kerarai heard the sound of children's voices at his sister's place. This surprised him, because he had believed his sister to be childless. "I'll visit her and see if she'll let me have one of her children," he decided.

Burumnaskai heard her brother coming towards her place the following morning and immediately hid her children in the ground at the foot of a banana tree nearby. When Kerarai arrived, there was not a child to be seen. Burumnaskai greeted him and said: "My good brother, what brings you here? Is there something you want?" "I would like one of your children—a little girl or a little boy, either will do," Kerarai replied. "I have no children," Burumnaskai told him. "Oh well, in that case I'll be on my way," said Kerarai, and he went back to his home. However, he determined to listen very carefully in future to all that went on at his sister's place.

Whenever Burumnaskai had to go and work in her garden, she did not take her children with her, but left them at home, hidden in the ground at the foot of the banana tree. Moreover, she gave them strict instructions that they were to stay there without making a sound until she came back, and the children obeyed her. Therefore, Kerarai quickly established two facts: children laughed and played at his sister's place while she was at home; children did not laugh and play at his sister's place while she was absent from home. But that Burumnaskai had children was certain, so he went to her again before long and asked for one of them.

"Let me have one of your children," he begged, "just one to play in my house." But Burumnaskai, who had hidden her children at the first sound of his approaching footsteps, again refused to let him have one. "I have no children," she said. And as on the previous occasion of his asking for a child, he departed without having seen Burumnaskai's children and returned alone to his silent place.

The following day Burumnaskai hid her children as usual before setting out for her garden, but this time she forgot to sweep the ground clean around the banana tree, and when Kerarai came along soon after she had gone, he saw the footprints made by the children while they played. There was proof that his sister had lied to him. Furious, he shot arrows into the ground all round the banana tree. Then he returned to his home and lay down. Presently he began to snore.

Burumnaskai felt lazy and disinclined to work in her garden that day, and before very long she began to worry about her children. The feeling that all was not well with them grew inside her, so she hurried home. She saw the arrows in the ground at the foot of the banana tree and called loudly to her children. When they did not answer, she wept.

After a while she dried her tears and looked for the murderer's tracks. She found them almost at once. "My brother is no longer 'my good brother'," she said. "He killed my children. Their bodies lie underground. I am going to kill my brother."

Kerarai was still snoring when Burumnaskai arrived at his home. He did not hear her pile brushwood around it and set fire to it, only waking when it was too late to escape from the blaze. "Who did this?" he screamed. "Your sister. I, your sister. You are about to die for killing my children," said Burumnaskai.

The spirits of Burumnaskai's children became banana suckers, and before long their heads appeared above the ground around the tree[1] where they had formerly played.

1. This banana tree was a *kurub*, a variety which "has always grown at Mua". The suckers of every *kurub* are called *burumnaskai*.

KARUM   [Told by Salome Bosen at Kubin, 3 November 1967]

Some girls who were sisters once lived at Baugain.[1] There was a *mai* tree not far from their home which gave them ripe, red fruit for the plucking. This fruit (also called *mai*) they first cooked in an earth-oven and then ate.

One day, when a young man named Karum came for a share of the *mai*, he and the girls decided to go and play hide-and-seek (*utai sagul*) in Tulu Sarka (*sarka*, creek) while the fruit was cooking. The girls hid first, diving into the water and stirring up the muddy, mangrove-fringed water until they were out of sight of Karum who had to find them. When it was Karum's turn to hide from the girls, it took a very long time to find him.

At the end of the game, Karum and the girls returned to the earth-oven and opened it up. It was empty! "Someone has stolen our *mai*!" cried the girls. "Who would do such a thing! There must be a *dogai* about," said Karum, pretending surprise when, in fact, he knew all about it. While the girls were looking for him in Tulu Sarka, he had run to the earth-oven, stolen and eaten the *mai*, run all the way back and slid into the muddy water without being seen. No wonder it had taken the girls so long to find him!

This happened not once, but many times. Karum and the girls plucked *mai*, put them in the oven to cook, and, while they were playing hide-and-seek in Tulu Sarka, the earth-oven was robbed. In the end, the girls became suspicious of Karum.

1. On Mua.

36

The very next day, the youngest sister stayed behind when the others went to Tulu Sarka and hid near the earth-oven. Thus she saw Karum steal the *mai*.

All went to Tulu Sarka the following day, and the moment Karum dived into the water, the girls ran back to the earth-oven. They reached it ahead of Karum and so were able to catch him in the act of theft. They then beat him to death.

Just before he died, Karum said: "*Isu! Isu!* (Too late! Too late!) I robbed your earth-oven many times before you found me out."

Karum's spirit became the lizard which lives amongst the mangroves. Watch, and you will see him dive into the water and swim about.

KUDULUK AND
KUI [Told by Lizzie Nawia of Kubin at Thursday Island, 25 July 1969]

Kuduluk

Kuduluk, a young cuckoo,[1] set out from his home one day in search of food. Before long he met Kui, a young curlew. "Where are you going?" Kui asked him. "I'm looking for food," replied Kuduluk. "Don't go away. Stay and talk to me," said Kui.

The two young birds talked for a while, and then Kui said: "Would you like to play a game?" "What kind of game?" Kukuluk wanted to know. "*Umau sagul* (A game called death).[2] I'll teach you how to play it. Lie down and close your eyes, and I'll cry for you. I'll beg you to open your eyes, but you must take no notice of anything I say and just keep on lying very still with your eyes tight shut. Death is like that."

So Kuduluk and Kui played the game of death. Kuduluk lay down, closed his eyes, and lay very still. "Kukuluk! Kuduluk! Wake up! Open your eyes!" urged Kui, and he pretended to weep for his friend. Kuduluk did not move, and Kui kept on calling: "Kuduluk! Kuduluk! Open your eyes!" But Kuduluk played the game very well and continued to lie very still. At last Kui said: "It's time to get up now, Kuduluk. That's how the game is played. You can open your eyes now and get up." Kuduluk stood up and said: "Was I dead? Is that what death is?" "Yes," replied Kui, "that's death. Now it's my turn to act dead."

Kui lay down and Kuduluk wept for him. "Kui! Kui! Wake up! Open your eyes!" called Kuduluk. Kui lay without moving. "Kui! Kui!

1. Informants described this bird as small and brown, like the Torres Strait pigeon in shape, but not so big. It builds its own nest. It is called *koko* in East Torres Strait.
2. *Uma*, death; *umau sagul*, death game.

37

The following details were given by the informant who tells this children's story. Children at Kubin fear the curlew, *kui*. [Called *kobebe* at Badu. I did not see this bird myself, but the Islanders call it "curlew" when they speak English.] Should they be playing out-of-doors in the evening and a curlew cry, they run for the shelter of their home. Nothing will induce them to set foot outside the house after they have heard a curlew. "That's Kui, the dead bird, calling," they say.

Open your eyes!" he called many times. Then he said: "It's time to get up now, Kui. Open your eyes and get up." But Kui did not stir. Though Kuduluk called him and cried for him all day long, Kui never once so much as fluttered a single feather, and at last, just before sundown, Kuduluk left him lying still and cold on the ground and returned to his home.

His mother asked him why he had stayed away so long, and he told her: "I met a young curlew, Kui, and we played a game called death. Kui taught me what it is like to be dead. First I pretended to be dead, and then it was Kui's turn. Only, Kui would not get up at the end of the game as I had done. I called him and called him. I told him the game was over, but he would not move. He will never move again. Today I learned that death comes to birds and animals and humans. Kui is dead."

BURUM   [Told by Lizzie Nawia at Kubin, 3 November 1967]

A long time ago there was a very big pig on Mua. It was a man-eater. If a man went to his garden alone, this savage boar attacked him and ate him. Anyone who passed within smell of it was chased by it and eaten. There was no one who could describe the pig, because all who had actually seen it had been killed and eaten by it. But everyone had seen its tracks.

At last the head man called the people together and said to them: "We will leave our island and go to Badu. Prepare your canoes and load them. We will go today."

So the people of Mua[1] abandoned their homes, and by the end of the day there was no one left on the island but a pregnant woman whose husband had died a short time before. She had begged for a place at each of the canoes in turn, but all had refused to take her. She wept when she saw them go.

The woman gave birth to twin sons. When they were old enough, she made bows and arrows for them, and they learned to shoot.

One day her sons said to her: "Mother, is there no one on this island but us?" And only then did she tell them about Burum,[2] the savage boar.

"Once," she said, "there were many people on this island, but they became so terrified of Burum, the man-eating pig, that they went to Badu."

"Mother," said the boys, "we will kill Burum today." When she tried

1. Lizzie said that there were many people living in the interior of the island at that time.
2. *Burum*, pig.

38

to hold them back, they told her firmly: "We will hunt for Burum and kill him today. We will be back before night for our evening meal."

The two boys found the boar's tracks and followed them up the side of a hill to a big boulder, at the foot of which the monstrous beast lay asleep on the ground. They climbed the boulder and shot arrows into the pig until it was dead. Then they climbed down to the ground, removed two of the arrows from the pig, and set out for home.

The woman shed tears of joy when she saw the blood-stained arrows. "My sons," she said, "we will go to the beach and light a big fire."

This they did, and the fire was seen at Badu. The head man said: "What does the fire at Mua mean?" To some of the young men he gave the order: "Go and find out."

The young men went across to Mua. As their canoe drew close to the beach, they saw a woman dancing around the fire. Soon afterwards they had her story.

"Burum is dead," she told them. "Tell the people of Mua who are living at Badu that Burum, the man-eating pig, is dead. My sons killed him, my twin sons who were born after the people of Mua abandoned their homes."

The news was taken to Badu, and next morning the Mualgal who wished to go back to their island were permitted to do so. A few old women were so beside themselves with joy at the thought of returning to Mua that they said they would roll all the way up the hill to their former home.

MUTA [Told by Dubi Eseli at Kubin, 5 November 1967]

Muta of Totalai walked south across the island of Mua to Kubin, where he planned to spend several days digging up *bua*, a kind of yam that he felt like eating. He made a temporary shelter for himself near the beach called Mipa.

One night as he lay in his camp, he saw flickering lights appear at Zurzur, a point north of Mipa. Soon he realized that they were moving south, and before long he picked up the sound of paddles. Presently he heard canoes beaching and people talking. Whoever they were, they were coming straight towards him.

And then he saw them. They were carrying strings of dugong and turtle meat and *guiar*—the stingray that is eaten only by *markai*. His visitors were *markai*!

The *markai* placed their food on the ground near his shelter.

Immediately a big area of ground round about became as clean as if it had just been swept: all the grass disappeared, and the fallen leaves and undergrowth as well. Fireflies swarmed, lighting up the air and the trees. The *markai* women sat down and gave suck to their babies to prevent them from crying, and the *markai* men began to dance. Muta lay watching them, head on hands.

It was not long before feathers fell from the head-dresses of the dancers. The *markai* leader said: "There is a human watching us." However, the dancing resumed and continued until daybreak, when the ground opened, and *markai*, canoes, and food disappeared inside it.

Night after night the *markai* came to Mipa from Zurzur. Muta took particular notice of the dancers' head-dresses, because he had made up his mind to make a head-dress exactly like those of his visitors and join in the dancing.

One morning he walked along the beach and picked up the feathers that he needed. Then he made the head-dress, put it on, and shook his head. He was satisfied with his handiwork.

Muta had his meal early that evening and, as soon as the flickering lights appeared at Zurzur, went to the beach at Mipa and swam out until the water was up to his chin. Now he draped his head with seaweed and stood watching the *markai* canoes approach.

The *markai* leader saw Muta's head and thought it a rock covered with seaweed. "Keep away from this rock," he called to those who followed him. The outrigger of his own canoe almost scraped Muta's head, but the others avoided it more easily.

Muta followed the last of the canoes as it ran in to the beach. He helped the *markai* unload the dugong and turtle and *guiar*, and walked with them to their dance ground. The *markai* women settled themselves with their babies, and when the *markai* men began to dance, Muta danced with them, his eyes on their leader. Almost at once, however, the leader's head-dress fell from his head. "Stop!" he ordered the dancers, at this proof that there was a human in their midst.

Now the *markai* had been dancing in pairs. So when the leader asked each dancer in turn to name his partner, and of them all only Muta could not comply, the identity of the human was quickly established. Terrified of what the *markai* would do to him, Muta fled from Mipa.

Muta ran across the island, his only thought to reach his home at Totalai. Close behind him, the *markai* drove him relentlessly all night long.

At dawn, when Muta was within sight of Totalai, the *markai* disappeared into the ground. Muta's feet pounded on. They bore him into his house, and then he dropped down dead.

RARAMAI [Told by Wees Nawia at Kubin, November 1967]

In former times there were many villages on the island of Mua, but the people did not live in them all the time. Sometimes they abandoned them for weeks on end—when, for example, they went to their garden lands, or hunted, or, perhaps, merely wanted a change of scene.

Now in those days there was a village called Parbar on the western side of the island and a village called Sagan on the eastern side, and the people of those two places, being good friends, showed their friendship by sending each other presents of food. Thus, when the men of Parbar speared dugong or turtle they sent meat to Sagan, and when the men of Sagan speared dugong or turtle they sent meat to Parbar. That was the custom.

One day, boys who were delivering a present of meat from Sagan to Parbar unexpectedly heard singing as they approached Palga, halfway between the two villages. They had not known that anyone lived in that part of the island, so they dropped the strings of meat that they were carrying and went to see who it was. Not far away they found Raramai, a blind old woman, lying on her back on the ground.

When one boy said, "Let's get a big log of wood and put it across her neck—she can't see us," the rest agreed and helped him do it. Afterwards they picked up the strings of meat and continued their walk to Parbar. Later in the day they returned to Sagan by a path which avoided Palga. They told no one at either village what they had seen and done.

Raramai had struggled for a long time to free herself from the log which pinned her by the throat to the ground, but her efforts had grown feebler and feebler and at last ceased. Poor woman, she had made her home at Palga, thinking to use the leaves of the pandanus which grew there to make mats. She had harmed no one.

It was now the turn of the people of Sagan to send a present of food to Parbar, and this they did as soon as the men brought home a dugong. The boys who took it across discovered Raramai's body and, feeling sorry about the manner of her death, removed the log.

They told the news to the people of Sagan and to their own people at Parbar when they returned, but no one at either place shed light on the sad end of Raramai, for the culprits kept their secret well.

Today nobody lives at Parbar or Sagan, but the women of Kubin Village[1] go to Palga when they decide to weave mats. They say that the best mats are made from pandanus which grows at the spot where Raramai used to live.

1. At the southern tip of Mua.

YELUB AND HIS DOG

[Told by John Manas at Kubin, 27 October 1968]

There is a Mabuiag expression: *"Umail lak mabaigal (Men are like dogs)."*

At Murray Island, on the opposite side of the Strait, the Meriam say: *"Wi le uridli (They [that is, dogs] are men)."*

★

Yelub of Palga[1] had no wife. He lived by himself and never shared the food he brought home with him at the end of each day with the people in the village, but ate all of it himself. To his dog he threw only bones.

Now the dog knew very little about Yelub, for when it woke in the morning Yelub was already gone—to wherever it was he went—and he did not return until late afternoon. When he came back—from wherever it was he had been to—he cooked a meal and ate it, threw some bones to his dog, and then slept.

One afternoon as the dog lay waiting for its master to return, it spoke its thoughts out loud: "Yelub, all day long you go from place to place to eat food. You begin to eat when the sun comes up; you are still eating when the sun goes down. You eat fish and meat from dawn until dark, yet all you give me is bones." It did not know that it had been overheard by its master who had returned earlier than usual from hunting.

Yelub coughed, to let the dog know he was back, and went straight to the creature. "Dogs are like men," said Yelub. "Dogs and men should eat the same food."

He said the same thing to the people of Palga. "Feed your dogs well," he counselled them. "They think like us and feel like us. It has been our custom to eat meat and throw the bones to our dogs. That is wrong. We should share the meat with them, for, truly, dogs are like men."

1. On the island of Mua.

42

USIUS

[Told by Katua Namai at Kubin, 2 November 1967]

Formerly many people lived at Usul Nguki in the centre of the island of Mua. Each of the men had a stone fish-trap on the reef at Gerain, which he visited at low tide. The fish a man caught in his trap were his.

Usually all the men of Usul Nguki went to Gerain in company, but on one occasion a man named Usius stayed behind. His wife, Drak, overheard what the men said to her husband after they returned: "There are many fish in your trap. This time we will give you some of our fish. In future, however, you will have to go and get fish for yourself." She chided Usius for his laziness, and he promised to go to Gerain at the next low tide.

The moon was very bright that night. Usius woke when it was high in the sky and, thinking it was daytime, said to Drak: "I am going to my fish-trap." Halfway to Gerain, however, he had a change of mind and decided to go instead to his garden at Gisan and collect some sugarcane.

Hardly had he reached Gisan when he heard laughing voices behind him. He broke off some stems of sugarcane, stripped off the leaves and threw them away to the north of him. Almost at once the leaves were thrown back at his chest. "Perhaps I should throw the leaves in a different direction," he thought. So he threw them west. But again they were thrown back at him. He tried throwing them south and east—each time the leaves were immediately returned to him. "Someone is having a joke with me. I'd better leave this place," he decided.

After he crossed the creek near Gisan, Usius saw who had tricked him —*markai*! There were many of them, and they had a leader. "It's you who have been teasing me!" he cried. The *markai* said nothing. Suddenly they rushed at Usius, grabbed hold of him, and pulled him to the ground.

Usius wrestled with them and managed to break free. He tried desperately hard to escape, running first in this direction, then in that. It was useless. There were *markai* at the tops of trees who shouted to their companions: "There he goes! That way!" He tied stalks of grass together in order to trip the *markai*. But they caught him many times and, only by struggling with all his might, was he able to tear himself from their grasp —to run again, hopelessly, blindly. The fearful chase lasted till just before dawn when the *markai* suddenly disappeared. Usius collapsed, unconscious.

When he woke, he lay for a while with his eyes shut. He felt warm.

"It must be day-time," he thought. So he stood up, looked around him, said, "Yes, of course it's day-time," and walked home to Usul Nguki.

Drak was waiting for him. "Where are the fish?" she asked. Usius told her the story of his horrid encounter with the *markai* during the night. "There! You see? When I tell you to do something, you should do it. That's what comes of going off and doing something else. Go and rest while I cook something for us," said Drak.

Usius lay down. Soon afterwards Drak called him to come and eat, but by then he was dead.

GORA AND THE BUK [Told by Katua Namai at Kubin, 3 November 1967]

On the seaward slope of a tall hill at the northern end of Mua there is a spring of water, Purup, which is surrounded by big boulders. Formerly these boulders were used as a lookout by the people who lived at the foot of the hill in the village called Gisan.

There is no sign of this village today. What follows is the story of a man named Gora who lived at Gisan a long time ago when it was a big community.

Every morning Gora used to climb up the hill to Purup, where he had a small shelter made from leafy boughs.[1] Once inside it he could not be seen by the birds which came to the spring for water, and it was easy for him to shoot as many of them as he needed for food for himself and his family. He put a mark on his bow for every bird that he killed.

One day when he returned from Purup, he found Gisan deserted except for his wife and children. He asked where everyone had gone. "To the gardens near Narasaldan," his wife told him. "We will go and stay at Purup until they come back," Gora said.[2]

Throughout the time that they camped beside Purup, Gora's wife and children slept inside the bough shelter at night, and Gora lay down outside it across the entrance. He kept a big fire alight all night long for warmth.

As he was drowsing off on the second night at Purup, he heard something or someone moving towards him and the sound of a seed-pod dance-rattle (*gua*). His wife and children were asleep. He lay very still.

Presently he saw a *buk*[3]—a *markai*, the most dreaded kind of *markai*.

1. This shelter has a name, *urui mud* (literally, "bird house"). It was the custom at Mua for a man to erect an *urui mud* if he intended to make a practice of shooting birds at their regular watering-place.
2. Informants said that at Mua an entire village would be deserted for up to several weeks at a time when the people decided to go and work their garden-land. After the work was completed, the people returned to their village.
3. Wees Nawia of Kubin said that his grandmother (from Muralag) distinguished between four kinds of ghost: *mari*, which wore feathers on its head —sometimes as many as three or four; *markai*; *buk*, which made the sound of a shaken *gua* (old-time dance-rattle) and was especially to be feared; and *padutu*, which might occasionally be seen after sunset while the sky was still red. A *padutu* wore a single feather and had a red stripe across its forehead.

Silently he willed it to come closer: "Come on. Come on. I'm not afraid of you." He moved his hand to the fire and grasped a burning log. The *buk* came nearer. When it was almost upon him, Gora hurled the log of fire at it, striking it on the right cheek bone. The *buk* turned and fled down the hillside.

At the foot of the hill the *buk* whistled. "Go home! Go back to Kibu!"[4] shouted Gora. The *buk* whistled a second time. "Go home to Kibu!" shouted Gora. After that there was silence.

4. Kibu was the home of the spirits. It lay somewhere beyond the horizon. (See also footnote 5 of "Aukam and Tiai", in this section.)

GOBA   [Told by Wees Nawia at Kubin, 8 November 1967]

Amongst the Mualgal (people of Mua) who were living on the eastern side of the hill called Gunagan[1] was a man who had a young son named Goba. When this man said to his wife one day, "There's a good low tide today—I'll go and spear some fish," she warned him to be on his guard against raiders from the neighbouring island, Badu. He intended to leave his son at home, but the boy pleaded so hard and so long to be allowed to go that he yielded, against his better judgment, and took the boy with him.

Father and son walked to Isumulai[2] on the western coast of the island and went out on the reef and fished—unaware that they were watched the whole time by members of a warring party from Badu whose canoes were beached on the other side of the nearby point, Karbai Gizu. After they had filled a basket with fish, they picked up some big *bu* shells which were lying on the reef and began their journey back to Gunagan.

Both Goba and his father felt very thirsty by this time. When they reached the spring, Uma,[3] they halted for a drink. Goba then complained of hunger, so his father lit a fire and roasted some fish, although he knew it was extremely dangerous for him and his son to dally alone in the bush. "Should we be attacked," he told Goba, "run away and climb a tree. Hide amongst the branches and leaves. Make no movement. Utter no sound."

Soon after they sat down to eat the cooked fish, the father glimpsed movement in the scrub nearby. "Run!" he whispered to Goba and when the boy had gone stood up to face the men of Badu who were about to

1. This hill is not far from the spring, Uma.
2. The big boulder, Karakar Kula (which was formerly a giant, an *adiad*) is at Isumulai.
3. From which Kubin Village draws its water supply today.

45

strike him down. "Don't kill me," he said to them, "I am a friend." The men of Badu clubbed him and afterwards removed his head with a bamboo knife (*upi*). Goba, watching from a tree, saw his father killed. He shut his eyes before the moment of his father's beheading. When he opened them he saw his father's headless body lying on the ground and the retreating figures of the men from Badu, one of whom carried his father's head.

Goba stayed up the tree until long after sunset. Late at night he climbed down and ran all the way home to Gunagan, where he told what had happened to his father. "Take us to your father's body tomorrow," the men said.

Next morning Goba led the Mualgal to his father's body. They covered it with stones.

[**After finishing the story, Wees Nawia added this detail**]:

The events related in this story happened just prior to the coming of Christianity to Torres Strait in 1871.

Goba was about eight years old when his father was killed by the raiders from Badu. The mound of stones beneath which his father's bones lie is approximately a quarter of a mile from the spring, Uma.

Goba married. He cut off his wife's head with an axe one day when she displeased him.

stories from

BADU *Mulgrave Island*

BIA

[Told by Father Mara at Badu, 22 October 1967]

Bia, an aborigine (*kawaig*), lived at Cowal Creek on Cape York Peninsula. He ate fish and wild yams (*saur*). He had magical powers.[1]

Every day he walked along the beach, either south to the mouth of the Jardine River, or north to Red Island Point, and he always took his spear (*dikun*)[2] with him, a spear which had some of his own magic power in it. He used to throw the spear ahead of him, walk to it, pick it up and throw it again, all the way there and back. He used a woomera when throwing his spear.

On the way back from Red Island Point one day, his spear landed at Alau, skidded along the sand and buried itself to its full length just above the beach. Bia followed its track and found it; when he pulled it out, water gushed from the hole. There has been a spring of water at that spot ever since.

The thought came to Bia one morning that he would visit the islands which lay to the north of his home at Cowal Creek. From the dilly-bag in which he kept his aids to magic he took out a small, magic canoe and a feather. He put the magic canoe into the sea, stuck the feather in the canoe, and spoke magic words. These caused the feather to become a sail and the canoe one big enough to hold a man. Bia stepped into the canoe and sailed to Muralag.

He landed at Dakanu. Now if he were to be able to play with his spear at this new place, he had to have a long beach like those at his former home, so he went round to the west side of the island and looked for one. At the first long stretch of sand he saw, he threw his spear. It came to rest in the roots of a mangrove tree. This island, Bia decided, did not suit him. So he sailed further north.

Kunai (Goode Island)[3] did not please him. Warar (Hawkesbury Island) did not please him. At neither was there a beach where he could throw his spear. At Warar he looked north and saw Badu and Mua. He chose Badu as the next island that he would visit.

Bia landed on the south-west coast of Badu at a spot on the beach near the big rock called Kudal. A man named Itar lived near by. He greeted Bia, and the two men became friends.

Bia and Itar lived together at Kudal for some time. They ate fish and

1. *Nui pui-mabaig*, he magic-power person.
2. *Dikun*, a spear used in play.
3. Goode Island seems to have two names, Kunai and Palilag.

yams. The variety of yam which Itar dug was *bua*, a kind unknown to Bia. Bia, on the other hand, dug *saur*, the yam which he had found and eaten at Cowal Creek, and he now taught Itar about it. Each man was delighted to learn of a new food.

One day Bia threw his spear along the beach which stretched north of Kudal. He had not used all his strength in throwing it, so it did not travel very far. Yet Bia spent a long time looking for it before he found it, because the sand where it landed and afterwards skimmed along the surface was hard-packed—there was no track to lead Bia to his spear. Eventually he found it at Mekeina Kausar. Then he threw it back to Kudal, and it landed beside the rock on the beach.

Another day, after throwing his spear to Mekeina Kausar, he threw a second time, further north, to the very end of the beach. It was very hard to find. For a while he thought it was lost for good. "My beautiful spear, where are you? Have you buried yourself like a crab in the sand? I do not want to lose you," said Bia. He went to the soft sand-ridges behind the beach. There was no trace of the spear. At last he found it, further inland from the shore than he had expected it to be, buried to its full length in the middle of a patch of scrub, and, when he pulled it out, beautiful, clear, sweet water gushed from the ground.[4] "This is my water. I found it with my spear. This water will never stop flowing," he said. He was very happy.

On the long walk back to Kudal, Bia threw his spear twice only, the first time, just before he set out, the second time from Mekeina Kausar where it had come to rest. At Mekeina Kausar he hooked his spear to his woomera and threw with all his might. When he reached Kudal, he saw Itar lying on the beach, dead: his spear had pierced his friend's side and killed him. Bia wept.

Afterwards he carried Itar to the edge of the sea and, before throwing the body into the water, said: "Itar, my good friend, you will become a fish and live in the sea. You will look for food only at night. During the day you will rest safe and sound inside a hole in a stone."[5]

Bia had no wish to stay at Kudal any longer, so he left at once in his magic canoe, sailing round Zigini Ngur to Wakaid and then leaving Badu and crossing to Parbar on Mua. From Mua he sailed to Iem, a small island from which Gumu (Mabuiag) was clearly visible. He chose, however, to go east with the next morning tide past Gebar (Two Brothers Island) to Iama (Yam Island), which place he reached before sunset that day.

When he woke the following morning, Bia decided to play with his spear and, walking to the beach,[6] threw it over a rocky point at the end of the stretch of sand. When it landed, its tip pierced the ground. Bia easily found his spear. When he pulled it free, water flowed from the shallow hole. "This is my water," he said, "but, because my spear only went into

4. This spring is called Iaza. It has never been known to fail.
5. Itar became the Epaulette Shark, *Hemiscyllium ocellatum.*
6. In front of the present-day village.

50

Mota Charlie, one of the story-tellers.
Mota is sitting facing the spring created
by Bia's spear. The spring is at Iaza on
the island of Badu.

the ground a little way, it will sometimes fail. In a drought, this spring will go dry."[7]

Next day, Bia again sailed east with the morning tide. It took him to Kailag (Yorke Island), where he did not go ashore, not liking the beaches for spear-play, and to Erub (Darnley Island), where he landed at Badog.[8]

Bia slept the night at Badog and in the morning walked round to the east side of the island. At the beginning of the long beach called Isem, he threw his spear, and it fell on the far side of the headland at the end of the beach, burying itself to half its length. At that spot,[9] once again Bia's spear found water. Bia said: "This is my water. The spring is good. Nevertheless, it will dry up at times, because my spear did not bury itself completely."

Mer (Murray Island), suspended above the horizon east of Erub, was not visited by Bia. He saw Mer, but he did not go there. From Erub he sailed south. With his magic to help him and a good north wind from behind, he reached Cowal Creek in one day. He sailed up the creek for a short distance and then, standing up in his canoe, hooked his spear on the woomera and threw it. "Where my spear stops, I will make my home," said Bia.

The spear flew through the air to the hills inland and half-buried itself in the ground at a place where tall grass grew. Bia lived there by himself for a while. Later, he had a wife with him.

Bia's spear had been his plaything, a magic toy, which he had never used for killing men. He was a man who had magical powers; he was not a fighting man. Therefore, when he had reason after a time to believe himself to be in danger of an attack by enemies, he said to his wife: "We must leave this place. It is not safe for us to remain here." And the two walked towards the coast. Not far from the mouth of Cowal Creek, Bia embraced his wife and, holding her tight in his arms, jumped into the running water. He spoke magic words, and at once he and his wife became a pair of mating turtles (*saulal*) which were carried out to sea by the tide.

Ever since, the first pair of mating turtles in the season of mating turtle have always been seen floating on top of the water near the entrance to Cowal Creek. Other couples quickly follow the first and make their way north. Before long, the sea which lies between the two mainlands is dotted with mating turtle.

7. This spring is called Ngurnguki at Yam Island (*ngur*, point; *nguki*, water).
8. The church stands there today.
9. In Mogor.

52

WAD AND
ZIGIN   [Told by Ben Nona at Badu, 25 October 1967]

Long ago there were two brothers, Wad and Zigin, living near the spot on the beach which came to be called Wadan Wibad. Wad's home[1] was a little to the north of Zigin's.

Both men were hunters. Wad was an expert, a champion, and he always gave his younger brother a half share of everything he speared in spite of the fact that Zigin was lazy and seldom went out.

In the season of mating turtle, there was never a day when Wad was not out in his canoe hunting. On the beach in front of the place where he lived there was always a long row of turtle lying on their backs, white bellies uppermost, that Wad had speared. When he wanted to eat turtle, he killed one of them, cut it up, and gave half the meat and fat to Zigin.

But Wad found it very difficult to do all the work by himself, and one day he asked Zigin to go with him and steer the canoe. Zigin said: "I won't go with you—I might get wet. Besides, after playing my drum all night I'm tired and I'm going to sleep today."

For a while longer Wad continued to work alone without the help of his younger brother, and he still gave him a half-share of his turtle meat and fat. The day came, however, when Wad said to himself: "I'm going to teach that lazy brother of mine a lesson."

Next day, Wad caught some turtle, brought them ashore and cut them up. This time he kept all the best parts for himself and to his brother gave no fat (*tupai*), no eggs (*wibad*), only shoulder meat (*pagasiu madu*), the worst cut from a turtle.

Zigin was furious. "I'll go out and catch turtle for myself," he raged. "I'll block the tide and prevent it from reaching Wad—*usalai*[2] will bring no more turtle to Wad. My elder brother will sit out there with dry lips (*Kau ni nika kuruig tepad gudalnga*). He'll catch nothing. *Kulis* will drive all the turtle to the bottom of the sea and keep them there, and there'll be no *usalai* for Wad. I'll have my revenge on him for giving me shoulder meat only!"

The following morning, Zigin went to Kabar Gizu,[3] walked out into the sea, and stood in it all day long, facing west. But he caught no turtle. *Usalai*, blocked by Zigin, diverted itself to his left. It swept the turtle

1. The school stands very close to where Wad lived.
2. In Torres Strait, tide is thought of as flowing either from west to east, or from east to west. There are names for special conditions of tide. Thus, *usalai* is the tide when it is flowing strongly from west to east in the afternoon. It is the tide when turtle are caught. *Kulis* is the tide when it flows from east to west. Turtle are not caught with *kulis*.
3. The rocky point at the southern end of the beach beside which he lived.

53

south to the small island called Tiki, and Wad got them. (A rock marks the spot off Kabar Gizu where Zigin stood in the sea that day.)

The next day, Zigin walked south of Kabar Gizu to the beach called Dual Butu before going out and standing in the sea. *Usalai* again diverted itself to the left of him and this time carried the turtle between Tiki and neighbouring Iargas, a small island south of Tiki. Again, Zigin caught no turtle, and Wad caught many.

"What I have done has had no effect," thought Zigin. "I'll have to stand still further south, between Urakaran and Gizu.[4] Wad won't catch turtle if I do that. My elder brother will surely sit all day long with dry lips."

So, the day after, Zigin stood in the sea off Gizu and, at mid-afternoon when *usalai* began to flow full and strong, Zigin, who had spent the night playing his drum, was fast asleep. Turtle swept by on both sides of him. And Wad, as always, caught many turtle.

Day after day, Zigin stood in the sea out from Gizu. And every evening when he returned home, he saw a row of white bellies on the sand in front of Wad's place. Zigin never brought back a single turtle, for every day, by the time *usalai* arrived, Zigin, exhausted from playing his drum the night before, was asleep on his feet.

One day, Zigin died while he was standing in the sea out from Gizu. He died of starvation.

Wad continued to hunt daily and spear turtle. He had proved himself to be a cleverer man than his younger brother and he was proud of it. One day when he was cutting up turtle, he allowed the sea to wash the eggs high up the sand. "*Wadan wibad.* (Wad's [turtle] eggs.) This is my place," he said.

Wad's turtle eggs turned to stones which lie on the beach just south of the school. They are still there, at Wadan Wibad.

A ring tide swirls around Zigin when the tide is low—he never moved from the spot at which he stood in the water trying to prevent *usalai* from carrying turtle to his elder brother, but turned to stone and became a rock on the bed of the sea. He has not been forgotten. "*Ni mata keda Zigin mid,*" say the people of Badu to a lazy man, "*kai gam daidamalnga* (You are just like Zigin—a very lazy fellow)."

4. The rocky headland since called Zigini Ngur.

54

THE FOUR BEAUTIFUL DAUGHTERS

[Told by Yopelli Panuel at Badu, 25 October 1967]

Long ago at Wakaid there was a man who had four beautiful daughters, Madainab, Mainab, Damanab, and Kotinab.

One day he told them that they would be going that night to hunt for turtle by torchlight. In the evening they made their way by canoe to Kubin, and from there, south to the big reef a short distance away, where they released suckerfish (*gapul*). They did not know that they were being watched by a sorcerer who was using evil magic against them.[1]

Presently one of the suckerfish attached itself to a turtle. Madainab, the eldest daughter, jumped into the water to catch the turtle and was taken down deep by it. She never came up. "Madainab, my beautiful daughter," said the father after he had set sail for the return journey to Badu, "the spot at which you died shall be named for you."[2]

By the time the canoe reached Zigini Ngur,[3] the second daughter, Mainab, was so ill that the father decided to take her ashore at the small beach nearby. She died there. The father and his remaining two daughters built a *sara*[4] (platform) and placed her body on it. They then returned to their canoe.

"We cannot return to Wakaid,"[5] said the father. "We shall go to Argan." And as they sailed for the west coast of Badu, he said to the girl who lay on the *sara*: "Mainab, my beautiful daughter, men will call the beach where you died by your name."

When the father and Damanab and Kotinab reached a certain small bay between Barabaras and Argan they landed, to be greeted by the young men who were camped close by.

That night the young men danced, and Damanab fell in love with one of them. She did not sail with her father and her sister when they left in the morning, instead remaining with the young man whom she had chosen for her husband from among the dancers. From a distance the father looked back at her and said: "Damanab, my beautiful daughter, your home shall be called by your name."

The father and his youngest daughter went ashore for the last time at Koteid. After they had been there for a while, news of the beautiful girl

1. Another informant said that the sorcerer had been engaged by the brother of the father of the four daughters. This brother had refused to join the turtle-hunting expedition when asked, and, since he was jealous of his brother and was piqued by the latter's going off without him, decided to harm him.

   The brother's name was Idunab. He lived about half a mile north of the village called Wakaid, in the area near the creek which bears his name: Idunab.
2. Where Madainab died there are several small reefs. These have the name, Madainab.
3. On Badu.
4. The platform on which a corpse was laid.
5. See footnote 1 for the possible explanation of this remark.

6. At a later date, a man named Dokere cut up a turtle (of the big-headed kind known as *maiwa*) on top of this stone. He left the carapace on it, and the carapace afterwards turned to stone. Both stones are usually referred to as Maiwal Kula (*kula*, stone, rock).

When the story of the four beautiful daughters is told, the father is sometimes called Maiwal. Properly speaking, however, that name derives from an incident in the story about Dokere.

spread to a nearby village. "Let us go and dance for her," said the young men. "Let us see if she will choose one of us to be her husband."

So the young men decorated their bodies and set out with their drums to dance for Kotinab. Presently she chose one of them.

"Kotinab, my beautiful daughter," the father said at parting from his youngest child, "your name will live on, for the place to which you are going will henceforth be known as Kotinab. Later, I shall come and make my home within sight of you."

This he did, turning to stone on the reef,[6] not far from the southern end of the beach called Kotinab.

DOKERE [Told by Mota Charlie at Badu, 26 October 1968]

A long time ago, a man named Dokere who lived at Argan caught a big-headed turtle (*maiwa*). He did not want the blood of the turtle to be taken away by the tide when he removed the flesh from the carapace on the reef, therefore the cutting-up would have to be done at the right kind of spot. Turtle on shoulder, Dokere went in search of it.

He examined the reef at Tudui, Iaza, Waru, Zigini Ngur, and Sisal Ngur, in that order. There was nowhere suitable at those places. Not until he reached Koteid on the opposite side of the island to Argan did he see what he wanted. There, not far out from the beach, was a big rock with a flat top and around it a pool of water which had been left behind by the tide.

Dokere walked to the rock, laid the turtle on its back on top of it, and cut the flesh from the carapace. The blood of the turtle he emptied into the pool, where it would remain until the incoming tide brought it ashore. Replacing the meat in the shell, he carried it back to the beach and cooked it in an earth-oven. After eating, he slept all night long.

In the morning he woke with a raging thirst. First, he took the shell of *maiwa* out to the rock where he had done his cutting-up the previous day and, laying the shell on top of it, said: "This rock shall be called Maiwal Kula (Turtle-with-a-big-head Rock)." Then he began to look for water to drink.

He walked back round the island all the way to Iaza without finding a drop. At that place he struck inland and before long came to a beautiful, big pool from which flowed fresh, cool water. Dokere, parched, jumped into the water and swam and drank. He drank so much that his scrotum burst, and his testicles fell to the bottom of the pool.

Only then did Dokere climb out of the water. "This is my water (*Dokeren nguki*)," he said. "It will never go dry. My testicles will remain at the bottom of it for ever."

Both Dokere's testicles and the shell of *maiwa* which Dokere left on the rock at Koteid turned to stone. The stream of water (Bubul Nguki) which flows from the pool discovered by Dokere has never been known to stop running.

SESERE   [Told by Mota Charlie at Badu, 27 October 1967]

This is the story of a man named Sesere who lived by himself at a spot north of the village called Tulu. At that time there were a number of small villages south of Tulu—Bait, Bokan, Zaum, Aubu Kösa, Kulkai, and Sisal Ngur. The place where Sesere had his home is remembered as Seserengagait, Sesere's place.[1]

One morning at low tide when Sesere was walking about on the reef spearing fish—this was his daily custom—he noticed reef grass that had been nipped off short in mud that had the appearance of having been disturbed by a big fish eating. He had never seen anything like it before. Another day he saw a kind of excreta washed up by the tide that was different from any he had previously seen.

Sesere puzzled over these strange new signs. What kind of animal was visiting the reef? Was it good to eat? He would have to catch it and find out, but as he did not know how to set about doing it, he would have to obtain help from his parents who were dead.

So he went to the cave in which he kept their skulls, removed them, washed them, and rubbed them with the scented leaves of *takar* and *matua*, and then he addressed them: "*Amadual, babadual* (mother, father, both of you), give me a good dream tonight. Strange animals are grazing on the reef. What are they? How should I catch them?" That night he slept with his head close to the skulls.

1. *Gagait*, place.

57

The light-coloured dugong of West Torres Strait. Note the harpoon in the left shoulder.

In sleep he heard the sound of *awarpali* (finger-nail-flicking), and soon afterwards saw his parents. They said: "*Purkur!*[2] What do you want? Climb the hill tomorrow. Search until you find a place where many small birds are twittering. Everything you need to catch *dangal* (dugong), the creature whose spoor you have recently seen, will be there."

When he woke next morning, Sesere pushed the skulls away, saying: "You gave me a bad dream last night." But almost at once he pulled them back and, clasping them to him, said: "No, no. It was a good dream." And as soon as he had eaten, he climbed the hill behind Seserengagait and walked about until he reached the place described to him by his father and mother. There, leaning against the trunk of a tree—in which, and above which, many small birds twittered in tremulous flight—were *wap* (dugong-hunter's spear), *kuir*[3] (barbed harpoon), *kodai amu*[4] (rope), and poles for building a *niat*[5] (dugong-hunter's platform). All these things Sesere carried to his home.

2. Another informant, Jomen Tamwoy, used the word *purupuru*. I could not obtain a meaning for either *purkur* or *purupuru*.
3. Inserted into one end of the *wap*.
4. *Kodai*, a strong vine; *amu*, rope.
5. Or *nat*.

58

At low tide that afternoon, Sesere drove a *narapat* (marker stick) into the spot at which a dugong had left off eating at the previous high tide (to indicate the site for a hunting platform). Then he erected the platform and placed on top of it *wap, kuir,* and *amu*. When the water covered the reef that night, Sesere went to the platform and waited for the dugong to come back and resume feeding. Presently he harpooned it.

After that Sesere always had dugong to eat. Some of the meat he cooked in an earth-oven, some he smoked on a rack over his fire. He had meat to spare, and this he strung and suspended from the roof of his house. He had no need to spear fish.

After a while the people of Tulu became curious about Sesere; why did he no longer go to the reef daily and walk about with his fish-spear? One of the men made the shape of a dog from the spathe of coconut fronds, went into it, and ran to Seserengagait to find out. Sesere saw him coming and thought: "This must be a dog from the big village." He called it to him: "Come here, dog. Would you like some dugong meat?" The man inside the dog ran for the meat which Sesere threw to him, gulped it down, and then he ran back to Tulu. "Sesere is catching dugong," he told the people. "He gave me some dugong meat to eat. There are strings of meat, both fresh and cooked, hanging from the roof of his house."

The following day three men in the guise of dogs ran from Tulu to Seserengagait and, after being fed dugong meat by Sesere, returned to their village. The day after, five went to Seserengagait. This time they did not run away immediately after they had been fed but lay down and fixed their eyes on Sesere, who, finding their behaviour odd, walked away from his house. When he returned, the dogs had vanished, and some strings of meat had disappeared.

Many men ran to Seserengagait as dogs on the next visit, and, as on the previous day, they lay down after they had been fed and stared at Sesere.

Sesere stared back at them, taking particular notice of their eyes. "These dogs have the eyes of men," he decided. So he left his house, but for a short time only, and came back in time to see the dogs running away with strings of meat in their mouths. He shot an arrow at one of the dogs and killed it. And that night he asked his parents' skulls for a dream which would tell him how to fight the men of Tulu who would certainly come in strength to avenge the death of their kinsman.

In the morning all the men of Tulu put on their fighting gear and marched to Seserengagait, where Sesere was waiting for them inside his house. "Come out!" shouted the head man of Tulu, "Come out!" And after Sesere appeared, the head man said: "Look up at the sun (*Goigoika nagi*)! We are going to kill you. Take your last look at the sun!" Then the men of Tulu rushed at Sesere, ready to bring down their clubs on his head.

Sesere changed into a willy-wagtail and flew to the top of a man's head. Another man swung his club at Sesere but missed him completely, because Sesere flew away at that instant, and he only succeeded in killing his kinsman. Sesere flew from head to head, always saving himself from his attackers and causing the men of Tulu to strike each other dead. Thus, by following the advice given to him by his parents when they visited him in a dream the night before, he outwitted the men who had come to kill him. Only one man lived to return to Tulu.

This man summoned the men from the neighbouring small villages—Bait, Bokan, Zaum, Aubu Kösa, Kulkai, and Sisal Ngur. Together they went to Seserengagait. But of them all, only one survived, for Sesere again changed himself into a willy-wagtail and tricked the men into killing each other.

The villages appealed to a number of *dogai* to go and kill Sesere, but the *dogai* were no match for the willy-wagtail against whom they had to fight, and soon all were dead.

After that no one came near Sesere. He went on living by himself at his place, spearing dugong, and living well on their meat. He shared it with nobody.

From Sesere, however, came the knowledge of how to make *wap* and *kuir* and *niat*, and with it, the ability of men to hunt and catch dugong for themselves ever afterwards.[6]

6. Jomen Tamwoy, who also told the story of Sesere, gave a different ending from Mota Charlie's. Jomen said:

Sesere grew tired during the fight against the men from the villages south of Tulu and tried to escape by hiding inside a *bu* shell (Australian Trumpet Shell, *Syrinx aruanus* Linne). When his enemies smashed the *bu* shell with their clubs, he flew to a bush. Then his enemies swore at him and said: "You will be a bird for ever and ever. You will never leave this place, and as you flit about in the scrub you will call: '*Sesere pude, Sesere bubung kupai ia pude* (Sesere went and hid inside a *bu* shell).' "

Sesere   *Artist* Ngailu Bani

IAWAR

[Told by Mota Charlie at Badu, 26 October 1967]

Iawar lived by himself at Italnga. He was an excellent gardener. Everything that he planted—bananas, yams, and other fruits and vegetables—grew well and grew fast, so fast that while he was still planting, those plants which he had only just put into the ground had sprung up behind him and matured, and were swarming with fruit-flies attracted by the rich, ripe smell of their fruit.

On the high ground, Madubau Kal—not far from Italnga—there lived some men, *madubalgal,*[1] who watched all that Iawar did. They wanted to enjoy the same, quick harvests as Iawar, so they visited him and asked him to come and show them how he planted.

Iawar went to Madubau Kal and taught the *madubalgal* how to plant. But he did not give away all his secrets. Therefore, although the *madubalgal* followed Iawar's instructions, they did not obtain the results that they observed from Iawar's planting in his own garden at Italnga.

So the *madubalgal* asked Iawar to come and show them how to plant as he did. In fact, they asked him to come many times, because, no matter how often Iawar taught them, what they planted never grew so fast or so well as what Iawar planted for himself.

At last the *madubalgal* became angry and suspicious. "Iawar is making fools of us. He is holding something back from us. Why do our plants never grow like his?" they said.

Once more they invited Iawar to come to Madubau Kal. When he arrived, they knocked him down, overpowered him, and put a string through the hole in his nose. Then they hauled him—by means of the string—from Madubau Kal, along the high, grassy place called Kaideilu, to the foot of the hill, Wabau Pad—the route is clearly to be seen today as a strip of grass on which no trees grow, though many grow on either side of it—and from Wabau Pad to Tulu. At Tulu they put him in a canoe and took him across to Totalai on the island of Mua. From Totalai they dragged him past Baua to Bulbul, whence they dispatched him by rainbow to Erub (Darnley Island).

While the *madubalgal* were dragging him along on Badu by the string through his nose, Iawar gathered up all the good soil. This he held in his hands until he reached Erub, and then he used it for the gardens which he made on that island.

1. An informant said that a *madub* was a lazy, stupid, apathetic person; the *madubalgal* (plural of *madub*) had so little success with their planting because they were just that—lazy, stupid, apathetic fellows; and in the story of Iawar was to be found the origin of the idiomatic expression in current use at Badu for a lazy, stupid, apathetic person: "*Ni madub.* (You are just like the *madubalgal.*)"

BIU [Told by Sesa Bani at Kubin, 5 November 1967, and Jomen Tamwoy at Bamaga, 15 November 1967]

Gitalai the crab lived in the mud at the foot of a mangrove tree. Biu,[1] a seed pod which grew at the top of the tree, fell into the mud below and broke Gitalai's back.

Gitalai called loudly to a man named Goba: "Goba, bring your axe and chop Biu's head off!" Goba came and chopped Biu's head off.

Biu called to Fire: "Fire, come and burn Goba!" Fire came and burnt Goba.

Goba called to Water: "Water, come and quench Fire!" Water came and quenched Fire.

Fire called to Gudigad:[2] "Gudigad, come and drink Water!" Gudigad came and drank Water.

Water called to Kimus:[3] "Kimus, come and pierce Gudigad's belly!" And when Kimus came and pierced Gudigad's belly, all the water inside her ran out.

Kobebe, the night curlew, began to wail for all who had died: for Biu and Gitalai and Goba and Fire and Water and Gudigad.

"*Kia kia iarage,*"[4] mourned Kobebe.

"*Baiama sesere ku-ku-ku,*" cried Baimut[5] and his companions.

After, the air was still.

1. *Biu*, a variety of mangrove; the seedling pod of this mangrove; the edible pulp of its pod.
2. Gudigad could not be identified with certainty by the informants. Jomen Tamwoy thought that Gudigad may have been either a woman who habitually drank enormous quantities of water—Goba's wife, perhaps—or a *dogai*.
3. *Kimus*, an arrow which is tipped with cassowary bone (or claw). *Kimus* was more deadly than any other arrow.
4. *Iarage* = *iagar* (alas!).
5. *Baimut*, a small grey bird. It has a yellow breast.

KUAKA [Told by Wipa Waiat at Badu, 19 October 1967]

When Tagai and Kang set out from Mabuiag in their canoe one day, they had their sister, Kuaka, on board with them.

She made herself a nuisance by moving from stern to bow and from bow to stern, never sitting still, and forever calling her own name: "Kuaka!

Kuaka! Kuaka!" Her fidgety behaviour made Tagai very angry. "Be quiet! Sit still!" he ordered, at the same time striking the poling stick against the side of the canoe.

Kuaka obeyed for a while, and then she became restless again. "Stop it!" shouted Tagai, intensely irritated by then. But Kuaka, seemingly, could not.

Tagai emptied every one of the coconut shell water-containers (*kusul*)[1] on board the canoe. A short time afterwards he said to his sister: "You and I will go ashore at Mui Wakaid on Badu and fill the *kusul*."

Tagai and Kuaka carried all the *kusul* to the pool in the scrub behind Mui Wakaid. They filled some and took them back to the canoe, leaving behind those that were still empty. No sooner had they reached the canoe, however, than Tagai sent Kuaka back to fill and fetch the remaining *kusul* by herself, and she had not gone far, when he poled the canoe out from the shore. By the time Kuaka came back from the pool, he was well out to sea.

"Come back," called Kuaka, "I am your sister."

"I will not have you on board the canoe," replied Tagai. "Stay where you are. Badu will be your home."

In vain Kuaka pleaded with Tagai to put back for her. She was still calling to him when the canoe disappeared from her sight.

Presently she changed into a brown bird. From that time she has never done anything else but fly from tree to tree, never stopping long in any one place, but always restlessly hopping and flitting about. And, as she did in Tagai's canoe, so now she still calls her own name, over and over again: "Kuaka! Kuaka! Kuaka!"

The bird which Kuaka became. The sketch in the corner shows Kuaka standing on the beach at Badu, imploring her brothers, Tagai and Kang, to come back for her.

Artist Ngailu Bani

1. Always carried in pairs. *Kusu* is the singular form of the word.

TUBU AND THE SEVEN SISTERS   [Told by Lassie Eseli at Badu, 25 October 1967]

Seven girls—seven sisters— and a youth named Tubu used to go to Kulkai for *mai*, Tubu climbing the tree and knocking down the fruit, the girls filling their baskets as it fell. Then he climbed down and filled his own basket.

The girls treated Tubu shabbily, leaving only green, unripe fruit for him. He knew it, but said nothing.

After every visit to the *mai* tree, Tubu and the girls went down to the beach and cooked their fruit, the contents of each basket being kept separate from the rest: inside the earth-oven there were eight individual heaps of *mai*. And while they were waiting for the *mai* to come out of the oven, they played a game of hide-and-seek in the sea.

The girls always hid first, and while he was looking for them in their hiding-places under the water, Tubu would be thinking to himself: "You took all the ripe red *mai* and left only green ones for me, but I'll be even with you." And when it was his turn to hide, no sooner was he out of sight of the girls than he changed into a garfish (*zaber*), skipped along the top of the water until he reached the beach, and then changed into a little lizard (*zizuruk*, or *sizuruk*). Very quickly, he ran across the sand, went into the earth-oven, ate the seven heaps of ripe fruit belonging to the girls, and afterwards returned to the sea in exactly the same manner as he had left it.

It always took the girls a long time to find Tubu, the youth, when he hid from them. And, of course, at the end of the game when the earth-oven was opened, the girls always found that their *mai* had vanished.

After a while they began to suspect Tubu of playing a trick on them. "Why does it take us so long to find him when he hides? We'll have to catch him in the act. Tomorrow we won't waste time looking for him, but go straight to the earth-oven."

So the following day they were ready for Tubu, and when they saw a garfish skip along the top of the water towards the shore, they followed it in. Thus they were in time to see the garfish change into a lizard and run over the sand to the oven and go inside it. "That's the way he's managed to rob us, is it?" said the girls. "Very clever, Tubu, changing yourself into a garfish and a lizard. But not clever enough!" And they uncovered the earth-oven at once.

The little lizard lay very still, ashamed to look at the girls who had found him out. "We're going to kill you, Tubu," the girls said.

But Tubu pleaded with the girls not to kill him inside the earth-oven: "Let me go down the beach, to the edge of the sea. You can kill me then." The girls agreed to his; only, just as they were going to kill him, Tubu said: "If you kill me here, my blood will be wasted.[1] Mui Wakaid would be a much better place to kill me. I'll run from here to Mui Wakaid, and you can kill me there." At Mui Wakaid Tubu said: "Why don't you kill me at Dogai Wak (*wak*, bay)? It doesn't make any difference to you where you kill me, does it? You can easily catch me and kill me at Dogai Wak." And once more the girls agreed to put off killing Tubu for a little while longer.

Tubu reached Dogai Wak ahead of the girls, ran down into the sea, and changed into a fish—a sand flat-head.[2] The girls chased him with sharp-

1. Taken away by the sea.
2. *Platycephalus arenarius* Ramsay and Ogilby.

64

pointed sticks, but Tubu swam out to deep water and they could not catch him. "Go back to Kulkai and stay there for ever," Tubu ordered them.

And this they did. When they got back to Kulkai they walked to a spot on the reef at the edge of the channel between Badu and Mua and turned into rocks: seven rocks which are called Ngokazil.[3]

Meanwhile Tubu had been teasing the *dogai* whose home was the bay, Dogai Wak. That day she had gone fishing off the point not far from her home, and Tubu annoyed her by swimming underwater and tickling her feet. She tried to spear him with a pointed stick, but he was too quick for her and escaped into deep water where she could not follow.

"Tubu," said the *dogai* when she saw him come to the surface a little while after, "for the rest of your life you are going to have to follow the tide. You will go out with the tide and come in with the tide."

"*Dogai*," replied Tubu, "you're never going to move from the spot where you're standing right now."

The *dogai* turned to stone. She is the rock about seventy-five yards from the point at one end of the bay, Dogai Wak, so-called because it was once her home.

3. *Ngawakazil*, girls. *Ngawakazil* is pure Mabuiag. *Ngokazil* is dialect. The two words have exactly the same meaning. *Ngokazil* is used at Badu.

THE DOGAI OF ZURAT
[Told by Father Mara at Badu, 20 October 1967]

The people of Badu[1] went to the island of Kulbai-kulbai for a visit. For the most part the men either worked in their gardens or hunted during the day, but sometimes they played *tukutuk sagul*, the game in which spears are thrown at a target—a drifted log, or the trunk of a wild cotton-tree— to the accompaniment of the words:

> *Muta garu muta.*
> *Sara garu sara.*
> *Tana ina muigubalgal ia-umaike.*
> *Pagane, pagane, pagane, pagane.*[2]

At night they danced.

1. Badu, a former village site at the south-western end of the island of Badu.
2. This chant, used by young men while engaged in the sport of throwing spears at a target, was given—with only minor variations—in stories told at most islands of West Torres Strait. The first two lines were said to be "magic words" or "sorcery talk". Translated word-by-word, the last two lines read: "They here, *muigubalgal*, speak. Spear! Spear! Spear! Spear!" No one was able to identify the *muigubalgal*.

One morning while they were playing *tukutuk sagul*, they noticed turtle tracks on the beach of the neighbouring island, Zurat. Gabukaikai said: "I'll get the eggs." And he set out at once on a *kauta* (one half of a canoe which has split lengthwise), lying face downwards on top of it and paddling with his arms.

Instead of returning to Kulbai-kulbai as soon as he had collected the turtle eggs, Gabukaikai went to the swamp on Zurat for the fruit of an *aubau* tree, which, he remembered, grew there. He ate all the fruit that had fallen to the ground and then climbed the tree. Presently, while he was plucking and eating ripe *aubau*, he looked down and saw a long-eared *dogai* approaching. Gabukaikai shook with fear.

For a while the *dogai* was unaware of his presence at the top of the *aubau* tree, because she had her eyes on the ground, looking for fallen fruit. By and by she said out loud: "It is several days since I was here. Why is it there are no ripe fruit? What has happened to them?" And only then did she glance up at the top of the tree and see Gabukaikai. "So! You're the culprit, are you?" said the *dogai*. "Throw me some of the green fruit (*bukeral*)."

Despite his terror, Gabukaikai had been casting about for a means of escaping from the horrible creature. When she asked him to throw her some fruit, he threw one in the direction from which she had come. The *dogai*, who had very long legs, took one step towards it and reached for it with a long, skinny arm. He plucked another *aubau*, and this time he threw harder—the *dogai* had to take two steps in order to reach it. Gabukaikai plucked a third *aubau* and threw it with all his strength as far as he could.

The *aubau* fell outside the *dogai*'s cave home. The moment she began to move towards it, Gabukaikai flashed down the tree and fled to his half-canoe. Too late the *dogai* saw him running away. She tried to catch him, but, by the time she reached the beach, Gabukaikai was halfway across to Kulbai-kulbai, paddling for dear life. "Why did you run away from me?" she called after him. "I would not have harmed you." Gabukaikai did not answer. He did not stop paddling until he reached Kulbai-kulbai.

His friends had observed his hurried departure from Zurat, and when they now asked the reason for it, Gabukaikai told them a half-truth. "I was chased by a *dogai*," he said.

That night, Gabukaikai and the rest of the men on Kulbai-kulbai discussed how they should set about catching and killing the *dogai*. Next morning, armed with harpoon-spears and ropes, they went to Zurat in a body and walked to the cave in which the *dogai* lived.

She was fast asleep when they arrived. She had been weaving a basket, the men saw, but, like all *dogai*, she was a sleepy-head and had dozed off in the middle of her work. The men whispered among themselves and decided to harpoon her in the shoulder. One of the men threw his harpoon-spear, aiming at that part of her body.

This woke the *dogai*, and she screamed with pain. She caught sight of Gabukaikai and said: "I saw you yesterday. You stole fruit from my *aubau* tree, and then you ran away." To the other men she said: "He robbed me, but I did him no harm. Why have you come and hurt me?"

The *dogai* tried to escape from the men by running away towards the eastern end of the island, but the harpoon was embedded in her shoulder, and the men held the rope that was knotted round the head of the harpoon, so she did not get far. She tried to bury herself in the sand, but the men pulled her out. She ran again, jabbering, *"Dadipara, kadipara, dadipara, kadipara,"*[3] and tried to bury herself a second time. Again the men hauled her out. The third time the *dogai* tried to bury herself she chose a patch of very soft sand (*saibardar*) and was very nearly successful—she got so far down that the whole of the rope was played out. But the men put up a tremendous struggle and they managed to tear off her arm complete with shoulder-blade (*zug*).

After that the men returned to Kulbai-kulbai, where they tied the *zug* to the log that they had been using for *tukutuk sagul*. They spent the rest of the day throwing spears at the *zug*.

> *Muta garu muta.*
> *Sara garu sara.*
> *Tana inu muigubalgal ia-umaike.*
> *Pagane, pagane, pagane, pagane,*

intoned the men as they threw their spears. And every time a spear struck the *zug*, the *dogai* screamed with pain in the sand at Zurat.

That night the older men said: "*Dogai* are strange creatures. This one may come in search of her arm." (They were right—the *dogai* was on her way to Kulbai-kulbai at that moment.) "If she can get close enough to her *zug*, it will spring towards her and rejoin itself to her body."

In the end, everyone decided that the best thing to do was throw it into the sea between Zurat and Kulbai-kulbai. This they did, and it then turned into the rock which has ever since been called Dogai Zug.

3. See footnote 1 of "Saurkeke", in the section, "Stories from Mabuiag".

MUTUK [Told by Yopelli Panuel at Badu, 26 October 1967]

Long ago a man named Mutuk lived in Argan, a village on the west coast of Badu. He was expert at hunting and fishing—his luck never failed, and, besides, every fish he speared, every dugong he harpooned, was fat. But he never shared his catch with anyone but his own family. He gave nothing to the rest of the people in the village and, what was a more serious offence, he gave nothing to the sorcerers in the *kod* at the foot of the hill nearby. The sorcerers decided that Mutuk would have to be punished.

The day the sorcerers used their power on Mutuk, he threw in his fishing line from morning till late afternoon without getting a bite and was on the point of returning home when he hooked a big fish. Slowly he drew it towards him, lifted it from the water, and saw it was a snapper (*puad*). Then it struggled and jumped until it freed itself from the hook and fell back into the sea. Mutuk leapt after it with his spear—straight into the open mouth of a shark (*baidam*), poised, tail down, waiting to receive him.

At first Mutuk had no idea what he had fallen into. It was very dark, and he could see nothing. He felt round him with his hands and guessed that he was inside a shark.

The shark swam north from Badu in the direction of Daudai. As it swam in deep water, Mutuk felt cold. When it swam over reefs, Mutuk felt warm. It swam for several days, and then Mutuk was tossed about inside its body as the shark threshed frenziedly in its efforts to escape from the sandbank on which it had stranded. Mutuk knew and felt what had happened, though he could not see, and immediately began to cut his way out with a sharp piece of *akul*[1] (shell) through the stomach and back of the shark which had swallowed him. It was slow work, but at last he saw daylight above him and, not long afterwards, clambered out.

Mutuk looked around him. This was Boigu, the island to which his sister, Gainau, had gone when she married. Somehow he must find his sister and enlist her help before the Boigu people learnt that there was a stranger on their island. After a lot of thought, Mutuk decided to go and hide in a tree near the village well, Mai. All the women would go to Mai to fetch water, and, with any luck, he might see his sister alone when she came to fill her *kusul*.[2]

So Mutuk went to Mai. There was no one about when he reached it, so he walked down the bank to the water for a drink. As he bent low over

1. *Akul*, a bivalve shell found in mangrove swamps.
2. *Kusul*, coconut shells used as water-containers.

the water, he saw his reflection—there was not a hair on his head. He was completely bald from having been inside *baidam*'s belly for days on end. Mutuk drank, and then he climbed a tree beside the well and settled down to wait for his sister.

Many women came to Mai during the afternoon. He could see them, but they did not see him, because he kept himself well hidden amongst the leaves. He began to think that his sister might not come, after all. Very late in the afternoon, however, he saw her approaching and, as she stooped to fill her *kusul*, waved a hand at her. Gainau saw it reflected in the water, and then, as he put his head outside the screen of leaves, her brother's face gazing up at her. "Mutuk!" she gasped. "Mutuk!" She looked away and back. Mutuk's hand waved to her again, and she heard his voice: "It is I, Mutuk, your youngest brother. Is that you, *kuikuig* (eldest child in a family)?" Mutuk climbed down from the tree, and the two embraced.

Gainau agreed to help her brother, and the two set off for the village together. However, Gainau told him to wait outside it while she went ahead and talked to her husband.

Mutuk's brother-in-law spoke to the other men in the village and told them that Mutuk should be allowed to stay because he had willingly given Gainau to him for wife. For that reason Mutuk was brought in to Boigu village as a welcome guest, and that night a feast was given in his honour. Three days later the Boigu men took him back to Badu by canoe.

They appeared off Argan two days after the death feast (*tarabau ai*) had been held for Mutuk. The Boigu canoes set Mutuk ashore and immediately afterwards set sail for Boigu without any of the Boigu men having set foot on Badu.

Mutuk's wife and children ran to meet him. "If only you had come the day before yesterday!" she said, weeping for him. "That was the day of your farewell feast. Now you will be killed. Why did you not ask the Boigu canoes to wait for a while? We might all have gone with them."

News of Mutuk's return came to the ears of the sorcerers at the *kod*. "Kill him," the sorcerers ordered the men of Argan.

Mutuk saw the men coming towards him with their clubs and ran away. Many times he called back to his pursuers: "Spare me! I have a wife and children." They might as well not have heard. Through the scrub and along the beach, past Damanab and Gaubut, around the point called Barabaras, Mutuk ran for his life, the men of Argan close behind. They caught him between Barabaras and the rock called Tagain and clubbed him to death. Mutuk turned to stone.

At the moment of his killing by the men of Argan, flying-foxes took off from Badu and flew to Boigu. When Gainau saw them she recognized them as a bad omen and realized that her brother was dead.

WAWA

[Told by Mota Charlie at Badu, 26 October 1967]

While he was out on the reef fishing one day, a man saw a pair of mating turtles stranded in a shallow lagoon. He was far from his village, there was no one in sight, and he needed help to bring them in to the beach. So he called out at the top of his voice,

> *Kauki adidiu niaiginga?*
> *Waurari saurari ipal!*
> *Waurari saurari (o)!*
> *Kabau (o)!*

which was his way of saying: "Ho there! Are there any *adiad* (supernatural creatures of enormous size, bush devils) around here? I need help to bring mating turtles ashore."

There was no reply, so he called again:

> *Kauki adidiu niaiginga?*
> *Waurari saurari ipal!*
> *Waurari saurari (o)!*
> *Kabau (o)!*

Presently he heard a great rumbling sound and, when he looked in the direction from which it came, saw what looked like a hill moving towards him. As it came closer he saw that it was, however, not a hill, but Wawa, a hump-backed giant.

Wawa said, in a very loud voice: "Where are the turtles?"

"Out there on the reef, left behind by the tide," replied the man.

Wawa and the man walked out to the lagoon.

"Put the turtles on top of my hump," ordered Wawa, "and when you have done that, you climb on, too."

Then Wawa walked back across the reef, the two turtles and the man on his hump, and deposited them on the ground behind the beach.

"We'll cook the turtles at once," said the man, and he set about collecting firewood and stones for making an *amai* (earth-oven).

When he began to cut up the female turtle, Wawa said: "Call me when you have cut the meat from the shell." This he did, and Wawa came and drank the blood that had collected in the shell and ate the guts.

70

The man cut up the male turtle.

Again Wawa drank the blood that collected in the shell and ate the guts. Then he lay down and went to sleep.

The man replaced each lot of flesh in its own shell, laid both shells in the bottom of the *amai*, which he then sealed with leaves and sand, and sat down under a tree to cool off after his hard work.

Wawa was snoring loudly by this time. The man began to think: "When they are cooked, I could remove the female turtle from the *amai* and leave the male for Wawa. If I were very quiet, I could do it without waking him."

At the right moment, silently, stealthily, he withdrew the shell and flesh of the female turtle from the *amai*, raised it to his shoulder, and strode home.

His wife and daughter ran to meet him, very happy to see that he brought with him a turtle that was already cooked. They ate every part of it, giving no share to their relatives and friends.

Late in the afternoon Wawa woke up and went to the oven. When he saw only one turtle, the male, tough, dry, pale of flesh, he was filled with rage. However, he ate it.

Then he summoned his fellow bush-creatures, and together they all marched to the village, arriving at sunset. They tracked the man to his house.

Wawa stood beneath it, his company of bush devils (*bupau uruil*) just outside, and held out his *kimus* (arrow tipped with cassowary claw). The *adiad* began to chant:

> *Umai muli muli pai muli (a)*
> *(A) namalka mata mitaka*
> *(A) mai (e)*

The man said: "So, you want a dog (*umai*) to eat, do you?" He threw them a dog.

It landed on the tip of Wawa's *kimus*. Wawa tossed it to his companions, who tore it apart while it was in mid-air and then gulped down the morsels.

> *Burum muli muli pai muli (a)!*
> *(A) namalka mata mitaka*
> *(A) mai (e)*,

chanted the bush devils.

"So, you want a pig (*burum*) to eat, do you?" said the man. He threw out a pig. Wawa caught it on the tip of his *kimus* and tossed it to his companions who grabbed and devoured it as they had the dog.

Kazi muli muli pai muli (a)!
(A) namalka mata mitaka
(A) mai (e),

chanted the bush devils.

When they heard the word *kazi* (child) the husband and wife felt sick, for they had only one child, a girl. The husband went this way, the wife went that way, each of them begging relatives and friends for a child. But they returned without one, everyone they asked having said: "You did not share the turtle with us. You must give your own child to the bush devils."

Sadly the man and his wife returned to their house, where Wawa and his companions were now chanting:

Kazi muli muli pai muli (a)!
(A) namalka mata mitaka
(A) mai (e).

The parents called their daughter to them. They embraced her and wept on her. Then they threw her to Wawa, who caught her on the tip of his *kimus.*

Wawa did not throw the girl to his fellows. Instead, he took her in his arms, and then he led the bush devils back to the bush where they belonged. As they disappeared from sight, they could still be heard singing:

Kazi muli muli pai muli (a)!
(A) namalka mata mitaka
(A) mai (e).

GREEDY GOBA

[Told by Siailo Baira at Badu, 25 October 1967]

In former times, the men of Argan—a village on the west coast of Badu—used to catch many turtle. From the turtle, oil was obtained.

The people of Argan once sent a man named Goba with a baler-shell of oil to give to their friends who lived at Koteid on the east coast of Badu, but when he reached the hill, Kianpalai, in the centre of the island, he put the shell on the ground and went on without it.

At Koteid, Goba told the people that many turtle had been caught at Argan, and much oil obtained. "Why did our friends not send us some oil? Here we have nothing but *biu sama* (balls of cooked *biu* pulp)[1] to eat?" they said. In spite of their disappointment, however, they sent Goba away with a present of *biu sama* for Argan.

On the way home, Goba stopped at Kianpalai and set down the basket of *biu sama* beside the baler-shell of oil. Then he mixed the oil with the *biu sama* and ate the lot. After that, he felt lazy, so he lay down and slept. When he woke up, he completed the rest of his journey.

The people of Argan were very surprised to see him return empty-handed. "Why did our friends at Koteid not send us *biu sama*?" they said. "Here we have nothing but turtle to eat."

They sent Goba with another present of oil for Koteid. Again he arrived without it, having left it, as before, at Kianpalai. Goba set out from Koteid with *biu sama* for Argan, but they did not reach the people for whom they were intended—Goba feasted at Kianpalai as he had on the previous occasion.

The people at each village began to suspect Goba of stealing.

Once more Argan sent Goba to Koteid with oil. This time men followed him as far as Kianpalai and then waited, hidden in the scrub, for him to come back from Koteid. When they saw him begin to prepare his rich meal, they sprang out from the bushes, grabbed hold of him, threw him to the ground and covered him with stones.

Goba died beneath the weight of the stones. You can still see the mound beneath which he lies buried at Kianpalai.

1. *Biu* is a variety of mangrove. The pulp scraped from its seed-pods is first soaked and then cooked to render it edible. (See footnote 1 of "Tawaka, the Greedy Man", in "Stories from Mabuiag", for the recipe for preparing *biu sama* given to me by Maurie Eseli at Mabuiag in October 1967.)

A *sarup* is a castaway.

In former times, a *sarup*'s head was in danger no matter at which island he landed. Should his presence be suspected by the people of any island which he might chance to reach—including his own—he would be hunted and killed.

An informant at Murray Island (in East Torres Strait) told me that if a canoe overturned more than about thirty yards from the shore, all who had been on board it became *sarup*. Their own people seeing the incident would not go to their help but would try to prevent them from landing. If any of the *sarup* succeeded in landing, they would be killed unless a powerful friend or relative chose to receive them and was able to intervene. It was thought that exposure to these things, the cold of deep water, salt, sunburn, thirst, and shark-danger, affected *sarup* in such a way as to make strangers of them.

He also said that this attitude towards *sarup* still exists in Torres Strait, and because of it men who are shipwrecked are extremely reluctant to return home, instead preferring to go and live on the Australian mainland. When he spoke of his mother's cousin who had been on board a lugger which was lost during a cyclone, I asked him what he would feel towards this man if he should chance to meet him. He replied: "I would feel sorry for him, but he would be a stranger to me. He would not be the person he was before his boat went down."

At Yam and Yorke Islands (in the Central group) and at Badu (in West Torres Strait), I was told that in the old days, once a man was presumed dead by his people, they performed his death dance. After that he was nothing to them but a *markai*, a ghost. So the *sarup* who managed to return to his island came either as a stranger to his people or, if his death dance had been performed, as a ghost. A *sarup* was a man without hope from the moment that his canoe sank.

1. *Surka*, the jungle fowl or "scrub-hen", *Megapodius tumulus*.

BEUG AND THE SARUP

[Told by Yopelli Panuel at Badu, 30 October 1967]

When the women of the village of Waruid went to the mangroves at Tulu to look for crabs one day, two of them, Sui and Milu, took a different path from the rest and came out on the beach from the scrub at Seserengagait. There Sui, who was a short distance from her companion, discovered in the sand above the high-water mark a man's footprints which led up from the sea.

Sui was overjoyed: the footprints could only have been made by a *sarup*. She could hardly wait to tell her husband, Beug, so that he could hunt the wretch down.

Sui said nothing to Milu or to the other women when she and Milu caught up with them, and she kept the discovery to herself all day long. She could not, however, give her mind to the job of looking for crabs, so that, when it was time to go home, she had only three, whereas everyone else had many.

When the men and children of Waruid went to meet the women at the end of the day, Beug immediately noticed that his wife had something on her mind—her footsteps dragged, she did not chatter like the rest of the women, and she had brought back very few crabs. So he said to her: "What have you to tell me? Is there something the matter? Speak out."

The secret burst from Sui. "My good husband," she replied, "this morning I found tracks made by a *sarup*. There is a *sarup* on the island. I have found a head for you!"

Beug made plans. He told his wife to prepare food for him and then go to sleep. He himself would make ready his bow and arrows and grease his club (*gabagaba*). He would set out when *surka*[1] called just before daybreak.

At dawn next morning Beug saw the footprints at Seserengagait. "My wife was not mistaken," he said. "These are indeed the tracks of a *sarup*," and he began to follow them.

They led north—through Mazar, past Maiwal Kula, along the beach, into the scrub, and back to the beach at Kotinab. They climbed a hill and returned once again to the beach, this time at Kurturnaiai Wak (*wak*, bay). Beug saw that he was nearing the end of the hunt, for the last prints were newly made. When he reached the point called Dugu Ngur, he heard the *sarup* crying. "I hear you," thrilled Beug, "I hear you. You are up there on the hill, very close to me. I am going to drink your blood. Your head is mine." Beug bit his tongue in the frenzy of bloodlust.

The *sarup* sat on a rock, looking towards Gebar, his home island, weeping bitterly for himself, for the two companions who had set out with him and been drowned when their canoe overturned, and for the wife and children whom he would never again see.

Beug was now so close to the *sarup* that he heard him choke out the words: "Gebar, you are far away. There is a fog between me and you." He crept closer, and then he bent down and dislodged a stone in order to make a sudden noise. The *sarup* saw Beug and sprang to his feet; he backed away, whimpering: "Don't kill me. I am a friend. I have a wife and children. I cannot go back to Gebar, because it is too far away."

Beug leapt at him. "Look up at the sun!" he screamed. "You will never see it again. Your head is mine!" and he smashed the man's skull with his *gabagaba*. "Sui, my good wife," he said as he struck.

Beug grabbed the *sarup*'s head, severed it with his *upi* (bamboo beheading-knife), and let the useless body drop to the ground. Then he danced down to the beach and washed the head in the sea. Afterwards he made a grass basket,[2] put the head in it, and set out for home.

"I only speared turtle eggs," he told his wife when she asked if he had found the *sarup*. "Cook them," he said, as he handed her the basket.

Sui shouted with joy when she saw what was in it. She ran to her husband and rubbed noses with him.

The news spread through the village. All the men came to visit Beug and praise him for what he had done. Each held the head in his hands and said: "If only I had been there! If only I had had the luck to know about the *sarup*, this head would be mine."

Beug stored the head with others that he had taken.

2. The kind that is made on the spot when turtle eggs are found.

WAII AND SOBAI

[Told by Mota Charlie at Badu, 25 October 1967]

The two brothers, Waii and Sobai, were head men of the village of Waruid. They were renowned as fighters, having successfully fought against the men of the other villages on Badu and of islands around Badu.

At that time, the leading warrior at Tudu (Warrior Island) was a man named Kaigas. He had heard of Waii and Sobai and, jealous of his own reputation, told the men of Tudu that he wanted to go to Badu and fight the two brothers. The men of Tudu told him that Waii and Sobai would cut off his head, but they agreed to accompany him.

The Tudu canoes were run in at Kotinab, at the north-eastern end of Badu. Three men were sent to spy out the land and find out where Waii and Sobai lived. When they learnt this, they returned to Kotinab. The warriors put on their fighting gear and set out in two columns led by Kaigas. It was then about midnight.

That evening, Pitai, Waii's eldest son, had gone to visit a girl, and the pair were talking outside her home when Pitai caught a glimpse of men moving among the trees and bushes nearby. Immediately he went to his father and told him what he had seen, and both then watched carefully for signs that an enemy was about to attack Waruid. There were none. Waii said that what Pitai had seen was a *mekat*, the lighter colour of the air in gaps between trees. But Pitai insisted that he had seen *dari* (head-dresses of white feathers),[1] and after that, Waii spread the alarm to the whole village.

Just before daybreak, Waii and Pitai came out of their house and saw the two lines of Tudu warriors with Kaigas at the head. Waii said to Pitai: "Go back inside the house. I'll fight these men single-handed."

Waii stole silently towards Kaigas who was unsuspecting of his enemy's approach until the moment when Waii moved in the action of shooting the arrow from his bow—he was standing on dry cabbage-palm leaves and one crackled under his feet. Kaigas, hearing the sound, crouched down to listen. Waii's arrow found him in the back and killed him.

The Tudu warriors saw it and yelled their battle-cry: "I-I-I-U-O!" It was answered by the fighting men of Waruid: *"Imano! Imano! Imano!"* Waii and Sobai shouted: "We two, Waii and Sobai, fight together all the way."

1. Made from the feathers of the white reef heron, *karbai*.

76

The fighting was long and hard. But the Badu men in the end put to rout their Tudu opponents and chased them back to Kotinab. They pressed them hard and killed many. When a Badu man killed a Tudu man, he placed his personal mark on the body—a stalk of grass, perhaps, or a twig—to identify it and enable him to collect every head which was rightfully his when the fighting was over.

Outside a small village, Kudungurki (a very short man) overtook a Tudu man who turned and stood his ground, bow at the ready. Kudungurki, who was very quick-witted, shot an arrow at his enemy's bow and split it lengthwise. A mother and daughter who saw this feat were so filled with admiration for Kudungurki that both instantly wanted him.

Another Tudu man tried to escape his pursuers by hiding in a waterhole. A Badu man heard him jump into the water, ran to the edge of the hole, waited for him to come up to the surface, and then shot him in the right side of the neck.

Those of the fighting men of Tudu who survived the defeat swam out to their canoes as soon as they reached Kotinab.

One man who had come to Badu with the men of Tudu had had no part in the fighting. He was a Badu man who had married a Tudu girl, and, when all the other men went to fight Waii and Sobai, he had been left behind in charge of the canoes. So angry and so humiliated were the Tudu warriors because of the crushing blow delivered by Badu, that no sooner had they boarded their canoes than they killed this man, cut off his head, and waved it at the top of a poling stick towards the victors standing on the beach.

The Tudu canoes sailed home.

Waii and Sobai lived to be old men. When they died, the people whom they had led for so long honoured them by taking their heads to Kanig, a small island several miles from Badu. The heads of the warrior brothers, Waii and Sobai, were never to be confused with those of lesser men.[2]

2. The skulls of Waii and Sobai are still at Kanig.

PITAI

[Told by Wipa Waiat at Badu, 19 October 1967]

The Mualgal killed Pitai of Badu, a very handsome young man.[1] This story tells how the fighting men of Badu avenged him.

They sent word to Mabuiag by canoe asking for the help of its warriors —*Zugutiam*[2]—to take the head of the man who had killed Pitai. It was readily promised, and a day fixed for the Mabuiag men to come to Badu.

Two equal heaps of chips were made by placing one chip at a time in each heap in turn. Each chip represented a day, and chips were added to each heap until the desired number of days had been counted off. One heap remained at Mabuiag, the other was taken back to Badu. Every day, a chip was removed from the heap at Mabuiag and a chip from the heap at Badu. When none remained in the heap at Mabuiag, that island sent its canoes to Badu. When none remained in the heap at Badu, that island expected the arrival of the canoes from Mabuiag.

On the day thus appointed, the Mabuiag canoes made their landing at Garaz[3] on Badu. Those who were married men made their way overland to Koteid. The single men stayed with the canoes and brought them round after dark when they could not be seen by watching eyes across the channel at Mua.

As soon as the single men of Mabuiag arrived at Koteid, a feast began. It was held in the dark. Every fire had been extinguished. No torches flared. Nothing betrayed the presence of *Zugutiam* on Badu.

Late that night the warriors of Badu and Mabuiag poled their canoes across to Parbar on Mua, where they made their landing inside Kai Kasa (a tidal creek) amongst the mangroves. They slept there until early morning, and then they advanced on the Mualgal.

★

After the death of Pitai, the fighting men of Mua went to Poid[4] and waited for the retaliatory raid by Badu. For many days they kept watch towards the south-west and the north-west, from either of which directions the attack by Badu would be made. They saw nothing to suggest that their enemies were preparing to fight—nothing to indicate that *Zugutiam* was about to strike.

Even when the warriors of Badu and Mabuiag were almost upon them, only one of the Mualgal had any presentiment of danger. This man,

1. Very handsome young man, "*mina bupurul kazi*".
2. *Zugu* is the name of a reef close to Mabuiag; *tiam*, creature (here, shark). The warriors of Mabuiag are as deadly as the shark of the reef, Zugu. They are that shark.
3. *Garaz*, stone fish-trap on the reef. The place derives its name from the fish-trap.
4. South of Parbar. An older name for Poid is Adam.

78

Sibari, said: "Is that *dari* (head-dresses) I see? Are those two lines of men coming towards us?" His companions laughed at him. "Where are the canoes?" they scoffed, their eyes fixed on the approaches from Badu.

Sibari sprang to his feet, dusted himself and said angrily: "I'm leaving. I intend to live." As he ran away, the jeers of the Mualgal followed him. He had gone only as far as Mug[5] when he heard the cracking of skulls at Poid. "My poor friends. *Zugutiam* has struck," grieved Sibari.

He ran until he was exhausted and had to slow down to get his breath back. He walked a few steps and began running again. Occasionally he looked back at Poid—the dust of battle rose in the air as if whipped up by a whirlwind.

When he reached Waga, the women and children, who had stayed there while the men were at Poid, ran out and met him. "Where are the rest of the men?" they asked. "What men?" replied Sibari. "Of all who went to Poid, only one survives. I am husband for all of you." The women and children wailed. Not until the young boys became men would Mua fight again.

5. Poid obtained water at Mug.

★

Bu shells were blown on board the canoes as the victors poled back to Badu. The skull of the man who had killed Pitai capped a spear driven into the bow of the leading canoe.

When the warriors of Badu and Mabuiag leapt ashore, dancing began. "For how long have we wanted this head? Not until *Zugutiam* struck did we get it," said the people of Badu. The dancing continued all night long.

The people of Badu showed their gratitude to the people of Mabuiag for their help in avenging Pitai by giving them half of their island. From that day, all the land on Badu north of a line drawn from Kulkai on the east coast to Wam on the west coast belonged to Mabuiag.

stories from

MABUIAG *Jervis Island*

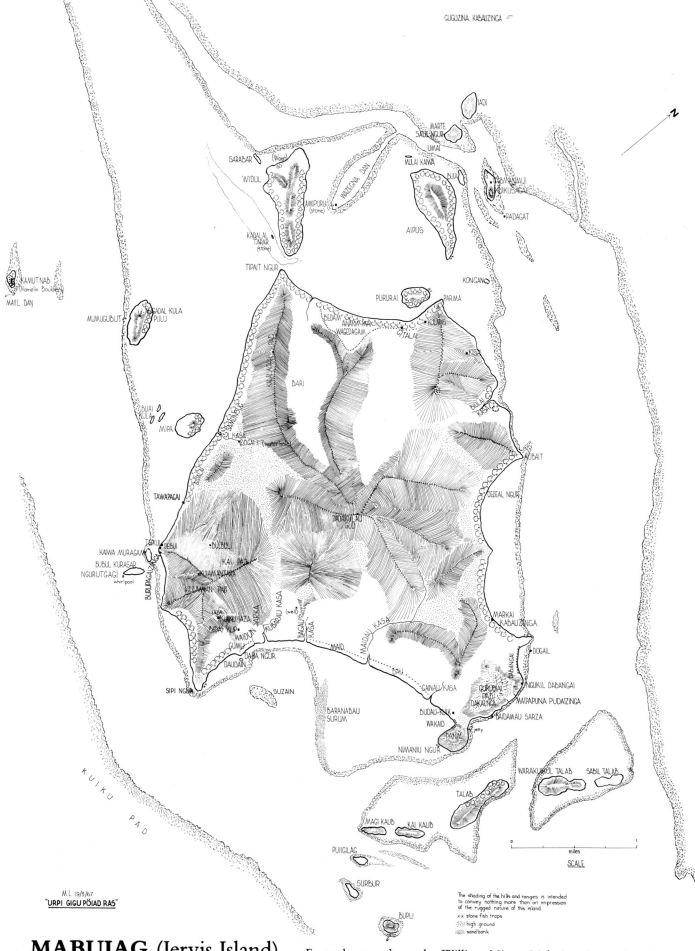

GUGUZINA KABAUZINGA

IADI

MARTE
SABILNGUR

UMAI

SARABAR   (Waia)

WIDUL   MULAI KAIWA

BUAI

DONA MAUI
KUIKUSAGAL

AMIPURU
(stone)   PADAGAT

WAIZGNA DAN

AIPUS

KADALAL
TAPAR
(stone)

KAMUTNAB
(Hamelin Boulder)   TIPAIT NGUR   KONGANO

MAIIL DAN   PURURAI   PARMA

KADAL KULA   DEDAM   AWANA MAI
MUMUGUBUT   PULU   WAGEDAGAM   KULABA
                                                                GITALAI
                                                                                      KISA

BARI

BUAI
KULA   KASA
          MIPA   DOGAI I (waterhole)

SAMU JUL   KUBAIT

TAWAPAGAI   DEDEAL NGUR

DADAKULALI
GUD

TERKUI DEIBUI
KAIWA MURAGAM   •BULBULI
BUBUL KURASAR   KAI PAD
NGURUTGAGI   •KULAMANTARA
          whirlpool
BURUPAGAIZANGA   KULAWAIN PAD   MARKAI
                                                               KABAUZANGA
          JAZA
          KUBAU IAZIA   KUBAU KASA
          DISAI KUD   WAIDUN SARKA (well)   DOGAIL
                      GUMU   DAGAU
                           KASA   MAID.   DABANGAI
          DABA NGUR   MAIDAU KASA   NGUKIL DABANGAI
          DAUDAIN   GURUDIAI
                                              BIAU   PAD   MAIPAPUNA PUDAIZINGA
SIPI NGUR   SUZAIN   GAINAU KASA   DAKALNGA
                                          BUDAU-KULK   BAIDAMAU SARZA
                    BARANABAU   WAKAID
                    SURUM   PANAI jetty
                                    NIMANIU NGUR

                                                        WARAKUIRUL TALAB   SABIL TALAB

                                              TALAB

                                    MAGI KAUB KAI KAUB

KUIKU   PUIIGILAG

PAD

M.L. 19/3/67   SURBUR
"URPI GIGU PÖIAD RAS"

                                                        BUPU

The shading of the hills and ranges is intended
to convey nothing more than an impression
of the rugged nature of this island.
x x stone fish traps
      high ground
      sandbank

miles
SCALE

MABUIAG (Jervis Island)   From the map drawn by William Min at Mabuiag, September 1967

HOW FIRE WAS BROUGHT TO TORRES STRAIT

[Told by Maurie Eseli at Mabuiag, 6 October 1967]

Long ago when animals were close relatives of men and could freely take human form, there were many goannas and lizards and snakes living at Nelgi (Double Island). Their leader was Walek, a frill-necked lizard.

In those days there was no fire in Torres Strait, and cooking was done on stones heated by the sun. For example, when a fish was caught it was placed on top of a hot stone. As soon as a part of the fish became soft, the fish was removed from the stone and the cooked part eaten, and then the rest of the fish was returned to the stone for cooking, bit by bit. The reptiles at Nelgi often wished they had something better than sun-heated stones for cooking their food, and as they often saw smoke rising up from the northern mainland, the idea began to take shape amongst them that it might be connected with heat and cooking. One day they asked Karum, the monitor lizard, to go and find out.

So Karum set out. But he did not go far and was soon back at Nelgi, trying to warm his cold body on top of a rock. "The tide was too strong for me. I could make no headway against it," he told the other reptiles.

At the time, Walek was sunning himself on top of a white ants' nest. "Walek," said the reptiles, "will you go to Daudai and find out about smoke?" "Yes," said Walek, "I'll go."

Before he left Nelgi, the reptiles hung seedpod rattles around his neck and placed a head-dress of white feathers on his head. "Watch the islands to the north," he said as he ran down to the sea. "When you see smoke go up on those islands you will know I am on my way home."

Walek, whose legs were stronger than Karum's, swam until he reached Daudai. He landed at Mawat, changed into human form, and went to Masingara, where his sister, a woman named Ubu, lived. Walek told her how food was cooked at Nelgi and, seeing her cook food with fire, asked

This myth was also told at Kubin (by Lizzie Nawia, 3 November 1967) and at Saibai (by Alfred Aniba, 8 September 1967). Each of these versions is slightly different from the one told at Mabuiag. Lizzie Nawia gave Zuna (a small island off Prince of Wales Island) as the home of Walek (whom she called Waleku) and the reptiles, and she said that Walek was accompanied to Daudai and back by Sigai, the flying-fish. She also said that Waleku ran across Mua. Alfred Aniba used the Saibai name, Iku (instead of Walek or Waleku), and named Muri (Mt. Adolphus Island) as the home of the reptiles.

No one in East Torres Strait told me the story of how fire was brought to Torres Strait.

Walek, who brought fire to Torres Strait from the northern mainland
Artist Ngailu Bani

if he might have a live coal to take back to his people. Ubu agreed to let him have it and invited him to spend the night with her. She promised to give him the coal in the morning.

Before he fell asleep that night, Walek noticed that the coals in her cooking fire went out, one by one, and became black. He observed, also, that his sister had coals of fire between the fingers of her right hand. These coals glowed and did not fade.

Next morning, Ubu gave Walek a coal from her cooking fire, and Walek said goodbye to her and walked away. No sooner was he out of her sight than he changed into his lizard form, ran down to the sea at Mawat, and extinguished the coal in the water. Then he ran all the way back to Masingara, and approached his sister in human form. "My coal of fire went out," he said.

Ubu gave him another one. This time, in saying goodbye to her, Walek asked her to scrape palms with him,[1] and as their fingers curved into each other's hands, he hooked one of his fingers around a coal between two of her fingers and removed it. Then he ran away as fast as he could, popped the coal into his mouth, changed into his lizard form, and made all speed to the beach at Mawat.

"Come back!" called Ubu. "You have stolen Surka's fire. The coals between my fingers belong to my children. Bring back the coal that belongs to Surka,[2] my daughter." But Walek paid no heed to his sister's plea, and soon he was far from Masingara, swimming towards Saibai.

He went ashore at Saibai, set fire to some grass with the coal, and after returning the coal to his mouth, swam to Gebar (Two Brothers Island). There, also, he went ashore and lit a fire. He lit fires at Gitalai (Pole Island), Sauraz (Burke Island), and Nagi (Mt. Ernest Island), and the reptiles at Nelgi, seeing these fires, said: "Walek is coming. Walek is on his way back from Daudai."

When Walek reached Nelgi, he threw the coal to his brothers, ran to a white ants' nest, and lay on top of it with his mouth open. His tongue had been badly burnt, so his brothers brought healing medicine and dressed the sore place.

In that manner fire was brought to Torres Strait. From Nelgi it was taken to other islands in baler shells, and soon every island had fire.

Walek's tongue healed, but a scar remained, and it never faded. It is still there today. Go to Badu or Mua and look at the tops of white ants' nests. Before long you are sure to come across Walek sunning himself on top of one of them, Walek the frill-necked lizard who carried a coal of fire in his mouth from Masingara to Nelgi. And when he opens his mouth, you will see on his tongue the red scar left by the coal of fire which he stole from between two fingers of Ubu's right hand.

1. *Get pudan*, the old style of greeting and leave-taking.
2. *Surka* is the mound-building jungle fowl or "scrub-hen".

SISTERS WHO QUARRELLED

[Told by Dakanatai Kiris at Mabuiag, 7 October 1967]

Once upon a time two sisters, Widul and Marte, lived with their brother Umai at the north-western end of Mabuiag. Widul had a daughter named Sarabar, and Marte had a daughter named Iadi.

One day Widul and Marte quarrelled. Widul threw a spear at Marte, which split her down the middle, at the same instant as Marte threw several spears at Widul. Marte's spears pierced the top of Widul's skull and stuck in it.

Umai put a stop to the fight between the two sisters—as their brother, he had the right and the duty to do it—by moving them far apart from each other and sending them to places of his choosing on the reef which surrounds Mabuiag.

The sisters and their daughters became islands. Umai turned to stone and has ever since stood guard over them at the edge of the passage through the reef between Marte and another island, Aipus. He can be seen at low tide. Widul stays south of him and keeps her small daughter, Sarabar, behind her. Marte's place is north of him, and she also keeps her daughter, Iadi, behind her.

For a long time, pandanus trees grew at the top of Marte—they were the spears that were thrown at her by her sister, Widul.

KAMUTNAB

[Told by Maurie Eseli at Mabuiag, 5 October 1967]

Kaumain, head man of Pulu,[1] had many wives of whom the most important was Kamutnab. This woman was his first wife, and she had borne him many children. The other wives were childless.

People often came to visit Kaumain, and every time, just before a party was due to arrive, he told Kamutnab to shave off his beard. It was a task she heartily disliked.

One day Kaumain received a message from the people of Bau[2] asking if they might come to Pulu. Kaumain was agreeable and, as usual, called Kamutnab to come and shave him.

1. Pulu is a small, rocky, high island within the home reef of Mabuiag.
2. On Mabuiag.

85

This time Kamutnab flew into a tantrum, picked up the bamboo knife (*upi*), advanced on her husband—and sliced off his double chin as well as his beard. Furious, Kaumain ordered her to leave Pulu. So Kamutnab gathered up her children, walked out into the sea with them, and sat down.

At that instant, Kamutnab and her children turned to stone—and so, also, did Kaumain and the remaining wives. None of them has moved since that day, not even the baby whom Kamutnab was carrying on top of her head. Kaumain, chinless, with all but one of his many wives at his feet, stands at the southern end of Pulu staring at the wife who took his children with her when she moved out and sat down in the sea.

[**After finishing the story, Maurie Eseli added this detail**]:

Kamutnab and her children have been given another name by Europeans —they call them Hamelin Boulders.

Kaumain staring at his wife, Kamutnab, and her children (Hamelin Boulders)

WAMEAL

[Told by Dakanatai Kiris at Mabuiag,
25 September 1967]

Long ago when there was a village on the northern side of the island of
Pulu, the boys and girls who lived there spent far too much time making
string figures (*wameal*). They became obsessed with the game. Their
parents tried to put a stop to it, but the children would not obey.

One night a huge boulder fell from the sky and killed every one of the
children.

This enormous rock is still at Pulu. It is called *Augadal Kula* (sacred stone).

DEIBUI AND
TEIKUI

[Told by Ephraim Bani at Mabuiag, 9 October 1967]

Two brothers, Deibui and Teikui, used to go fishing with their spears on
the home-reef at the south-western end of Mabuiag. They were excellent
fishermen and always came home with long strings of fish.

But they sometimes quarrelled. Then, instead of cooking their fish on
one spit (*iu*)—as was their custom when they were friendly—they parted
company and cooked on separate spits.

The spirits of Deibui and Teikui went up to the sky, south-west of
Mabuiag, and became two small, white star-clouds (*kunar*).

The brothers behave in the sky as they did on earth, quarrelling and
making up, only to quarrel again. Sometimes the star-clouds, Deibui and
Teikui, are far apart, but they always move in towards each other after
that. The kind of regard the brothers have for one another at any particular time is plain to be seen by all.

The human forms abandoned by Deibui and Teikui became rocks.[1]
Young men leave food at these rocks before they fish on that part of the
reef where the two brothers fished before they went up to the sky. The
offering ensures that, like Deibui and Teikui, they, too, will go home with
long strings of fish.

1. At their former home, near Burupagaizinga, the spot at which Kuiam's
father landed when he arrived at
Mabuiag from the southern mainland.

THE SAGA OF KUIAM

[Told by Maurie Eseli at Mabuiag, October 1967]

When Kuiamu, a man who had magical powers, decided to leave his home at Waterhole on the southern mainland,[1] he first plucked a stalk of grass and threw it to obtain the bearing he should take. The stalk fell to the north of where he stood, so he travelled north.

After he had been walking for some time, he saw a man coming towards him. This man, too, was following a route indicated by thrown stalks of grass. Kuiamu screeched at him like a cockatoo,[2] at which the man collapsed on the ground, twisting his left arm and his left leg in falling. After he had passed the stranger, Kuiamu plucked a stalk of grass and threw it back at him; whereupon the man immediately stood up, completely recovered from his injury. Both men then continued on their separate ways, Kuiamu to the north, the other to the south.

At Paira,[3] Kuiamu saw that island-studded sea lay ahead of him. He had magic which enabled him to walk on water, and this he now employed, attaching a piece of wood to each of his legs and then bending his legs backwards at the knees. Thus shod, in a kneeling posture, Kuiamu walked on. After passing by many islands, he came to Nagi and from that island crossed to the large island of Mua where he landed at Pabi. He walked through Kubin and then went up the west coast as far as Parbar, thence across the narrow stretch of intervening water to the island of Badu. Upon landing, he found the remains of an old camping spot. There was no one about, and he walked on to the northern end of Badu. To the north lay yet another large island—Mabuiag.

At Mabuiag, Kuiamu walked ashore at Burupagaizinga and removed his magic "shoes". He plucked a stalk of grass and threw it, again obtaining the direction: north. This led him round the point called Dada Ngur to the small creek, Bagau Kasa, where he sat down and looked for signs that would tell him if there were people on the island.

That day, a man who lived at Budaukuik[4] had gone into the scrub to cut vine for rope. As soon as he came out, he saw Kuiamu and crept towards him, intending to kill him. Kuiamu, however, heard him approaching from behind and leapt to his feet, biting his tongue[5] in the rage which instantly possessed him. Woomera and spear at the ready, Kuiamu was about to kill his would-be assailant, when the latter made overtures of friendship.

1. Kuiamu live in Waterold [Waterhole, a spring of fresh water at the back of the beach not far from Cape Direction] on Millines land [Mainland, i.e., the southern mainland, *zei dagam daudai*]. From Redrockey to Redecstsen [Cape Direction] Kuiamu always troubled [travelled] anting [hunting] for Cangaro [kangaroos] and Posomes [possums]. When he want eat dugong he go with little canow cross to Loz [Lloyd] Island.
   —Copied from Esili Peter's Notebook.

   Esili Peter was born at Mabuiag in 1886. His daughter, Mauari (or Maurie) lent me her father's Notebook during my visit to Mabuiag in October 1967.
2. Kuiamu's magic travelled with this sound to the man whom he intended to injure.
3. The tip of Cape York Peninsula.
4. To the east of Bagau Kasa, in the area called Bau. The present-day Government school-teacher's house is at Budaukuik.
5. . . . bite is tonge, meaning saw [show] is magice to this man . . .
   —from Esili Peter's Notebook.

After scraping palms with Kuiamu, this man daubed Kuiamu's left arm with clay in the manner to show that he enjoyed the friendship and protection of a man of Budaukuik and, having made signs to Kuiamu that he should sit down and wait, hurried to his people to tell them the news. His two brothers and the head man consented to Kuiamu's coming to live with them.

One afternoon while the men of Bau were on the beach throwing spears at the trunk of a cotton tree for target practice, Kuiamu sat on the sand watching the sport. He laughed at their efforts, for these men sometimes missed in their aim, and, when presently some of the men told his adoptive brothers to invite him to join in the play, he was amused, knowing his superiority to all the men of this place at spear-throwing. His turn came at the end of a round. He threw, and his spear went straight through the log, splitting it in two and burying itself in the sand beyond. "My husband!" screamed Kuinam, one of the women onlookers, for she immediately desired Kuiamu. Tömagan, her brother, took her by the hand and led her to Kuiamu, beside whom he made her sit. In that fashion, Kuinam was made Kuiamu's wife.

For a time, Kuiamu and Kuinam lived at Budaukuik, but one day, Kuiamu told his wife that they would make their home apart from the rest of the people. They built their house at Gumu.

There was constant friction, however, between Kuiamu and Kuinam, for the custom of the people to whom Kuiamu belonged on the mainland was to sleep out-of-doors beside a fire at night-time, and in this he persisted, despite Kuinam's protests that he should sleep indoors on a mat. At last Kuiamu became so angry with Kuinam's nagging at him about it that he left Gumu one night and returned to his old home at Waterhole. The next morning, Kuinam followed his tracks to the beach and down to the edge of the sea.

Tömagan, learning of Kuiamu's departure, invited his sister to return to Budaukuik and make her home with him, but she refused to do so, saying that she must remain at the place where her husband had left her. Instead, Tömagan went and lived at Gumu.

Kuinam was pregnant at the time that Kuiamu deserted her. To the son who was born to her she gave the name Kuiam.

★

The youth Kuiam became curious about the woomera and spears which his mother kept in her house at Gumu and one day asked whose they were. Upon learning that they had belonged to his father, he asked if he might have them and thereafter practised with them daily until he was expert in their use.

6. The *zugubal* of West Torres Strait looked like humans while they inhabited the island world, but they were super-human in their strength and performance.

Tagai and Kang, leaders of the *zugubal* mentioned in the story of Kuiam, could increase their stature to giant proportions. They possessed powers which enabled them to summon thunder, lightning, wind, and rain to their aid, and they could control the moods of the sea. They introduced the method of catching turtle with sucker-fish, and they imposed conditions on the habits and habitat of sea-creatures.

The *zugubal* went up to the sky and became bright stars (*zugubal tituil*) soon after humans appeared in Torres Strait. As stars, the *zugubal* ever afterwards ushered in seasons, and caused rain, wind, tides, and calms. When they "dived into the sea" (disappeared from the night sky for a time), they splashed up water which fell as rain. They (in particular, Tagai) directed men in their gardening activities. They were guides for men at sea.

7. *Zugubau pula, zugub* stone or rock.
8. *Naigai dagam daudai,* literally, north-side mainland, i.e. New Guinea.
9. When Tagai and Kang dive into the sea, they splash up water. This water is the first rain of the north-west season, *kuki*. Tagai's left hand is the Southern Cross.
10. The *zugubal* whom Tagai sent to the sky are seen as constellations known to the people of Mabuiag as Dedeal (eight stars), Gapukuik (five stars), Gitalai (six stars), Bu (eight stars), Usal (six stars), and Utiamal (six stars).

Usal and Utiamal are the *zugubal* whom Tagai bound. The other four constellations are made up of the *zugubal* who floated away unbound in formations which looked like the breast-bone of a turtle (*dedeal*), the

As he grew to manhood, Kuiam's thoughts turned to fighting, and the idea took shape in his mind that, in combination with his skill at handling his father's weapons, the wearing of emblems endowed with his own magic power would make him invincible. These emblems he would carve from the shell of the hawksbill turtle (*unuwa*); to obtain the shell of *unuwa* he needed the help of *zugubal*.[6]

The day that Kuiam reached this decision, the *zugubal* were at Maiil Dan, a lagoon in a reef to the south of Mabuiag. Their leaders, two brothers —Tagai, who was keen-sighted, and Kang, who was blind—left the canoe and went walking on the reef to spear fish. It was very hot, and before long the *zugubal* who had stayed behind with the canoe felt thirsty. The only drinking water belonged to Tagai and Kang—it was stored in a cluster of coconut shells suspended from the side of the canoe into the sea to keep it cool. The *zugubal* crew swam to ease their suffering, but this in no way relieved their thirst, and at last the temptation to broach the brothers' drinking vessels became so strong that, one by one, they pierced the coconut shells with fish-teeth and drank.

Tagai and Kang caught no fish; they, too, were hot and thirsty. When they returned to the canoe, Tagai accidentally bumped one of the coconut shells as he was climbing aboard, causing the rest to clatter against each other. Tagai heard the hollow empty sound and was furious with his crew for their theft of the water. "I will kill every one of them," he whispered to Kang.

The brothers commanded that the canoe be poled to a big rock[7] some distance away on the reef, and there ordered the crew to dive for crayfish. Tagai went to the stern and drove his poling stick into the eyes of each *zugub* as he returned, crayfish in hand, to the surface of the water. Soon all the crew were dead. Their bodies drifted around the canoe, empty eye sockets streaming strands of blood, which, as they were carried away by the current, formed what looked like a rope of blood to Tagai.

Some of the dead *zugubal* Tagai bound together with vine. The rest floated away in groups. All he sent far-away to the sky at the east of the northern mainland (*naigai dagam daudai*),[8] saying, as he despatched them: "Later, Kang and I, too, will make our home in the sky, but you will never visit us. When you wish to appear in the sky, use the *zugubal*'s signal, thunder; hearing it, Kang and I will dive into the sea,[9] and you may then travel south of Daudai. Do not, however, come to that part of the sky which is south of Mabuiag—your place is to the north of that island."[10] Tagai gave them work to do in their future home, and then he and Kang returned to Gumu, there to be met by Kuiam.

★

Kuiam gave Tagai and Kang their orders. They were to catch a sucker-fish (*gapu*) and use it to obtain the turtle that he wanted. His instructions were given in detail; nothing was left to chance. When the brothers left Gumu, they understood that Kuiam required every part of the turtle to be brought back to him.

Tagai and Kang planned their task. They decided to go to Tiki, a small island off the southern tip of Badu, for octopus bait; to Tidiu, a reef, to catch *gapu*, the sucker-fish; to Garirai, a reef which lies to the north of Mabuiag, for *unuwa*, the hawksbill turtle; and to Mawai (Wednesday Island) to remove the flesh of *unuwa* from its carapace.

They were at Tiki very early the following morning, but, try as they might, they could not find an octopus until the sun was high in the sky. Then they saw a big one. "You are a *zugub* octopus," they told it, "and you are henceforth subject to this rule: you may never leave your hiding places in the rocks at Tiki until late in the morning."[11]

In order to reach Tidiu, the brothers poled their way north through the passage between Badu and Mua. A strong wind blew from the south-east. Off Adam[12] they caught a big white cat-fish, a *waibe*, which, when it was placed in the bottom of the canoe, spoke in grunts. The brothers thought it said:

> *Peokainu peokainu kazia sauwaia ririma sasabi Sarabaria Muruka Waibenia (e).*

> (I lie here gasping for breath—I, who have relatives at Sarbar, Muri, and Waiben.)[13]

Using octopus for bait, Tagai and Kang caught a sucker-fish at Tidiu and then poled to the reef called Garirai, where they soon captured a hawksbill turtle (*unuwa*).[14]

From Garirai Tagai and Kang made all speed to Mawai. They used their elbows as poling sticks—as they had done since the moment of their setting out that morning—for that was the custom of *zugubal* who wished to travel fast by canoe. At Mawai they carried the turtle ashore and cut the flesh from its shell. After this had been done, they replaced the flesh in the shell, carried it to the canoe, and left for Gumu.

Kuiam came down to the beach to meet them. There he spread a mat on the sand and laid out every part of the turtle—carapace, flesh, and organs. The liver and *kunai baba* (the two parts right at the tail end of the shell)[15] were missing. He asked Tagai and Kang if they had eaten the liver. "We ate nothing," they said. "We can only have forgotten to replace it in *unuwa*'s shell-back," they told him. They sped back to Mawai to search for the liver and the *kunai baba* and found them underneath the leaves upon which they had placed the turtle for cutting up.

10. (*continued*)
head of a sucker-fish (*gapu kuik*), a crab (*gitalai*), and a *bu* shell (*Syrinx aruanus* Linne).
Usal is known to Europeans as Pleiades, the Seven Sisters.
The Tagai myth is an important one at Murray Island in East Torres Strait, but there Tagai, his friend, and his crew are known simply as men who afterwards became constellations. They are said to have come from Deudai (New Guinea).
Tagai is associated with gardening at Murray Island by a particular group of people. He is also associated with gardening at Saibai—North-West Torres Strait—by the people at that island who have *deibau* (a yam) as their *augad* (totem).
11. This is still the case. Octopus are never found at Tiki early in the day.
12. On Mua.
13. This translation was suggested by Fr Mara at Badu.
14. *Unuwa* was caught at the spot called Gauma.
15. Used for making fish-hooks.

All that Kuiam had given them to do they had done, and that in less than a day. But they were by now very hungry, so, during their journey back to Gumu they anchored at Usar, a rock off the north-western end of Mua, Kang staying in the canoe while Tagai went ashore to look for fruit.

Tagai found a tall, heavily-laden *kupa* tree. Increasing his stature until he stood higher than the tree, he began to pluck and eat the ripe, white fruit. He spat out the seeds to the ground below.

Now this *kupa* tree was the property of a woman of Mua. She had not visited it for several days, and chose to come to it while Tagai was robbing it. She brought with her a number of baskets to fill. However, just as she set them down, a seed which bore teeth-marks fell close to her. Then she noticed Tagai's feet and, following up the length of his body with her eyes, recognized a *zugub*. Terrified, she ran from the spot.

Tagai, glancing down, saw the woman and knew that she would tell her people she had seen him. So he stamped his feet, and there came thunder and lightning and a deluge of rain. But it was a very narrow storm, limited in extent to the path taken by the woman in her mad, erratic flight: no matter which way she ran, she was trapped inside a torrential downpour, on either side of which the sun shone brightly. There was no escape for the woman, and she died.

Kang heard the thunder and laughed. He knew that a human must have discovered Tagai's presence on Mua, for *zugubal* always raised storms if they were surprised in their secret existence. Tagai told him the whole story when he presently returned to the canoe, bringing *kupa* fruit for Kang in the bag which he wore over his left shoulder.

Tagai and Kang departed for Gumu, fingernails flashing in the sunlight as they poled their canoe with their elbows. Before long Kang told Tagai to leave the poling to him. The wind dropped shortly afterwards, and Kang said: "See! I have caused the wind to stop blowing." Tagai replied: "There is still a slight breeze. There are ripples on the water." Tagai poled then, and immediately there was dead, flat calm. "There is no wind now," said Tagai. "The air is so still that we can hear the twitter of birds in Daudai. I can see fish swimming in the coral below. I stopped the wind blowing."

When they reached Gumu and gave the parts missing from *unuwa* to Kuiam, he told them that he needed no more help from them and they might go where they chose. A strong wind sprang up from the south, a wind to send Tagai and Kang on their way.[16] It took them first to Dauan and then to Saibai.

16. *Zugubau iawarau gub*: literally, *zugub* journey wind.

★

One evening, Kuiam lay on the beach at the mouth of the little creek, Waidun Sarka, cutting the turtle which Tagai and Kang had brought him. In shaping the two emblems, Giribu and Kutibu, which he intended to wear when fighting, he used the crescent moon for model. To each he added movable pieces—a full set of turtle-shell replicas of the legs, eyes, nose, and mouth of the sand crab (*butu kupas*).

The bigger of the two emblems, Kutibu, Kuiam made to wear on his chest; Giribu, the smaller, was for wearing on his back. Each was a sacred object, Kuiam's personal *augad*, which he endowed with magical power from himself (*nuid nungi puiu parapar wanadin nungu kösar augadia*). They became living things, and he fed them with the thick, rich blood of the small rock cod, *mata kurup*.

The day after he fashioned Giribu and Kutibu, Kuiam told his uncle, Tömagan, to cut young, green coconut leaves and make a skirt for him to wear. When it was finished, Kuiam dressed himself in it, and put on armlets and leglets. On his chest and back he wore his two *augad*. "What do I resemble?" Kuiam asked his uncle. "You look like a big rock with waves breaking against it," Tömagan told his nephew.

Kuiam went to the beach and, seeing people coming to Gumu from Panai, ran towards them. They fled. Some believed him to be a ghost; but all were afraid, even those who recognized him. Kuiam then ran to Gumu, from time to time dashing into the sea and drinking salt water. Seeing this, Tömagan said: "Whatever has Kuiam done?" For Kuiam's behaviour was that of one in a frenzy from killing.

Kuiam ran inside the house at Gumu, where his mother sat weaving a mat. He stood on a strip of pandanus leaf that she was putting into her work. Kuinam, now blind and old, swore at the culprit. "Mother," said Kuiam, "it is I, your son, whom you have cursed." "Oh Kuiam, my good son," burst from Kuinam. Kuiam left the house without speaking.

The following day he went to Bidai Kup, a small, fertile spot at Gumu, and dressed himself as he had on the previous day. Then, after running round and round Bidai Kup until he was fighting mad, he went to his mother who, as usual, sat weaving. "Mother," he said, "look at me." Kuinam raised her head in his direction. Kuiam drove his spear (*takul*, a pronged spear) into both her eyes, killing her.

Tömagan, who had witnessed the scene, now shook with fear. "Kuiam has killed his mother. I am nobody to him now," he thought. Certain that he, too, was about to die by his nephew's hand, Tömagan ran away and hid in some bushes.

Kuiam went looking for his uncle, calling him to come. Tömagan answered—in a voice that quavered weakly. Kuiam told him to prepare their canoe for a journey, and to place in it his, Kuiam's, fighting gear and the two *augad*, Giribu and Kutibu. Before stepping into the canoe, Kuiam held up his woomera which, of its own accord, turned in his hand until it pointed due north. Kuiam and Tömagan sailed in that direction.

Late in the afternoon, they anchored on the reef at Beka, some distance north of Mabuiag. Kuiam immediately sent Tömagan to catch rock cod for feeding the *augad*. He himself remained in the canoe, decking his body in fighting attire and holding aloft his woomera. It first turned itself to the north towards Daudai, but afterwards moved slightly to give the exact indication of where Kuiam was to fight—Boigu—and then it fell from Kuiam's hand into the canoe. Tömagan, who had been watching Kuiam, was sure that Kuiam was going to kill him.

When Tömagan came back with the rock cod, he and Kuiam fed the *augad*, cutting the fish and holding it close to the nose of each. As the blood dripped on to Giribu and Kutibu, the *augad* sniffed audibly and the blood disappeared.

Next day, uncle and nephew sailed to Boigu, making their landing at Kadalau Bupur. Kuiam went ashore at once to look for people to kill. Tömagan stayed with the canoe.

Kuiam came to a house which had two doors. After setting fire to one of them, he went and stood outside the other—through which the people inside were forced to emerge when the flames caught the other end of the building. Kuiam killed them as they came out. The only person at Boigu who escaped him was a woman who managed to run away.

Kuiam went to the canoe to fetch two bamboo beheading knives, one for himself and one for Tömagan, whom he told to come with him and help remove the heads of the Boigu dead. He soon found, however, that Tömagan was awkward and squeamish in the performance of this task. "Uncle," said Kuiam, "that is not the way to remove heads. This is the way to do it," and he showed Tömagan the correct action, to the rhythmical accompaniment of the spoken words, "*Wati kuik* (Bad head). *Boma kuik* (Useless head)." All the heads were afterwards strung together with vine and taken to the canoe, together with some dugong flesh which the Boigu people had had at their house.

It was Kuiam's intention to sail to Daudai from Boigu, but he changed his mind and put in at Saibai. There he found no one until he overturned a baler shell (*merewal*). Inside it was a man. Kuiam asked him where the rest of the people lived at Saibai, and was told that there was no one but himself on the island.

From Saibai Kuiam sailed to Dauan, and at this island he stayed with the canoe while Tömagan went ashore to see if it was inhabited. Tömagan found some people and told them that they must prepare a friendly welcome for Kuiam—they must spread a mat for him and bring him *biu*[17] and green coconuts for food and drink.

17. Food prepared from the seedling pod of a variety of mangrove.

94

The effect of this hospitality upon Kuiam was to make him feel friendly towards the people of Dauan. Having eaten and drunk, he said: "Dauan is my island. The coconut palms at this island will always bear big fruit. The *biu* will always be fat."

He went for a walk along the beach. Presently he threw his spear, and it landed a short distance back from the shore; when he pulled it out of the ground, water gushed up. "This is my water," Kuiam said. "It will never go dry."

From there Kuiam walked to the top of Tögani Pad (a hill). For a time he stood gazing south across the sea towards Mabuiag, tears streaming from his eyes as he thought of Kuinam whom he had killed. "Mother," he said, "you do not see this sun go down." Then he turned his face north and saw smoke going up in Daudai.

★

Kuiam walked inland from the coast of Daudai through long grass until he came to the place called Zibar. There he saw a long house with a single door at which a grey-haired man sat. He set fire to the rear of the building, and then he ran to the front of it and killed the old man. When the building caught alight, the people inside it woke up and rushed to the door to escape. Kuiam speared all of them, saying as he killed each: "*Mawa keda*." "*Mawa keda, mawa keda, mawa keda . . . ,*" chanted Kuiam, until all were dead. Lest one or two should have escaped and be planning to take him unawares, he dropped to the ground and lay still for a while. But there was no sound; nothing stirred; so he got to his feet and looked at the bodies that lay around him. "*Aiau dumaniu itamar kibuia get mataik* (I am like poison vines and bushes killing all whom I touch)," he said. "*Ngai amana Kuinamna kazi ibaidau tamanu dani makamaka pudaumaka* (I, Kuinam's son, my legs adorned with fringing made from branches of the fig-tree, take very big steps). *Ngai surka, ngai keu* (I, the jungle fowl, I call)."

Kuiam walked to Toga, not far away, and killed every person at that place, in the same manner as he had at Zibar, afterwards cutting off their heads . . . "*Wati kuik. Boma kuik. Wati kuik. Boma kuik.*" He took cane from a vine which grew nearby and strung the heads, and then he went back to Zibar to remove the heads from those whom he had killed earlier . . . "*Wati kuik. Boma kuik. Wati kuik. Boma kuik.*" These heads, too, he strung, before setting out on the return walk to the canoe.

All this time Tömagan had waited in the canoe. He was doubly afraid: Kuiam had been gone so long that Tömagan feared his nephew was dead and, thought Tömagan: "Someone may see that I am alone and kill me." But at last he saw Kuiam approaching. It was black night, and Kuiam was lit up by swarms of fireflies, his body spattered with blood from the string of heads which trailed from his left shoulder to the ground behind him.

Kuiam in Daudai (New Guinea)
Artist Ephraim Bani

18. Actually, "*Ngau iarkapul paipa ladun* (My curly hair stands on end)".

Kuiam called to his uncle to run the canoe in and, after he had loaded the heads, summoned a north-west wind to take them home.

By the time they passed Dauan, the heads smelled foully; in addition, the canoe was leaking badly. "*Mina wati gangul gul a kuparal gul ngalbai pungaik* (What an evil-smelling, maggot-ridden canoe we sail)," said Tömagan as he baled out the water. "What is that you say?" asked Kuiam. Tömagan replied: "*Bilan saia bagia pudema Iabina Kap kulai sika susul pagaz wagel mudan araik* (You are like the rock, Iabina Kap, behind which I [Tömagan] shelter like a little fish)"—meaning by this, that Kuiam's strength and prowess saw them through every danger that they encountered on their journey. They were, in fact, quite close to Iabina Kap at the time, and soon afterwards sailed safely by it. To Tömagan it seemed that they escaped from Iabina Kap as a fish escapes, when the hook pulls out through the side of its jaw. "Uncle," said Kuiam, "I thrill to your words."[18]

96

Kuiam put in at the island of Gebar because he was thirsty and, when the people of that island gave him water to drink, said: "Gebar is my island. There will always be plenty of water at Gebar, and its coconuts will always grow big." He asked for a new canoe after he had drunk, saying that his own leaked badly.

By then, the people of Gebar were speaking out loud about the dreadful smell which came from Kuiam's canoe. Tömagan counselled them to stop, warning them that Kuiam was quick-tempered and might take offence at their words.

After Tömagan had loaded the new canoe[19] with the heads from Boigu and Zibar and Toga, the last stage of the journey began. Kuiam went ashore at Niman[20] and, climbing the rock-face close to the beach, held aloft his woomera. It pointed to Pulu, a small, rocky island off the west coast of Mabuiag. Soon afterwards they reached Gumu.

Tömagan made an earth-oven and placed the heads in it, covering them with sand. Presently he removed them and cleaned them of all flesh. He placed the skulls in a heap.

19. The old canoe later turned to stone.
20. On the south-eastern tip of Mabuiag, at the part of the island which is called Panai. Kuiam's footprint is in a rock at Niman.

★

Daily, Kuiam ran from Gumu to the top of the big hill close by, keeping a constant lookout for approaching canoes. None came.

One day, he held up his woomera as he stood watching and, when it pointed to Pulu, knew that he must fight there.

That night, he and Tömagan crossed to Pulu by canoe and landed at the sandy beach since called Mumugubut. Kuiam went ashore alone and, finding a man asleep beside an earth-oven, killed him with his spear. The man's backbone broke with the sound of wood snapped in two, waking the rest of the people at Pulu. Kuiam thrust his spear this way and that way—"*Mawa keda, mawa keda, mawa keda*"—until all were dead.

Back at Gumu, Tömagan cleaned the heads and added them to Kuiam's heap of skulls.

Kuiam saw three canoes approaching from Mua when he climbed to his look-out the following day, so he ran down the hill to the beach at Gumu and signalled them ashore with his woomera. When the men landed, he killed them. Tömagan placed the cleaned skulls on the mounting heap.

The people at Mua waited in vain for their canoes to return, their fear increasing as the day wore on that Kuiam had killed their kinsmen. Under cover of darkness, another three canoes sailed across to Mabuiag, these men going round to the western side of the island and hiding in the mangroves at the mouth of I Kasa until daybreak.

In the morning, Tömagan walked across the island to Sipalai,[21] to which place the people of Bau had gone to live after Kuiam killed his mother,

21. Not far from I Kasa.

believing that Kuiam might kill his mother's people, too, if they remained within sight of Gumu. Seeing Tömagan, the people from Bau mistook him at first for Kuiam. Tömagan told them the reason for his visit: he had come there to look for rock cod for feeding to Kuiam's *augad*, being afraid to go to Sipingur as he usually did for this purpose, in case men from Mua should be hiding there, waiting for the opportunity to avenge their dead.

While Tömagan was turning over stones on the reef outside the mangroves at Sipalai, the men of Mua left their cover at the mouth of I Kasa, took him by surprise, and killed him. They cut off his head and put it at the top of a poling stick which they stood upright in the bow of one of their canoes. Kuiam saw it as they approached Gumu, blowing *bu* shells and beating the sides of their canoes with their hands, and he was immediately filled with grief and foreboding. "I, too, shall die today," he thought.

Very soon, the fighting began. Kuiam killed a number of Mualgal (men of Mua), but they were too many for him. He changed into a swallow (*katakuik*) and flew to Bidai Kup to gain a temporary respite, but

Gumu, where Kuiam lived. The green patch in the centre is where Kuiam rested after he changed into a swallow. This patch is called Bidai Kup.

his enemies quickly found him and hunted him into the open. Kuiam returned to his human form and fought on. The peg at the end of his woomera broke. Forced to retreat, he ran backwards up the side of the hill which he had climbed daily in the past when going to his look-out.

When he reached the waterhole, Kuiku Iaza, halfway up the hillside, the *augad*, Giribu, detached itself from his back and fell into the water, lodging itself in the roots of the *iwir* tree which grew beside the pool.

Still retreating, still warding off his enemy pursuers, always with his face towards them, Kuiam was at last struck down by the Mualgal on top of the hill which bears his name—Kuiaman Pad. Some of these men thought to remove his head with their bamboo knives, but their leaders prevented them. "Kuiam's head was a good head, a head which teemed with ideas, a clever head (*kapu kuik, wakain tamamal kuik, kutinau kuik*)," they said, "unlike ours, which are bad, useless, stupid heads (*wati kuikul, boma kuikul, kutingi kuikul*)." One man had already grazed Kuiam's throat with his knife before the Mua leaders began to speak, and blood from the dying Kuiam splashed the leaves of the small, stunted ti-trees which grew at that spot.

The Mualgal covered Kuiam's body with stones and went down the hillside called Iaza to Gumu where they slept that night.

In the morning, some of the women walked from Sepalai to Gumu for news of Kuiam and the Mualgal. One of them went to Kuiku Iaza to fetch water—to be smitten silly by the sight of Kuiam's *augad*, Giribu. She tore back down the hillside to Gumu, where the Mualgal were sitting, as if in a *kod*.[22] She could not speak, but from her throat came a series of grunts, "Ee-ee-ee-ee", and she pointed with her hand towards Kuiku Iaza.

The Mualgal followed the woman to Kuiku Iaza, where she showed them the *augad*. They saw its eyes move—they thought them like those of the sand crab (*butu kupas*)—and they plunged their hands into the water to grasp Kuiam's sacred emblem. The *augad*, however, retreated deep down in the water and disappeared inside the roots of the *iwir* tree.

One man ran to Gumu to fetch a coconut-leaf mat (*potawaku*). This was spread beside the pool and attracted the *augad* from its hiding-place; but the *augad* disappeared when the mat was pulled closer to the edge of the water.

Another man ran for a mat made of soft pandanus leaves (*minalai*), in the hope that Giribu would show a preference for that kind of mat. But the *minalai* proved to be as unattractive to Giribu as the *potawaku*.

The Mualgal then discussed the possibility that Kuiam had stored his *augad* in a wrapping of ti-tree bark when he was not wearing them. So

22. I.e., as if for serious discussion, or for a ceremony.

Maurie Eseli, one of the story-tellers. She is standing on Kuiam's hill, indicating leaves "stained with Kuiam's blood". Kuiam's home, Gumu, is beside the sea in the middle distance.

they tried to lure the *augad* with the bark of three different kinds of ti-tree, *zöi ub, pöitai ub,* and *musil ub.* The smooth bark of *zöi ub* brought Giribu into sight again; the dusty bark of *pöitai ub* brought it close to the surface, so that its eyes protruded above the top of the water, and even when they moved this strip of bark very close to the edge of the pool, the *augad* only retracted its eyes. Finally, they tried the bark of *musil ub:* the effect on Giribu was immediate, and it leapt from the pool on to the strip of bark. The Mualgal quickly folded the bark over the *augad* and carried it down to Gumu.

100

When the Mualgal sailed back to Mua the following day, they took Giribu with them. They hid it in a hole beneath a big stone to keep it safe for their people. After the missionaries came to Torres Strait, this hiding place was given the name, *Satanan Kupai* (Satan's navel).

No one knows what happened to Kutibu. Kuiam was wearing it when he fell forwards, struck down by Mua clubs.

DOGAI I [Told by Maurie Eseli at Mabuiag, 10 October 1967]

The girls and boys of Wagedagam[1] on the island of Mabuiag used to play a game called *mudaidau sagul*. In the morning the boys went off to spear fish on the reef, and the girls went to the mangroves to look for crabs. In the afternoon all met at a pleasant spot where an exchange of gifts was made, each boy giving the fattest fish he had speared that day to the girl whom he favoured, and this girl giving him in return the fattest crab she had found. It was the rule that only fish and crabs which had yellow eggs inside them could be given.

One day a girl cooked all the crabs that she had found that morning and brought them to her mother for safe keeping while she played with the other girls until it was time for the exchange of gifts. When she ran home for her best crab, she discovered that her mother had eaten every one of her crabs—she had nothing to give. Her partner waited for her in vain: the girl was at home, crying her heart out.

She was still crying at sunset. Her mother could not stop her, nor could her mother's sisters, even when they pretended that *dogai* I was coming to take her away. "*Dogai* I is very near. *Dogai* I will get you," they threatened, but the girl kept on crying regardless of anything that they said or did.

Now at the mention of her name, *dogai* I experienced a strange bodily sensation (*gamu zilmai*). Knowing all that had happened at Wagedagam in the afternoon she said: "That little girl is still crying and someone has threatened her with me. Someone is using my name to frighten her." *Dogai* I decided to steal the girl.

The girl was still crying at midnight when I set out to run over the hill and across Bari to Wagedagam. She sent magic ahead of her, which caused everyone to fall asleep—everyone but the mother and daughter.

Dogai I is an important mythical figure at Mabuiag. The name I (pronounced *ee* as in "feet") had its origin in an incident which occurs towards the end of the story. Two physical features at Mabuiag, a well and a creek, bear the name, I.

Dogai I eventually went up to the sky and became a constellation (identified by Haddon, in *Reports*, V, 16, as "the star Vega with the adjoining group of small stars which represent one arm held out"). This constellation is associated in West Torres Strait with the onset of the season of the south-east wind (*waur*), and for this reason Dogai I is often referred to as *Waurlaig* (south-east-wind-person).

1. People whose totem (*augad*) was *kadal* (crocodile), i.e. *kadal augadalgal*, lived at Wagedagam, on the island of Mabuiag. *Wagedagam* means "the other side"—in this instance, the north-western side of the island.

The mother was still trying to quieten the girl. "Don't cry," she said. "It's very late. *Dogai* I will hear you and take you away." But it was no use, the girl went on crying, and presently the mother, too, slept. *Dogai* I crept into the house, snatched the girl and made off with her, jabbering as she ran: "*Dadiapara, kadiapara, dadiapara, kadiapara.*"

The little girl called to her mother many times, more and more loudly as she was taken further and further away from her home. The women at Wagedagam heard her cries and ran to try and save her, but *dogai* I had too great a start for them to be able to catch her.

When *dogai* I passed the *putil* trees on the north-western side of Wagedagam, she gouged an eye from the girl with a finger. The girl screamed. *Dogai* I, still running, soon afterwards removed the other eye from the girl, who again screamed.

When I reached her home amidst the rocks on the side of the hill, she tried to make the girl stop crying and, because she was unsuccessful, became very angry. Grabbing her by the legs, *dogai* I swung her up and then down, cracking her head against a rock. Then she rubbed the girl backwards and forwards, backwards and forwards, against a boulder until there was no skin left on her. After that she placed the body on her lap and began to rock it—as if to put it to sleep.

All this happened during the absence of the men from Wagedagam on a hunting expedition for dugong and turtle. They returned the morning after *dogai* I's theft of the girl, and all the women except the girl's mother went down to the landing to help unload the canoes. Afraid to face her husband for fear of what he would do to her when he heard about the loss of his daughter, the poor woman asked her youngest sister to meet him and tell him the story and herself went some distance away to Awana Mai where she sat down alone, sick at heart.

So the father received the news from his wife's sister and, as soon as he had taken his share of the meat and fish obtained during the hunt to his home, went to the head man (*kuiku garka*) and told him all that had happened.

The head man ordered the men of Wagedagam to search for *dogai* I until they found her. Arming themselves with harpoon-spears (*wap*), harpoons (*kuiur*), and ropes (*amu*), the men were soon tracking the *dogai* across Bari, up the hill and down the other side. When they caught sight of I, she was still sitting down; she held the girl's body in her arms and was rocking it from side to side as if to soothe it to sleep.

The men crept towards I, the girl's father in the lead. When he was close to the *dogai*, he harpooned her in the shoulder. I threw the child away and tried to escape from the men by screwing herself into a solid wall of rock.[2] The men threw a rope around her and tried to haul her out, but *dogai* I

2. The well, I, is said to have come into existence at this spot as the result of *dogai* I's screwing herself into the rock. The creek which runs down to the sea from this well in the wet season is called I Kasa.

The well called I, which is said to have
come into existence as the result of *dogai*
I's screwing herself into rock

103

continued to turn her way into the rock—all they managed was to tear off her right arm at the shoulder. "Now I have only one arm to use when I hunt for crabs," said *dogai* I.

After the *dogai* had disappeared from their sight, the men took her arm back to Wagedagam and told the boys to throw it to the sharks in the sea. But the boys said: "We won't throw I's arm into the sea straight away. Let's hang it up on a tree and use it for spear play (*tukutuk sagul*). We'll throw it to the sharks when we've finished our game." And they threw spears at I's arm until sunset. Then, instead of throwing the arm into the sea as they had promised, they left it hanging on the tree.

After dark, fireflies (*zagul*) swarmed around the arm, lighting it up, so when *dogai* I came in search of it late that night, she saw it from a long way off at Bari. She ran towards it, scratching herself at the part where her arm had been torn off and calling:

Zug nguzu zug a ngapa mariu a kawa utu a.
(Arm, arm, come to me. Join here.)

When she came close to the tree, the arm and her shoulder reached out for each other by sending out tendons. The arm was finally drawn to her shoulder so fast and with such force that the two made a loud noise at the moment of impact. "I!" squeaked the *dogai*. "Now I have two hands to use when I look for crabs." Then she ran back to her home.

Everyone at Wagedagam heard the sound of the arm rejoining itself to its shoulder. "That would not have happened if you had thrown the arm to the sharks as we told you," the men said to the boys.

UG [Told by Tabitiai Mooka at Mabuiag, 29 September 1967]

Once upon a time there were living at Dabangai a widow and her only son, Tabepa, a handsome young man for whom all the young girls were crazy.

That her son found favour with these girls did not please his mother at all, for she intended him to marry Ug, a spirit girl of Kibu, the land beyond the horizon to which the ghosts of dead people go. Again and again she told him: "You are to marry Ug of Kibu." But Tabepa continued to spend far too much time in the company of the girls of Dabangai for his mother's liking, and in the end she decided to go and make a home for herself and her son at Wagedagam, the opposite side of the island.

They settled at Kulapis, outside the main village of Wagedagam, and before long all the young girls of Wagedagam were throwing themselves at Tabepa. His mother became very angry. "You are to marry Ug of Kibu," she reminded him often.

His mother's frequent mention of Ug worried Tabepa. What kind of girl was she? Was she beautiful? As for Ug, whenever Tabepa's mother mentioned her, she experienced a strange bodily sensation (*gamu zilmai*). "Someone is using my name at Gigu (an old name for Mabuiag)," Ug said at those times. She made up her mind to escape from Kibu and visit Wagedagam in order to satisfy her curiosity about the young man for whom she was intended as a bride.

Ug stole away from Kibu one night after the spirits had gone to sleep. She took some strings of dugong meat for a present for Tabepa's mother. Outside Tabepa's house she called: "Tabepa! Are you asleep?" Tabepa woke and said: "Who is it?" "It is I, Ug, the girl whom your mother wants you to marry." Tabepa went to the girl, and they talked until just before daybreak, when Ug said that she must hurry back to Kibu.

After leaving Kulapis, Ug ran to the rocks on the mudbanks, Gatani. There she went down to Apangab, the road under the sea, and ran along it until she came to sandbanks (Guguzina Kabauzinga, ghosts' dance place) the other side of the small island, Iadi. At Guguzina Kabauzinga, Ug stood for a while and looked back at her sweetheart's home. "*Urpi Gigu pöiad ras* (Gigu, so rich that the sea around you is filmed with the oil of turtle and dugong. Dusty, windswept Gigu)," she said. Then she re-entered Apangab and sped to Kibu, arriving just in time to light up the *markai* (spirit) dancers. Had she been late, she would have been missed, for she was a beautiful girl; as such, it was her duty to hold a torch of burning palm-leaves while a dance was in progress.

Tabepa felt very tired the morning after Ug's visit to him. It was late when he got up. His mother thought that he looked sick. The girls of Wagedagam were hanging about at Kulapis, so he told them to go to a big fig-tree (*dani*) on top of Kalalagau Pad and wait there for him. "I'll tell my mother that I'm going to the reef to spear fish. With that excuse, I'll be able to escape from her and join you later," he said.

After they had gone, Tabepa picked up his spear and walked down to the beach. Then he walked along past the mangroves until he reached the point, Tipait, and climbed up to the girls. The *kutai* and *bua* (yams) that they had cooked while they were waiting for him to come were ready to eat.

Tabepa and the girls spent the afternoon together on Kalalagau Pad.

He told them about Ug's visit to Kulapis, explaining that Ug was the girl whom his mother wanted him to marry.

Tabepa's mother saw him walking back with the girls and scolded both him and them. Tabepa said nothing.

Ug visited him again that night. "Not tonight, not tomorrow night, but the night after that I shall take you to Kibu," she told him. Tabepa said that he would go with her. She stayed with him until dawn and then hurried back to the spirit land.

Tabepa spent the afternoon on Kalalagau Pad with the girls and arranged to meet them again for the last time the following afternoon, when he would say goodbye to them before going to Kibu with Ug. When Ug visited him that night she reminded him that the next time she came they would set out for Kibu together.

Tabepa felt infinitely sad after he said goodbye to the girls the following afternoon. When he lay down to sleep in his house, sleep would not come. His body began to chill, and shortly afterwards he heard Ug calling his name. He had said nothing to his mother about Ug's previous visits, and now he left her for ever without a word of farewell.

At Gatani, Tabepa asked Ug how he was to enter Apangab. "Catch hold of my grass skirt," Ug told him. They came up at Guguzina Kabauzinga and looked back at Wagedagam. *"Urpi Gigu pöiad ras,"* said Ug in praise of her sweetheart's home. Then they re-entered Apangab and travelled the long road to the home of the spirits.

Ug hid him in her house and, when she had to go and light up the *markai* dancing that night, made him promise to stay indoors until she returned.

The *markai* dancers advanced in two lines, but hardly had they begun to dance when feathers fell from their head-dresses. "We are being watched by a human," they said. Ug dropped her palm-leaf torch. "Come close," she said, "for I want all of you to hear what I have to confess." "Is it about the human at Kibu? Do you need help?" asked the *markai*. "My fathers," said Ug, "I brought the human here to be my husband." "Let us see him," said the *markai*.

The *markai* approved of the handsome young man as husband for Ug, and the next morning they escorted him round their village. In the party was a *markai* named Baz.

Baz had long been in love with Ug, but Ug had never felt love for Baz. Fiendishly jealous of Tabepa because he had been accepted by Ug, Baz had concealed a small club (*malpalau nai*) under his arm before leaving his house that morning. He was going to kill Tabepa.

The chance to do so occurred when Tabepa complained of thirst during the walk round the village and was taken to the well. While he was drinking, the *markai* stood around him in a circle. Baz struck Tabepa a death-dealing blow between the eyes with his club as Tabepa was straightening after quenching his thirst.

The other *markai* growled at Baz: "You should not have killed the human. We promised Ug that no harm would befall her husband. There has never been a human at Kibu before."

Ug heard almost at once that Tabepa was dead and ran to the well. "I hate you," she stormed at Baz. "I never loved you. Tabepa did you no wrong." Then she wept bitter tears.

MAIWASA

[Told by Repu Dugui at Mabuiag, 22 September 1967]

Two brothers, Konowe and Bainu, lived in a village on the small island, Iadi. Konowe had a son named Maiwasa, and Bainu had a son named Gizu. Both Konowe and Bainu were expert hunters.

Every morning, Konowe used to sit on top of a rock and keep a good look-out for turtle and dugong. If he saw one of these creatures, he went straight back to the village and organized a hunting party.

When Maiwasa grew to manhood he became an expert hunter like his father, Konowe, and his father's brother, Bainu. Like them, he was *zogoau garka*—a man who had magic which enabled him to see dugong and turtle when ordinary men saw none. He never missed when he threw his harpoon-spear (*wap*), and whenever he went fishing he returned with a long string of fish.

Now there was a big snake (*unar*) in a cave on Iadi. She used to watch Maiwasa all the time he was out on the reef, and, because she found him very attractive to her, she decided that she wanted him for a husband.

One day she went to the reef while Maiwasa was fishing. Maiwasa, who had had no luck up to that time, saw her head in the water and, mistaking it for a baby turtle, speared her. As he lifted her up with the prongs of his spear, scales fell from her body and stuck to fish—till then, fish had no scales.

"I want you to be my husband," the snake told Maiwasa. But Maiwasa had no desire for a wife who was a snake, and he told her so and killed her.[1] Then he went home to his father at Iadi and recounted all that had happened.

The following day Maiwasa went to Dauan to hunt dugong . . .

Two versions of this story are told in Torres Strait, one at Mabuiag, the other at Dauan, where it goes by the title, "Kusa Kap". The principal difference between the two versions is the way the story begins.

At Mabuiag, a Mabuiag origin is ascribed to the hero, Maiwasa. At Dauan, the details relating to Mabuiag are omitted. The rest of the story, in which the action relates to Dauan and a small island off the coast of Papua, is told in greater detail at Dauan than at Mabuiag.

This tale is the beginning of the story told at Mabuiag. It should be read in conjunction with "Kusa Kap", in the section, "Stories from Dauan".

1. Another informant at Mabuiag said that when Maiwasa refused to take the snake for wife, the snake changed into a *dogai*—but not before she had thrown Maiwasa to Dauan. As a *dogai*, she followed him to Dauan, and as a *dogai*, she watched him at that island as she had at Iadi. It was her firm intention to grab him at the first opportunity and make him her husband.

107

THE MARKAI OF TAWAPAGAI

[Told by Dakanatai Kiris at Mabuiag, 10 October 1967]

There used to be a village in the district of Wagedagam called Urabal Gagait, and at Buru, a place in that village, there lived a mother and daughter.

One day the mother told her daughter that they would go and fish on the home reef north of Pulu.[1] There the daughter found something that looked like a rope of living flesh. It was very long. She called her mother to come and look at it. "It may be good to eat," the woman said when she saw it. So they cut a piece from it and took it home and cooked it.

"We'll throw it to the ants and see what happens to them after they eat it," said the mother. "If it doesn't kill them, we'll know that we've found a new food for ourselves." The ants ate it and did not die. The mother said: "We'll go to the same place tomorrow and get some more." This they did, and they cooked it and ate it themselves this time.

Day after day, mother and daughter obtained their food from the strange thing that the daughter had found.

"You look plump and well-fed," the children of Urabal Gagait said to them when they visited Buru one day. "What have you been eating?"

Now the mother and daughter had found that the new food yielded a lot of fat when it was cooked, and they had been skimming this off and storing it in baler shells. They sent the children home with a shellful of it and told them to tell their parents to go to the reef and get some of the rich food for themselves.

So, for a time, all the people of Urabal Gagait cut daily portions from the edible rope of flesh, in so doing, working their way over the reef from the spot north of Pulu, where it had been discovered by the girl from Buru, towards the mangrove islet, Mipa. The day came when, after they finished cutting off their food, they found themselves at the south-eastern tip of Mipa, opposite Tawapagai on Mabuiag where a man was swimming just outside the mangroves.

Actually, this man was a *markai* (ghost) who, for a long while, had daily felt himself growing weaker. When he saw the people on the other side of the narrow channel that separates Tawapagai and Mipa, he said to them: "Why have you been chopping off my penis?"

No sooner had he spoken than he died and turned to stone. He became the big boulder which stands in the sea outside the fringing mangroves at Tawapagai.

1. Pulu, a small rocky island inside Mabuiag's home reef.

Landtman in *The Folk-Tales of the Kiwai Papuans* (Helsingfors, 1917), pp. 422–24, gives a tale, "The Man with the Enormous Penis", which he collected at Mawata, on the Papuan mainland.

AMIPURU [Told by Maurie Eseli at Mabuiag, 6 October 1967]

Artist Ephraim Bani

When Amipuru of Wagedagam was fishing with his spear between Paidai and Tipait one day, he saw a pelican swimming in the sea between the two small islands, Widul and Pururai. He decided to catch it and give to his children for a pet.

So he broke off some branches of mangrove and, with them for camouflage, waded and swam towards the pelican. Just as he reached it, however, it took fright and rose up from the water. Amipuru managed to grab one of its legs with one hand and held on tight.

The pelican flew into the air and circled Wagedagam. Then it flew across Mabuiag to Kuiam's hill and Bau and out over the passage between Mabuiag and Kuiku Pad (Jervis Reef).

Amipuru held on for dear life. Sometimes he changed hands. He was waiting for the pelican to fly over soft mud before he let go.

Eventually the pelican returned to Wagedagam and flew out over the mud offshore from that place. Amipuru loosened his grip and fell like a stone, to sink to his neck in mud.

The people of Wagedagam saw him fall, and they tried to dig him out.[1] It was useless. Faster than they dug away the mud from around him, the sea rushed in with the rising tide. Before long the poor man was in imminent danger of drowning, because the water was up to his mouth.

"We can't do anything for Amipuru," the people said, so the head man cut off his head with a bamboo knife.

Amipuru's wife and children wept.

1. The removal of the mud by the people in their efforts to save Amipuru is said to have created the lagoon, Wazegna Dan.

109

SAURKEKE

[Told by Repu Dugui at Mabuiag, 25 September 1967]

Once upon a time there lived on the island of Bupu a man named Paiwain, his wife, Utaga, and a *dogai* named Saurkeke.

Every morning when Saurkeke woke up, she used to leave her home, a *buda* tree, and go down to the sea and wash her grass skirt. Then she climbed up the hill to a flat stone and danced on it, singing as she danced:

> *Saurkeke gima zazilnga.*
> (Saurkeke is wearing her short grass skirt.)

After that she walked down to the reef and collected limpets from the rocks.

One morning when Paiwain was fishing on the south-eastern side of Bupu, he saw Saurkeke coming towards him. He dropped his line and chased her back to her home.

This went on for many days, Saurkeke trying to come close to Paiwain, and Paiwain chasing her away. At last Saurkeke called to him one morning: "You will not let me be your friend, so I shall go to an island where the men are like brothers to me."

Actually, Paiwain had nothing against Saurkeke so long as she kept her distance. In fact, he was glad to have her at Bupu, for she was not a bad *dogai* as *dogai* went, so he now begged her not to leave. Saurkeke, however, would not be persuaded, and she pushed a log into the sea, stretched out along it, wrapped her arms round it, and drifted away from Bupu with the tide. As she floated along on top of the water, she sang:

> *Napai ngapai nga wa nga baltaika?*
> *Doke doke töribu töribu.*
> (Who is this floating along?
> *Doke doke töribu töribu.*)[1]

Near the island called Surbur, waves almost tore Saurkeke from her log: the tide was on the turn, and there is a swirling current at that spot at such times. She groped with her feet for the bed of the sea, but could not reach it because it was too far away. (A small reef formed there afterwards.) The tide took her close to Dabangai Ngur, a point on Mabuiag, and again

1. When I asked William Min for a translation of this, he just said: "*Dogai* language, which is very hard to translate."

she felt for the bottom of the sea with her feet, once more finding that the water was too deep. (Here, also, a small reef formed.) Finally she washed up at Padagat, a spot at the eastern edge of the reef which surrounds the island of Kuikusagai.

That day seven men of Aipus[2]—Iamata, Buibuigi, Salgaigi, Unuwakab, Unuwatur, Uta, and their nephew, Aipazar—had gone to Kuikusagai in their canoe to fish, and while Uta was walking about on the reef with his spear he saw a log cast up at Padagat. He went to it and, seeing what he took to be roots on its under-side, tried to break them off. They were not roots, however, but Saurkeke's fingers—she was still clinging to the log—and she shrieked with pain. Uta yelled, terrified: "What's this? A *dogai*!" And he ran away as fast as he could, Saurkeke jabbering at his heels: "*Dadiapara, kadiapara, dadiapara, dadiapara.*"[3]

Halfway along the reef from Padagat, Uta went inside a hole in a boulder not far from the beach. He had to remove stone-fish and stingrays from the hole, but after that he was perfectly safe, and Saurkeke could not reach him. She stood outside his hiding place for a long time, but the tide came in and eventually she was forced to go ashore, where she climbed to the top of the ridge in the middle of the island and went into the small cave, Gabmanmui.

While Uta walked about on the reef with his spear, the rest of the party fished from the canoe outside the edge of the reef. They saw Uta running away from a *dogai* and, believing Uta needed their help, told Aipazar to pull up the anchor. Aipazar said: "Don't be silly. There are no *dogai* at Kuikusagai. Now at Sasi you can see *dogai* walking about at all times of the day, but Kuikusagai is a different kind of place. That's not a *dogai* chasing Uta. What you see are two boys, Waimugi and Samugi, chasing garfish." Against their better judgment, the brothers stayed where they were and continued to fish until the tide covered the reef. Then they poled their canoe in to the beach. During the day they had caught many crayfish and a big rock cod.

After they had placed the rock cod in an earth-oven to bake and cooked the crayfish, there was still no sign of Uta, so they called to him: "Uta, where are you? We caught a rock cod and some crayfish. Come and eat." Uta heard them, but he would not leave his shelter on the reef because he was afraid of being grabbed by the *dogai*; nor would he reply to his brothers, except with a whistle. "Come, Uta. Come and eat crayfish claws," the brothers called again. Not until it was almost dark did Uta leave the hole in the rock and go to his brothers' camp.

Later in the evening, Iamata walked down to the beach to see if his canoe was safe, and found that it had split lengthwise and the outriggers were drifting out to sea. Sad at heart, he was strolling along the beach

2. A neighbouring islet.
3. "*Dogai* language". See footnote 1. In "The Dogai of Zurat", in the section, "Stories from Badu", this gabble was given as "*dadipara, kadipara*", i.e. without the middle syllable "a".

when he saw a hawksbill turtle coming up to lay its eggs. He turned it on to its back and walked back to his brothers.

Soon all but Uta fell asleep. Uta was still eating crayfish claws. Saurkeke, who had been watching the brothers and Aipazar from Gabmanmui, now crept towards the camp and, the moment Uta began to drowse, put a hand inside the earth-oven, hooked a finger through the jaw of the rock cod, and dragged it out. And at that instant, Uta, whose head had been nodding, jerked awake.

"The *dogai* is stealing our fish," he yelled. "She sneaked to the earth-oven when my eyes closed for a moment." Aipazar said: "That's a lie. You stole the fish yourself." But Uta was able to convince his brothers that he was telling the truth, and all of them gathered sticks and grass, plucked brands from the fire, and then followed the *dogai*'s tracks to Gabmanmui. Outside the cave they lit a fierce fire, and before long Saurkeke was yelling with pain. Aipazar said: "There's no *dogai* in this cave—one of you men is making that noise."

In the morning the men climbed up to Gabmanmui. On the ground inside the cave they saw a skull and the head of a rock cod.

Iamata and his brothers and Aipazar returned to Aipus on the two halves of the canoe which had split lengthwise the night before, taking with them the rest of the crayfish and the hawksbill turtle. When they arrived at Aipus, Aipazar took more than his fair share of the crayfish and scoffed at Iamata when he said: "Tomorrow I shall go to Gumu[4] and visit my nephews. They have a new canoe which they will give me in exchange for the shell of the hawksbill turtle I found at Kuikusagai." "The people of Gumu will cut off your head," Aipazar told him. "They will not," said the people of Aipus, "because his nephews live there."

Next day when the reef was dry, Iamata set out for Mabuiag on foot, and, as he walked away from Aipus, Aipazar said to the people: "Say goodbye to Iamata. You will never see him again."

When Iamata arrived at Gumu, the youths of that place were throwing spears at two logs,[5] so he sat down behind some bushes on the bank of Kuburau Kasa and watched them for a while.

> *Muta garu muta.*
> *Sara garu sara.*
> *Tana ina muigubalgal ia umaika.*
> *Pagane! Pagane! Pagane!*[6]

4. On Mabuiag.
5. *Tukutuk kalakau sagul*, target play.
6. The magic chant used at islands in West Torres Strait to ensure accurate aim in target play.

chanted the boys as they took aim. Presently Iamata's nephews threw their spears and missed the target completely, the spears travelling in the direction of the bushes behind which Iamata was screened, and when they

112

ran to retrieve them they saw their uncle. "Are you a ghost or a human?" they asked him. Iamata assured them that he was their uncle in the flesh and explained the purpose of his visit.

His nephews invited him to spend the night with them, and in the morning loaded their new canoe with a present of yams. They accompanied their uncle in the canoe as far as Dabangai, and then they left him and walked back to Gumu.

Iamata was seen by his people as he came towards Aipus, and they ran to the beach to meet him. Aipazar reached him first and helped himself to most of the yams.

GIGI   [Told by Saku Mooka at Mabuiag, 27 September 1967]

One night the men of Dabangai planned a hunting trip to Anui.[1] While they were making their preparations the following morning, a young boy named Adiad asked his father, Gigi, if he might go, too. Against his better judgment, Gigi finally agreed to take him. He and Adiad sailed alone in their own canoe.

The hunters spent several days at Anui, harpooning enough turtle and dugong to fill every canoe with fresh meat. Then they set out on the return journey to Dabangai. Gigi and Adiad were the last to leave.

They had still not reached home when all the other canoes had finished unloading. Everyone stood around on the beach, watching for Gigi and Adiad, but the day wore on, and there was still no sign of their canoe. Gigi's wife asked the men who had returned for news of her husband and son, but they could tell her no more than that Gigi and Adiad were the last to leave Anui. That night she wept, believing both her husband and son to have perished.

★

When the canoe sank on the way back from Anui, Gigi tied his son to one of the outriggers and told him that he would try and swim to Mabuiag for help. Adiad pleaded to be allowed to swim, too, but Gigi refused to let him make the attempt. "Stay here until I come back," he insisted.

1. A reef several miles distant from Mabuiag.

113

Gigi managed to reach Buia.[2] He walked along the beach to the north-western end of the island and looked towards the spot at which his canoe had sunk. "Adiad, my son," he grieved.

Three *dogai* were watching Gigi from the top of the hill on Aipus.[3] They had had their eyes on him since the moment he set foot on Buia. "Our husband," they said.

Late in the afternoon Gigi began to feel very thirsty. There was no water on Buia, so, as the tide was out, he decided to walk across the reef to Aipus and look for some there. Not far from the top of the hill he found a pool and drank. Then he climbed to the top of the hill—and was grabbed by the *dogai*. "You are our husband. You must stay here and never leave us," they told him.

Straight away the three *dogai* dug some yams and roasted them for Gigi's evening meal, but what they brought him were the charred skins— they had scraped out the fleshy part and thrown it away! Gigi explained that it was the fleshy part he wanted, so they gathered it up and gave it to him.

Many days passed. The *dogai* fed Gigi on yams which they dug on Aipus, but the time came when there were no more yams on Aipus to be dug, and then the *dogai* said to their husband: "You will have to stay and look after our home while we go to Widul[4] and dig yams for you there. Don't you run away, Gigi."

Before very long, there were no more yams to be dug at Widul, and the *dogai* had to go to Mabuiag for yams for Gigi's evening meals.

First of all they dug at Awana Mai. Then they had to go to Dawalnga, and after that to Kai Pad. Each new place they went to was further from Aipus than the last. One night they told Gigi that there were no more yams at Kai Pad and they would have to go to Bulbul.

After the *dogai* left for Bulbul next morning, Gigi said: "It will be very late when they arrive home today. Bulbul is a long way from Aipus. If I run fast, I should be able to reach Dabangai before they get back." But in order to be able to gain a little more time for himself, he took a louse from his hair and put it in one half of an *akul* (shell)[5] which he placed on the ground in the middle of the *dogai*'s home. "Louse," said Gigi, "when the *dogai* return this afternoon they will say: 'Gigi, where are you?' Then you say: 'I am still here.' " And with that, Gigi ran down the hill.

That morning there was a very low tide, so the whole reef was dry, and Gigi was able to run all the way from Aipus to Dabangai. His people saw him from a distance and ran to meet him. "Gigi, where have you been? What happened to you?" they wanted to know.

Gigi said: "I'll tell you all about it later on. Right now there's no time to be lost, because three *dogai* will be coming for me pretty soon. They've

2. A small island within Mabuiag's home reef.
3. The islet mentioned in the previous story, "Saurkeke".
4. Another small island within Mabuiag's home reef.
5. *Akul*, a swamp shell—a bivalve— formerly used for cutting.

had me for their husband all this time, but I ran away from them this morning."

All the men armed themselves with bows and arrows and clubs and harpoons and spears, and then everyone got into the canoes and went out to the edge of the reef. Gigi said: "They should have arrived back at Aipus from Bulbul by now. Keep a sharp look out."

Presently a cloud of small butterflies (*peitawal*) flew towards the canoes. Soon afterwards dragonflies (*kuipul*) appeared. And then everyone saw the three *dogai* off Dabangai point.

"Gigi! Come here, Gigi!" ordered the *dogai*.

"You come here!" Gigi countered.

"You are a bad husband," shouted the *dogai*. "We dug yams for you every day and fed you well, yet you ran away from us."

"You come here!" Gigi called.

The *dogai* advanced on the canoes and were harpooned by the men of Dabangai.

The three *dogai* turned to stone at the edge of the reef. They are still there. The people of Mabuiag call them *Dogail*.[6]

6. The correct plural of *dogai*.

WAIAT [Told by Maurie Eseli at Mabuiag, 6 October 1967]

This is the story of a man named Waiat who was a very powerful sorcerer. He had another name, Naga. Most people called him Naga.

Naga lived on Widul with his wife, Waba, and his daughter, Gainau. He had a sister, Kuda, who lived at Wagedagam[1] on Mabuiag with her two sons, Waimugi and Samugi.

No hair grew on Naga's face—he was beardless like a woman, and he had breasts like a woman. His sister Kuda had a beard like a man, and she had no breasts.

Kuda had a big drum (*warup*)[2] which she beat every night for her sons to dance to. Naga heard it at Widul.

Naga's favourite pastime was a game which he played with a seed-pod rattle (*gual*) tied to the end of a length of vine. He used to throw the rattle over the branch of a tree and let it fall to the ground, and then jerk it up by

1. Not far from Widul.
2. This drum had two names: Izalu and Zapulu.

115

pulling on the vine-rope. In falling to the ground the rattle went: "Lu! Lu! Lu!" As Naga jerked it upwards it went: "Wo! Wo! Wo!"

One day Naga visited his sister at Wagedagam and told her to give him her drum, her flat chest, and her beard, promising her his breasts in return. The exchange was made.

Not long afterwards Naga was out in his canoe hunting for turtle. When he caught one he said to the men who were crew for him that day: "No one but me may put a knife into this turtle. It is mine, Waiat's. It belongs to feather-bearded Waiat."[3] Then he ordered them to return to Widul and after they had carried the turtle ashore, told them that his nephews, Waimugi and Samugi, would dance for him that evening in the red afterglow of the sun.

He gave instructions for cooking the turtle in an earth-oven and sent some men to Bedam[4] to cut young, white coconut fronds. "Perform this task secretly," he commanded. "Drag the fronds under the water on your way back to Widul. Should anyone see you, either while you are cutting the fronds, or while you are bringing them back, kill him."

While the men were cutting the fronds, Naga's wife and daughter walked past Bedam on their way to fetch water from the well, Awana Mai. The men killed them.

Naga questioned the men upon their return to Widul. "Did anyone see you?" he asked them. "Your wife and daughter saw us," the men replied. "Did you kill them?" pressed Naga. And when they told him that they had killed Waba and Gainau, he approved their action.

That evening Naga stuck feathers of the white crane to his face with beeswax, and then he began to beat the drum that he had obtained from his sister, Kuda. Presently his nephews came into sight. To Naga it looked as if they were dancing at Saul Ngur, the southern point of the neighbouring island, Marte, whereas, in fact, they were dancing at the northern end of Widul. Waimugi and Samugi danced to the beat of Naga's drum until it grew late. Then they lay down, covered themselves with mats, and slept. Naga was still beating his drum. The men at Widul fell asleep to the sound of Naga's drum.

> (Wa) ngai Izalu (wa) (wa) Zapulu (wa),
> (Wa) ngai taitalgar sika (wa) taitalgar (e),

sang Naga, recalling the sympathy and encouragement (taitalgar) that he had always received from the wife whom he had had killed.

> (Wa) ngai Izalu (wa) (wa) Zapulu (wa),
> (Wa) ngai taitalgar sika (wa) taitalgar (e),

mourned Naga.

3. Waiatan baba-sigamai waru (feather-bearded Waiat's turtle).
4. A small part of Wagedagam.

116

Waimugi and Samugi woke during the night and, feeling hungry, cut some meat from the turtle that Naga had caught that morning. Afterwards they went back to sleep. Naga was still singing and beating his drum.

At last he stopped. His nose was streaming, for he had wept the whole time he had sung and beaten his drum. Now, in clearing his nose, he removed so much mucus that when he threw it at a stone it hit so loudly as to startle the sleeping birds at Tipait Ngur.[5] They flew up into the air.

Naga felt hungry, so he went to his cooked turtle for meat. When he found that flesh had been cut from it, he walked to his sleeping nephews and, seeing turtle grease around their mouths, killed them by driving the pointed end of a *bu* shell into their eyes.

Afterwards he returned to his quarters, got his *walsi iana*,[6] hung it over his shoulder, and walked to the beach. There he took from his *walsi iana* the feathered wing of a man-o-war hawk and blew it into the water, where it transformed itself into a canoe. He stepped into the canoe and, at that moment, heard a drum beating to the south.

Naga travelled towards it and so came to Koteid on Badu. He asked the people of that place if the drum he had heard was theirs. They said that it was not. They had heard a drum south-east of Koteid.

He sailed south-east to Widui on Mua and there learned that the people had heard a drum in the direction of Totalai. At Totalai the people told him that they had heard a drum at It. At It the people said that the drumbeats came from the island of Nagi.

So Naga returned to his canoe and, as he sailed away from Mua Point to cross the sea to Nagi, pulled all the feathers from his face and flung them shorewards. Some fluttered halfway up the hill before they fell to the ground, but all turned to white stones (which you may see today).

There was no one at Nagi. Naga saw coconut-leaf dancing skirts scattered about on the ground and the ashes of a dead fire. That was all. But he could hear a drum, and the sound came from the east. He sailed east and came eventually to Waier.

5. A point at the north-western end of Mabuiag.
6. *Walsi iana*, bag in which a sorcerer kept his aids to magic when he travelled. It was made from teased bark fibre.

KAMA   [Told by Dakanatai Kiris at Mabuiag, 28 September 1967]

The older boys of Dabangai[1] often went to Gainau Kasa at night and played. A young boy named Kama used to follow them.

Kama's mother always worried about her son when he went to Gainau Kasa. "My son," she warned, "you are too young to go off like this. One of these nights the older boys will come home without you. You will go to sleep, and they will forget you." But Kama insisted on going. "I won't get lost. I won't get left behind," he used to say to his mother.

One night he fell asleep under a *bodau* tree while the older boys were playing and when they were ready to go home they did not give Kama a thought. "Where is Kama?" his mother asked the moment she saw that her son had not come back with them. The boys ran all the way to the *bodau* tree at Gainau Kasa, but he was not to be seen. He had been stolen by *markai*.

The *markai* kept Kama for three moons. Then they decided to give him back to his parents. They took him as far as a spot in the mangroves north of Dabangai, and, after giving him a message for his mother and father, sent him on alone from there. Kama was to tell his parents that the *markai* were going to leave a present of dugong and dolphin for them at that spot.

When Kama was out of sight, the area around the *markai* denuded itself of trees,[2] and the *markai* danced.

The people of Dabangai saw Kama walking towards them. "Kama! Kama is coming!" they shouted. They ran and met him. When they reached him they said: "You have the stink of *markai* on you." Kama said nothing.

His mother's brothers told his mother that she was to take him down to the sea and make him swim in order to rid him of the foul smell that emanated from him. Still Kama said nothing. His jaws were locked tight.

The following morning his mother made him swim in the sea again. Afterwards she rubbed his body with cream of coconuts, and then, clean and sweet-smelling, Kama recovered the power of speech.

When his parents heard from him about the present of dugong and dolphin meat, they went to Markai Kabauzinga and brought it back to Dabangai.

1. *Dangal augadalgal* (people whose *augad* [totem] was *dangal* [dugong]) lived at Dabangai on Mabuiag.
2. The people of Mabuiag call this spot Markai Kabauzinga (*markai* dance-ground). It is a patch of bare ground in striking contrast to the mangrove-fringed coastline immediately north and south of it.

118

TAWAKA, THE GREEDY MAN

[Told by Maurie Eseli at Mabuiag, 4 October 1967]

The people of Wagedagam sent a man named Tawaka with a gift of *biu sama*[1] for their friends at Bau,[2] but Tawaka arrived at Bau empty-handed, having left all the *biu sama* at Dadakulau Gud, a spot on top of the high ridge between Wagedagam and Bau.

The people of Bau were surprised to see Tawaka and asked him why he had come. "Just to see you," he told them. When he said he was going home, they brought strings of dugong meat for him to take to their friends at Wagedagam.

Tawaka climbed up to Dadakulau Gud, sat down and ate all the *biu sama* that he had left there earlier in the day and the dugong as well. He rested for a while after he had finished eating and then walked the rest of the way to Wagedagam. The people were surprised that he brought no present for them from their friends at Bau.

The same thing happened several days in succession: Tawaka set out from Wagedagam with *biu sama* for the people of Bau, and he began the return journey from Bau with strings of dugong meat for the people of Wagedagam. But the gifts of food were never received by those for whom they were intended—Tawaka ate the lot at Dadakulau Gud on his way home.

After a while the people of Wagedagam became suspicious of Tawaka, for they could scarcely believe that their friends at Bau had not reciprocated with gifts in kind. So some of the men followed him one day, in order to learn what happened when Tawaka went to Bau.

They went no further than Dadakulau Kula. There they hid behind some bushes and waited for Tawaka to come back. They let him eat every scrap of the dugong meat that he should have taken to Wagedagam and every one of the *biu sama* that he should have given to the people of Bau. Then they rushed from their hiding place and killed him with their clubs.

After covering his body with stones,[3] they walked home to Wagedagam and told the people about Tawaka's greed.

1. *Biu sama*. In former times in the Western Islands of Torres Strait, *biu*, the rod-like depending seedling of a species of mangrove, was a staple item of diet. It was not eaten raw, needing careful preparation and cooking to render it edible and palatable.

    The embryo seedlings of *biu* were plucked when they turned yellow-green in colour. Each was then nicked lengthwise. When a sufficient number had been treated in this way, they were placed in an earth-oven and cooked for approximately one hour, after which the sand and leaves were removed from the earth-oven, and the *biu* taken out and allowed to cool. They were then placed in a basket and the basket and its contents steeped in fresh water for three days.

    At the end of that time the basket was taken from the water and the pulp scraped from each seedling. Finally, the pulp was squeezed with hands (to rid it of excess moisture) and shaped into balls (*sama*) which were stored in dry baskets.
2. On the opposite side of Mabuiag.
3. The heap of stones beneath which Tawaka is said to have been buried can still be seen at Dadakulau Gud.

CROCODILE PLAY

[Told by Manase Bani at Mabuiag, 27 September 1967]

Awailau Kasa (wa) (a) (a) (a) (a)
(A) (a) (a) nguzu lag (a) (e).
Ubiri kubiri, Ubiri kubiri,
Dum sena dum, dum sena dum.

(Crocodile, Crocodile, Awailau Kasa is
your home. That's your place.)

Kutal Mazia bau bau tapia,
Iut (e) (ia) singe iut (e) (ia),
Kutal Mazia bau.

(The reef, Kutal Maza, looks like a
crocodile being drawn through the
water by a string through its jaw.)

1. *Kaigas*, the shovel-nosed ray, *Rhynchobatus djiddensis* (Forskal). *Kaigas* men were men whose totem was *kaigas*.
2. The opposite side of the island to Sipingur and Panai.
3. A creek on Badu.
4. It reached to the shoulders and had an opening for the man's mouth.
5. The informant said that the mask was used for crocodile play (*kadalau sagul*) which included song, dance, and distribution of food by the *kadal* people to members of the other, smaller groups of people (*kaigas*, and *dangal* [dugong] *augadalgal*). He said that the mask was given to a member of the Cambridge Expedition by a man named Gizu.

One cloudy night when there was scarcely any light from the moon, some *kaigas* men[1] of Sipingur killed a crocodile by mistake while hunting for dugong. They took it to the people of Wagedagam[2] who, seeing it, burst into tears, because their totem was crocodile (*kadal*). They mourned it for many days afterwards.

So the men of Sipingur went to Awailau Kasa,[3] harpooned another crocodile and examined it very carefully. Then they returned to Mabuiag and made a turtle-shell replica of it in the form of a mask which could be slipped on over a man's head.[4]

When it was finished, the men of Sipingur took it to the men of Wagedagam and gave it to them, saying: "We have made this crocodile for you."

The people of Wagedagam dried their tears and danced round their plaything.[5]

120

WAIABA [Told by Manase Bani at Mabuiag, 27 September 1967]

A party of men, all of whom were young and unmarried except one named Waiaba, set out in a canoe to hunt turtle and dugong.

At Sarbi, a small island close to Mua, they went ashore and dug up many nests of turtle[1] eggs. Afterwards they paddled to Mua and landed at Totalai, where they visited the gardens belonging to the people of that place and dug up many yams. These they loaded into their canoe, and then they returned to their homes at Mabuiag.

Several days later they decided to go again to Sarbi and Totalai for turtle eggs and yams.

By that time, however, the Mualgal had discovered the theft from their gardens and were constantly on the watch for strangers. Therefore, when they saw a Mabuiag canoe approaching, they said: "These must be the men who stole our yams. Let us welcome them appropriately." And they spread a mat in the shade of a tree close to the beach and placed stone-headed clubs beneath the mat.

Upon arriving at Totalai, Waiaba said to the young men: "Stay with the canoe. I shall go alone to the gardens." The Mualgal watched from behind bushes as he walked across the beach, and then they clubbed him and cut off his head. One of the Mualgal held it up for the men in the canoe to see. The canoe put back to Mabuiag immediately.

A plan was formed at Mabuiag to avenge the killing of Waiaba, and the men made ready their fighting gear. The two Kuiam *augad*[2]—crescentic emblems of turtle-shell—were rubbed with the scented leaves of *takar* and *matua*. "The Mualgal have sparked off a mighty blaze (*Ina Mualgal kai mui nitungul*)," said the men of Mabuiag.

Meanwhile at Mua the people of Totalai had moved some distance inland to Töit, knowing full well the retribution that would be exacted for Waiaba's head. They likened the coming fight to the fire which results from setting alight dead grass which has stood for several years without burning off (*Ina ngalpa senakai kai mui ngari guit waiangul*).

Many canoes were paddled across from Mabuiag to Mua. They arrived after dark and, in the middle of the night, ran into the mangroves where they were screened from sight. At first light, the men went ashore and formed into two lines, each under the leadership of a man who wore a

This tale was given as a factual account of the last fight between Mabuiag and Mua. I was told that it took place shortly before the London Missionary Society began its work in Torres Strait in 1871.

1. Of *unuwa*, the hawksbill turtle.
2. Replicas of the legendary *augad*, *giribu* and *kutibu*, fashioned by Kuiam for his own use in fighting.

Mabuiag warriors. When the men of Mabuiag fought, they advanced in two columns led by two men who each wore a replica of a Kuiam *augad* and a special head-dress with "owl" or "ghost" eye-pieces. The men they led wore head-dresses of white feathers known as *dari*. Concerning the *augad* worn by the leaders, one warrior wore an *augad* on his chest, the other wore an *augad* on his back. The custom goes back to the story of Kuiam.

Artist Ephraim Bani

3. "The shark of Zugu"—synonym for the fighting men of Mabuiag. *Zugu* is a reef close to Mabuiag.

Kuiam *augad*. In this formation they moved silently through the *zanga* trees, their presence on Mua known only to *surka*, who called an alarm from time to time.

Very early that morning, a woman and her small daughter walked some distance from Töit to pluck fruit from a *kupa* tree. While her mother was filling her baskets, the little girl saw the two leaders of the Mabuiag fighters. Frightened, she ran to her mother and buried her head in her mother's grass skirt. "What are they?" she whispered. "Are they ghosts?" When the mother saw them she said: "Daughter, the shark of Zugu[3] is streaking towards its prey for the kill (*Kai senakai zugutiam walmai-ima*). See, behind the two *augad* are the feather head-dresses (*dari*) of the men whom they lead. That is why *surka* has called so often. We must try to warn the people at Töit." They were too late.

Before the mother and daughter reached their people, the men from Mabuiag had already begun to shoot arrows at the Mualgal; soon they were fighting at close quarters with their clubs. The dust raised by pounding feet on dry earth was like smoke. When it settled, all the Mualgal were dead but one man who had managed to escape by running away. He was pursued, killed by a blow from a *gabagaba*, and beheaded.

GI OF DABANGAI

[Told by Maurie Eseli for Jimmy Luffman at Mabuiag, 14 October 1967]

Gi, whose totem was *dangal* (dugong), lived at Dabangai on the island of Mabuiag. He had two wives, one, a woman of Mabuiag, the other, a *markai* (ghost). The eldest child by the Mabuiag wife was a son, Anu; the eldest child by the *markai* was also a son, Wizu. Gi lived with his human wife during the daylight hours; he spent the nights with his *markai* wife.

It sometimes happened that a man lost the *kuiur*[1] from his *wap*[2] when he was hunting dugong. As soon as he arrived back at Dabangai, he sought out Gi and told him of his loss. That night, Gi would go into the bush and tell the *markai* about it. The *markai* would search for it until they found it and then bring it to Gi who would give it to its owner the next morning. A man who lost a harpoon could count on getting it back if he enlisted Gi's services.

Gi used to visit Mari Kula,[3] a boulder on top of the big hill, Kai Pad. Sometimes he would see a ghost standing beside it, the ghost of a living person. In every instance, that person died soon afterwards. One day, he saw the ghost of his grown-up son, Anu, at Mari Kula. Sad at heart, he returned to his home at Dabangai. Anu died that afternoon.

Gi told his wife that, with the help of his son-in-law, he was going to take Anu to a spot on the beach a little to the east of Kuburau Kasa (a creek) and stay with him throughout the night while Anu took the living form of a dugong.[4] In the morning, his son-in-law and male relatives would come to Kuburau Kasa, and, together, he and they would take Anu's body on a stretcher made from bamboo poles to Muwaukazi, near Maid, for placing on a *sara*.[5] He had very good reasons for wishing to have Anu's *sara* at Maid, because that was where he went at night to visit his *markai* wife; he would, therefore, be able to see his son's body every time he visited her.

So Gi spent the night near the mouth of Kuburau Kasa—thick scrub used to grow there, but Gi never feared to be alone at night—and placed Anu's body on the *sara* at Muwaukazi the following morning. He spent the rest of the day at Dabangai and returned to the *sara* after dark, intending to learn how Anu's ghost left his dead human body.

Gi saw lights like flames appear at the tip of every branch at the top of every tree which grew at Muwaukazi. Soon afterwards a *markai* peeped out of the ground and looked all around before he finally emerged fully. Gi saw that this was a very strange *markai*—he was, in fact, only half a *markai*. Buli was his name. Buli had only half a face—one eye, one nostril,

1. *Kuiur*, detachable barbed harpoon.
2. *Wap*, long, heavy spear, into one end of which the harpoon (*kuiur*) is inserted.
3. Mari Kula—literally, ghost stone (*mari*, ghost; *kula*, stone).
4. His *augad*, i.e. totem. Maurie Eseli said that the old belief was that, during the night after he died, a person took the form, and behaved in the manner, of the animal creature which was his totem.
5. It was customary to place a corpse on a platform called *sara*.

123

one ear, half a mouth—half a body, one leg, and one arm. He carried a drum which he now began to beat. Immediately, many white-clad *markai* came up out of the ground—men, women, and children, amongst them Gi's wife, who carried a baby in her arms, Gi's child. Gi went to her at once.

Buli beat the drum a second time. Hearing it, the male *markai* formed themselves into a row. He beat it once more, and the *markai* began to dance. Their leader was Wizu, Gi's eldest son by his *markai* wife. Wizu held a club in one hand.

Wizu danced towards the *sara*, and Anu's ghost left the body on the *sara* and ran to meet Wizu. When the two came close together, Wizu hit Anu's ghost on the head and said: "*Ni markai Kabarimai* (You are *markai* Kabarimai)." After that, both Wizu and Anu's ghost, *markai* Kabarimai, led the dancing, and as they danced they intoned these words:

> *Ngalbai kuikul gubarka ulmeukaka,*
> *Pai taparid sika matui nageumaka,*
> *Ngalbai markai, Wizuwal a Kabarimaiwal.*

> (We, the leaders of the dance, we who wear
> *markai* eyepieces, we cause the dust to
> swirl upwards with our movements, we two
> *markai*, Wizu and Kabarimai.)

The dancing continued until close on daybreak, at which time all the *markai* sank down into the ground, and Gi was left suddenly alone at Muwaukazi.

One day, Gi went in search of *markai* and did not find them for a long time. When, at last, he saw them—at Budaukuik—they were standing in a circle, heads bowed, silent, staring at something which lay on the ground. He asked them the reason for their unusual behaviour. One of the *markai* said: "*Dabangai mudna Bauaka tamaik ngalmun gul palga-paleka* (When the people of Dabangai move to Bau, our canoe will be wrecked)." Gi asked where their canoe was. "It lies on the ground in the middle of this circle of *markai*," he was told. Gi pushed the *markai* aside.

On the ground lay a body wrapped around with a mat, and Gi recognized the toes which protruded from the bundle as his own. He went home to his wife at Dabangai and told her what he had seen, and then he burst into tears.

The people who lived at Dabangai soon learned why Gi wept. The head sorcerer forbade them ever to move to Bau, saying that he and his fellow sorcerers would kill anyone and everyone who went there to live.

Three days later, missionaries of the London Missionary Society arrived at Mabuiag[6] and landed at Dabangai. Before long they persuaded the people of Dabangai to go and live at Bau. The night of the day that they went to their new home, Gi died.

6. In the year 1872, or thereabouts.

124

stories from **DAUAN**

DAUAN

PAD. hill
DAN. lagoon
KULA.stone
GIZU. point
BUTU. sand

KURUP KULA

TURAMANA BUTU

SIRISIR

DAN

GIGU

UKAMANAM KULA

SESEI

BARI

MEMEN

GINGUR

SUGU

KAUDAB

KAUDAB'S canoe and amu

KAUDAB'S dugong

the stone on which KAUDAB

cut up his dugong

BURUGUD

DOGAI

MARUGA

ARUTANIPIU PAD

SIWABAL PAD

SIABU

VER

ZUD

GIZI

MEKAL PAD

a MEKAL PAD'S cave

USAUKUIK

BAKAR

BUTAILZ PAD

LATAIL PAD

TAUTAI

SAMEN

KOMAL KULA

DOGAIL DAN

ANGAGALGAU SUGU

KABAIN

MET

COTERUN

KOGAS KOGAS-sago growsher cave

MANAN

MAWAL KULA

BADUKUT

WARAU DAN

ZAMAN

MARBAI KATAN

SAN

TRUMAT ABU

WARZID

KATANBUNA PAT

BULI

TAUGIN

KUMUN village

KADAU

BOIGUTURAU KULA

KOD

WAKAID

KUPAMAU KULA

ZOGAIL KULA

GAWA GIZU

GAGAN

SAIWALAB

GAGAT

MAWAL GIZU

SIGAIN KUP

KABAI'S landing place

BUTU

N

SCALE

½

Miles

0

M.Lawrie 14/10/68

KUSA KAP [Told by Anau Mau at Dauan, 12 October 1968]

Kaudab lived at Burugud. He was an expert dugong hunter. He used to spend the daylight hours when the tide was low examining the reef for signs that dugong had grazed and making preparations for hunting at night. When Kaudab saw dugong tracks, he knew which kind of dugong had made them: whether a male or a female, or a female and child (*apukaz*). He spent the night hours on the dugong platform (*nat*) which he had erected close to the spot at which a dugong had stopped eating grass the previous night. After he harpooned a dugong, his crew helped him take it ashore, where he cut it up on top of a big, flat rock. This meat he shared with the rest of the people at Burugud.

Kaudab was never far from his harpoon (*kuiur*) and dugong spear (*wap*). If he was not using them, the *wap* stood against the *mekei* tree beside which he lived, and, close beside it on the ground, were his *kuiur* and *amu* (rope) and *topi iana*.[1]

Not far from Burugud lived a girl named Bakar. She often heard people speak about Kaudab's prowess as a dugong hunter, and she used to ask her parents what kind of creature a dugong was, never having seen one because she was not permitted to leave her home. She was a very beautiful girl, so beautiful that she was not expected to do any work. So Bakar spent her days sitting cross-legged on a fine mat (*minalai waku*). She was *wakuniaingawakaz*.[2]

And there was *dogai* Giz. Giz knew all about Kaudab. She used to sit in a stone look-out above the rocks at the edge of the reef and watch him all day long, because she wanted the handsome young man with the soft red hair[3] as husband. She regarded Kaudab as hers and, because she was a very jealous *dogai*, never let him out of her sight.

One morning while Kaudab was out on the reef his relatives went to Bakar's parents and asked for Bakar as wife for him. They consented to the match, so Kaudab's relatives returned to Burugud and came back later in the day bringing Kaudab with them.

Kaudab was wearing a *kadik* (bracer) on his left arm and *musur* (woven armlets) on both upper-arms, and he carried his bow and arrows. Bakar sat waiting on her fine mat, unsmiling. Kaudab shot an arrow marked

1. *Topi iana*, the bag in which he kept his aids to magic. This bag, or travelling basket, was made from the teased fibres of the bark of a tree.
2. *Wakuniaingawakaz*, mat-stay-girl (*waku*, mat; *niai*, stay, sit; *ngawakaz*, girl).
3. Kaudab's hair was wavy, not tightly curled. It was said to have been bleached red by sun and salt water. According to Anau Mau, red hair was admired. He said the copper-red colour (*kiris*) was the result of constant exposure to sun and salt. Thus, a man who spent a lot of time fishing and hunting came to have hair this colour. Red hair could also be obtained by dyeing it, the method being to rub the hair with a mixture of salt water and ashes of burnt *wongai* skins (*wongai* [or *ubar*], the wild plum of Torres Strait).

127

with red ochre (*parma*) into the ground beside her. Then he and his relatives took Bakar to her new home at Burugud.

Giz saw and was furious. "You go first, but I'll come after. You'll suffer before long, my girl," Giz threatened from a distance.

Kaudab continued to hunt for dugong, and Bakar now went daily to the reef. Giz watched Bakar, waiting for a suitable moment to seize her and send her away from Dauan.

One day when Bakar was walking on the reef looking for octopus, Giz willed the young wife to come close to her—Giz was in her usual place, the stone look-out above the rocks at the edge of the reef—and, when Bakar came near, went down to a pool and changed into an octopus.

Up to this time, Bakar had not seen a single octopus. Now she saw a big one. From her basket she took bait—*mokan*[4] tied to one end of the mid-vein of a dry banana leaf—and dangled it above the pool to lure the octopus from its hiding place under a rock. When the octopus emerged fully, Bakar grasped its head and tried to whip it from the pool, only to be wrapped round by the tentacles of the octopus and dragged into the water.

Bakar knew this was no octopus, but a *dogai*. "Kaudab," she called. "Come here! Come quickly! I've been caught by a *dogai*." But Kaudab was a long way off, so he did not hear her.

Giz took Bakar down to the entrance to Apangabia-taian—the tunnel under the sea—and sent her by this route to the island of Kusar.[5] She then changed her appearance to that of Bakar and went to Kaudab's home at Burugud.

That afternoon when Kaudab announced he would be leaving soon to go hunting, Giz prepared food for him—she knew the duties of a wife. But she was very clumsy and, instead of using tongs to remove the roasted food from the hot stones, used her fingers instead. "*Ia ga ie!*" she cried, when she burnt her fingers. "*Pak za za, Kaudab, ga ie, ngazu aiai e*[6] (Where are the tongs, Kaudab, my husband)?" Kaudab looked at her in astonishment. What crazy cackle was this coming from his wife? Then she broke wind very crudely, and he understood: she was not Bakar, but a *dogai* who looked like Bakar.

★

After she had walked for a long while in the tunnel under the sea, Bakar came up to the top of the water to see how far she had still to go. (A reef, Namul Maza, marks this spot.) Kusar lay not far ahead, so she returned to the tunnel and came up again at the tiny, mangrove islet, Kazi Kusar, off Kusar.

Bakar sat down and looked around her. Where would she sleep? There was a small patch of dry ground not far from where she was sitting, so

4. *Mokan*, a sea "toad" which puffs itself round and globe-shaped when caught.
5. Near the coast of New Guinea.
6. *Dogai* were said to speak a confused gabble of the Island tongue. Here, Giz was trying to say: "*Iagar* (alas!) *Pak na lag* (where are the tongs), *ngazu Kaudab* (my Kaudab), *ngazu alai* (my husband)?"

Wellington Aragu posing as *dogai* Giz. Giz "used to sit in a stone look-out above the rocks at the edge of the reef and watch Kaudab all day long".

she broke branches from a ti-tree-like shrub called *saur* and made a shelter from them at that spot. For food she ate seeds from *kusa* trees.

The following day when she bathed in the sea, she noticed that her breasts floated in the water, a sign to her that she was pregnant.

Bakar gave birth to an egg. Because it had come from her body she looked after it well, and from it hatched a baby eagle for whom she cared as much as if it had been a child in human form. She named it Kusa Kap, after the *kusa* seeds (*kapul*) which she had eaten.

Kusa Kap grew fast. He began to learn to fly. The day soon came when his wings were strong enough to take him to the top of a dead tree. From it he looked down at the sea and, spying some mullet, swooped down and caught one. He flew back with it and dropped it in Bakar's lap. Bakar said: "Why have you brought me a fish? You know we have no fire to cook it. However, it is the first fish you have caught, so I shall eat it."[7]

From that day, Kusa Kap regularly caught fish in the sea, but though he always brought some to his mother, she always refused to eat them. So Kusa Kap ate all the fish himself. He grew huge.

That was what Bakar had been waiting for. She needed a big, strong son to fetch the things that she wanted from Pösipas, a woman who lived on the mainland. "My son," she said to Kusa Kap one day, "fly to Pösipas and sit down beside her. She will ask you whose son you are and name several people. When she says my name, nod your head up and down. When she asks why I sent you to her, fly to a bundle of *ubu*[8] bark, to *mod* (string),[9] to *upi* (a bamboo knife), and to her fire. She will understand that I want these things from her and give them to you. Most of all, I need fire from her fire."

So Kusa Kap flew to Pösipas in Daudai and behaved exactly as his mother had told him. Thus Pösipas learned that he was Bakar's son and that Bakar had sent him to ask for things that she needed. "How will you take *ubu* and *upi* and fire to your mother?" Pösipas asked. For answer Kusa Kap turned his back to her. Pösipas tied the roll of *ubu* to his back with *mod*. He turned and faced her. Pösipas hung the *upi* from his neck with *mod*. Kusa Kap then snatched a coal from her fire and flew up into the air. He circled once above Pösipas and afterwards flew straight to Bakar, landing at her feet. "Now we have everything we need," said Bakar. "I'll look after the fire and cook the fish that you catch."

Next morning, Kusa Kap flew to the top of a mangrove tree and watched the sea. The tide was high. Presently he saw a strange animal, a young dugong (*kazi dangal*). Its behaviour was very odd. It spent a short time at the surface of the water and then went down to the sea-bed. He wondered if it were good to eat. He flew out and hovered above the spot where it was feeding and, when it came to the surface again, examined it very

7. The catching by a boy of his first fish is an important occasion.
8. *Ubu*, a ti-tree which has bark like sheets of paper.
9. Made from the bark of the yellow-flowering hibiscus tree.

130

closely. The next time it came up, he seized it with his talons and took it to Bakar. Bakar cut it up and cooked it.

But there was more meat than she and Kusa Kap could eat. "My son," said Bakar, "take some of this food to Pösipas." Kusa Kap turned his back to his mother, she tied some cooked dugong to his back, and he flew to Daudai with it. When he returned to Kazi Kusar, he brought with him vegetables and water and tongs (pak) for his mother.

Kusa Kap caught many dugong. His mother cooked them and regularly sent him to Pösipas with a present of cooked meat. And every time he came back with gifts from Pösipas for his mother.

One day Bakar said to her son: "I want you to go to Dauan. Fly along the coast of Daudai to Gidigidsugu and then fly south to the island which was formerly my home. Your father lives there, not far from a beach behind which there is a grove of coconuts. If you see a dugong platform on the reef outside such a beach, a canoe at a landing place nearby, and a wap leaning against a mekei tree, you may be sure you have found the right place. Now go to your father for me."

Kusa Kap found his father at Burugud and sat down beside him. Kaudab asked whose son he was and named several women, and when he said, "Is Bakar your mother?" Kusa Kap nodded to signify, "Yes". "Did she send you to me?" asked Kaudab. Kusa Kap flew to the steering oar (walnga) of his father's canoe, to the canoe itself, and to the top of the mast. Then he looked towards Daudai. Soon afterwards he flew back to his mother, leaving Kaudab with the knowledge that his real wife, Bakar, was alive and was somewhere to the north of Dauan.

"Did you find your father?" Bakar asked her son. Kusa Kap nodded. "Fly back to him," said his mother.

Kusa Kap returned to Dauan, circled Burugud and alighted on top of the mast of his father's canoe. While Kusa Kap had been absent, Kaudab had been preparing for the journey which was to take him to Bakar, and he now set out. With Kusa Kap to guide him, he soon reached Kazi Kusar and was greeted by Bakar. "Oh Kaudab, my good husband! You have come to take me home," she rejoiced.

And after Bakar had told Kaudab about dogai Giz and the birth of Kusa Kap and her life at Kazi Kusar, Kaudab and Bakar boarded the canoe and sailed back to Dauan. Kusa Kap went with them, riding at the top of the mast as before.

Like Kaudab, Kusa Kap now knew all about the dogai who had harmed Bakar. When the canoe landed at Burugud, he flew round in circles until he saw the false Bakar—dogai Giz—at his father's home near the mekei tree, and then he swooped down, caught her with his talons, and flew high into the air with her.

Only then did *dogai* Giz learn that Bakar had been brought back to Dauan by Kaudab. "It doesn't matter what happens to me now," gabbled *dogai* Giz, "because I got what I wanted. I lived with your father for a long time as his wife. I punished that woman for taking him. I saw him first. He was mine. She should never have been his wife. But look what I did to her!"

Kusa Kap heard her. He let her fall, grabbed her before she fell very far and flew on. He dropped her again, only to grab her with his talons, and carry her further away from Dauan. In that way he tormented *dogai* Giz for a long time—dropping her, grabbing her, flying with her, dropping her, grabbing her, flying with her. Giz vomited and excreted from terror and pain.

All the while Kusa Kap had been working further and further south of Dauan. He looked back, saw that Dauan was far away, and flew very high. Then he let go of *dogai* Giz for the last time and flew back to Kaudab and his mother, Bakar.

Dogai Giz fell into the sea and turned to stone. Ever since, that part of the sea has been called Dogail Malu (*dogai* sea).

KABAI [Told by Anau Mau at Dauan, 12 October 1968]

Kabai had an argument with the other men at Dauan one day about sun and moon, day and night, and *kubil*, darkness. Kabai said: "Sun and moon are two different things, and darkness is another thing altogether." Everyone else said: "You are wrong, Kabai. There is only one thing, *kubil*, darkness, and it changes its form into sun and moon. *Kubil* is day, and *kubil* is night, whether black or moonlit." "I'll go and find out," said Kabai.

So Kabai slung over his shoulder his *topi iana*—the bag which contained his aids to magic—and went down to the canoe landing place on the beach where there are two big flat stones, took a feather from his *topi iana*, and threw it into the sea. The feather became a canoe (*babagul*, [magic] feather canoe), and Kabai set out in it.

Zei, the south-west wind, bore him swiftly to Augar Gizu, a point on the coast of Daudai near Mabudauan, where he was met by a man named

Gamia who, after asking Kabai where he was going, invited him to spend the night ashore. Next morning, Kabai asked Gamia to provide him with a good south-west wind and, with its help, sailed east along the coast of Daudai to Zagwan.[1] He slept there that night and the following day continued his journey east.

Kabai sailed on and on, day and night, night and day, out of sight of land, and at last reached Kibukut, the home of the spirits, at the end of the world. As he was running in to land, fruit of *kuzub* trees growing in the water at the edge of the sea fell on his head, immediately causing his hair to turn white—in that instant he became an old man.

After Kabai stepped ashore, he addressed his canoe with magic words. It changed into a feather again and he put it in his *topi iana*. Then he set out to explore the strange place to which he had come.

For a while he saw nothing to indicate that people lived at Kibukut, but then he came to a house; only, there were no foot prints on the ground around it. He went into the house. There were many skeletons lying on the floor, and, though he searched every corner, that was all he saw—skeletons. He returned to the spot at which he had landed and waited. The sun set. It began to grow dark.

Inside the house, the skeletons changed to ghosts of human appearance and began to talk. Hearing the voices, Kabai walked back to the house and entered it.

"Who are you? Where have you come from? What do you want?" he was asked.

"The men at Dauan say that day and night, and sun and moon are only *kubil* in different forms, but I say that sun and moon and *kubil* are three different things, each separate and distinct from the other," Kabai told them.

"You are right," said the ghosts. "Sun, moon, and night-without-light are three, not one. We have in our gardens light-coloured plants, plants less light in colour, and plants which are very dark. The first belong to the sun, the second to the moon, and the third to *kubil*, darkness. You were right all the time, Kabai. Spend the night with us in this house, and tomorrow we will show you the three kinds of plants."

Kabai lay down on the floor in the centre of the house, and the ghosts lay around him in a circle; but while he was asleep, the ghosts changed back into skeletons, and Kabai, seeing them when he woke just before daybreak, left the house and waited outside for them to reappear as ghosts. This they did later in the morning when they said: "We are going to our gardens to fetch the plants that we promised to show you."

While the ghosts were away, Kabai walked to the beach and transformed his magic feather into a canoe. Soon afterwards the ghosts loaded it with

1. A village in the Fly River delta.

three kinds of taro and three kinds of sugarcane, piling them in three heaps. In one were the light-coloured taro and sugarcane which belonged to the sun, in another, taro and sugarcane which belonged to the moon, neither very light in colour nor very dark. In the third were the dark-coloured taro and sugarcane of *kubil*, darkness, night-without-light.

Kabai walked back with the ghosts to their house and slept in it again that night. In the morning he went straight to his canoe. "Give me a north-east wind (*naiger*) to take me home," he called to the ghosts, and *naiger* at once blew strong. One ghost came and put a coconut in the stern of his canoe. "Shorten my journey to Dauan," said Kabai to this ghost as he set sail.

During the day, midway between Kibukut and Bramble Cay, Kabai saw a big, round piece of pumice floating in the sea. He caught it and placed it in his canoe. He reached Augar Gizu that evening, spent the night with Gamia, and crossed to Dauan in the morning. His journey from Dauan to Kibukut had taken many years, but it took him only one day to return from Kibukut to Dauan.

When Kabai set out from Dauan, his wife was pregnant, and he had told her that if the baby was a girl she was to be given the name, Kadau. When he arrived home, his daughter was a grown-up girl. She ran down to the beach to greet him. His wife followed.

Kabai showed the taro and sugarcane to the people of Dauan. "You see?" he said. "These plants belong to the sun, these to the moon, and those to *kubil*. Sun, moon, and darkness are not one, but three." The men had nothing to say. Kabai had proved his point.

He and his wife and his daughter, Kadau, took the piece of pumice and the coconut from Kibukut to the opposite side of the island. He placed the pumice in a pool of water in a low-lying area at Burugud and planted the coconut close by. And when that had been done, Kabai, his wife, and Kadau walked to the big rock called Boiguturau Kula and sat down on top of it.

Anau Mau, who told this story, and his friend, Elisala Bigi, showed me a piece of pumice in the fork of a mango tree at Burugud. This, they said, was the pumice brought back to Dauan by Kabai; they had placed it in the tree for safe-keeping. The tree has grown round it and over it until it is now almost part of the tree.

Anau and Elisala also showed me a coconut palm at Burugud. Kabai's coconut, they said, had grown into a tall palm and borne fruit for many years. It developed a branch which pointed straight to New Guinea. When the palm died, "old Naiama" replaced it with a coconut which had fallen from it. This grew into the coconut palm which I saw.

GABAI
[Told by Elisala Bigi at Dauan, 12 October 1968]

Gabai lived at Buli,[1] a village on Dauan. Most days, he used to walk round the island reef to Badukut and Burugud, spearing fish as he went, and then

1. In front of the present Mission House.

134

return home by the overland path. But sometimes—when low tide occurred very early in the morning—he went out from Badukut to a lagoon called Dogail Dan before coming in at Burugud. What he did depended on the tide.

Now whenever Gabai went fishing he was watched by a number of *dogai*. "That's a fine-looking man. Look at his red hair! What a handsome fellow he is!" they used to gabble away to each other. The *dogai* decided that he would make an excellent husband for them, so they began to plan how to catch him.

The head *dogai* was Mekial Pad. The other *dogai* were Katauna Piti, Taugin, Kauar, Toran, Samun, and Usau Kuik. Their names are the names of places on Dauan—each of the *dogai* had her home at the place by which she was known. Thus, for example, *dogai* Mekial Pad lived in a cave on the side of the hill called Mekial Pad.

Mekial Pad said one day: "Tomorrow, some of us will watch Gabai from my cave, and some of us will go to Burugud and change into a cluster of fruit at the top of the *mekei* tree which grows there. Gabai will be hungry when he comes in from fishing. He'll see the ripe fruit and knock them down—and find them change into *dogai*. We'll easily catch Gabai then." The other *dogai* agreed that this was a very good plan.

Gabai was very hungry when he came in from the reef the following day. ("He's coming!" called the *dogai* in the cave on Mekial Pad to the *dogai* in *mekei* form.) After walking through the mangroves at Burugud, he came to the *mekei* tree and, seeing the ripe *mekei*, knocked them down with a stick.

The plan had worked. Gabai was grabbed by the *dogai* and taken to the cave on Mekial Pad—the *dogai* had got the man they wanted for husband. Gabai thought: "For how long will I have to stay with these *dogai*? Will I never be able to escape?"

The next day, the *dogai* went away and dug yams, before they set out, placing a big, flat stone on top of the cave to prevent Gabai from escaping during their absence. After they returned, they roasted the yams, scraped away the charred, crusty, outside part of the roots and gave that to Gabai for his meal. They began to eat the floury part of the yams themselves. "Give me some of what you are eating," said Gabai. The *dogai* obeyed their husband.

After he had eaten his meal of yam, Gabai felt thirsty. "Bring me some water," he said. The *dogai* left the cave and came back with their urine. Gabai sent them to fetch fresh water, and again the *dogai* obeyed their husband.

Gabai was held prisoner by the *dogai* for so long that he came to think he would never escape. His seven *dogai* wives were all heavily pregnant.

He was painfully hungry the whole time. The *dogai* never forgot to seal him in the cave when they left him by himself. Gabai was in despair.

One day, not long before the *dogai* were due to have their babies, Gabai said to them: "Cut down a *kusi* palm and bring me some of its wood." The *dogai* had no idea why he wanted them to do this and said so. "I have nothing to do during the day while you are away. Bring me some *kusi* wood, and I'll be able to make something from it," he explained. The *dogai* brought him the wood, and the next time they went to dig yams, he fashioned seven pointed sticks (*kusiu buru*) from it and hid them.

The *dogai* gave birth to their children.

One morning, not long afterwards, they said to Gabai: "We are going to a distant part of the island to dig yams today." And they left their babies behind in the cave with Gabai. Hardly were they gone when Gabai took the seven pointed sticks and drove one each into the soft spot on top of the head of a *dogai* baby, killing all seven. Then, using all his strength, he lifted the stone away from the top of the cave.

Gabai now took a louse from his head and said to it: "If the *dogai* call out and say, 'Are you there, Gabai?' answer, 'I am here.'" Then he climbed out of the cave and began to run down the hillside. His legs were so weak that he often stumbled and fell. After a while his legs became stronger, however, and he eventually reached Kadau, not very far from Buli. He looked up at the sun and saw from its position in the sky that the *dogai* would soon be returning to Mekial Pad. Gabai ran as fast as he could the rest of the way to Buli.

The people in his village were very surprised to see him—they had thought he was dead. They told him that they had searched for him, but gave up when they could not find him.

Gabai told them the whole story of his capture by the *dogai*, and then he said: "There is no time to be lost. Those *dogai* will come looking for me and they'll be so angry that they will kill everyone of us if we are not well prepared to fight them. Load seven canoes with food and water. See that there is a harpoon and spear in each. And then everyone must get into the canoes and go and anchor in the sea between Buli and Kadau."

Gabai continued: "These signs will herald the approach of the *dogai*: thunder and lightning, wind and rain; a swarm of mosquitoes followed by a swarm of sandflies; and finally, a cloud of butterflies. When you see the butterflies, you will know that the *dogai* are close at hand."

Then Gabai led the people down to the beach, and, when all the canoes had been made ready, they got into them and stood out to sea between Buli and Kadau. Gabai took his position in the leading canoe.

When the storm which broke soon afterwards was at its height, Gabai signalled to the canoes behind that the weather would soon clear. The calm fell. And, just as Gabai had said, the mosquitoes and sandflies and butterflies appeared in turn.

Now the *dogai* were seen coming round Boiguturau Kula. They ran down to the beach at Kadau and began to chant:

> *Gabai maia bui (e)*
> *Gabai kupuri mai*
> *Gabai mata keda ti-i-i-i-ti.*

They sang this song four times—the words are *dogai* language, and it is impossible to say exactly what they mean. *Dogai* tried to speak like Island people, but they muddled their speech.

Each time they sang the song, they faced a different direction, raised their legs up and down in time with the words, and, when they came to the end of them, stooped low and charged forward, head out. Four times they did this—charging to the south-west, the north-west, the north-east, and the south-east. When they charged south-east, however, they did not break off but continued the movement and waded out to the canoes.

They went straight towards Gabai in the leading canoe. "Why did you run away from us? We looked after you and fed you. Why did you run away?" they stormed at him. Gabai said to the *dogai*: "Each of you go to a different canoe." And the *dogai* obeyed.

Mekial Pad swam to Gabai's canoe, and Gabai harpooned her. Her fellow *dogai* were harpooned by men in each of the other canoes. All the *dogai* swam back to the shore where they cut the ropes from the harpoons embedded in their backs, and then they ran back round Boiguturau Kula, discussing as they went what they should do now; should they go back to the cave on Mekial Pad and watch Gabai while he fished on the reef every day, or should they go to another island and so never see him again. They decided to leave Dauan and go to another island.

When they reached the well called Usau Kuik, the *dogai* jumped into the water and made their way underground to another well, Sapu. There they came up and went and made sharp-pointed, stone chips with which they cut the harpoons from their backs. Afterwards they returned to Sapu.

The seven *dogai* travelled under the bed of the sea a long way and came up at the reef, Sapul Maza. They looked back at Dauan. Ahead lay Gebar. They went down under the sea again and before long arrived at Gebar.

The *dogai* from Dauan talked things over with the *dogai* who lived at Gebar. All the *dogai* from Dauan were determined to stay at Gebar, so Mekial Pad said to the *dogai* of Gebar: "We're not going back to Dauan. You'll have to go and live at Dauan."

And that is what happened. The *dogai* of Gebar went and lived at Dauan, and the *dogai* of Dauan stayed on at Gebar.

TAIKOKO [Told by Anau Mau at Dauan, 21 September 1967]

A man named Taikoko lived beside Amakuduluna Mai.[1] A girl named Butu lived at Wakaid. They were in love with each other. Every day, Taikoko fished on the reef outside Wakaid, and Butu watched him.

Over his shoulder Taikoko wore a basket[2] in which he put fish as he speared them; but there was a hole at the bottom of the basket, so the fish fell straight through to the reef. His hair was copper-red, bleached to that colour by sun and salt water. While he was walking on the reef at Wakaid, he used to sing:

> *Taikoko ke! Taikoko ke!*
> *Nginuai nginuai Butu na ge?*
> *Nginuai nginuai Butu na ge?*
>
> (Taikoko! Taikoko!
> Butu, my sweetheart, where are you?)

One day Taikoko returned to his home after fishing, to see Butu's reflection in the water of Amakuduluna Mai. Believing what he saw to be Butu herself, he dived in after her. He struck his head against a submerged log and was killed outright.

When Butu saw that Taikoko was dead—she had been hiding in a tree which grew beside the well—she dived in to him. She, too, struck her head on the log and died.

1. A well on Dauan.
2. A fishing basket, *abata*.

KOGIA

[Told by Elisala Bigi at Dauan, 12 October 1968]

In Böibai, a village near a tributary of Mai Kasa, there lived a young boy named Malnga. One day his father found a small, stumpy, black snake which had a spike at the tip of its tail. He took it home and gave it to Malnga for a pet—not knowing that the snake was really a man who had gone inside a snake form.

Kogia was kept in a cave and fed well. At the end of a day's hunting, the men of Böibai always threw him a pig and a wallaby, but Kogia grew so fast and became so huge that very soon a pig and a wallaby were too small a meal for him. Before long his body filled the entire cave, and he suffered from hunger the whole time. He began to plot how to obtain more food.

Late one night, he set out for the village. So enormous was he that, when his head arrived at the village, part of his body still lay in a coil in the cave. He opened his mouth, and from it beamed light which enabled him to hunt for food. Thus he quickly found the people's *bereg* (food rack) upon which were cooked pigs and wallabies. Kogia extinguished the light by closing his mouth, and then he swallowed every animal on the *bereg*. Afterwards he returned to his cave and slept.

Henceforth, Kogia made a regular practice of robbing the *bereg* in the village. The people were at a loss to explain the theft of their food, but it did not occur to them to suspect Malnga's pet.

One night the men decided to watch for the thief and catch him in the act. They had eaten a heavy meal that evening, however, and, one by one, they fell asleep, all except a man who had yaws on both legs. The cold night air made his sores very painful, and this kept him from feeling drowsy. So, when Kogia arrived at the village and directed the beam of light from his mouth at the *bereg*, this man saw who was stealing their food. In the morning, he told Malnga's father about Kogia's thieving ways, and Malnga's father went to the cave, beat Kogia, and told him to leave Böibai.

Kogia crawled away into the scrub and coiled up inside a thick patch of lawyer vine. Later in the day, the children of Böibai found him and teased him by shooting toy arrows made from coarse, long grass called *magad*

Two stories about Kogia are told at Dauan. Both are recorded here.

According to informants at Dauan, the first is also told on the Papuan mainland "in the Tuger country, from Jerai to Gamar-Mai (just east of Buzi)". I do not think it has been previously recorded.

The same informants at Dauan said that the second story is also told on the Papuan mainland, "from the coast at a point north of Dauan east to Sui (a village near the mouth of the Fly River)". Wirz (*Folk-Lore*, 1922) recorded it during a brief visit to Dauan in 1929. Haddon (*Reports*, I, 43) dismisses it as "of little interest or value". Certainly it came into being after contact with European influence had been made—there is reference in it to a *markai gagai* (ghost bow, i.e., gun) which made the noise (*nur*) of thunder—but when, I do not know. The fact remains, however, that the people of Dauan told it in 1968 as one of their important myths.

1. *Magad*, blady grass. At a number of islands in West Torres Strait, the children play a game, *magadau sagul*, in which they use sections of the leaves of blady grass, eight or nine inches in length, in such a way as to fire the mid-veins as toy arrows. Williams describes and sketches this game in his study of the Morehead River people, *Papuans of the Trans-Fly* (Oxford, 1935), pp. 441–42.

Today, small, harmless, stumpy, black snakes, each with a spike at the tip of its tail, are often seen at Dauan. The people say that they are found at no other island in Torres Strait, and they call them *kogia*, believing them to be descended in some way from Kogia, the man who changed into that kind of snake and came to their island to live. Indeed, some say that Kogia, the man-who-is-Kogia-the-snake, still lives in Kogian Kula—Kogia's cave. Some nights a light is seen moving about on Lalau Pad: Kogia is looking for food as he formerly did at Böibai when he robbed the people's *bereg*. Sometimes, between Lalau Pad and the beach at Gulkun, they see a track which has been made by a big snake.

(A reliable informant said that he had seen a *kogia* at Mabuiag in 1939. It disappeared, and has never been seen since.)

at him.[1] Pricked and irritated, Kogia climbed a tree and wound himself round a branch.

When the children told Malnga's father that they had seen Kogia, he went to look for the snake which had been his son's pet and, finding him, invited him to return to Böibai. For answer, Kogia uncoiled himself from the branch of the tree and crawled further into the scrub. Malnga's father tracked him through long grass the following day, but he did not catch up with him. No one at Böibai ever saw Kogia again.

Kogia travelled south-east to Garber, where he could see the tip of the highest hill of Dauan. He thought he would like to make his home at that place, so, after collecting seedlings and seeds—of *urwaba*, sago, *pud* (the small variety of bamboo used for making arrows), and red-flowering hibiscus—and putting them in his *topi iana*, he set out for Dauan.

From Garber he crawled to Gidigidsugu; from Gidigidsugu he crawled to a spot on the landward side of Sigabadara; from there he crawled to Sirpupu; and from Sirpupu he crawled to Pad. At Pad he saw that Dauan lay to the south-west—and he had travelled too far to the east. So he went back to Gidigidsugu, crawled to the canoe landing place, entered the sea, and began to swim towards the island at which he wanted to settle.

It was a very long swim. Kogia became breathless from swimming so far. More than once on the way he excreted, the waste matter from his body turning to reefs.

Eventually he reached Dauan. He landed at Gulkun and spent the night on the beach. But he did not sleep. "I must leave this open spot on the sand. If I stay here, people will find me and kill me," he worried. As soon as it was morning, he left the sand and crawled up Lalau Pad (a hill) where, before long, he found the cave which became his home.

The seeds and seedlings which Kogia had brought from Garber were planted by him as he crawled from Gulkun to the cave on Lalau Pad. The sago grows a short distance from the beach at Gulkun, *pud* at Pudalnga, and the red-flowering hibiscus and *urwaba* at several places on Lalau Pad.

★

Kogia looked north to Daudai from his cave on Lalau Pad one day. The air was so clear that the northern mainland seemed poised above the horizon somewhere between sea and sky. He thought of Meseda, his friend who lived at Sui, and was so overcome with longing for the sight of him that he decided to pay him a visit.

Kogia crawled down to the beach at Gulkun and changed into his human form. He took his magic feather from his *topi iana* and threw it into the sea, whereupon the feather became a canoe (*babagul*); then, after obtaining a south-west wind by magical means, he set out on his journey.

He sailed past many villages on the coast of Daudai, through Tora passage, and so, at last, reached Sui.

The visit to Meseda was a long one, and, at some stage of it, Kogia obtained a wife, a woman named Sagaru.

Kogia had a gun, a *markai gagai*,[2] which he kept secretly stored inside his wife, only taking it from its hiding place if he intended to go hunting. On those days, he used to tell Sagaru to open her mouth and, when she did so, would reach inside her throat with his hand and pull out the gun. Meseda hunted with *gagai* and *taiak* (bow and arrows). He did not know that Kogia had a *markai gagai*.

Every morning, the two friends used to go and work in their gardens. Often they spent the afternoon hunting, when Kogia always shot many pigs and wallabies (which he always shared with Meseda), but Meseda was not so lucky. The latter found it hard to understand that Kogia never missed with his bow. And there was another thing that puzzled him: the sound of thunder (*nur*) that he heard from time to time where Kogia was hunting. He began to think that Kogia's bow must make this sound when it was fired. His own bow did not make the sound of thunder; therefore Kogia's bow must be different from his. He decided he would not go to his garden the following day, but stay at home and, while Kogia was away working, visit Sagaru. He would ask her what kind of bow Kogia used.

This he did. "Sagaru," he said, "tell me the truth. What kind of bow does Kogia use? Is it a real bow made from bamboo (*marap*), or is it a *markai* bow?" "I don't know," the woman replied. "When Kogia fires his bow, it makes a sound like thunder, and I jump with fright. Tell me, what kind of bow is it that Kogia uses?" Meseda persisted. Sagaru was silent for a while, and then she said: "If I give you Kogia's *markai* bow, he will kill me."

"So," thought Meseda, "Kogia has a *markai* bow, and Sagaru is looking after it for him."

"Let me see it," Meseda ordered. "Come close," said Sagaru, and she stood with her mouth wide open. Meseda looked down her throat to the muzzle of Kogia's *markai* bow.

"Let me use it," Meseda now begged. "No," said Sagaru, "for if you shoot with it, Kogia will hear, and there will be enmity between you and him." "Give me the *markai* bow," Meseda entreated. "I'll go away and fire it, and then bring it straight back. Kogia will still be my friend." For a while Sagaru would not yield, but in the end she took it out and gave it to her husband's friend.

Kogia's body did not perspire while he was working in his garden that day. Besides, he felt lazy; so, before long, he lay down and rested—only

2. *Markai gagai*, gun. (*Markai*, ghost, European; *gagai*, bow. Ghosts were believed to have pale skins; therefore, when the first Europeans arrived in Torres Strait, the people of Torres Strait believed them to be ghosts, because they had pale skins. There was, of course, no word for gun in either of the languages of Torres Strait. The newly-come *markai* wounded and killed with a weapon which he aimed and fired as a man used his bow to shoot arrows; so the term *markai gagai*—ghost bow—quickly evolved for the European's gun. Europeans are still called *markai* in West Torres Strait.)

to be startled by the same kind of sound as his *markai* bow made when he fired it. He left for his home at once.

Having obtained possession of Kogia's wonderful bow, Meseda hurried to a spot near Kogia's garden and shot a pig with it. Then he returned to Sagaru, gave her the *markai* bow, and went to his own home. There he cut up the pig. Afterwards he took some of the fresh meat to her.

Kogia saw it as soon as he reached home. He threw down his gardening tools and said to Sagaru: "You didn't give my *gagai* to anyone, did you?" Sagaru denied having done so. "Tell the truth," Kogia ordered. "There is still blood on this meat. Who gave you this meat?" "Meseda gave it to me," Sagaru told him. "Did you give him the *gagai*?" pressed Kogia. "No, I did not," the woman lied.

Before long, however, Kogia had the truth from Sagaru, and then he flew into a rage with both her and Meseda. "Why didn't you ask me first? Why didn't Meseda wait and ask me himself?" stormed Kogia. Meseda came along, and a fight started between the two who had been close friends. Eventually Meseda got the better of Kogia and threw him to the ground. "You lied when you said you were sad for the sight of me," Meseda told Kogia. "Leave Sui. Go back to Dauan."

Kogia felt sick with shame. He told Sagaru to prepare for the journey to Dauan. When the canoe was loaded, Kogia asked Meseda to give him a north-east wind. Husband and wife left with it, sailed through Tora passage and spent the night at Daru.

After Kogia left Sui, Meseda began to feel sorry for what he had said and done, and the more he thought about Kogia's act of friendship in coming to visit him, the more he wished to make peace with Kogia. So, the day after Kogia's departure for Dauan, Meseda set out in his canoe and tried to catch up with his friend in order to ask him to return to Sui.

As Kogia was preparing to leave Mabudauan, he saw a canoe approaching and knew it would be Meseda coming after him. But he did not go down to meet him. He let Meseda come to him, and when Meseda said, "I've come to take you back to Sui," Kogia replied: "You sent me away. I feel shame. Go back to Sui. I am going to Dauan. We are still friends, but nothing will change my mind about returning to Dauan. Let *naigai* (the north-east wind) take me the rest of the way home, and as soon as I arrive, I will stop it and send you a south-west wind to blow you to Sui."

Naigai, the north-east wind, dropped when Kogia landed at Gulkun on Dauan, and *zei*, the south-west wind, began to blow. It blew day and night until Meseda reached Sui, when Meseda magically caused it stop, in that way letting Kogia know that he had arrived home safely.

Kogia and Sagaru climbed Lalau Pad and settled down in Kogia's old home, the cave which he had found when he first came to Dauan.

142

THE KIWAI RAIDERS

[Told by Simona Naiama at Dauan, 14 October 1968]

Abai, a woman who lived in the village of Buli on the island of Dauan, received a baby pig from friends on the northern mainland, together with the message that she should look after it for them until it grew up. This she did, and the pig grew big and fat, so fat that it could not walk. She then told the people of Buli to kill it, and when that had been done, the pig was eaten.

Now the pig had never belonged to Abai—she had merely been looking after it for the owners, her friends. Therefore, when they heard that their pig had been killed and eaten at Dauan, they were exceedingly angry and sent a message to Kiwai saying that they wanted the people of Dauan to be punished for their offence. The Kupamal,[1] more than willing to fight at Dauan, immediately got together their fighting gear—clubs, bows and arrows, and bamboo beheading-knives—and loaded their canoes for the journey.

They set out late in the afternoon and reached Augar Gizu at sunset. It was *naigai* time, the season of the north-east wind, and they had been helped on their way by a steady breeze. After dark, they sailed on. *Naigai* was still blowing, and it stayed with them the rest of the way to Dauan, where they arrived late that night. They landed at Sigain Kup, a small cove, armed themselves, and climbed up the rocks at the back of the beach to an enormous boulder which they tried to roll down into the sea. They believed that if they could do so they would have proof at the outset that their combined strength was sufficient to overcome the people of Dauan. They could not budge it.

They went to the boulder-strewn area further back from the shore and, as it was not time to commence the attack on Buli, drew pictures with *parma* (ochre or red clay) on the undersurface of a huge rock while they waited.

The Kupamal set out for the village while it was still dark, advancing through scrub in two columns. The two leaders ordered some men to remain hidden in the bushes; the rest they sent into the village where they were to disperse. Men were to steal into every house, and each man was to lie down beside a sleeping occupant.

Just before daybreak, a Dauan woman got up and went to the bushes,

1. The fighting men of Kiwai in the Fly River delta.

143

to the spot where the Kupamau leaders were hiding. They shot arrows at her. "People of Dauan," she yelled, "there are enemies here! Either Gumulgal[2] or Kupamal—I don't know which." Wakened by her cries, the people of Dauan tried to dash from their houses, but every Kupam was ready to seize and club the victim he had marked, and few escaped. The Kupamal cut off the heads of the dead.

One man who got away—a man named Kang—had been able to snatch up his bow and arrows, and he limped off, pretending to be a cripple. The Kupamal saw him when he reached a rock, near the monument which commemorates the "Coming of the Light" to Torres Strait, and urged one of their number, Kamumu, to go and kill him. "Kamum'! Mm! Mm!" they pointed. Kamumu did a frenzied dance and brandished his *gabagaba* at Kang. Kang shot an arrow into Kamumu's heart.

Kang walked on a little further—to the site of the present-day Church. Another Kupam had gone out to kill him. Kang shot him through the heart also. He killed a third Kupam at very close range at Markai Katam.[3] The arrow used by Kang for this shot was a *bisikuik,* one which had a man's head carved on the head and a poisoned tip—with this arrow a man never missed. But it was the last of Kang's arrows, so, after he had fired it, he began to run away up the steep hill behind Markai Katam. Halfway to the top, he turned round and yelled down at his enemies: "Kupamal, come and get me!" But none of the Kupamal took up the challenge, all giving up the chase and going back to rejoin their comrades.

A Kupam who had had no part in the pursuit of Kang presently heard voices in the bushes behind the well at the back of the village and stole towards them. He saw a woman—Abai—and her children.

Abai, hearing no sound of fighting for some time, and believing, therefore, that the battle had ended, had gone to the spot at which she had prepared *biu* the day before and was feeding her children. The Kupam killed the small children and struck Abai a glancing blow with his *gora-patutu*, a small club. She dropped to the ground, unconscious. Her eldest son—a big boy—ran away and sat on top of the big rock called Kangan Gul (Kang's canoe). He looked down on his mother and the dead children, and then he ran without stopping to the top of the hill.

The Kupam stood astride the body of Abai, sharpening his *upi* (bamboo beheading-knife) with his teeth, his eyes sometimes on the woman, sometimes glancing around him. Consciousness returned to Abai. She looked up, saw the Kupam, and shut her eyes fast. She was lying on her back with arms outstretched. Now, always watching the Kupam through half-closed lids, she gradually moved her arms in to the middle of her body. The Kupam took his eyes off her—Abai brought her hands up, grabbed his genitals and wrenched savagely. He died of it.

2. Men from Gumu, by which name the island of Mabuiag was often called.

3. The well which supplies the village with water today.

Above: The Kupamal "landed at Sigain Kup, a small cove, armed themselves, and climbed up the rocks at the back of the beach to an enormous boulder which they tried to roll down into the sea".

Below: Rock painting on the under-surface of a boulder above Sigain Kup, the work of the Kupamal

Rock painting on the under-surface of a
boulder above Sigain Kup, the work of
the Kupamal

146

Those men of Dauan who had escaped hid on either side of the path through the scrub between Buli and Sigain Kup and stoned and killed many of the Kupamal as they were returning to their canoes with the strung heads of their victims.

Some Kupamal reached their canoes. They sailed away with a south-west wind and came to Gawal Maza off Saibai—where the beacon is.

Two men, Iamaru and Kaigas, who lived at the western end of Saibai Village, saw the Kupamau canoes and said: "Where have they come from? Let's go and find out." They put a canoe into the water and questioned the Kupamal. On being told that the Kupamal were on the way home from Dauan, Iamaru and Kaigas went to one of the canoes and looked under a mat. They recognized the heads. While Iamaru and Kaigas were killing the men in that canoe, the other canoes sailed away.

These were seen at Mawat by Gamia, who went with other men to find out where they had come from. When Gamia and the men of Mawat saw the Dauan heads, they went from canoe to canoe and killed every one of the Kupamal except those in the single canoe which managed to escape.

Thus, of all the canoes which sailed from Kiwai for the punitive raid on Dauan only one returned.

Outrigger canoe riding at anchor at high tide, outside Saibai Village

stories from **SAIBAI**

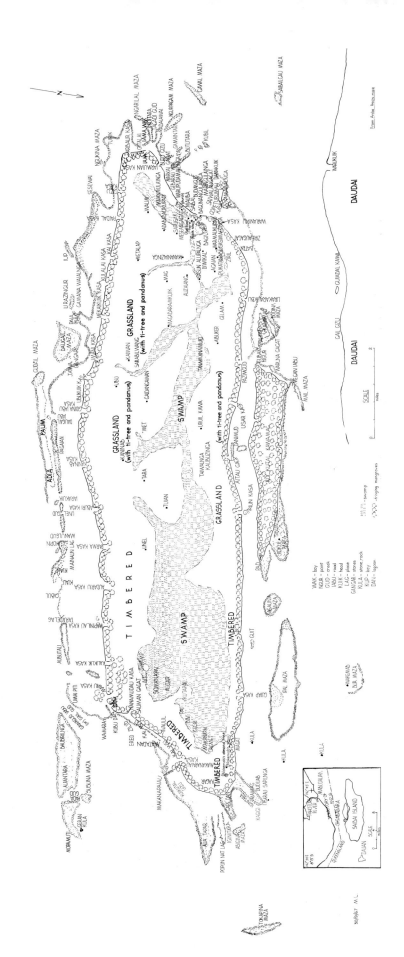

SAIBAI

Key:
WAK – bay
NGUR – point
GUD – creek
IADU – road
KUIK – head
LAG – place
GANGAR – stones
KULA – stone rock
KUP – bay
DAN – lagoon

GRASSLAND
(with ti-tree and pandanus)

SWAMP

TIMBERED

DAUDAI

SCALE
miles

From Anba, Anca maps

Low tide off Sabai Village, exposing mud flats

Mesea (or Melewal)   *Artist* Kala Waia

THE FIRST MAN
AT SAIBAI

VERSION A

[Told by Wake Obar (for whom sam [cassowary] is augad) at Saibai,
 27 August 1967]

The first man at Saibai was Mesea. He is usually called Melewal, because
his home was a big baler shell of the kind called *melewal*. No one knows
how he came to Saibai. The spot at which he lived bears his name: Meseangagat (Mesea's place). From time to time he used to leave his shell and
go for short walks.

Nima and Poipoi, two brothers who lived at the eastern end of Saibai,
once visited Melewal. After walking across the swamp they arrived at
Bagunangulainga.[1] From there they walked a short distance west to
Meseangagat where they saw lying on the ground pieces of bamboo such
as are used in making bows and arrows. Each said to the other: "Someone
must live here." So they called out: "*Köimega* (friend), are you here?"

Melewal left his shell, walked towards them and greeted them. He asked
them where they were going, and was told: "We are looking for our
sister, Ereu. We intend to search for her along the coast of Daudai."
Melewal said: "Where is your canoe?" Nima and Poipoi told him that
their canoe, Binibin,[2] was in their *topi iana*.

The two brothers walked north and went down to the beach. While
they were putting Binibin into the water, they saw a pair of mating turtles
floating on top of the sea, so they named the spot at which they were
standing Saiwalaugagat (mating turtle place).

From Saiwalaugagat Nima and Poipoi crossed to Daudai and sailed
east.

1. The site of the present-day school.
2. The canoe, Binibin, was a magic one.
Nima and Poipoi had a half-coconut
shell in their *topi iana*. When they
wanted to travel by sea, they removed the half-coconut shell from
the *topi iana* and stuck a magic feather
in it; the shell then transformed itself
into the canoe, Binibin.

VERSION B

[Told by Aniba Asa (for whom deibau [a wild yam] is augad) at
 Saibai, 25 August 1967]

Melewal and Budia are called *muruig*, because they are "first people":
no one lived at Saibai before Melewal and Budia. Budia arrived earlier
than Melewal, whom he saw crawl from the sea with an *alup* shell, a
different kind of baler shell from *melewal*, on his back. Budia said to the
newcomer: "Who are you? If you are a man, answer me." And, upon
learning that the stranger was indeed a man, he invited him to live at
Saibai.

Before Melewal came, Budia lived in a hole in the ground. Now he said: "Henceforth I shall live on top of the ground. My home will be a *bu* shell. You are to live inside a baler shell."

Both men used to leave their shells and go for walks, Melewal as a man, Budia as a willy-wagtail (*seseku*).

Many years went by.

Two men came to Ait: Nima and Poipoi. They and their sister, Ereu, walked to the other end of the island[3] and lived for several months at Magadaramkuik.[4]

One day Ereu asked permission of her brothers to go to the reef and catch crabs. When she failed to return, Nima and Poipoi left Magadaramkuik and went to look for her. One of them had Binibin, a magic canoe, in his *topi iana*.

They walked across the swamp towards the northern coast of Saibai, coming out close to where Budia and Melewal lived. Expecting to find

3. The western end.
4. Not far from the well called Mag.

Budia (as willy-wagtail)

Artist Kala Waia

two men whom they had observed from a distance, they saw no one. "Does anyone live here?" called Nima and Poipoi. At that, Budia—who had changed into a willy-wagtail at the approach of the strangers—flew down from a tree and took human form. "I have a friend who lives in a baler shell," he told the brothers. Melewal now left his shell, and the four men exchanged greetings.

Budia and Melewal asked Nima and Poipoi where they were going. "We are looking for our sister. Have you seen her?" the brothers said for answer. Budia and Melewal replied that they had not and invited Nima and Poipoi to spend the night with them, but the brothers refused to stay.

Before they took their departure, Budia said to them: "After you go, I shall return to my former home under the ground, never to be seen again. Tell my people who come after me that I will leave two remembrances of myself for them: a hole which will sometimes appear in the ground at the spot where I live,[5] and the bird, *seseku*, into which I changed."

5. Alfred Aniba said: "When Budia feels cold, his body shakes. That causes the hole in the ground to appear. The hole never appears when the ground is hard."

Aniba Asa, one of the story-tellers

Enosa Waigana, one of the story-tellers

NIMA AND POIPOI

[Told by Enosa Waigana at Saibai, 25 August 1967]

For a while two brothers, Nima and Poipoi, and their sister, Ereu, lived at Magadaramkuik.[1]

One day Ereu obtained permission from her brothers to go and hunt for crabs on the reef, and while she was looking about for them she was noticed by a man named Gamia who was sailing back from Dauan to his home at Maiad, a village on the Papuan mainland which can be seen from the island, Daru. Gamia came and asked her to go with him; she agreed, and the pair then travelled together in the canoe, hugging the coast of Daudai as they journeyed east.

Nima and Poipoi set out in search of their sister the morning after her failure to return from the reef. In their *topi iana* they had Binibin, the half-coconut shell which was their magic canoe. When they reached the well, Mag, they drank from it before walking across the swamp to the sea. From Sarusak they saw a man walking about near the beach.

They emerged from the swamp at Bagilgagat and learnt soon afterwards that the man whom they had seen was Mesea (or Melewal, because he lived inside a baler shell of the kind called *melewal*). Mesea greeted them and asked where they were going. Nima and Poipoi told him they were looking for their sister and would be sailing east along the coast of Daudai. "Where is your canoe?" Mesea asked. "Our canoe, Binibin, is in our *topi iana*," they replied.

Nima and Poipoi spent the night with Mesea at his place (Meseangagat— *gagat*, place). Next morning they walked north for a short distance and, on looking at the sea, saw a pair of mating turtles (*saiwal*), so they named the spot at which they were standing, Saiwalaugagat. From here they went down to the beach and put Binibin into the water. Next they stuck a magic feather (*warka*) in Binibin, and so soon as the feather quivered in the wind, Binibin transformed itself into a canoe, and the feather became a sail. Nima and Poipoi stepped into the canoe and, after magically procuring a following wind, crossed to the mainland opposite.

They reached Daudai at the mouth of a river and named the spot Warukuik (*waru*, turtle; *kuik*, head) because they saw a turtle's head appear above the surface of the water there, and when they saw a small sandy beach a little further on they gave it the name, Butulwarukuik (*butu*, sand,

1. A grassy region at the western end of Saibai.

157

sandy beach). Before long they saw a *kuzub* tree[2] in the sea outside the fringing mangroves, and round one of its branches a carpet snake (*guiad*), so that spot they called Guiadal Kawa (*kawa*, an islet).

Nima and Poipoi continued to sail east, naming those places which interested them for one reason or another: Göil Gizu;[3] Köi Kupad;[4] Buiai Gizu,[5] because when they looked east from Köi Kupad, they saw a big pig on the reef at that point; Sapural Kawa;[6] Mabudauan, a hill on the mainland, because as they passed it they chanced to look back at the high island, Dauan; Kawa, a small island in the mouth of a river; Malu Kawa,[7] a small island south of Kawa in a deep part of the sea; Kubakil Kawa,[8] because while they were talking about the single pandanus tree on this small island, one of the brothers coughed; Augarmuba,[9] a point of land on which there were good trees.

East of Augarmuba, Poipoi began to feel that they should turn back, but Nima wanted to go on, and before long the two brothers expressed their thoughts to each other on the subject. They named the place at which this discussion was held Köisarköisarburupagaizinga.[10] Afterwards Nima sailed on alone.

The sun set as Nima passed the point of land which he named Tere Gizu.[11] He saw the lights of a village—Maiad, where his sister had gone with Gamia, though Nima was unaware of it—and, a little while after, sailed through a passage which he named Mabuadadakas. Not far from Sui, Nima put Binibin ashore and rested for two days.

On the third day he saw a fishing canoe coming towards him from Sui and changed into a stork (*kaiarpitu*). The men in the canoe tried to kill the bird with their bows and arrows, and then Nima changed into his human form and shot those who had attacked him, killing all but one man, and him he wounded in the thigh. This man he sent back to Sui with the message that it would take more than one canoe to overcome Nima.

The following day several canoes were sent from Sui to fight Nima. Nima saw them coming and, as on the previous day, changed into a stork at their approach. Once again, the men of Sui fired arrows at the bird, after which Nima fought them (in human form), uttering magic words as he sent his arrows towards his enemies:

> *Panibabura, panibabura.*
> *Ju mari mare. Ju mari mare.*[12]

He spared a man to take a message to Sui: "*Gagaur poibamiz!* (String every bow!)"[13]

Every man from every village at Sui accepted the challenge. Nima changed into a pig before the fighting began, and into human form before he fought back.

2. Apparently a variety of mangrove.
3. *Göil*, stones; *gizu*, point.
4. *Köi*, big; *kupad*, bay.
5. *Buiai*, big pig.
6. *Sapural*, flying-foxes; *kawa*, islet.
7. *Malu*, sea, deep water.
8. *Kubakil,* coughs, coughing.
9. *Muba*, point.
10. *Köisarköisar*, many; *buru*, arrow-tip made from the wood of that name; *pagai*, strike or hit; *zinga*, [place] belonging to—i.e. the place where many thoughts were directed to a single topic, as arrows would be shot at, and hit, a target.
11. No meaning was obtainable for *tere*.
12. I was unable to obtain an adequate translation for these words.
13. "String every bow!" That is to say: "It will take every man from every village at Sui to bring me down."

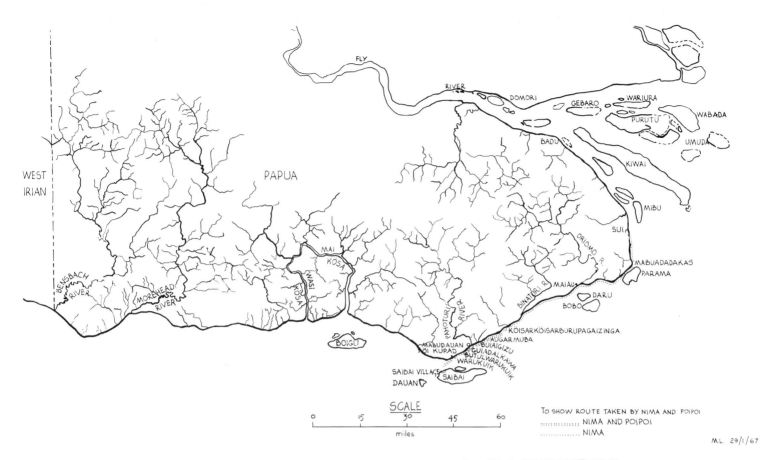

Map labels: FLY RIVER, DOMORI, GEBARO, WARIURA, PURUTU, WABADA, UMUDA, BADU, KIWAI, WEST IRIAN, PAPUA, MAI KOSA, WASI KOSA, ORIOMO R., SUI, MIBU, BENSBACH RIVER, MOREHEAD RIVER, PAHOTURI RIVER, BINATURI R., MAIAU, MABUADADAKAS, PARAMA, DARU, BOBO, KOISARKOISARBURUPAGAIZINGA, AUGARMUBA, BUIAIGIZU, GUIADALKAWA, BUTULWARUKUIK, WARUKUIK, MABUDAUAN, KOI KUPAD, BOIGU, SAIBAI VILLAGE, SAIBAI, DAUAN

SCALE
0 — 15 — 30 — 45 — 60
miles

To show route taken by Nima and Poipoi
::::::::::::: NIMA AND POIPOI
.... NIMA

M.L. 29/1/67

ROUTE TAKEN BY NIMA IN BINIBIN

Outline copied from Department of Lands Map, Brisbane, 1966

Nima and Poipoi with Binibin
Artist Kala Waia

Atituku, atituku,
Ju mari mare. Ju mari mare,

intoned Nima, as he fought the men of Sui,

Panibabura, panibabura.
Ju mari mare. Ju mari mare.

Then his bow broke, and he changed into a pig again.

Some men wanted to kill the pig, but others said: "This pig, Agabe, is an *augad* (a sacred creature, a god). We should keep it and guard it well."

Agabe was enclosed with canes and worshipped by men at Sui for a time. Later, however, there was a difference of opinion amongst the men, some saying that Agabe should be killed, others that Agabe should be set free. In the end, Agabe was taken out of his pen and sent inland.

★

No one knows what happened to Poipoi after he parted company from Nima at Köisarköisarburupagaizinga. Ereu married at Maiad and stayed there. Nima, as the pig, Agabe, became a source of strength for the men of Saibai.

Before young men were permitted to fight in Daudai, they had to go through a ceremony which was held in the *iut*, the men's house from which all women were excluded. Beforehand, men went across to the mainland and charmed Agabe from the scrub by singing for it:

(E) Agabe tumuruda.
Nima Nima (da)
Tumuruda.
Nima Nima (da)
(Sa) (e).

And hearing this song, Agabe came to them and allowed itself to be taken to Saibai, where it was killed in the *iut* and fed to the young men. Afterwards they were given bows and arrows. In future, whenever there was fighting to be done in Daudai, they fought along with the other Saibai men.

THE STORY OF AIT
KADAL   [Told by Enosa Waigana at Saibai, 27 August 1967]

People lived at Ait. They were gardeners and hunters [of dugong].

Once there was a very beautiful girl at Ait whose name was Usalal. Her father was dead, and she lived with her mother, Ua.

Usalal was so beautiful that every young man wanted her for a wife, but her mother and her mother's brother refused to allow her to marry, because they thought none of the young men was good enough for her.

After a time Usalal's uncle became so angry with the young men who came courting her that he shot her in the belly with an arrow.

So Ua built a shelter for her daughter outside the village where none of the young men could see her. The brother forbade his sister to visit her daughter, not even permitting her to take food and water to her. He told her that he would shoot her as well if she disobeyed him.

Usalal lay inside the shelter, weak and helpless from pain and hunger. All she could do was look up at the sky. Often she called to her mother. She made a song which she used to sing over and over again:

> *Jial (a) naki gar (a) (a) walmanu (a) (a) (waia) (a)*
> *Ama gar (a) ama ama (a) (ua) (a) (a) (waia) (a).*

> (The clouds overhead pass this way and that.
> Mother! Mother! Alas! Alas!)

Ua soon knew her daughter's song by heart. She could not bear to hear Usalal crying to her, and, despite what her brother had ordered, she decided to visit Usalal secretly at night and comfort her.

Early one morning just before daybreak, Ua heard Usalal singing softly to herself. She crept unseen to the shelter, but when she went inside she saw that her daughter had died. "My good daughter," said Ua, "I did not know this would be my last visit to you."

★

People continued to live at Ait.

One year when no rain fell, there was scarcely any food or water, and there was nothing to eat but dugong, which the men hunted, and crabs, which the women found in the mangroves.

Ait, an island at the south-eastern end of the Saibai swamp, was formerly the headquarters of one of two groups of people on Saibai whose sacred ancestor animal (*augad*) was *kadal* (crocodile). The other group lived at the north-western end of the island.

No one has lived at Ait since the early years of London Missionary Society influence in Torres Strait when the entire population of Saibai was induced to go and live in one village. But the descendants of the people who used to live at Ait continue to identify themselves as members of Ait Kadal, thus distinguishing themselves from the descendants of the other group, who belong to Village Kadal.

The episodes related in "The Story of Ait Kadal" represent knowledge of their past inherited by the Ait Kadal people.

After a time, the women became so weak that they died as they searched for crabs. They became black birds (*kaukuk*)[1] and sang to those women who still lived and came to the mangroves:

> *(Waia) (e) (a) (ua) (e) (a) (bumere) (bumere)*
> *Maiau kaukuk (a) Sarkau kaukuk (a)*
> *(Waia) (e) (a) (ua) (e) (a) (bumere) (bumere)*
> *Kau-kau-ku-ku-ku!*
> (Kaukuk of Maia and Sark.
> Kau-kau-ku-ku-ku!)

When the men and women went to their gardens, their digging sticks (*pabu*) on their shoulders, the spirits of the dead women accompanied them, too, flying round them as black birds and singing:

> *(A) pabu patanu (a) patanu*
> *(A) pabu pabu patanu.*
> (Dig with your digging sticks!
> Dig, dig with your digging sticks!)

Dugong meat kept some of the people alive until the rains came.

★

One day all the men of Ait went to hunt dugong. They caught many and brought them ashore at Saumangagat, their landing place on the southern coast. They left the dugong and the canoes here and walked to Ait, which they found deserted, their wives and children having gone to sleep at Taiwalnga a short distance away.[2] The men decided to spend the night at Ait and join their wives and children in the morning, all except Dogei who said: "I shall go to Taiwalnga and tell the women that we caught many dugong."

That night some Kupamal[3] came across to Saibai. They landed at Alil, hid their canoes in the mangroves, and made their way through the swamp in the dark. They reached Taiwalnga and surrounded it, attacking at daybreak and killing everyone who had slept there that night except one woman and her daughter, who managed to escape and run off towards Ait. The Kupamal pursued them.

The men of Ait woke to the sound of screaming women and clubs thudding against skulls. They ran for Taiwalnga, with the famous fighter, Waria, in the lead. He was the first to see the mother and daughter fleeing with Kupamal at their heels.

Waria pretended to be lame and bent himself double, using this ruse to tie a small club (*gorapatutu*) to his ankle. He called to the woman, telling her to run straight to him. When she and her daughter were safe behind

1. *Kaukuk* also means "empty".

2. When all the men were absent from Ait, and it was defenceless against a chance raiding party, the women removed to Taiwalnga for safety's sake.
3. Men of Kiwai.

162

him, he straightened himself and shouted at the two Kupamal: "Here stands Waria!" The pair of them turned tail and fled, but Waria caught them almost at once and drove his club into their skulls.

He ran on. When he was recognized by the rest of the Kupamal, they too fled back across the swamp into the mangroves, trying to reach their canoes at Alil and escape. He killed many of them.

That morning, Papat, a Saibai man of Iam, which is at the southwestern end of the island, set out to visit a friend at Ait. When he had gone halfway, he heard of the raid by the Kupamal and determined to have a share of the heads. Though he ran as fast as he could, he did not, however, reach Alil until the only Kupamal to escape were drawing away in one of the canoes.

Waria and Papat walked back through the mangroves to Ait, killing any Kupam whom they found trying to hide. The few whom they missed eventually died of hunger.

For a long time afterwards the men of Ait discussed the raid by the Kupamal, at last coming to the conclusion that these warriors possessed some magical object from which they drew their strength. They decided to steal it, travelling to Kiwai in the canoes left by the Kupamal.

At Kiwai they visited each village in turn, but learned nothing until they arrived at the last. There they captured a man and forced him to betray the location of the thing they sought.

Two men from Ait, Zangaur and Kinaur, followed the captive to a thick patch of scrub. He led them by a secret path through otherwise impenetrable, thorn-covered vines to the clearing within. On the ground lay a stone which glowed.

Zangaur and Kinaur took it back to the canoes where they told the waiting men that they had found the object of their search. All then returned to Saibai, beached their canoes at Alil, and strode triumphantly home across the swamps to Ait.

They called their treasure Adibuia,[4] for it shone by day and night. Adibuia was born of a beautiful girl of Kiwai, who, when her parents would not let her marry, had formed the habit of exposing her body to the moon and had become pregnant by it. Adibuia made the warriors of Ait invincible, and thereafter, before setting out to fight, they obtained strength from Adibuia by ritual observance.[5] No warrior of Ait who approached Adibuia in this manner died in a battle.

For a long time Adibuia was kept at Ait; then, for greater secrecy, it was removed to Diwikal.

★

4. Adibuia: *adi*, big, great; *buia*, light.

5. At this point, Enosa interrupted his recitation to give the following explanation of the phrase "obtained strength":

Each time, a warrior smeared Adibuia with red clay (*parma*), anointed it with coconut oil (*wakasu*), and placed on it a garland (*kedi*) of vine. This done, he ordered the rest to put on their fighting gear.

One by one each advanced towards Adibuia, touched a hand to it, to his eyes, to his ears, so that the enemy should neither see nor hear him as he crawled towards them; touched his bow and his arrows to Adibuia, so that the string should not snap as he fought, and that the arrows would fly swift and true.

The leader laid aside his bow and arrows and went again to Adibuia, bearing in his hand a circlet—like an armlet or anklet—made from dried grass. He put it on the ground, stepped inside it, and attempted to run round Adibuia keeping his feet within the circlet. Stumbling, falling, pushing himself to his feet, he completed the circle, thus ensuring that the enemy would stumble and fall during the forthcoming battle.

Finally, Adibuia was asked to send its strength ahead to where they would meet the enemy.

A warrior of Ait

Artist Kala Waia

Warriors of Ait
obtaining strength
from Adibuia,
the stone that
glowed

Artist Kala Waia

Lifu missionaries arrived at Saibai Village. They sent a man named Baira, who belonged to Village Kadal, to Ait to tell the people to leave their home in the swamp at the other end of the island and come and live with them. The people of Ait agreed to do this, but did not make the move because they feared they would own no land and they would lose their independence.

A year later Baira went again to Ait to call the people to Saibai Village, and this time they went.

As they walked across the swamps, the men and women and children repeatedly looked back at Ait, sorrow in their hearts, tears in their eyes. A song broke from them:

> Lag gar nupaipa kunia wanan (a),
> Ngau gar mai (a) mai (a) ulaipa,
> Ngau gar mai (a) mai (a) ulaipa.
>
> Lag gar nupaipa pusia taraipa.
> Ngai gar lagapa kunia taman (a).
> Ngai gar lagapa kunia taman (a).

(My home, my place,
I look back at it from a distance.
It is left behind. I cry, I choke with grief.

I cannot see it for the fog of my tears.
We come this way, leaving behind for ever
The home, the place to which we belong.)

When they reached Saibai Village, Baira met them and took them to his house. Men of *tabu augad* (*tabu,* snake) went there to greet them. Later, Baira and the men of *tabu augad* gave them garden land and land where they might build homes. They also provided the young men with wives.

On the first night at Saibai Village, one of the men from Ait could not sleep for the sound of the sea and went back to Ait. However, in the morning he returned to his people.

The people of Ait brought Adibuia from Diwikal to Gasun Alupalnga to have it closer to them. Later, they moved it to a spot on the high ground in the swamp between the village and the well called Mag, naming this spot Akananiaizinga,[6] because they loved the stone like their own grandmothers. Soon afterwards all the trees around Adibuia died, killed by its power, and land which had previously been covered with scrub was laid bare.

When Dr. McFarlane[7] visited Saibai, he saw a light shining in the swamp and asked what it was. When the people told him that it was Adibuia, he said that he would take it away with him. He did, and nothing is known of Adibuia since that day.

6. Akananiaizinga: *aka,* granny; *niai,* stay, sit, rest; *nga,* place. *Aka* was the affectionate nickname by which Adibuia was called after the people of Ait moved to Saibai Village. Adibuia ("*Aka*") was a very heavy, round stone, about 10–11 inches in diameter.

7. Rev. S. McFarlane, LL.D., of the London Missionary Society. Dr. McFarlane visited Torres Strait in 1870 and returned in 1871 to embark on sixteen years of pioneer work in this region. He retired in 1887.

WAKEMAB   [Told by Nawia Elu at Saibai, 25 August 1967]

Saibai is a long, narrow island hemmed by mangroves. The interior is largely swampland in which there are raised areas called *kawal* (islands—singular, *kawa*). Today the islands in the swamp are used as garden lands, but formerly people lived on many of them.

The setting of this tale is the eastern end of Saibai. Of the places mentioned, Kagar is an area which includes forest land behind fringing mangroves; Makanapai, Igelai, Bin, Pai, Augar, Somanapai, and Ait are islands in the swamp.

One day a man left his home at Makanapai in the swamp to go and fish on the reef. When he reached Kagar, he saw a man named Wakemab sitting on the ground in the shade of an almond tree.

"*Köimega* (friend)," said the man from Makanapai, "are you the only person living at this place?"

"*Köimega*," replied Wakemab, "no one lives here but me. Where are you going?"

And when the man from Makanapai told Wakemab that he was going fishing, Wakemab wanted to know where he intended to sleep that night. "If I may, I should like to stay here with you and go home tomorrow," the man from Makanapai told Wakemab, and then he went off to fish.

When he returned in the evening, Wakemab said: "It's too hot to sleep here tonight. We'll take some mats with us and find a cooler spot." And he led the way to the natural jetty of sand and dead coral that runs out into the sea from Kagar. Some distance from the shore, Wakemab put up two mat shelters, one for himself and one for the man from Makanapai. His own he made waterproof, unlike that for his guest.

Presently the tide turned and water began to enter the tent of the man from Makanapai. "*Köimega,*" he called to Wakemab, "I'm up to my ankles in water." "I, too," replied Wakemab.

The water continued to rise. "*Köimega,*" called the man from Makanapai, "the water is up to my waist." "To mine also," replied Wakemab, and he began to beat his drum and sing,

> *Wakemaba köi maba.*
> *Kui dara meuria meuria,*

a song which praised himself as a big man, and foretold the death of the other man.

"*Köimega,*" called the man from Makanapai, "the water is up to my chest." "To mine also," replied Wakemab, and he went on singing:

> *Wakemaba köi maba.*
> *Kui dara meuria meuria.*
>
> (I'm the better man of the two.
> The other man will be killed by me.)

166

The partly submerged natural jetty of sand and dead coral running out from Kagar, at the eastern end of Saibai

"*Köimega,*" called the man from Makanapai, "the water is up to my neck." "To mine also," replied Wakemab, who by this time was beating his drum faster and singing more loudly.

'*Köimega!*" shouted the man from Makanapai, "I'm out of my depth. I'll drown!"

Wakemab did not answer him. Instead, he beat his drum very fast and sang:

> *Wa nga Wakemaba?*
> *Ngau gula dakanu bubuama.*
> *Kuradara matamiza*
> *Kut boi wunariz.*
> *Sam tete ngau gula.* Oi!

> (Who is Wakemab?
> My canoe is the best canoe.
> This man's end is upon him.
> My canoe is the winner. Oi!)

When the tide began to ebb, Wakemab sang to a slower drum-beat:

> *Wakemaba köi maba.*
> *Kui dara meuria meuria.*

And now he sang of himself as a man who had proved his superiority, because the other man was dead.

At daybreak the jetty of sand and dead coral was dry. Wakemab took down his mat shelter and went to that of the man from Makanapai, removed the man's head with a bamboo knife and strung it through the neck and out through the mouth, threw the body into the sea, and walked in to the shore with the head.

Not far from the almond tree under which Wakemab lived was a *surka* mound.[1] This was used by Wakemab as his *sibui,* the place where he stored bones, and in it he now put the head of the man from Makanapai. Afterwards he returned to the almond tree, and before long was fast asleep.

When he woke at the end of the day, he saw two men walking towards him from the direction of Makanapai. They greeted him as friend and asked if he lived alone at Kagar. "*Köimega,*" replied Wakemab, "there is no one but me." And in answer to their question, "Have you seen our friend who came this way to fish yesterday?" Wakemab countered by asking which way they had come. The moment they told him that they had walked across the swamp, he said: "He went the other way—outside the mangroves, along the reef. Do you plan to return to Makanapai tonight?" "We would rather stay here tonight and go home in the morning," the men told him.

1. The nest of *surka,* the mound-building jungle fowl or "scrub-hen".

Wakemab persuaded them to go with him to the jetty, saying that it was a cool and pleasant place for sleeping, and the following morning he buried their heads in his *sibui*.

Several men arrived at Kagar from Makanapai that evening. In the morning, Wakemab added their heads to his *sibui*.

And so it went on. Wakemab slept all day. At night he sang and beat his drum while his visitors drowned. And at last there were no men left at Makanapai.

The women of Makanapai appealed to the people of Igelai, asking for their help in finding the men who had not returned to Makanapai. Before long the women of Igelai were asking help of the people at Bin, and then the women of Bin were asking for help from Pai, those of Pai from Augar, and those of Augar from Somanapai. Finally the women of Somanapai sent to Ait.

"*Ait bubuam!*[2] (No one can vanquish Ait!)" Ait rallied to the call for help from its neighbour in the swamp. Three men went to Kagar from Ait. They did not come back.

The following day eleven men of Ait set out for Kagar. One had yaws and could not keep up with the rest, so he was told to go home. The others made all haste by the coast route, and when they arrived at Kagar were told by Wakemab that the men who had visited him the previous day had returned to Ait by way of the swamp. They accepted Wakemab's invitation to spend the night with him.

It was the man who had yaws who learnt what happened to men who went to Kagar. He did not return to Ait when sent back, but followed his ten companions at a distance and climbed an *ubar* tree near Wakemab's place. He saw the men of Ait accompany a fat, tall, bald-headed man out on to the bank that runs out from Kagar and, abandoning the *ubar* tree for a mangrove tree at the edge of the sea, listened all night long to a drum. And in the morning he saw Wakemab remove the mat shelters, cut off the heads of ten men of Ait, string them, and walk back to the shore. The man who had yaws slid down the mangrove tree and made off through the swamp as Wakemab strode back to the almond tree after visiting his *sibui*.

The man who had yaws told what he had seen to the women at Makanapai, Igelai, Bin, Pai, Augar, and Somanapai, and then he told the people at Ait.

"*Ait bubuam!*" Every man at Ait armed himself with bow and arrows and *gabagaba* (club with circular stone head). Every man of Ait went to Kagar.

Wakemab lay with his head on the ground, asleep. He had killed so many and killed for so long that "the blood had come to his eyes" (*kulka*

2. *Bubuam*, the white cowry shell (*Ovula ovum* Linne) which was a valuable commodity for purposes of barter. A single *bubuam* could be exchanged for a canoe in New Guinea. The expression, "*Ait bubuam!*", conveys the idea of strength and wealth, the strength and wealth of the people of Ait. Although it is nearly a hundred years since the people of Ait abandoned their island home in the Saibai swamp in response to repeated requests from early missionaries, "*Ait bubuam!*" is still the proud motto of those who have Ait blood: "No one can beat me."

purkia amaiz). He was torpid from over-much killing. One of the men called him: "Wakemab! Wakemab!" Wakemab could scarcely open his eyes. "Wakemab! *Köimega!* Get up!" Wakemab forced himself to his feet. Then two men felled him with their clubs.

Wakemab crawled away from the men of Ait on hands and knees through the mangroves to the sea. "You killed all the men from Makanapai, Igelai, Bin, Pai, Augar, and Somanapai. You killed men from Ait," said the men who had come to avenge their dead. "You came too late. Those heads are in my *sibui*," Wakemab replied. He crawled on further, and then he looked back and said: "Where I go now, no man will ever come. I will kill every man who comes anywhere near me."

He reached the sea at Magat, a little to the west of Mamag, the natural jetty of sand and dead coral to which he had lured so many men to their death, and crawled into the water. He crawled out into the sea, twice looking back at the men who stood watching him,[3] and after a long while reached deep water and was swept away by a current.

It took him towards Malu Kawa, an island near the coast of Daudai. He began to feel cold. This place suited him. The water was very deep. Wakemab sank to the bottom of the sea and turned to stone, not far from the reef called Bur Maza.

Men fear Wakemab. Logs that drift towards the place beneath which he lies on the bed of the sea are drawn deep down into the water by a swirling current and reappear a long way off. No one ever goes anywhere near Wakemab.

3. There is a rock (*kula*) at each of the spots from which Wakemab looked back at the shore.

Wakemab crawling out into the sea after being clubbed by two men of Ait
Artist Kala Waia

170

SUSUI AND DENGAM

[Told by Timothy ("Susui") Akiba at Saibai, 5 September 1967]

Susui and his sister Dengam lived in a small village a little to the north of Kibul.[1] They left their home and followed a river[2] downstream to where it entered the sea.[3] As they walked, they sometimes took stones from their *topi iana* and threw them into the water. The last of the stones was thrown into the mouth of the river.

They crossed to Saibai and made a home for themselves in the scrub at the place called Tanamanamuid. Every day they went in search of food.

Sometimes they went out at night, too, when, to help them see, they used each to take something from their mouths and throw it to the ground where it lit up. They afterwards retrieved and returned the objects to their mouths. The people living at Saibai Village always knew when Susui and Dengam were looking for food at night, because they saw lights appear and disappear at different spots around Tanamanamuid.

From time to time, even now, lights are still seen at Tanamanamuid: Susui and Dengam, as the snakes into which they changed, still go searching for food at night.

Susui and Dengam were the "first people" (*muruig*) of the group at Saibai for whom *tabu* (snake) is *augad*.

Susui was bald.

Nothing else is known about Susui and Dengam.

1. On the Papuan mainland.
2. Marked Pahoturi River on maps.
3. Near Mabudauan.

There are today a brother and sister who bear the names, these having "come down" to them. Susui told this story. His sister Dengam is married and lives at Dauan, the small, high island close to Saibai.

KARBAI AND PUKAT

[Told by Timothy Akiba at Saibai, 5 September 1967]

Karbai is the white reef heron. It is *augad* for a small group of people at Saibai. "*Karbai baba*" is the idiomatic phrase currently used for hair which is prematurely white. *Pukat* is a grasshopper.

Karbai and Pukat were a brother and sister who lived, long ago, at Gelam on the island of Saibai. Every day Karbai went out on the reef and fished; his sister plucked *biu* and prepared them for food.

One day, Karbai sent his sister to the reef to hunt for crabs. After she had caught many, she came close to Karbai, who asked her if she had had any luck. That night, Pukat cooked the crabs for the evening meal.

Pukat now began to desire her brother for husband, but, as he did not return her unnatural affection, the next time she caught crabs she kept the best ones for herself and gave the poorer ones to Karbai. She also gave him to eat *mabut*, a paste made from the pulp of *biu*, into which she had mixed some of her blood.

Some days later, Karbai went to the swamp to look at the reflection of himself in the water. To his amazement he saw that his hair was now white. "I am still a young man," he said to himself. "My sister has done this to me. I will punish her for it."

Karbai and Pukat continued to live together as brother and sister, outwardly happy enough as they went about their daily work of obtaining food. But underneath, Karbai seethed with anger against the injury done him by his sister, and Pukat took satisfaction from the harm she had worked on her brother.

One day Pukat went off to collect *biu*. When she had a basketful, she set about scraping them, and soaking and squeezing the pulp.[1]

Karbai took advantage of her absence to make a bird, using the wood of the tree called *buru* for its legs and beak, the spathe of nipa palm leaves for its wings, and the bark of the tree called *tapi* for its body. He hid it before his sister returned from her work.

Henceforth, whenever Pukat was away from home during the day, Karbai went inside the bird which he had fashioned and practised flying. Upon her return, Pukat always called to her brother: "Are you here, Karbai?" And Karbai always replied: "I have been here the whole day long." This state of affairs continued until the day that Karbai could fly well.

The following morning Pukat announced that she was going to the reef for crabs. No sooner had she gone than Karbai entered the bird and flew

1. The place at which Pukat performed this task is called Pukatanabiusasimaizinga.

172

into the air. He circled his home and then flew to the reef where he was seen alighting by Pukat at the moment she emerged from the mangroves. "What a lovely bird!" she thought. "If only I could catch it and give it to Karbai!" Karbai began to walk about looking for food, and Pukat ran towards him. Karbai, however, flew up at her approach and went to another spot on the reef.

Pukat now set down her basket and again ran towards the beautiful bird; but again it flew away from her and alighted some distance away. This happened many times, Karbai always keeping beyond his sister's reach, tantalizing her and punishing her for her treatment of him in turning his hair white. Pukat called to her brother: "Karbai! Karbai! Come and help me catch this bird!"

Not until Pukat was exhausted from the chase did Karbai come out of the bird and stand before his sister as a man. Then he said to her: "To whom are you calling? I, whom you thought a bird, am your brother Karbai. You mixed your blood with *mabut* which you gave to me to eat, by that means causing my hair to turn white." And Pukat, sorrowful for what she had done, confessed.

Karbai said: "I am no longer your brother. I am about to fly to Daudai, from which place I shall never return. You will often see birds like the one I made on the reef outside the fringing mangroves of the mainland opposite. They will remind you of me." After that, he went back inside the bird form which he had created, circled in the air, and flew across the sea to Daudai.

SUI [Told for Kadam Waigana at Saibai, by her grand-daughter Marypa, 8 September 1967]

A man and woman left Saibai and made what was intended to be only a temporary home for themselves and their two children, a girl named Sui and a small boy, on the mainland opposite their island. Not long after their arrival in Daudai, however, the man died, and the woman and the children did not return to their island.

The woman treated Sui very badly, denying her food and ordering her to eat her little brother's faeces. She used to say to her daughter before she

Sui, a swamp bird—white, with black on its back—is *augad* for a small group of people on Saibai. The myth recorded here should be compared with the versions obtained by Landtman (*The Folk-Tales of the Kiwai Papuans* (Helsingfors, 1917), pp. 426–29).

went to her garden, leaving the boy behind in his sister's care: "Look after him well, and when his bowels move, eat the excrement." And after she returned from gardening she always asked if Sui had obeyed her instructions during the day. "Yes," replied Sui, when, in fact, she had buried the child's faeces. But the woman always found out that Sui lied to her, because immediately afterwards she called to the excrement of the little boy's bowels, "Where are you?", and it answered from wherever Sui had buried it: "Here I am." Even when Sui threw the excrement into the sea, it still answered the woman's call to it.

At last Sui decided to run away from her mother and, to enable her to do this, she made a bird form, using the light wood of a *buat* tree for the body, *koia* for the wings, the wood of *buru* for the beak, *guruad*, a kind of pigweed, for the legs and feet, and *timikapul*,[1] shiny, hard, red seeds which have a black spot, for the eyes, and learned to fly in it. The bird was fashioned during her mother's absence and kept hidden in the bush until Sui had mastered the art of flying by daily practice.

One day Sui's mother ordered her to dig up the excrement that she had buried and insisted that her daughter eat it, and then Sui ran to the bush, entered the bird, and flew back to her mother. Sui circled around her in the air. "Sui! Sui! Come and catch this bird for your brother!" called the mother. Sui flew lower. "Sui! Sui! Catch this bird!" the mother called again. For answer, Sui alighted on the ground, stepped out of the bird and said: "It was I whom you wanted for my brother. You have treated me shamefully, and I am going to leave you." With that Sui went back inside the bird she had made and flew away.

She flew inland. Presently she looked down and saw a man sitting on the ground in his garden. She landed near him, came out of the bird, and walked to him when he signalled her to approach with his hands. This man, Murke, could not speak, because his lips were joined together, but he made it plain to Sui by signs that he was glad to see her and led her to the shelter in which he stored the fruits of his garden. He was rich in garden produce, and, when Sui told him how her mother had treated her, he made her sit down and placed a bunch of bananas on each side of her. After she had eaten her fill, he invited her to live with him.

Sui lived happily with Murke for a long time, but she always wished that he could speak. One day he indicated that he wanted her to rid his head of lice. While he lay with his head in her lap, he fell asleep and began to snore. Sui stole away, found a very big shell (*saimer*),[2] and filled it with clay. After putting the shell on the fire to heat, she took a bamboo knife and cut his mouth, and then she dressed the wound with hot clay. "My daughter," said Murke, plain and clear, "what have you done to me?" Sui cooked soft foods for him until his mouth healed.

1. *Timikapul*, the seeds of the twining plant, *Abrus precatorius*.
2. A very big variety of edible shell-fish found in mangrove swamps.

174

Sui   *Artist* Kala Waia

LA WAIA
-9-67

An invitation arrived from an inland village some distance away for Murke and Sui to attend a *gum*, a party to which the people of many villages are bidden. Sui and Murke set out, taking bamboo pipes of water with them for the journey, and arrived at the host village after the dancing had begun.

Murke immediately joined in the dancing (*badara*),[3] and Sui was in the act of lighting a bundle of palm leaves to show up the movements of the dancers, when she heard her mother's voice saying: "Sui! Is it you, Sui?" "Yes," replied Sui. "Your brother is here. Come home with us after the end of this dance," her mother ordered. Sui refused to go.

The dancing went on all night. Just before daybreak, Murke, who felt very thirsty and hungry, slipped away and ran all the way home. He drank water and began to eat—and suddenly died, smitten by stabbing pain in the region of the liver.[4]

When the dancing ended, Sui looked round for Murke and could not see him. She asked all the dancers in turn if they knew where he was and finally received the answer: "He complained of feeling hungry and thirsty. He must have gone home." She found his tracks soon afterwards and, seeing them, felt sad that he had left without telling her.

Sui saw him lying on the ground at their home and thought he was asleep. She sat down beside him, and then she saw ants running into his mouth and knew he was dead. Tears streamed from her eyes. "Murke," she sobbed, "you took me into your home and cared for me well. I was a child when I came to you, and now I am a young woman."

After a while she went to Murke's garden and brought back fruit and vegetables. These she heaped in his *saualag* (the shelter in which garden produce is stored). Next she dragged Murke to the *saualag*, and then she set fire to it. Finally, when it was burning fiercely, she threw herself into the flames.

3. An old style of dancing in which the dancers carry bows and arrows and step backwards and forwards with bent knees.
4. *Sib pagadin*, liver "spear thrust".

yellow-bellied black snake with a thin red stripe from the tip of its head to the tip of its tail.[4] Kongasau, the ghost whom she had believed to be a man, had changed into a snake.

Adasakalaig searched for Kongasau until day broke. But she could not find him, and she never saw him again.

4. This venomous snake is greatly feared at Saibai today.

Artist Kala Waia

WAMALADI [Told by Gamia Asse (for whom umai [dog] is augad) at Saibai, 5 September 1967]

Wamaladi was a man. He lived with his wife and daughter at Maian-mulainga. Every day the three of them used to go and work in Wamaladi's garden at Waum.

When his daughter grew up, Wamaladi was stirred by desire for her body and, one day while his wife was temporarily absent from Waum, he said to the girl: "If you should see the leaf of a banana tree struck by an arrow, find out the direction from which it travelled—whether from the north, or from the south, or the west—and then walk straight to the man who shot it from his bow. First ask him his name, then take him as husband."

Wamaladi left his daughter and went to Markaigagat where he examined his reflection in a pool of water. He was not a handsome man. Now, in order to make himself attractive to his daughter and, at the same time, conceal his identity from her, he altered the shape of his nose by fixing pieces of wax on it. Then he hurried back to Waum and shot an arrow at a banana leaf close to his daughter. She saw it and, obedient to her father's instructions, walked straight to the man who had fired the arrow.

Wamaladi bade her sit at the foot of a banana tree, and then he sat down beside her. Rain began to fall, so he stood up in order to shelter her from it with his body. When the rain stopped, he sat down again. Showers of rain continued to fall, and, at every one, he stood up to keep her dry. By doing this, however, he himself became thoroughly wetted, and water began to lift the wax on his nose. Presently a piece of wax fell off. The girl noticed it, but paid it no heed. Wamaladi picked it up and replaced it on his nose.

The rain did not ease, and, despite the man's efforts to shield his daughter from it, before long she was thoroughly drenched. Suddenly all the wax with which he had remodelled his nose fell off in one piece and dropped between the girl's legs, and she looked up at the face above her. "Father! It's you, father!" she cried. "Go away from me!" yelled Wamaladi. And he fled.

At this moment the mother arrived on the scene and, seeing a man running away from her daughter, asked who he was. "That is father," the girl said.

Wamaladi ran all the way home to Maianmulainga; but he did not stay there because of the shame he felt. He went into the mangroves and lived there for some time all by himself.

One day he dressed himself as an old woman, tying a skirt round his waist and donning a wig (*dum*) which gave him the appearance of having a big head of hair. Skirt and wig he made from the teased fibre of the trunk of a banana tree. Thus disguised, he set out for Waum, before he reached the area, shaking his legs in aboriginal fashion, performing in turn towards east, west, south, and north.

Women who were working at Waum that day saw Wamaladi approaching and called out: "Granny, come here! We will spread a good mat for you to sit on." Wamaladi replied, "I know the custom, but I prefer to sit by myself at a little distance from you," because he was afraid of being recognized if he came close to the women. Presently he said: "You have worked so hard at gardening and fishing today that you will be very tired tonight. Don't bother to cover your knees with your skirts when you lie down to sleep." The women did as Wamaladi had bid them, and during the night he went to every one of them. When he heard the first twitter of the birds he left Waum. It was nearly daybreak.

Wamaladi visited many places—Metalap, Koiwan, Darkam, Ubu, Kaninab, and Tara. At each he was accepted during the day as an old woman; at each he ravished the women while they slept at night.

He went to Tuian, but there he learned that all the men from Waum to Tara had joined in one big party and were hunting for him. So he hurried to Maianmulainga and, after removing his skirt and his wig, changed into a crow. The men who had come armed with bows and arrows and clubs to kill Wamaladi reached Maianmulainga in time to see him fly north towards Daudai. They felt sorrow for him.

METARAWAI

[Told by Alfred Aniba at Saibai, 6 October 1968]

At Waum on the island of Saibai there once lived a dwarf-sized man named Metarawai. Wherever he went he always took his bow and arrows, because he liked to practise shooting at targets as he walked along.

In order to reach his garden at Metalap, Metarawai had to walk across a stretch of flat ground. In some places the grass grew short and spindly, in others it grew tall and thick. He avoided the latter, because he would not have been able to see over the top of the long grass, nor would he have had room to draw his bow.

A very small man, he used a very small bow, and the arrows that he shot did not travel far. It occurred to him one day that if he had a longer bow his arrows would travel much further.

So he made a very long bow, one out of all proportion to his height— only to find that he could not bring it into the vertical position for firing ahead. The only way he could use the new bow was to shoot arrows straight up at the sky, and when he did that the arrows fell to earth at his feet.

The grass still grows in short, spindly tufts along the way that Metarawai walked from Waum to Metalap and back.

ROA KABUWAM

[Told by Aniba Asa at Saibai, 28 August 1967]

Roa was an expert hunter. He was also a generous provider, sharing his kill with the people of Saibai Village at the north-western end of the island and the people of Ait at the eastern end of the swamp. As proof of his skill as a hunter, the *sibui* (place where bones, human or animal, are heaped) on which he saved the bones of the dugong and turtle he speared grew to be taller than himself. Its height was the measure of his generosity.

182

Roa Kabuwam, the people called him, likening him to the pellets of beeswax (*wam*) stuck to the centre (*kabu*, chest) of the skin at the end of a drum. As the wax gives sweetness to the sound of the drum, so Roa gave happiness to the people with the food he brought to their midst.

Roa knew where to hunt, the times to hunt, how to make harpoon and spear and rope, how to erect the platform from which to spear dugong. He knew everything about hunting that had been learnt and handed down by his ancestors. Some men lived to fight. Roa lived to hunt and provide food for the people. He loved his *wap* (harpoon-spear) as he loved his children.

When he returned from hunting, he scraped the meat from a dry coconut, squeezed the milk from it, and rubbed his *wap* with it. Roa's *wap*, which he had made himself from heavy *tulu* wood, became black and beautiful with this care. If he was not out hunting it stood near his *sibui* at Budiangud, close to his home. It was more than a hunting weapon. It was the symbol of a way of life.

When other men were hunting, they shouted as they jumped from the dugong platform to harpoon the animal that had returned to graze. They needed the help of the men who waited silently some distance away in a canoe, either to bring the dugong ashore, or to disentangle them from the rope that was attached at one end to the harpoon, at the other to the platform.

Not so Roa. When Roa hunted he did all the work himself. The men slept in the canoe until morning. Some nights he harpooned as many as six or seven dugong.

It was the same with turtle. Roa was so strong, so able, that he needed no help from anyone.

The people did not mind if Roa came ashore while he was hunting and quenched his thirst with coconuts from their gardens. Seeing the dry husks on the ground they smiled and said: "Ah, Roa has been here."

Roa was a big man with bulging muscles. The hair on his head grew long, his body was hairy. His fingers were covered with warts. His fingernails were long, like eagle's talons. He had a wife named Badi, and sons.

The years went by, his name continually on everyone's lips. Roa, Roa Kabuwam, Roa, Roa . . . There was far too much talk of Roa.

One day Roa went by canoe to the reef called Zangal Maza to look for places where dugong had grazed, taking with him as crew his sons and some other men. It was a day when big waves broke over the reef.

As he was poling his canoe over Zangal Maza, Roa saw a crayfish. Immediately he jumped into the water and followed it down to a hole in a rock. He caught hold of it and tried to return to the surface of the water, but was prevented from doing so by a big wave. Again and again he tried to escape from the hole, but it was always the same: every time he was kept under by a big wave. He was trapped. Roa knew then that someone was using *maid* (sorcery) against him.

Roa thought of his sons and made a desperate effort. This time he freed himself and reached the surface, the crayfish still grasped in his hand.

He climbed into the canoe and embraced his sons. He was embraced by the rest of the crew after they had heard his story.

That day Roa speared three dugong before returning to Budiangud.

Although Roa now knew that the sorcerers (*maidalgal*) were his enemies, he went on as before, hunting, fishing, and sharing with the people of Saibai Village and Ait.

One night when the moon was full, Roa went pig-hunting. Before long he saw a mob. Dropping to his hands and his knees, he began to crawl towards them, his bow in his left hand, his arrows in the right. At the moment of his releasing an arrow, six sorcerers appeared, shouting at the pigs and calling his name.

Roa said: "Why have you come? Are you going to kill me?"

"Yes," said the sorcerers.

One of them left the group and walked towards Roa. When he was about to bring down his club on Roa's head, Roa shot him in the thigh with an arrow.

Another sorcerer stepped forward. This man, too, Roa shot in the thigh. The rest fled.

Roa did no more hunting that night; instead, he returned to Saibai Village and told the women: "Should any man come home tonight and tell you he has a splinter of mangrove in his leg, he will lie. Men tried to kill me, and I shot them, not to kill, because I am Roa Kabuwam and do not kill men, but to make them afraid."

At last Roa began to grow old. He hunted less. Often he was quite content to stay at home.

One morning he decided to go to the garden called Adabadau Kupad. As he walked through the grass, two deadly black snakes slid towards him, one from the left, one from the right.

Roa might have made a move to save his life, but he had had enough of fighting the sorcerers. "It is better," he thought, "that I let them have their way. If I continue to thwart them in their attempts to kill me, they may turn their attention to my wife and family. It is better this way," and he stood perfectly still, allowing the snakes to sink their fangs in his ankles.

His people buried him, leaving his fingers and toes exposed until the flesh had rotted sufficiently to allow the nails to be easily removed. These they kept, precious relics of Roa the hunter, Roa Kabuwam, whose generosity, for a time, had sweetened the lives of all at Saibai.

HOW BAIRA
GOT A WIFE

[Told by Nawia Elu, great-grandson of Baira, at Saibai, 5 September 1967]

Baira lived at Saibai Village. His *augad* was *kadal* (crocodile). He was unmarried.

Nadai also lived at Saibai Village. His *augad* was *samu* (cassowary). He had four wives, of whom Aukam was first.

One day, after Baira had gone out on the reef in his canoe to fish, Aukam, who desired him, managed to escape from Nadai and run away. She made her way past Aibuker[1] to the mangroves and climbed a mangrove tree growing in the water at the edge of the sea at Urakaral Iabu. From it she watched Baira, who was fishing at Megan Iabu, and, when he put about to come ashore, she climbed down and signalled to him by splashing up water. Then she climbed up the mangrove tree again and waited for him to come to her.

Now Baira had no idea who wanted to see him, but he poled his canoe to the spot at which the signal had been made. Looking up, he saw Aukam. "What do you want?" he asked. "I have come for you," she replied. "Get into my canoe," he told her.

The two poled to the small landing-place, Gopeturumau Gagat,[2] left the canoe there and walked inland, taking with them all the fish which Baira had caught that day. They passed Diwikal and came to Warmau Kupad, where the people of *tabu* (snake) *augad* were living at that time. Both Baira and the men of *tabu* advised Aukam to return to Nadai, but this she would not do.

Baira now sent a message to the groups of people living at Ait—to *kadal* (crocodile) and *baidam* (shark) and *tabu* (snake)—calling them to fight with him and his men against Nadai who would most certainly do battle for Aukam: not only was Aukam Nadai's first wife, but also she was the mother of his son, Alis. Nadai sent back word that he would fight on a certain day.

On the day appointed by Nadai, the *kadal* men of Ait went early to the magic stone, Adibuia,[3] and obtained strength from it. At the conclusion of the ceremony, each man placed on his head a wreath woven from pandanus leaves turned white by heat, outward symbol of the invincible power derived by him from Adibuia. Seeing the *kadal* men of Ait thus adorned, Nadai, arriving later in the day, ordered his men to return home

1. A garden area.
2. Close to Gopeturumau Kasa.
3. The history of Adibuia is given in the story, "Ait Kadal". Adibuia was lodged at Diwikal at the time when Baira obtained Aukam for wife.

without firing a single arrow or dealing a single blow. Some were unwilling to yield without fighting. "*Sakanu mangalei* (The arrows will pierce our bodies)," said Nadai, and he led them back to Saibai Village after telling Baira that he might keep Aukam.

That is how Baira got a wife. Three children were born to them: two sons, Nawia and Kebesu, and a daughter, Mapu.

AGBURUG

[Told by Nawia Elu, great-grandson of Baira, at Saibai, 29 August 1967]

Formerly it was the custom for men of Saibai Village to sail across to mainland Papua (Daudai) whenever they wanted the flesh of kangaroo and pig to eat. They used to land at Warukuik and then walk inland to a big swamp, Sirpupu, and hunt.

On one of these hunting expeditions a man named Baira had no luck at all. By late afternoon, each of the other members of the party had shot as many as four or five animals. Baira had killed none. Feeling tired, he decided to have a short rest and smoke a pipe of tobacco. Afterwards, when he resumed hunting, he came to a place where tall grass grew and saw, to one side of it, an old man sitting on the ground eating raw kangaroo meat. The old man was Agburug.

Agburug invited Baira to join him and gave him some meat to eat. He asked Baira his name and where he lived. He told Baira that he would go to Saibai that night and visit him at his home.

Baira returned to Saibai empty-handed that day, and at sunset was standing outside his house waiting for Agburug, the old man whom he had met while hunting. He had no idea that Agburug was both man and snake and the man was usually concealed within the snake. Therefore, when Baira saw a snake crawling towards him, he was very frightened. Agburug said: "Do not be afraid. I am a friend who will do you no harm." And immediately afterwards he emerged from his snake form to reveal himself as the man whom Baira knew. The two men talked.

Agburg told Baira that he would like to live at Saibai. "Show me a place where I may settle," he said. So Baira pointed inland to his garden place at Koiwan. "On the northern side of Koiwan there is a patch of scrub, Sarabilwang. Live there. I will visit you every time I go and garden," he told his new friend. Presently Agburug changed back to his snake form and

Artist Kala Waia

went to his new home, where, in future, Baira always called on him both before and after he gardened.

Baira often warned Agburug not to leave Sarabilwang. "There are many men on Saibai. If any one of them were to see you, he would kill you," he used to admonish his friend.

For a long while Agburug never left the area of scrubland which was his home and searched for food only at night. But the time came when there was nothing left to eat at Sarabilwang, so he had to go further afield in order to appease his hunger. Eventually he had to travel so far to obtain a meal that he could not reach home before daylight.

One night Agburug crawled by way of the well called Met and the garden places, Kaninab and Tara, to the garden place, Tuian. Day broke and he was still at Tuian. On the way home he felt so tired that he decided to rest. He fell fast asleep, his head inside a bush, his body stretched out across the path which led from Saibai Village to Tuian, to be found by a big, baldheaded man named Jangaur who was walking to his garden at Tuian. Jangaur struck the snake a heavy blow with the stick which he carried. Badly wounded, Agburug slithered away into the grass and called back: "You hurt my leg. One day I will have my revenge on you."

Agburug managed to reach Sarabilwang, but by that time he was very sick. After dark he went to the mainland opposite Saibai. He stayed there for two moons, until he was fully recovered, before returning to Sarabilwang.

Baira saw him the following day when he came to garden. "Where have you been?" he asked. "I searched for you for a long time." Agburug told him all that had happened and, at the end of his story, added: "I must have my revenge. I am going to harm Jangaur." "On no account are you to kill Jangaur," said Baira, "for he is my father.[1] Furthermore, you must let him know why you punish him."

Next morning Agburug went to the spot at which he had been injured by Jangaur and lay across the path between Saibai Village and Tuian. This time he did not sleep; instead, he kept a careful watch for Jangaur, whom he presently saw approaching—Jangaur was on the way to his garden at Tuian. He waited very still until Jangaur was almost upon him—and then he struck, biting his enemy not badly, but hard enough to cause him to fall to the ground half-dead. Agburug returned to Sarabilwang.

Jangaur lay unconscious until late afternoon when he recovered sufficiently to be able to walk home. He felt very sick that night. Two months later he was still so sick that he had wasted away to skin and bone.

Throughout Jangaur's illness, Baira often begged Agburug to permit Jangaur to recover, but Agburug always refused, saying that Jangaur would not die.

The day came when Baira judged Jangaur to be at the point of death, for his lips were the colour of the grey fruit of the *aubau* tree. Again Baira interceded for Jangaur, and this time Agburug said: "I will visit Jangaur tonight. He must be alone, and his house must be dark." Baira went to Jangaur's relatives, told them why Jangaur had been sick for so long and passed on Agburug's instructions.

Agburug kept his promise. That night, as snake, he entered Jangaur's house and, coiling himself around Jangaur's body, squeezed the feeble, pain-racked man repeatedly, brought his head close to Jangaur's face, and licked Jangaur all over from head to toe. Then Agburug went back to Sarabilwang. In the morning Jangaur felt perfectly well.

Eventually Baira died. Agburug waited in vain for his friend to visit him. Lonely, believing himself to have been forsaken by Baira, in the end Agburug departed from Saibai and returned to Daudai where he made his home at Dabu.

1. Jangaur belonged to Ait *kadal* (crocodile), Baira to Saibai Village *kadal*. Jangaur was an important kinsman of Baira, but he was not Baira's actual father.

MAIGI   [Told by Enosa Waigana (Ait kadal) and Aniba Asa (deibau) at Saibai, 28 August 1967]

One day Maigi set out from his home at Ait to hunt dugong. He was successful and shared his kill with the people of his village. In the distribution of meat, however, one man, Piapi, received none. This was not intentional on Maigi's part—one of the other men may, perhaps, have forgotten to hand over the cut which was Piapi's portion—but Piapi chose to regard it as a personal slight and began to stir up trouble against Maigi. Kamana, Maigi's sister, learned what he was doing and told her brother.

Maigi became extremely angry when he heard this. "Piapi has always had a portion of every dugong I have killed in the past, and I am willing to share in like manner in the future. It is not true that I deliberately left him out on this occasion," he said. And he went to his brothers and told them that they were to help him fight Piapi.

Now Maigi's brothers thought that he wanted Piapi killed, whereas, in fact, Maigi meant no more than that they should wrestle with him and give him a sound thrashing. Piapi had gone to the reef to spear fish, and Maigi planned to catch him as he was on his way home to Ait. Maigi's brothers accompanied him to Somanapai as he asked and, when Piapi came along, killed him with their *gabagaba*.

Realizing that his brothers had believed themselves to be obeying his wishes, Maigi now took full responsibility for the death of Piapi. He told them to take Piapi's body to Saumangagat and cover it with leaves. They were then to return to Ait where they would say nothing about what had happened. He would give the news himself.

When Maigi arrived at Ait several hours later, his body was smeared with clay, and he held in his mouth a young *waba* plant which he had torn from the ground by its roots, signs that he had killed an important man. Seeing Maigi, the people were immediately afraid and looked about to see who was missing. When they learned that Piapi had not returned from fishing they understood that it was Piapi whom Maigi had killed, and fighting began between Maigi's people on the one hand—those who had *kadal* (crocodile) as *augad*—and Piapi's people on the other, those who had *baidam* (shark) as *augad*.[1]

1. Alfred Aniba said: "A little stream divides *kadal* and *baidam*."

189

2. The western end.
3. Kusei's grandson, Nawia Elu, was about 65 years of age in 1967.
4. This tree has two names. While it is young it is called *jangau* (or *zangau*); when it grows old it develops a hollow trunk and is called *aubub*.

When it came to the end of the story, Aniba's account differed from Enosa's.

Aniba said that Maigi sent word to Piapi's people at Ait and Saibai Village, telling them to come and kill him. Gemetu and Monga, sons of Maigi's sister, went ahead of the rest of the men from Saibai Village and hid near Tara. They stood between Maigi and those who had come to kill him, but Maigi told them the story behind Piapi's death and forbade them to intervene in future. Despite this, Gemetu and Monga defended Maigi on a second occasion. It was

Afterwards, Maigi told his brothers that he was leaving Ait and going to the opposite end[2] of the island to live. He, his wife, Sagaro, and their son, Kusei,[3] made their home at Tara, a place where bamboos suitable for making bows and arrows grew. They stayed there for many months, Sagaro and Kusei going into the mangroves at night and sleeping inside the hollow trunk of an *aubub* tree.[4]

Oppressed by the certainty that fighting between his people and Piapi's would never end while he himself lived, Maigi in the end sent word to the men of *kadal* and *baidam* at Saibai Village to come and kill him. When he saw them coming, he spread coconut leaves and banana leaves on the ground and lay on top of them, face downwards, pretending sleep. Baira (*kadal augad*) struck him first; the men of *baidam augad* followed, killing him with their *gabagaba*. It had been Maigi's wish that his brothers bury him at Augar, and this they did.

not until men came from Ait and Saibai Village the third time that Maigi was clubbed to death.

Aniba also said that Maigi had told his brothers to take his head to Augar and place it at the foot of the *waba* plant which grew there. All who saw it would be reminded of the reason why he, Maigi, had submitted to being killed: that the fighting between *kadal* and *baidam* should cease.

Aniba was eighty-five years old in 1967. He said that he had seen Maigi's head at Augar when he was a boy.

GIRBAR   [Told by Timothy Akiba at Saibai, 27 August 1967]

1. Mag is like a small dam. There is a well similar to Mag at Boigu (where it is known as "Mai"), and another at Waraber (Sue Island). Mag is still the principal source of water for Saibai Village, with which it has recently been connected by pipeline.
2. Timothy Akiba who told this story used *madubal* (*madub*, singular) for "spirits who live in wells". Another informant at Saibai preferred "*imagaral*" to "*madubal*" for such spirits, asserting that a *madub* was a bull-roarer used in raising wind.
   At Badu and Mua a *madub* was said to be a lazy fellow who would not work like others around him and would not join in group activities.

Late one afternoon, a woman named Girbar set out from her home at Jiril to fetch water from the well, Mag.[1] There, because the water was very low at this time, she had to climb down the bank to the bottom to fill her *kusul* (coconut shell water-containers).

By the time she had completed her task the sun had set, and, in a hurry to cross the swamp and reach Jiril before dark, she quickly slung the *kusul* over her shoulders and prepared to climb out of the well, only to find herself ringed around by *madubal*[2] who were standing on the top of the bank. "Girbar," said the *madubal*, "we have come to take you with us to the sky."

Now the woman had no wish at all to go with the *madubal*, but she had no choice in the matter; for she was only one, and they were many. So Girbar went up to the sky with the *madubal*.

The people in Saibai Village waited and watched for Girbar for many days and at last they saw her climbing down a very tall coconut palm at Bagunangulainga.[3]

Girbar brought with her three plants: banana, taro, and sugarcane, each a variety which had never previously been grown at Saibai. The people planted them, and they flourished for many years.

During a thunderstorm, the coconut palm by means of which Girbar had completed her journey back from the sky was struck by lightning, and its trunk split. After that the trunk developed two branches, one pointing south, the other pointing north, so that the palm had the form of a cross. It had already been the tallest coconut palm by far at Saibai, but the centre part of the trunk still kept on growing upwards, and it continued to bear coconuts.[4]

3. Where the school stands today.
4. Timothy Akiba said that he saw the rotting trunk of this coconut palm when he was a small boy. Timothy was about sixty years of age in 1967.

Artist Kala Waia

191

THE PET CROCODILE

[Told by Enosa Waigana at Saibai, 6 September 1968]

Long ago, say the people of Ait *kadal* (crocodile) *augad* at Saibai, there were eleven children—one boy and ten girls—who used to go for rides on a crocodile's back. That each child always sat at the same spot accounts for the names given to those parts of all crocodiles ever since. These names are the names by which the children are identified in the myth. Furthermore, these names have been, and still are, used for children in families which have *kadal* as their totem.

Not far from the mouth of the Oriomo River on the Papuan mainland, there was once a small village consisting of three families which had the crocodile for their totem.

In this village there were eleven children who, whenever the parents went to their gardens, were left at home in the care of a very old man. He was the oldest man in the village, and he never let the children out of his sight, neither the boy, Gaizu, nor the ten girls, Sabui, Kuikuit, Kuta-dan, Nataru kubi, Patait, Nubeza, Za-nubeza, Adata, Ulaita, and Mopata.

One day Gaizu's father went hunting for pigs and kangaroos and as he followed the river upstream came upon a crocodile egg.

Now when a single egg is laid by a crocodile it is a very special egg: it is like the son, or the grandson, dearest to a man's heart. Indeed, the same words are used to describe both this egg and a favourite male child: *kadalau poipiam kakur* (the crocodile's egg which must be carefully watched).

Gaizu's father took the egg back to the village, built a pen on the muddy side of the river bank, and put the egg inside it. When the egg hatched, he gave the baby crocodile to his son for a pet.

Gaizu and the girls loved the little crocodile and played with it every day. They called it Aka (granny) because it was as dear to them as their own grandmother.

The idea of letting Aka out of her pen did not occur to them until she grew big and strong. Then, one day, the thought flashed into their heads that Aka could take them for a ride on her back, and after that they could hardly wait for the day when their parents next went to their gardens and left them at home with the old man. And when that happened, no sooner were the parents out of sight than the children ran to Aka and coaxed her from her pen. "Aka," they said, "take us for a ride in the river."

Gaizu sat in front at Aka's nostrils. Behind him, in order, sat the girls: Sabui, Kuikuit, Kuta-dan, Nataru kubi, and Patait on her head; Nubeza and Za-nubeza on her back; and Adata and Ulaita and Mopata on her tail. In their hands they held leafy branches of *waba* and *kuruba* and *sam tete*, plants which grew close to their village, and as Aka took them downstream with the current, they sang with joy.

Ai dara besere nau nau a
Ai dara besere nau nau a

Pörki pörki siraria sörari gamada nau nau a
Pörki pörki siraria sörari gamada nau nau a

Aka went no further than the mouth of the river, waited there until the tide turned, and then swam back with the current.

When the parents came home in the evening, Aka was in her pen; and since neither the children nor the old man breathed a word about the ride on Aka's back, the parents had not the slightest idea of what had happened during their absence from the village that day.

Aka took them for many rides to the mouth of the river. Every time the parents left them at home with the old man, the children ran to her pen, let her out, hopped on her back, and in no time at all were on their way down the river. The parents did not learn what their children had been up to until it was too late to put a stop to it.

A day came when Aka swam beyond the mouth of the river to the open sea, where she fed for a while on floating seaweed and grass before going back inside the river and taking the children home.

Gaizu was very cross with Aka for her behaviour that day. After she was penned, he said: "Aka, open your mouth!" Aka opened her jaws wide, and Gaizu put his hands inside them and removed the seaweed and grass that she had eaten. "Look at what you ate!" he said, holding the mess close to her eyes, and with that, threw it full in her face. The old man thought to himself: "That crocodile will become bad-tempered."

From that time, Aka always swam beyond the mouth of the river when she took the children for a ride. And Gaizu always removed the seaweed and grass that she ate in the sea as soon as she was back in her pen.

The old man was very worried, and rightly so. For Aka, at first merely resentful of Gaizu's treatment of her, finally became angry and the next time she had all the children on her back, swam straight to the open sea and allowed her body to sink in the water.

"Aka! Aka!" cried the children, "why are you sinking? We're getting wet!"

Aka ignored the children. Besides, she was busy sending a message to all the crocodiles and sharks in the sea. Not until she had finished doing that did she come up to the top of the water, and then she began to swim—on and on, further and further from the mouth of the river. Late in the afternoon she swam past Daru (an island). "Aka," whimpered the children, "take us home." Aka took no notice of them.

Back at the village, the old man had climbed to the top of the tallest mangrove tree, the better to keep his eye on the children. He could see what was happening, and he said to himself: "That's the last we'll see of them."

East of the island called Bobo, Gaizu saw flurries of foam ahead. "Aka! There's a reef!" he warned. But Gaizu was mistaken.

When Aka sent her message to all the crocodiles and sharks in the sea, she told them to go to a certain place and wait at it until she arrived. What Gaizu saw was water churned by the creatures that had gathered at Aka's bidding. When Aka reached them she turned over with a splash so great that it was seen by the old man at the top of his tree. The children fell into the water and were eaten by Aka's friends.

That evening, the old man told the parents the whole story. When they heard it they turned their faces towards Bobo and wept.

The crocodile, Aka, the children's pet, never returned to the village.

BIU

[Told by Wagea Waia at Saibai, 2 September 1967]

Long ago at Saibai when the water in the sea was fresh and sweet to drink, a single mangrove, Biu, grew all by itself outside and beyond the unbroken wall of mangroves that ringed the island.

One morning a pod growing at the very top of Biu fell to the mud beneath and broke the shell of Gitalai the crab, who had made her home at that spot.

"*Igari! Igari! Igari!*"[1] cried Gitalai. "Biu, you have broken my back and caused me great pain. I shall ask Akul to punish you."

"Akul!" she called. "Come and cut Biu!"

Akul, the shell-fish, came at once and began to cut Biu with her shell. "*Igari! Igari! Igari!*" cried Biu. "Fire, come and burn Akul!"

Fire came and began to burn Akul.

"*Igari! Igari! Igari!*" cried Akul. "Water come and quench Fire!"

Water came and began to quench Fire.

1. *Igari* = *iagar* (alas!)

194

"*Igari! Igari! Igari!*" cried Fire. "Guzuguz, come and drink Water!"

And Guzuguz, the jelly-fish, came and began to drink Water.

Guzuguz drank till the reef lay bare. Then she drank all the water in the pools where the crabs had their homes; she drank all the water in the holes made by fish; she drank and she licked till the reef was as dry as a bone.

Presently Kimus,[2] a man who had gone out on the reef to fish that day, came upon Guzuguz. He drove his spear into the swollen, stranded jelly-fish.

"Bu-bu-bu-bu," gushed the water from the body of Guzuguz. "Bu-bu-bu-bu," bubbled the water as it flowed from Guzuguz out over the reef.

In the afternoon Maluigal[3] arrived at Saibai to hunt turtle. When they caught one, they pulled it aboard their canoe and cut the flesh from the shell. Then they removed the *il*[4] from the liver and threw it into the sea.

The bitter salt fluid of the *il* mingled with the sweet fresh water that covered the reef. Ever since the sea has been salt.

2. *Kimus* is the name of a deadly arrow tipped with cassowary claw.
3. Maluigal, deep-sea people. (*Malu*, the deep blue sea). Men from the islands of Mabuiag and Badu.
4. *Il*, gall-bladder.

AUKAM [Told by Wagea Waia at Saibai, 2 September 1967]

Aukam of Saibai wove mats by the light of the moon. The woman did no other work.

When the moon rose at night she took dry coconut leaves and began to weave. When the moon set she laid down her work and slept.

It was always her way—Aukam of Saibai wove mats by the light of the moon and at no other time.

The moon saw that she worked only when he was present and, believing the reason to be that she loved him, came down one night and took her up to the sky.

Within the bright circle of the moon's embrace Aukam still weaves her mats, as all may see.

DAUAN [Told by Wagea Waia at Saibai, 2 September 1967]

The people of the long, low island of Saibai tell this story of the small, high island of Dauan, their closest neighbour in Torres Strait.

Once upon a time, a little *zub* (foothill) named Dauan lived beside Meiai, a very high mountain in Daudai, somewhere to the north-east of our island.

Dauan always felt very lonely because the clouds hid Meiai's face from her, so one day she ran down to the sea and set out along the coast to find a new home for herself. For many days she travelled towards the west, seeing no place that pleased her until she reached Warukuik, opposite the island of Saibai.[1]

"I am sure Saibai would like to have me for her companion," thought Dauan. "She has no neighbours. Why, she must be as lonely as I." And with that, she crossed the water to Saibai.

"Saibai," said Dauan, "may I stay with you and be your close friend?"

"You may," said Saibai.

So Dauan chose a site at the edge of Saibai's home reef at Danakuik, offshore from Saiwalaugagat. Saibai was not at all pleased.

"If you stay there my people will have nowhere to go fishing or looking for crabs," she said. "You cannot settle at Danakuik. You will have to go somewhere else."

The little *zub* moved on towards the western point of Saibai, to Gebarau Wak. Again she asked: "Saibai, may I stay here?"

"Oh no," replied Saibai, "that would never do. My canoes anchor at Gebarau Wak, and so do the canoes that bring visitors to my people. When my reef is dry, Gebarau Wak is the only close anchorage I have for them. You must find another place."

Dauan moved on round the western point of Saibai until she came to Iama Wak.

"Sabai, please let me stay at Iama Wak," she begged.

"I cannot allow you to do so," said Saibai, "because my canoes go there to hunt and fish."

Then Dauan knew that there was no place at Saibai for her, for she had already looked east and seen the reefs that lay scattered in that direction.

"Saibai," said Dauan, "you do not want me to be your companion, so I shall leave you. Do you see where big waves break to the west of you? That is where I shall make my home."

1. Wagea said that some people believe Dauan left a part of herself at Mabudauan on the Papuan mainland. Dauan carried a basketful of fish, and some of these fish she threw out for Mabudauan before she went on to Warukuik.

196

"And," she continued, "I promise you this: 'When your canoes come to visit me I shall move away from you and call up big waves for the passage between you and me. When my canoes set out to visit you, however, I shall move close to you and give them a fair wind to make their crossing swift and smooth.' "

Whereupon the little *zub* moved out to the west and settled at the spot where she has remained to this day.

WARUPUDAMAIZINGA [Told by Alfred Aniba at Saibai, 5 September 1967]

A tortoise whose home was the Saibai swamp was suffering badly from heat.

Kuki (the north-west wind) had brought little rain that year, and the water in the swamp had quickly dried up. So although she walked from the eastern end of the swamp to the western—from island to island,[1] over glistening white salt-pans and sun-baked red clay, through tall, dead reeds and grass—nowhere did she find a pool in which to soak her poor, hot body.

At last she reached the place where the swamp is kept separate from the sea by a very narrow strip of land. Parched by then, she was climbing up on to it at the same time as a turtle came to the surface of the sea to breathe, not far out from the shore. "Come here, turtle!" the tortoise called, "I have something to say to you."

The turtle swam in, and the tortoise walked towards her. They met on the beach. "Turtle," said the tortoise, "will you change places with me? Will you live in the swamp so that I may live in the sea?"

"Would I have any friends in the swamp?" asked the turtle.

"Oh yes," the other told her, "there are prawns and crabs and tortoises in the swamp—you would have plenty of friends. I badly want to live in the sea," she continued, "but I may not leave the swamp until I find someone to take my place there: the number of living creatures in the swamp must always remain the same. You will like the swamp, I promise you. Only think of all the new friends you will have."

1. The higher patches of ground in the swamplands at Saibai are called islands (*kawal*—singular, *kawa*).

So the turtle agreed to change places with the tortoise and crossed the narrow strip of land to the swamp, and the tortoise walked out into the sea.

Within a short time the turtle was in agony, her head and her back and her flippers bone dry in the dusty swamp. Before long she was dead.

For a while the tortoise drifted along on top of the sea, cool and refreshed. Presently, when she felt hungry, she reached for the bottom of the water with her feet, intending to search there for food. She found, however, that she was out of her depth. There was nothing for her to eat on the surface of the water, so eventually she starved to death.

The people of Saibai have a name for the narrow place at which sea and swamp nearly meet—they call it Warupudamaizinga. In their language, *waru* means turtle and *pudamaizinga* means the place at which an exchange has been made. Even very small children know that Warupudamaizinga is the place at which the turtle changed places with the tortoise.

MIBU AND THE
COCONUT [Told by Alfred Aniba at Saibai, 8 September 1967]

A long time ago Mibu, a man who had a sore on his foot, left his home in Daudai and came to Saibai to live. When he arrived the village was deserted; he saw footprints on the ground, and fronds which had been cut from coconut palms, but every house was empty.

Mibu was very hungry after his long journey, so he searched for food. There was nothing to be had, however, but some coconuts at the top of a very tall palm. He could not reach them from the ground because they were too far up, and he could not climb up to get them because of the sore on his foot. Mibu tried to coax one to come down to him.

"Come down, coconut," he called to it.

The coconut did not stir.

"Coconut, good coconut, come down," he called.

The coconut showed no sign at all of having heard him.

"You are very sweet," Mibu cajoled it, "come to me."

But the coconut was not deceived by his flattery. "If I come down you will eat me," it said.

Mibu now looked round for a very long stick to knock it down and, before long, found a three-pronged fish spear which had been left behind by one of the men. With this he could reach the coconut. Thrusting hard, he pierced its shell with the pointed prongs of the spear, and pulled the coconut down from the palm.

And that is the reason why every coconut bears the thrust-marks of the three-pronged fish-spear—they were put there, in the first instance, by Mibu, a man who came from Daudai and made his home in Saibai Village.

AMAGI   [Told by Wagea Waia at Saibai, 6 October 1968]

Amagi and her little son, her only child, lived at Kagar, at the north-eastern end of the island of Saibai. She loved the boy dearly and denied him nothing—whatever he asked her to do she did; whatever he wanted she gave him.

Now the child was inordinately fond of wild plums (*ubar*—or *wongai* as most people call them today), not small ones, but big, choice fruit which are not easy to find. So when the *wongai* hung red and ripe from the trees, Amagi used to search for the kind that her son preferred. One day, however, she saw no big *wongai*, and she brought him small fruit instead.

"Mother," said the boy, "I do not want these *wongai*. They are far too small. I want big *wongai*."

"My son," replied Amagi, "I saw no big *wongai*. These are the best I could find."

"Go and look for big *wongai*," her son ordered, and, when she would not because she knew there were none to be had, he burst into tears.

At the time the two were seated on the ground in the shade of a *wongai* tree. Suddenly the boy saw what he craved—right at the top of the tree beneath which they sat was a big, sweet *wongai*. "Look, mother! That's what I want. Get that *wongai* for me!" he cried.

Amagi saw it and knew it to be out of her reach. "My son," she said, "I cannot. It is too far up. I cannot get it for you."

The child wept and stormed and would not be appeased. In the end the mother looked around until she found a long stick. With this in her hand, she climbed up the tree as far as she dared and then swung it at the fruit that her son demanded. The *wongai* flew away and fell into the sea beyond the end of Mamag, the natural jetty of sand and dead coral at Kagar. When the fruit hit the water it shattered to fragments.

"Get it for me," said the boy, who had not seen what happened to the *wongai*.

Amagi reasoned with her child. "My son," she told him, "it fell far out in the sea and burst."

"I want that *wongai*. I want it. I want it. Get it!" raged the boy.

Amagi walked down to the sea and began to swim out.

Her son stopped crying—he was worried about his mother. Now he called: "Mother! Mother! Come back!"

Amagi paid no heed to him. Presently she began to sing:

> *Amagi nangulpa titeria baltaipa.*
> *Amagi nangulpa titeria baltaipa.*
>
> (Amagi floats on top of the grey-green water.
> Amagi drifts away with the sea.)

"Come back! Come back, mother! Come back!" her son entreated her.

But Amagi took no notice of him. Instead, she swam further and further out—past the end of Mamag, past Ubarau Sapilnga, the spot at which the *ubar* had burst and then fallen into the sea as stones—until she was swept away by the tide.

DAGMET   [Told by Wagea Waia at Saibai, 2 September 1967]

Long ago there was a man named Sibika who lived by himself at Makanapai, an island in the eastern part of the Saibai swamp. Every morning he went to Kagar and speared fish. When he got back to Makanapai, he built a big fire and, after it died down, cooked his fish on top of a *iu* (rack, or spit) over the coals. Then he worked in his garden for the rest of the day.

Now when Sibika walked back from Kagar in the morning he took a path which followed the creek, Bulaimai Kasa, and, though he did not know it, passed close by a *dogai* named Dagmet whose home was a *surka* mound. And Dagmet, seeing fish on the prongs of his spear, used to grumble away to herself: "Why does he never leave one for me? I live near the path. You wait, Sibika. One of these days you'll go home with a fine lot of fish, but then see what happens."

200

Sibika was very lucky with his spear one morning, and that night, because he felt very tired, went to sleep early. Soon he was snoring.

By that time, Dagmet was on her way to Makanapai, preceded by swarms of butterflies and dragonflies. Sibika, she knew, would not have been able to eat all the fish he had taken home that morning and would have plenty left on his cooking rack. Near Makanapai she began to cackle:

> *Sibika, Sibika, ngi utuiuipa.*
> *Ina ngai Dagmet,*
> *War kaura abaiak, war kaura utuilag.*
>
> (Sibika, Sibika, you are asleep.
> Here is Dagmet, long-eared Dagmet,
> One ear to lie on, the other to cover her.)

Sibika did not hear her, nor did he stir when she sat down beside his *iu* and helped herself to his fish.

> *Sibika, Sibika, ngi utuiuipa.*
> *Ina ngai Dagmet,*
> *War kaura abaiak, war kaura utuilag,*

gibbered Dagmet, mouth full of fish,

Sibika, with his pronged fish-spear and
a string of fish

Artist Kala Waia

Wapi puime puime,
Rid puime puime.

(Sucking fish and bones.)

When she had eaten every fish, she walked back to her *surka* mound, gabbling and jabbering: "Sibika, you think you'll find fish on your *iu* for breakfast, but you won't, will you?"

Sibika went to his *iu* in the morning and found only bones and scales. He was very puzzled. There were no footprints on the ground. "Perhaps it was birds who stole my fish. Maybe eagles or crows," he reasoned. So he took his spear and went to Kagar for fish. Dagmet saw him as he went by and said: "There won't be any fish on your *iu* tomorrow morning either, my friend."

When Sibika found that his fish had been stolen a second time, he decided to keep watch for the thief who came in the night.

That morning he speared many fish. He cooked them, but ate none during the day, leaving all of them on the *iu*. At sunset he lay down, determined not to sleep until he learnt who was stealing his fish.

So he saw the swarms of butterflies and dragonflies, and he heard Dagmet's voice as she approached:

Sibika, Sibika, ngi utuiuipa.
Ina ngai Dagmet,
War kaura abaiak, war kaura utuilag.

He watched the long-eared *dogai* eat his fish and noisily suck the bones, and he never once stirred or moved hand or foot.

Again next morning he speared many fish, and again he cooked them and left them on top of his *iu*. But when he lay down, pretending sleep, he had beside him a small club.

Dagmet came and sat down beside the *iu*.

Sibika, Sibika, ngi utuiuipa.
Ina ngai Dagmet.
War kaura abaiak, war kaura utuilag,
Wapi puime puime,
Rid puime puime,

chanted Dagmet, mouth full of fish.

Sibika leapt to his feet, club raised and ready. "You're the one who's been stealing my fish," he said, and then he brought down his club on her head. Dagmet screeched: "Too bad, wasn't it? I stole your fish many times before you found out." And then she died.

Sibika set fire to her and burnt her on the spot. All that remained of Dagmet was a large piece of pumice (*met*) which is still at Makanapai.

Head of harpoon-spear (*wap*), with harpoon (*kuiur*). The carved end of the *wap* represents a shark's head.

stories from

BOIGU *Talbot Island*

Poised to jump with his *wap* and harpoon a dugong

BOIGU (Talbot Island)

N

SWAMP

142°15' EAST
9°15' SOUTH

KIASAS
KERPAI GIZU
AUGUD
PAUPANATAM
ADARIPATARA
DAINI
GUTATAU
NGUR
KERPA
KERPAI
WATI
KOBA
NANAI
GIWAI
BUTU
GANALAI
BAIDAM
SAMARA
MURIGIÑA
KOSA
KOI
KULPUGUD
KOSA
IUBU
GIBU
GUD
GEBALAP
KADAPAKUIK
KOWE
MARAPH TOGA
KAUSARAL TOGA
GIMA KOWE
KUFURIABD
WATI KOSA
KAWATAG
BEDAL TOGA
MAI KIDU
KATATA MAI
CHURCH
TEIANTARA
AL BUPUR
MOIM
PUTITALMAITARA
TUAM
PADIN
PALI
SERE
GORAMAB
STARKAZUB
SURUKUMAÑA
SURUM
KOIKUP

SURUMAL KAWA
SAPURAL KAWA
TUGERAUNIAIZINGA
AIMER-MUD
AU-BUZ

SCALE
0   1   2   3
Miles

August 1966
M.L.

mangroves
swamp
sand, mud

BOIGU

[Told by Moses Dau at Boigu, 9 October 1968]

The first people on the island of Boigu were two men, from whom the island got its name, and a woman named Met.

For some time the men lived not far from each other on the northern side of the island, but, because each was effectively screened from the other by dense scrub, neither knew of the other's presence. Nor did the two men know of the woman Met who lived at Padin on the southern side of the island.

One man lived at Kadal Bupur;[1] the other lived at Böibil Gizu—close to the garden land worked by him near Mai.[2]

One night, the man who lived at Böibil Gizu walked through the scrub to Kadal Bupur—to learn that someone lived there. He returned again the following night, taking with him a gift of the biggest yams that grew in his garden.

Now the man who lived by himself at Kadal Bupur had noticed the tracks made by his visitor and had decided to keep watch in case he should come again. So it was that the man from Böibil Gizu was greeted upon his arrival at Kadal Bupur the second night with the words: "Who are you?" When he replied, "My name is Boigu," the man of Kadal Bupur said: "My name is Boigu, too." Boigu of Kadal Bupur then invited Boigu of Böibil Gizu to come and live with him. The other agreed, but said that Boigu of Kadal Bupur must make his gardens near his at Mai where the soil was very fertile.

So the two men lived together from that time, and every day they went to their gardens at Mai.

One day, Met decided to walk across the island. When she reached Kawatag after making her way through the swamp, she went down to the beach and followed it until she came to Kadal Bupur. She saw a house, but there was no one in sight. She returned to Padin.

The next day she crossed the swamp again. This time she took notice of the gardens and the coconut palms between Kawatag and Mai. Again she found no one at home at Kadal Bupur—the two men were away working in their gardens. So once again she returned to Padin, still without having learned who was living on the island besides herself. When Boigu of Kadal Bupur and Boigu of Böibil Gizu arrived back from their gardens

1. The church is at Kadal Bupur.
2. *Mai*, a well. This is the well from which Boigu Village obtains its water supply today.

at the end of the day they saw the footprints—footprints made by a woman—and began to argue about who should have her.

Met came a third time from Padin, and was seen by Boigu of Kadal Bupur as she was walking across the clearing to Kawatag after she left the cover of the mangroves at the edge of the swamp.

Boigu of Kadal Bupur went to her. He had connection with her, and then he took her to his home.

After that, the husband and wife went together to the gardens daily, and Boigu of Böibil Gizu decided to live by himself again.

Back at his former home the night after he left them, he made a plan to go to Kadal Bupur and kill the other man.

Armed with his *gabagaba*, he set out from Böibil Gizu at dawn next morning, walked to the beach, entered the water, and swam to Kadal Bupur, reaching that place just as Boigu of Kadal Bupur threw in his line to catch fish for the morning meal. Boigu of Böibil Gizu, who had timed his arrival for that moment, grabbed the line, pulled it under the water, and allowed himself to be hauled ashore like a fish. Once there, he stood up, struck Boigu of Kadal Bupur a killing blow with his *gabagaba*, and immediately afterwards swam back to his home. He landed on the beach at Gerwai[3] and walked from there to Böibil Gizu.

Met, who had not gone down to the edge of the water with her husband to fish but had remained behind to stoke up the coals of the cooking fire (as Boigu of Böibil Gizu had known she would), knew nothing of what had happened. It was not until some time later that she went to look for him and found his dead body on the beach.

She was still crying that afternoon when Boigu of Böibil Gizu walked through the scrub to Kadal Bupur. He asked her the reason for her tears. She told him that her husband was dead. She also told him to go away, but he refused to leave and after a while was able to persuade her to place her husband's body on a *sara*.[4] When that had been done, she consented to go and live at Böibil Gizu.

Now all the gardens belonged to Boigu of Böibil Gizu and Met.

3. The school is at Gerwai.
4. *Sara*, a raised platform for corpses.

KIBA

[Told by Moses Dau at Boigu, 15 October 1967]

A man named Kiba lived with his brothers on the banks of the Mai Kösa, a river in Daudai which enters the sea opposite the island of Boigu.

One day, Kiba asked his brothers to go hunting [dugong] with him. They did not want to go, but Kiba insisted, and, in the end, they went with him. First they went to the small island called Kusar. Kiba cut vines for the ropes he needed, and his brothers plaited them for him.[1] Then they began to hunt.

Before long they saw a dugong which had come to the surface of the water to breathe. Kiba made ready to harpoon it. The dugong, however, swam off quickly in the direction of Kerpai, the most easterly point of Boigu. The men gave chase. Kiba jumped into the water and, while he was below, told the dugong to run to Buru.[2]

After they had passed Kerpai, one of Kiba's brothers asked if he might jump for the dugong. Kiba refused him permission. He was still angered by his brothers' reluctance to accompany him when he asked them to go hunting with him, and it was his intention to punish them by refusing to allow them to jump for the dugong, and leading them on an exhausting, fruitless chase. Thus he would jump himself every time and pretend to try and harpoon the dugong, whereas, in fact, he would merely be creating the opportunity to tell the dugong to go to far places.

Between Boigu and Buru, Kiba jumped with his *wap* (spear to which a harpoon is attached) and told the dugong to run straight to Buru.

Off Buru, the brother asked a second time if he might try his luck at harpooning the dugong, but Kiba again forbade him and again jumped himself. This time he told the dugong to run to Mabuiag.

At the small reef called Markai Maza,[3] Kiba caught the dugong. His brothers hauled it into the canoe, and the party sailed back with the south wind.

Kiba's brothers wanted to clear Kerpai, but Kiba ordered them to go across the island by way of Köi Kösa, the salt-water passage which divides Boigu in two.

By then the youngest brother was almost dead from thirst, so Kiba was forced to make a landing on the northern coast of Boigu a short distance from Kadal Bupur.[4] He ordered his brothers to stay with the canoe while he searched for water.

1. Aaron Anau of Boigu, who also told me the story of Kiba, interpolated an incident which Moses Dau would not admit to his version. This detail, which concerns a man and wife whose baby fell from its basket while they were fishing, is given by Landtman (*The Folk-Tales of the Kiwai Papuans* [Helsingfors, 1917], pp. 236–37).
2. An island between Dauan and Mabuiag. The English name is Turnagain Island.
3. South of Buru.
4. The point of land on which the church stands today.

Namai Pabai gave these details to supplement the story of Kiba:

From time to time people see a dugong in the muddy waters of Mai Kösa. Ordinarily dugong never frequent muddy water; therefore, the dugong seen in Mai Kösa is an unnatural dugong. And there is another strange thing about this dugong: men cannot catch it. A man sees the dugong and builds a *nat* (platform from which to harpoon dugong); only, the dugong does not come to the *nat*.

Aaron Anau told me that there is a "story stone" in the river off the village of Lom. It is shaped like a canoe—it is, in fact, Kiba's canoe, which turned to stone after it sank, taking with it the bodies of Kiba, his brothers, and the dugong which Kiba had harpooned.

The spirit of this dugong is believed to have entered the dugong which is (or are) seen in Mai Kösa.

Kiba threw his spear and obtained water at the spot where it landed, Katana Mai.[5] When he tasted the water, he found it to be half-salt; so he threw his spear again. Where it fell this time he obtained water which was sweet, at Mai Kibu. Kiba then went back to his brothers and pointed the direction that they were to take for water to drink.

The brothers picked up their water vessels (lengths of bamboo, *ngukiu marapal*) and hurried off. They drank greedily and forced the youngest brother to swim in the waterhole. After they had filled the bamboo pipes they returned to the canoe, and Kiba gave the order to cross to the mainland.

As they made their way back to the Mai Kösa, the spirits of Kiba and his brothers began to weaken, until outside Lom—the village upstream from the mouth of the river which was their home—the brothers lay dead in the canoe. Kiba felt himself near to the point of death, and he began to allow the canoe to sink. And the people standing on the bank saw the canoe slowly tip over and go to the bottom of the river, taking with it Kiba, his brothers, and the dugong which Kiba had hunted and finally killed.

DOGAI METAKURAB [Told by Aaron Anau at Boigu, 17 August 1966]

1. So called because he had yaws (*guigui*) on his legs and feet.

Guiguisanalnga[1] set out from his home at Tuam one day to poke at *surka* mounds. He went towards Tarkazub and was quite sure that he would find many eggs, for he was very clever at this kind of work. But though he visited mound after mound and prodded every one of them all over, he was out of luck. There was not an egg to be had.

At last he saw a mound which looked just right, one in which there would certainly be eggs. So he scratched away the earth and leaves and, sure enough, saw what he wanted. There lay three big eggs close together. Guiguisanalnga was very happy at that moment—not knowing that the eggs were attached to a *dogai*'s head. He put his hand over the middle one to lift it from the mound, only to discover that it would not budge. He pulled with all his might. Suddenly there was a noise, the mound parted, and out came *dogai* Metakurab—he had been tugging at an egg which was attached to the middle of her forehead. Guiguisanalnga rolled down the nest in his fright, and then he picked himself up and took to his heels.

Because of the sores on his legs and feet, Guiguisanalnga could not run fast, but he hobbled along as best he could. He was breathless when he arrived at Tuam. The people asked him why he was in such a hurry. "I must have a drink and something to eat," he gasped, "before I can speak."

"*Dogai,*" he said presently. "Coming this way." And he told them how, after a long search, he had at last found a mound with eggs in it; only, when he tried to remove one, it was stuck fast; he pulled and tugged, and a *dogai* came out with the egg. "This is a painted *dogai,*" he told them. "She is painted black and red, and she has an egg growing on each of her big ears. There is an egg in the middle of her forehead as well." With that, Guiguisanalnga got to his feet and moved on—he dared not waste any more time if he were to escape from *dogai* Metakurab.

"Is there one *dogai*, or are there many?" the people called after him.

"Only one," he called back. "You will know when she is approaching by these signs: first there will be a whirlwind; then there will be a swarm of sandflies; and after that a swarm of mosquitoes. When you see a cloud of big butterflies, the *dogai* will be nearly upon you."

The women and children of Tuam set out after Guiguisanalnga at a run. The men armed themselves with bows and arrows and stood waiting for Metakurab. When they saw her they fled.

They ran across Padin to Sere, where they found the men of that place preparing to make a stand against the *dogai*. There was no sign of Guiguisanalnga or the women and children of Tuam and Sere—they were strung out along the path to Köwe by then. The men of Tuam ran after them. There was no thought in their heads of joining forces with the men of Sere, who, in the event, proved no braver than the men of Tuam. Soon they also were running from Metakurab.

In this manner, the mad flight of the people of Boigu continued and grew, until everyone on the island except Bu of Kerpai was running in panic from Metakurab. It ended abruptly when they reached Gutatau Ngur, but only because there was no place left for them to run to.

Bu alone stood his ground, Bu of Kerpai. The whirlwind passed by him, the sandflies and the mosquitoes, and the cloud of big butterflies—black ones, with yellow, red, and white spots on their wings.

When Metakurab saw Bu, she knew she was about to die. "*Isu! Isu!* (What do I care!)" said Metakurab. "I hunted the people from every village on Boigu. I chased them from Tuam to Kerpai."

"You will die for it," said Bu. And he shot an arrow through her.

The spirit of *dogai* Metakurab is said to have gone up to the sky and become a constellation. (Haddon identifies it [*Reports*, V, 13] as Altair with a star on either side.) Since then she has been known as *Kukilaig*, the "person" (in the sky) associated with the north-west monsoon (*kuki*).

211

GEINAU
AND JEIAI   [Told by Aaron Anau at Boigu, 18 August 1966]

For many years, only two people lived at Mawat:[1] Geinau[2] and her sister Pöiteriteri.[3]

When they could no longer endure the lonely days, Geinau, the elder sister, prepared *nobipui* from the bark of a certain tree and used it on her body, the magic essence enabling her to bear a beautiful baby boy, Jeiai. He was perfect, but for the sores on his skin, and the sisters adored him.

Daily throughout his infancy, the sisters anointed him with *nobipui* and bathed him afterwards in the healing waters of Mawatau Kösa, which helped the condition although it did not cure it. Geinau and Pöiteriteri lavished on the wonderful male child a devoted care which brought him happily to early manhood.

At Pösipas, a small beach in Daudai opposite the island of Kusar, there was at this time a lovely girl named Panipan—the name means "lightning" —who had promised that the young man for whom she put out her torch during a dance should be her husband. Every day Panipan cut dead palm fronds for the torch she would hold in the evening to illumine the movements of the men who danced for her. Every night the young men of the village danced. But Panipan never extinguished her torch.

Until, at last, even Pisapu despaired of winning her. Of all the dancers none had performed so magnificently as he, for, truly loving her, every movement of his body, and every word that had sprung from his lips had perfectly expressed his consuming desire for her. Yet Panipan had not put out her torch for him. He decided to visit his sisters, Geinau and Pöiteriteri: they might know of a man at Boigu who would prove acceptable to Panipan.

Geinau and Pöiteriteri heard the sound of Pisapu's canoe as it was run up to the landing at Mawat and were immediately fearful for the safety of their beloved Jeiai, for if strangers learned of his existence he would almost certainly be taken from them. Swiftly they hid him in the undergrowth beneath a *soboro*,[4] ordering him to make no sound until they came back for him. For themselves, they would say nothing, do nothing that would cost them their treasure.

When Pisapu reached them, they had spread mats for their visitor and were busy preparing food.

1. Mawat is on the southern side of Boigu.
2. *Geinau*, the Torres Strait pigeon, *Ducula spilorrhoa.*
3. *Pöiteriteri*, a grey and white swamp bird which has a yellow bill.
4. *Soboro*, a tent-like cover worn by a person to keep off rain. It is made from the leaves of a palm similar to *nipa*, which are stitched together with fibre obtained from a variety of hisbiscus tree.

"Are there any young men at Mawat?" Pisapu asked.

"No," said the sisters, "there are no young men at this place."

"Where are your husbands? There must be men here," insisted Pisapu. "Where are your children?"

But though Pisapu plied the two women with questions until the sun was low in the sky, he did not obtain the admission that he sought. He would have to return the following day and trick them into revealing the whereabouts of the young man who was concealed at Mawat. His sisters were lying to him. He knew it, for he could sense their fear.

Jeiai was making a bow when he heard Pisapu's canoe grate on the sand next morning. As taught by Geinau and Pöiteriteri, he snatched up the bamboo and string with which he had been working and hid them beneath a bush, and then he took cover beneath the *soboro*, not knowing that he had failed to conceal a *mukub* (the knot at the end of a bowstring).

Pisapu saw it as he strode to the clearing in which the sisters lived. It proved to him beyond doubt that one man at least lived here, for only men made *mukub*. He picked up the bowstring and kept it hidden behind his back until he sat down, when he slipped it under the edge of the mat which had been spread for him by his sisters.

"Are you sure there are no men at this place?" he asked, taking up where he had left off the previous day. "One of you must have a husband. I do not believe that there are no men at Mawat."

Again the sisters denied the presence of men at Mawat.

Pisapu brought out the bowstring.

He told them about Panipan; of her refusal to take any man at Pösipas for her husband; and of her promise to marry the dancer for whom she put out her torch.

Any resistance to Pisapu's demand that Jeiai dance for Panipan would have availed the sisters nothing, so, although their hearts were broken, they agreed to allow Jeiai to go to Pösipas. They insisted, however, that he travel alone in his own secret way. They gave their word that he would arrive in time for the dancing that evening.

So Pisapu sailed back to Pösipas. With him went Pöiteriteri, who had hidden herself in his canoe.

At sundown, Jeiai took the *kuruai*[5] that hung from the roof of the sisters' house, stepped on it, and walked quickly along it as it extended before his feet in an arch through the air to the roof of Pisapu's house at Pösipas. Soon afterwards he took his place in one of the rows of dancers. Before long, Panipan put out her torch for him.

In the morning, Panipan sailed to Mawat with Pöiteriteri, but Jeiai returned by *kuruai*.

5. *Kuruai*—an arch; a rainbow; a magical aid to travel. Travel by *kuruai* is always in an arc. The *kuruai* in use today—as I was told—is a length of string to one end of which is tied a crocodile's tooth.

DAMAK AND DARAM

[Told by Ganadi Toby at Boigu, 16 August 1966]

Every day the boys and girls who lived at Mawat[1] used to walk across the swamps to the opposite side of the island and fetch water from the well called Mai Kibu. The boys walked in one line and the girls in another. And every day they were joined by another group of boys and girls—from a place to the west of Mawat—who were also bound for Mai Kibu.

It was the custom of all these young people to play *wai* before they commenced the walk back, using for the game the red fruit of the *wai* tree which grew beside Mai Kibu. They stood in a circle and threw a *wai* from player to player until it had passed through everyone's hands. Then they picked up their coconut shell water-containers, walked the short distance to Bedaltoga and played *wai* again. They played several times more, at other places along the way, but when they reached Kadapakuik they separated into their respective groups, the one going east to Mawat, and the other to the west of Mawat.

Only one thing marred the enjoyment of these happy trips to Mai Kibu: a young girl named Daram did not keep to her place in the line of girls. Instead, she walked with the boys.

The result was that the other girls grew to hate Daram and decided to punish her. Their chance came the day that Daram began to menstruate for the first time while they were walking to Mai Kibu.

By the time the boys and girls reached Bedaltoga on the way home, Daram was so racked with pain that she was unable to walk. Damak, her elder sister, wanted to stay with her and comfort her, but the other girls jostled her on and put their hands over her mouth, so that she could neither go back to her sister nor even call to her. Damak's eyes filled with tears when she looked back at Daram left standing alone in the swamp.

The boys reached Mawat first. "Where is Daram?" her parents asked. "She must have joined the girls," the boys told them. The girls arrived. "Where is Daram?" her parents asked. Damak told them what had happened.

The parents left at once to go to their daughter. At Bedaltoga they saw the red patch of ground where Daram had stood for a while. They could see that she had crawled west from Bedaltoga, and they followed her trail.

1. Mawat is on the southern side of Boigu. It should not be confused with Mawat on the Papuan mainland.

214

★

Daram, abandoned by her sister and her playmates, made her way slowly towards the Wati Kösa. She rested at a number of places.[2] At the edge of the river she lay face downwards in order to gaze at her reflection in the water. What she saw, however, was not Daram, the girl, but Daram, her ghost in the form of a blue fish. Daram, the girl, jumped into the river and became one with Daram, the ghost, the blue fish, which, when the parents saw it, was recognized by them as their daughter.

★

Time went by. Damak no longer walked to Mai Kibu to fetch water. Sometimes her parents took her with them to their garden; sometimes they left her behind at Mawat. She was often lonely.

One day when she was alone at Mawat, she saw a youth named Wölki walking on the reef with his fishing spear. She waved to him, and he came in to her. They talked until late afternoon, the time when her parents usually returned from their garden. Wölki was on his way back to his home at Samar before they arrived, and Damak did not mention her visitor to them.

Wölki came again, many times. He and Damak spent happy days beside the Wati Kösa.[3] Then the parents found out and forbade Wölki to come to Mawat.

Damak was broken-hearted. Alone during the day, she thought of Wölki and relived the time they had spent together. It welled from her in song. Sometimes she thought of Daram, her sister, and then she was infinitely sad.

One day Damak made a pelican form for herself and tried to fly in it. She kept it hidden from her parents, but every day, as soon as they had gone to their garden, she went into it and practised flying.

When her parents came home a little earlier than usual one afternoon, they saw a pelican standing on Giwai Butu, the big sandbank outside Mawat. They called to Wölki, who was fishing not far from Giwai Butu: "What bird is that?" Damak came out of the bird, showed herself to her parents, and then went into it again.

She flew from Giwai Butu to another sandbank, Adaripatara. Wölki ran after her. She flew on and came down at Paupanatam. Wölki called to her; but so, too, did her sister. She flew on.

She rested at many sandbanks: at Augud, Kiasas, and Baini; at Gidi-gidniaizinga, Jeiantara, and Putitalmaitara.

At Putitalmaitara she came out of the pelican and walked as a girl to the spot where her sister's ghost stayed in the Wati Kösa and threw herself into the water. Daram, the blue fish, swam slowly towards her.

2. There are patches of red clay between Bedaltoga and the Wati Kösa. They are said to be the places at which Daram rested.

3. Not the river mentioned earlier in the story. There appear to be two rivers of this name at Boigu, one on the northern side of the island, one on the southern. Damak and Wölki lay beside the latter.

WAIREG　　[Told by Ganadi Toby at Boigu, 19 August 1966]

At Kerpai there once lived a woman and her small son, Waireg. The child loved to eat the fruit of the *ubar* tree[1]—not all *ubar*, only big, choice fruit. So, every day at the time of year when the branches of the *ubar* trees hung heavy with ripe, red fruit, the mother used to go and fill her basket with *ubar*, always remembering to place the kind that Waireg liked best at the top of it. She never disappointed him.

One day, however, she returned earlier than usual. Waireg was still at play. His aunts paid her a visit and, as they sat talking, helped themselves to the fruit at the top of the basket; so that, when Waireg presently went to it for his *ubar*, he found only one of the kind that he preferred. He could not believe that his mother would treat him like that. "Mother, where are my fruit?" he asked. "At the top of the basket," his mother told him.

Waireg felt every piece of fruit in the basket. His mother was wrong— there were no big *ubar* in the basket. So he asked again what she had done with his *ubar*. "I put them at the top of the basket," she repeated.

Waireg began to cry. He cried until his mother grew weary of his crying—and so did his aunts and the rest of the people at Kerpai. He was still crying when the sun went down, and as he showed no signs of stopping, his aunts decided that something would have to be done about it: they pretended to be *dogai*.

One by one, each of the aunts jumped at him, made strange noises, threatened to hit him with a paddle—they acted for all the world like *dogai*. But Waireg only left off crying long enough to say to this aunt, "I know you're not a *dogai*. You're my aunt," or to that aunt, "You're not a *dogai* either. You're my aunt," and start up all over again. The aunts kept at it until they were exhausted, but Waireg was still crying.

At last everyone slept—everyone but Waireg and one old man.

Now ever since dark, a real *dogai* had been watching the people at Kerpai, and she had decided to eat Waireg. Seeing everyone asleep except the child—as she thought—she crept towards him and brandished a paddle at him exactly as his aunts had done earlier. Waireg, who was worn out from crying and was beginning to drowse, took no notice of her, thinking it was only one of his aunts trying to frighten him again.

The *dogai* came closer and closer, and then she killed him with the pointed end of the paddle by driving it through his body. After, she

1. *Ubar*, the wild plum of Torres Strait. *Ubar* is the Mabuiag word; the Meriam word is *eneo*.

216

picked him up from the ground and hurried off with him under her arm to her home, a *surka* mound; and when she was safely inside it, she began to eat Waireg from the feet up. By daybreak she had eaten every part of him except his head.

Waireg was missed by the people at Kerpai when they woke in the morning. They searched for him everywhere, only leaving off when the old man who had been watching the night before told them what had happened to the child. "Look at that blood," he said, "that's the place where the *dogai* killed him. Follow the trail of blood if you want to find out where she took him."

The people followed the trail of blood and came to the *surka* mound which was the *dogai*'s home. They decided they would have to kill her. So they gathered sticks and twigs and branches, piled them on the mound and set fire to them.

The *dogai* began to feel hot. Before long she felt so hot that she had to leave the shelter of her home and come outside. And there she stood, surrounded by the people, Waireg's head in her hands. "I have something to confess," she said, knowing herself to be about to die. "I ate one of your children." The people killed her then and threw her body into the fire.

Afterwards they went back to Kerpai, taking with them all that was left of Waireg. They made a *sara* and placed the head on it; and then they cried.

Geinau, the Torres Strait pigeon, eating the fruit of the wild plum, *ubar*. These are Western Island names—in the Eastern Islands, the bird is called *deumer* and the plum *eneo*.   *Artist* Segar Passi

GANALAI
DOGAI

[Told by Moses Dau at Boigu, 9 October 1968]

Once upon a time there were living at Mawat a man who was an expert dugong hunter and his brothers. At Ganalai, not far from Mawat, there was a *dogai* whose home was a *surka* mound.

One day when the dugong hunter was walking on the reef outside Ganalai, he saw grass that had been newly grazed by a dugong. So he built a platform close to the spot at which the dugong had left off eating and placed on top of it everything he would need to harpoon the dugong when it returned with the next high tide to resume feeding. Then he went home to Mawat. At sunset he told his brothers that he would need their help before long and went back to Ganalai, where he sat on his dugong platform and waited for the dugong to come.

It came when the water was knee-deep—at the same time as the Ganalai *dogai* was wading out to the dugong-platform. The hunter heard the sound of splashing behind him and thought it was made by his brothers. He whistled and shouted to them, telling them to anchor their canoe. The *dogai* kept on wading out, and only when the hunter glanced back to see why his brothers had not obeyed him did he see her. At once he laid down his *wap*.

The *dogai* grabbed hold of poles that supported the platform and began to shake them. The hunter climbed down into the water and began to wrestle with the *dogai*. She bit him, and he bit her; but whereas she only left toothmarks on the man, he removed skin and flesh from the *dogai*. Fighting every step of the way, the hunter gradually manoeuvred her back to the shore.

Both were exhausted. They collapsed on the beach panting, the man a little to the east of Ganalai, the *dogai* a little to the west. Later on, after she had recovered from the struggle, the *dogai* called good-bye to the man and went off to her home in the *surka* mound.

The hunter returned to Mawat and found his brothers asleep. He made a torch from dry palm fronds, lit it, and shook it over them so that pieces of burning leaf fell on them and woke them up. Then he told them what had happened.

In the morning, he and his brothers went to the *dogai*'s home at Ganalai and kindled a fire on top of it. The *dogai* came out when the heat grew too much for her and confessed her behaviour of the night before. Then the brothers killed her.

218

MÖIBU AND BAZI

[Told by Moses Dau at Boigu, 9 August 1966]

A long time ago there were no flying-foxes. Boigu is the place where they were created.

★

In the "before-time"[1] there were two men here at Boigu, Möibu and Bazi. Möibu was head of the cassowary (*sam*) people, and Bazi was head of the crocodile (*kadal*) people. They were both good hunters [of dugong].

Möibu was more important than Bazi, because there were more people in his group than in Bazi's, and yet he never gave good food to his family. Bazi always shared every part of the dugong he caught with his wife and children and friends, but Möibu always kept the fat of the dugong for himself. Bones, liver, guts, and ribs—*rida, siba, maita, bera*—were all that Möibu's wife and children ever got. *Rida, siba, maita, bera*, day after day, day after day. They were sick to death of bones, liver, guts, and ribs. Möibu's wife could stand it no longer, and she made up her mind to do something about it.

The next time the men went out hunting she cut some *iwai* (cloth-like fibre at the base of fronds) from a coconut palm and fashioned it into a big, strange frog-form.

When the men returned the dugong were butchered, and as usual Möibu gave his wife and children only the worst cuts—bones, liver, guts, and ribs.

Night came. Möibu's wife called out to Bazi's wife to come with her down to the beach. She told her to wait there for her until she came back. Möibu's wife slipped the frog-form over her head and hopped back to Bazi's wife, who called out to her friend in alarm. Möibu's wife hopped away, took off the frog-form, then came back and told of her plan that all the women should act out a frog play she had in mind. She poured out her complaints to Bazi's wife: "Every time Möibu spears dugong he only gives me bones, liver, guts, and ribs. I want some fat, too."

Bazi's wife agreed that this was not good enough and said she would help her.

As soon as the men had gone off to Kerpai on the next hunting trip, the women began to rehearse. They were ready by the time the men got back again.

That night all the women went off on their own, put on the forms that they had made, and hopped about like frogs. They hopped into the well,

1. "Before-time" is current Torres Strait pidgin for the old days prior to 1871.

219

they hopped out, and they hopped all the way back to the village, calling out like frogs.

The men began to ask each other what it was all about. They shouted to their wives who, they knew, had gone to the end of the village.

Meanwhile the women kept on hopping. They hopped round the men and over the men, and they sang a song which they sang over and over again:

> *Kata! Kata! Kata!*
> *Rida, rida, rida;*
> *Siba, siba, siba;*
> *Maita, maita, maita;*
> *Bera, bera, bera;*
> *Biamu! Biamu! Biamu!*
> *Patimu! Patimu! Patimu!*
> *E—O—E—O—E—O!!*

When the women could keep it up no longer they hopped away to the well and washed their bodies.

Next day Möibu lay with his head in his wife's lap for her to rid him of lice, and he saw paint marks round her eyes. Then he knew that the frog play had been acted out by the women.

The more he thought over it during the next few days, the more he felt the women would have to be given a lesson that they would never forget. An idea began to form inside his head. Now he had it. This was a punishment fit for women who mocked at men.

He found Bazi and told him. Bazi agreed that such behaviour from the women was not to be endured or forgotten. They put their heads together, and the plan grew down to the last detail.

In the morning Möibu and Bazi ordered every man and boy at Boigu to set out on a hunting trip.

They went to Kerpai and hunted.

They went to Mawat and hunted.

They went to Baidam and hunted, to Samar, to Kupugud, to Köwe, and to Pali.

During the day they speared dugong; at night they cut them up and cooked them.

Möibu and Bazi now told the rest of the party to remain at Pali for two days while he and Bazi went hunting on their own. Möibu was ready for the next part of his plan.

He took some light wood—the very light wood called *buat*—and made from it a creature, the like of which had never been seen before. He put it on, climbed a tree and made a noise: "*Ti-i-i-i! Ti-i-i-i!*" He thought: "What am I? There has never been anything like this. I shall call myself a flying-fox. *Ti-i-i-i! Ti-i-i-i!*" He hid the form and rejoined Bazi.

Back at Pali the next evening after hunting all day, Möibu went inside the new form which he had created, and showed the men his flying-fox dance. He asked them what kind of bird they saw, and when they could not say, he told them. He told them he was a flying-fox and that they must do as he did. He told them everything.

The following night they set out for the village, Möibu in front and Bazi and the men and the boys behind. They were flying-foxes now.

They flew to the top of a *nabe* tree and broke off every leaf. They reached the big well and sat on the *dani* (wild fig) tree. They stripped it of all its leaves. When they came to the *dani* tree at the village, they did the same, flying round in circles and calling: *"Ti-i-i-i! Ti-i-i-i!"*

The women were afraid and begged Möibu's wife and Bazi's wife to tell them what kind of bird this was. "This is something new. We have never seen birds like this," they said.

Then Bazi came out of his flying-fox form and said: "Why are you so surprised at seeing flying-foxes? You made a frog play. We know all about it, for Möibu saw paint marks on his wife's face. We are going to punish you by going away to Daudai and never returning. Every man and boy now leaves Boigu. The male children as yet not born you may keep, but us you will never see as men again." And the flying-foxes flew off and headed west.

Across the sea on the banks of the Wasi Kösa, there lived a man named Bazi also, and the night the flying-foxes came to Daudai he dreamt. He saw them, Bazi leading, come to a dead *jangau* tree and fly into it one after the other, Möibu going in last. And in his dream he saw a man who told him he must do certain things the next day. He and his wife should go to their garden and dig yams and bananas and prepare as if for a feast.

When he woke he looked for the tree, going from this one to that until he found the right one. And just as he had dreamed, he reached down inside it, pulled out the first flying-fox, who was really Möibu, then the next one, and the next, and the next, until there were none left. He looked round, and there stood the Boigu men. He shook with fear.

But Möibu and Bazi said to the man from the Wasi Kösa: "Boigu is no longer our home. We stay here with you."

They came to the garden where the woman was preparing the feast, just as her husband had ordered her. He told her not to be afraid, and the men sat down and ate. This was their place now.

Möibu said: "It was my wife who told the other women to act the frog play. She did it because whenever I speared dugong I gave her only bones, liver, guts, and ribs, never the fat. Nevertheless they should not have made fools of us men, for that no woman may do."

THE DISCOVERY
OF THE GARDEN LAND
AT PADIN [Told by Judah Ganaia at Boigu, 21 September 1967]

Daleko lived at the eastern end of Boigu at a place called Baidam. His two sisters, Kaku and Winama, were the wives of Uwagu who lived at Sere, west of Baidam.

One day, Kaku and Winama walked to a nearby river and followed it inland. They came to land which was suitable for making gardens[1] and hurried back to Sere where their husband, Uwagu, was busy making a canoe. The two women did not mention their discovery to him, but announced that they were going to Baidam to take *kutai* (a variety of yam) to their brother. They did not give the true reason for their visit to Daleko, that they wanted to tell him about the new garden-land.

The sisters spent the night with their brother and returned to Sere next morning. Daleko accompanied them. Kaku and Winama now told Uwagu about their discovery the previous day. Uwagu stopped working on his canoe, and the four walked to Padin to apportion the new garden-land. Daleko claimed the greater share; Kaku and Winama were left with a small part only.

Daleko spent the night at Sere and returned to Baidam the following day. His sisters stayed with their husband at Sere.

1. At Padin.

KERERUM [Told by Moses Dau at Boigu, 10 October 1968]

Kererum and his wife, Muikup, lived inside the hollow trunk of a *kuzub* tree which grew close to the water's edge at Samar. They had two daughters, Buia and Kokaper.

During the day Kererum used to fish on the reef outside Samar. When he brought back the fish he had caught, his wife cooked them, and the family ate them. The only time the girls spent outside the *kuzub* tree was while they were eating. The colour of their skin was pale from their prolonged confinement to the *kuzub* tree for safety's sake.

Kererum made up his mind to find out if there was anyone living near Samar. One night while his wife and daughters were asleep, he walked east to Baidam and from there looked across to Mawat, where, at that time, a number of people had homes. He returned to Samar and said nothing about his discovery to his wife and daughters, either then or later.

The people at Mawat caught many different kinds of fish. Kererum caught only three kinds: *kurup* (coral cod), *teibu keibu* (sand flathead), and *badar* (striped angler). When the people of Mawat came in from fishing, their baskets were full. Every night they slept soundly because they lay down with full stomachs.

Kererum paid a second visit to Mawat at night and, when he was sure that everyone in the village was asleep, stole to the food racks and removed choice, cooked fish. These fish he took back to Samar and gave to his wife and daughters.

After that Kererum went to Mawat every night and stole from the food racks. The people could not understand how the choice fish which they had set aside for the morning meal always disappeared while they slept. Eventually an old man stayed awake one night and watched. So it was that he saw Kererum appear, remove the fish, and make off with them. He followed Kererum to Samar and saw him go inside a hollow *kuzub* tree.

In the morning, the old man told the people of Mawat about Kererum, and the men went in a body to Samar. They set fire to the tree which housed Kererum and his family.

Kererum and his wife, Muikup, and their two daughters, Buia and Kokaper, came out. When the men of Mawat saw the young girls they wanted them. But Buia and Kokaper were not willing, and they attempted to escape by climbing up to a branch of the tree while Kererum, his wife beside him, was confessing to the theft of the fish.

Kererum and Muikup tried to save their daughters but were killed by the men of Mawat. Buia and Kokaper then leapt into the fire and burnt to death.

BUKIA

[Told by Moses Dau at Boigu, 10 October 1968]

Soon after they were married, a man and woman left their home at Boigu and crossed to Daudai, where they settled among the Wasi people. They built their home on the outskirts of the village. When a son was born to them they gave him the name, Bukia. The child had copper-coloured hair.

When the child was old enough to use a bow and arrows his father made a set for him. To begin with, Bukia shot birds; later, he shot bandicoots; before very long he could shoot pigs.

The father died while Bukia was still a boy.

One night he came to Bukia in a dream and told him to go to a certain place. There, he said, Bukia would see many pigs. Bukia was to take with him the arrow with magical killing power which he, Bukia's father, had made for his son before he died. Bukia was to tell no one of the dream lest it come to the ears of the sorcerers who lived in the village.

In the morning, Bukia went to the place described to him in the dream and shot a pig. He took it home to his mother.

Bukia returned to this place again and again, and shot a number of pigs every time he went there—four, or perhaps five, at each visit. One day he shot ten pigs—the men in the village were in luck if between them they brought back one pig at the end of a day's hunt. Another day he shot eleven pigs. The Wasi men decided it was time to find out where Bukia hunted, so they sent a man to ask him.

Bukia and his mother fed the man well and told him what he wanted to know. The man spread the news round the village, adding that he had seen the pigs which Bukia had shot that day—all were fat. The men were incredulous.

Again Bukia's father visited his son in a dream. He told him that he must now go to a different place to hunt. There Bukia had the same kind of success as he had enjoyed at the first place revealed to him by his father's ghost.

Meanwhile, the men in the village continued to have as little luck as they had had in the past. They went to Bukia's former hunting ground, believing that they would shoot many pigs, many fat pigs, but found very few, fat or thin. They were bitterly jealous of Bukia. They sent another man to ask where he was hunting, and then two sorcerers—Bukia's uncles by adoption—took a hand.

The next time Bukia went to hunt, his uncles—the sorcerers—changed themselves into boars, passed him unseen and were waiting for him when he reached the spot that had been revealed to him by his father in the second dream. At the instant of releasing the arrow made for him by his father before he died, Bukia's bow snapped in two. The boars attacked Bukia and savaged him, ripping him with their tusks. They kept at it until he lay dying.

Bukia called many times to his mother: "*Bukia, Bukia mari. Bukia waradima.* (Bukia is a ghost. Carry him home.)"

When her son failed to return, the mother became worried and set out to look for her son. Once she thought she heard his voice, and stopped to listen, but the sound was not repeated, and she decided that what she had heard was two branches of a tree rubbing against each other in the wind. She went on and presently found her son's body.

She wove a basket, placed her son in it and carried him home. She set him down on the ground while she heaped firewood around and on top of their *saualag* (the shelter in which a man stores everything that he has grown in his garden), and then she set fire to it. At the height of the blaze, she threw her dead son into the flames and leapt in after him.

WAWA [Told by Moses Dau at Boigu, 10 October 1968]

Early one morning a man who lived in a village in coastal Daudai walked down to the beach and saw a pair of mating turtles not far out from the shore. He needed help to bring them in, so he called: "*Kaimeg o! Kaimeg o! Ngabanai ipal walwal saiwal kab o!* (Friend! Friend! There are mating turtles here for us.)" No one answered from the village. He called again: "*Kaimeg o! Kaimeg o! Ngabanai ipal walwal saiwal kab o!*" Still there was no reply from the men in the village.

However, his cries had been heard by a *wawa*—a giant, of whom there are many in bush places—who, armed with bow and arrow, came out to see what was going on. The man was terrified. "What are you going to do with me?" he quavered. The *wawa* said: "You called for help, so I came."

The man offered the male turtle to the *wawa* as return for his help; but that did not please the *wawa*, who insisted that he must have the female; and since the man was in no position to bargain he had to yield to the *wawa*'s demand.

No sooner had agreement been reached than the *wawa* said: "Go and bring them in yourself, one at a time." When both turtles lay on the beach, the *wawa* said: "Cut them up." And when the flesh had been removed from both shells, the *wawa* said: "Make earth-ovens and cook the turtles." The man grumbled about having to do all the work, but it made no difference: if the giant from the bush gave an order, the man had no choice but to obey.

At last there was nothing left to do but wait for the turtles to cook. Worn out, the man sat down to rest. "Rid my head of lice," said the *wawa*. So the man searched for lice in the *wawa*'s head—and caught so many that they filled the two halves of a coconut shell.

Now while the man was engaged in cleaning the *wawa*'s head of hair—which was full of earth as well as lice—the *wawa* fell asleep. He was snoring loudly when the turtles had finished cooking. The man said to a louse which he had removed from the *wawa*'s head: "Presently the *wawa* will wake up and call out to me. When he does so, answer him with these words: 'I am still here.' " And then he quickly removed the female turtle from the earth-oven in which it had been cooked and hurried back to the village with it.

He told the people everything that had happened during the day. "We must build a house on very high stilts," he urged, "and we must build it quickly. The *wawa* is enormous. He will surely come here looking for me when he wakes and finds that I took the female turtle."

When the *wawa* woke up he could not see the man, so he called out to him: "Where are you?" The louse answered: "I am still here." And hearing that, the *wawa* went back to sleep. The next time the *wawa* woke up he was feeling hungry, so he went straight to the earth-oven in which the female turtle had been placed to cook. He was furiously angry to find nothing but an empty hole in the ground.

He summoned every bush giant in the neighbourhood and together they marched on the village, singing as they went:

> *Burum muli muli mu*
> *Pai muli (e)*
> (We demand a pig. We demand a pig.)

The people in the village heard the *wawa* coming and took shelter in

226

the house that they had just finished building. The *wawa* and his fellows surrounded it, still chanting,

> *Burum muli muli mu*
> *Pai muli (e),*

so the people threw them a pig. But it was not a pig that the head *wawa* really wanted, and he let it lie on the ground.

> *Usar muli muli mu*
> *Pai muli (e),*
> (We demand a kangaroo. We demand a kangaroo.)

chorused the *wawa* and all his friends. So the people threw out a kangaroo. The *wawa* had no interest in the kangaroo.

> *Mabaig muli muli mu*
> *Pai muli (e),*
> (We demand a human. We demand a human.)

shouted the *wawa*, and they kept on shouting until, in the end, the people threw them a child.

There were no more demands from the *wawa*—he had had his revenge on the man who had stolen the female turtle from the earth-oven. He and his companions shot arrows at the child and killed it, and then they went back to their homes in the bush.

DARAK AND GÖIDAN [Told by Judah Ganaia at Boigu, 16 August 1966]

Göidan and his wife Darak lived at Boigu Village.

Darak fell sick. After a long illness, she died one day when Göidan was away fishing on the opposite side of the island at a place called Sere. Her ghost, who looked exactly like Darak in life, immediately went to Sere and sat on the branch of a tree. She watched Göidan, who was out on the reef. But as Göidan never once looked in at the shore, he did not see his wife's ghost until he came in from fishing, and then he thought she was his wife in the flesh.

227

He was amazed to see Darak, for when he had left her that morning she was too weak to move hand or foot. He ordered her to return to Boigu Village, but she did not go. He walked to Padin, and she followed him.

Göidan lit a fire and cooked some of the fish he had caught, the whole time watching Darak from the corner of his eye. After he had eaten the fish he told her to wait at Padin while he fetched some water and then hurried away from the wife who was behaving so strangely. He bent low over the pool to scoop up water and saw, looking up at him from the surface of the water, his wife's face. Not his wife's face, but that of her ghost! Göidan ran, his only thought to reach his home at Boigu Village. And as he fled across the island through the swamps he was pursued by his wife's ghost.

Though fear drove him, he could not outrun her, for when she came to swamps and bogs she sank into them and travelled direct below ground— whereas Göidan had either to squelch through mud or take a long way round to avoid it. Thus when Darak's ghost was at the garden-land called Kausaraltoga and saw Göidan ahead at Gebalap, she sank straight down into the mud and very soon afterwards came up at Gebalap. Seeing Göidan still ahead of her at Gud, on the far side of another swamp, she went down again and came up at Gud. By then, Göidan had reached Kuituriabu.

His feet found the poles laid lengthwise which form the track through a big mangrove swamp and carried him to the grassland and gardens beyond. Ahead of him the path divided, one arm going to Boigu Village, the other to the sea. Breathless, witless, he sped towards the beach. He saw that his wife's body had been placed upon a platform (*sara*) at Kawatag— and he also saw her ghost standing beside the platform. He ran straight past both. At last he reached the beach.

Darak's ghost was waiting for him. She came towards him and killed him with a turtle-hook.

The people watching from the village did not see Darak's ghost throw the turtle-hook—all they saw was a swirl of sand between them and Göidan. They ran to meet Göidan, only to find his lifeless body with a turtle-hook in it.

PODEPODE AND
NGUKURPODEPODE [Told by Ganadi Toby at Boigu, 21 September 1967]

A long time ago there were two brothers living at Mawat (on Boigu). Ngukurpodepode, the elder brother (*kuikuig*), was bitterly jealous of Podepode, the younger brother (*kutaig*). Podepode had a very beautiful wife whom he, Ngukurpodepode, coveted, although he had a wife of his own; Podepode was more successful at hunting dugong than he; Podepode never shared with him the meat and fat of the dugong that he caught . . . In short, Ngukurpodepode hated his younger brother.

One day while Podepode was out on the reef looking for grass that had been newly grazed by a dugong, Ngukurpodepode decided to kill him by sorcery.

That afternoon, Podepode erected a *nat* on the reef close to where it was expected a dugong would resume feeding at the next high tide and told his helpers that he would need them very early that evening. Shortly after sundown Podepode climbed up on to the *nat*. His helpers waited nearby in a canoe, ready to go to Podepode's aid immediately he called out.

Before long the dugong came close to the *nat* on which Podepode stood waiting. It came to the surface twice to breathe. When it came up the third time, Podepode hurled his *wap* at it—the *wap* bounced straight back at him, striking his throat with such force that it killed him at the instant of impact.

Podepode had shouted as he threw the *wap*. The men waiting in the canoe heard him and immediately began to pole towards the *nat*. Very soon, however, they became filled with anxiety: expecting every moment to hear another shout from Podepode, they heard nothing—nothing at all. When they reached the *nat* they saw that the rope was still on top of it, uncoiled; there was no sign of Podepode. Presently they recovered his body from the water and took it in to Mawat. Then the wailing began. It continued all night long.

Next day the relatives of Podepode prepared a feast. It was attended by many people from Boigu Village, who returned to their home on the opposite side of the island when it was over, leaving behind at Mawat Ngukurpodepode, and Podepode's widow who stayed to mourn beside the *sara* on which Podepode's body had been laid.

Hardly were they out of sight when Ngukurpodepode began to solicit the woman. She refused him, so he raped her. Afterwards she fled from him, running across the island with all speed for the protection of her people at Boigu Village. All alone now at Mawat, Ngukurpodepode began to eat his brother's corpse.

Presently Ngukurpodepode changed into an eagle and flew after the woman. He overtook her at Baidam, changed to human form, and had connection with her. Then he changed into an eagle and flew back to Mawat where, as a human, he resumed eating his brother.

Ngukurpodepode interrupted his meal many times, always to fly to the woman. He caught her at Murigiai, Samar, Iubu, Gibu, Marapiltoga, Kabailtoga, Bedaltoga, and Mai Kibu.[1] Podepode's wife ran as hard as she could, but she was no match for Ngukurpodepode, who as an eagle could reach her swiftly whenever he chose. And every time after he had been with her, he flew back to Mawat and continued eating. When he returned from Mai Kibu, he began to eat all that was left of Podepode—his head.

Podepode's widow was seen by her people at Boigu Village as she sped along the path from Mai Kibu. When they heard her story, the men armed themselves and went to Böibil Gizu to watch for Ngukurpodepode the next time he came over.

Ngukurpodepode flew from Mawat to Mai Kibu, changed into a man, and set out for Boigu Village. The men who had been waiting for him let him walk as far as Dawa Iabu and then they killed him. Ngukurpodepode was glad to die.

1. The big well from which the people of Boigu Village obtain their water.

MAUI AND USURU

[Told by Moses Dau at Boigu, 9 August 1966]

A long time ago at Boigu there were two brothers, Maui and Usuru. Maui, the elder brother, had a wife, but Usuru was still a single man. They had an unmarried sister whose name was Bumai.

Usuru, an expert dugong-hunter, was always out hunting, and during his absence from Boigu on an expedition to Warul Kawa (Deliverance Island) one time, Bumai was married. The first he knew of it was the night of his return, when his friends hurried to him and whispered: "Your sister is married."

Usuru was furious, his rage being principally directed at his elder brother. Maui was already a married man, but he, Usuru, was still single—what chance was there now of obtaining a wife since he had no sister to give as bride-replacement?[1]

The next night he sailed to Dauan. He went to the place where the skulls were kept and told the men who were sitting down there what had happened. They gave him *gamada* (a drink made from the root of a New Guinea plant of the same name), and after it had taken hold of him he said: "Come with me. Let us kill the men at Boigu." But the men of Dauan replied: "We cannot do that. Those men are our friends."

Usuru left Dauan and sailed to Saibai. There, also, he went to the house[2] where the men stayed and asked for help at Boigu. "We will not go to Boigu," these men said. "The people of Boigu are our friends."

Usuru always travelled at night. The following night he set out from Saibai to seek help from the men of Kiwai. On the way he decided to call at "Old Mawat"[3] and see if the men of that place would take his side against Maui. They refused, and he went on to Kiwai, the home of fierce fighting-men.

There, when Usuru told of his wrongs and asked for help at Boigu, the men drank *gamada*—which made them wild—and said: "We will go with you." And as soon as they had prepared their canoes for the journey, they set out. They landed on the southern side of the island at Mawat and slept. When they woke Usuru said: "Come with me."

The men of Kiwai followed him across the island by way of Köi Kösa to the almond tree at Kadal Bupur where all the Boigu men were asleep in one house. Usuru took Maui by surprise, waking him and then striking him between the eyes with his club. At that, all the Boigu men sprang to their feet and said: "Why did you do that?" When Usuru replied, "Because of Bumai," they had nothing to say. Usuru cut off his brother's head. Then he wept.

Through his tears Usuru signalled with his eyes to the men of Kiwai that they were to go their canoes. He went with them, having now to repay the help given to him.

This he did by fighting and killing enemies of the men of Kiwai in Daudai during the period of blood lust which he experienced after killing his brother. He fought all the way to the Fly River, killing so often that all men feared him. On the way back, still fighting and killing, he was often attacked, and sorcerers tried their skills to encompass his death. But every attempt to bring him down failed, because he himself understood the art of sorcery. At Jibar he spared only the very old men. After that, suddenly he had had enough of killing.

Usuru then went to Mawat[4] and stayed with the people of that place.

1. An informant at Boigu said: "If a girl is taken from one tribe, she has to be replaced by a girl from the tribe to which she goes as a bride. There would be nothing left of a tribe if this were not done. The tribe would become weak." Another informant said that marriage was a reciprocal arrangement between the two families concerned. ("Tribe" is habitually used in the broken English of Torres Strait to designate a totemic group of people.)
2. A long house with a thatched, grass roof.
3. On the coast of Papua, opposite the island of Daru.
4. Opposite Daru.

231

For a long time he provided them with food, spearing fish for them daily, and hunting turtle and dugong for them at Wapa reef. After a while he began to think: "I have fed these people well, but they have not given me a wife. I shall go back to Boigu." The people of Mawat, however, did not want him to leave, so one of the men gave his sister to Usuru.

After three sons had been born to Usuru and his wife—Kibar, Kabai, and Sigai—and a fourth child conceived, Usuru had a longing to visit Boigu. So he set out, taking his wife and children with him. At the end of the first day's journey, he ran his canoe ashore and, after telling his family to remain with it until he returned, walked to Jibar and made peace with the people there.

Usuru came home to Boigu, and his daughter, Bumai, was born amongst his own people. He left her with them when he returned to Mawat. Many people living at Boigu today are descended from Usuru through Bumai.

MAU AND MATANG

[Told by Moses Dau at Boigu, 11 August 1966]

Long ago there were two warrior brothers of Boigu, Mau and Matang. Mau was the elder brother. They fought for the love of fighting, and very often for no other reason.

One day they received a message from their friend Mau of Arudaru, which is in Daudai[1] just across from Boigu. Mau bade them come quickly for yams and taro, which would otherwise be eaten by pigs.

Mau and Matang made ready to go to Arudaru.

Their sister wove the sails for their canoes. At mid-afternoon, just as she had completed them, she noticed a big stain of blood on one mat. She hurried to her brothers to tell them about it and so try to prevent them from setting out on their voyage.

Mau and Matang would not heed the warning sign, and they set off with their wives and children. They reached Daudai and spent the first night at Kudin. During the night Mau's canoe drifted away. The brothers sent the crew to search for it, and they came upon it at Zunal, the sandbank of *markai* (spirits of the dead).

1. The mainland of New Guinea.

232

As they drew close, they saw the ghost of Mau appear in front of the canoe. In its hand was a dugong spear decorated with cassowary feathers. The ghost went through the motions of spearing a dugong, then placed the spear in the canoe and vanished.

Next they saw Matang's ghost pick up the spear from the canoe, just as Mau's had done. It too made as if to spear a dugong. Then it replaced the spear in the canoe and faded from sight.

On reaching the canoe, the crew members found the spear in it.

On their return to Kudin they told Mau and Matang what had happened. The brothers were sceptical and refused also to heed this warning. They ordered the party to set out for Arudaru, which they reached after a day's walk.

The head man of Arudaru, whose name also was Mau, greeted them, with his own people and many others, gave them food, and said that he would give them the yams and taro the following day. With that the Boigu people slept.

In the morning they woke to a deserted village. Only Mau of Arudaru remained. He gave them breakfast and then presented Mau and Matang with a small bunch of green bananas: it was a declaration of war.

Despite the friendship between Mau of Arudaru and the brothers Mau and Matang, the brothers had lightly killed kinsmen and friends of his, and the first duty of Mau of Arudaru was to avenge them. The invitation to come across for yams and taro had been part of a considered plan.

For days past fighting men from the neighbouring villages had been gathering at Arudaru. There had been endless talking until the whole plan had ripened.

With rage in their hearts, Mau and Matang herded their party together and set out on the return journey.

Mau of Arudaru had hidden his fighting men in two rows in the long grass so as to form two rows of unseen men. He allowed the brothers to lead their people back until they were halfway through the lines of fighting men. Then he gave the signal to attack.

The Boigu people were trapped. The women and children and the crew members fled. Mau bade his brother break the first spear thrown at him. He himself with his bow warded off the first spear that was hurled at him, splitting the end and throwing it backwards between his legs, thus giving himself good luck in battle.

Matang warded off the first spear received by him, but did not break it as Mau had commanded.

Before long Matang was struck in the ankle by a *kimus*, the most deadly arrow. "I have been bitten by a snake," he cried, and fell dead.

Mau continued to fight and kept backing towards his brother's body until he stood astride it. He fought until nearly all his assailants lay dead. The rest would have fled, but Mau signalled to them to put an end to him, so that he might join his brother. And this they did.

Mau and Matang did not have their heads cut off as would have been done were they ordinary men. Their courage and skill in battle were honoured by their opponents. They sat the brothers against two trees. They tied their bodies to the tree-trunks, facing them south towards Boigu. On their heads they placed the warrior's head-dress of black cassowary feathers and eagles' wings, so that when the wind blew from the south the eagles' wings were fanned backward and when it dropped, they fell forward.

AUSI AND
DUBUA
[Told by Moses Dau at Boigu, 10 October 1966]

Ausi and Dubua were brothers. They lived in a village on the island of Kiwai.

One day, Ausi, the elder brother, asked Dubua if he would wrap a bunch of bananas for him. Dubua agreed and the following day went to Ausi's garden to do it. He did not know that Ausi had preceded him there and concealed himself in a patch of banana suckers.

Dubua made a ladder, placed it against the trunk of the banana tree, climbed up, and began to wrap the bananas. As he made the second turn of the dry banana leaves used for wrapping, Ausi shot an arrow into the right side of his body, piercing him to the heart. Dubua fell to the ground dead.

A ghost now, Dubua presently got to his feet, broke off the shaft of the arrow—leaving the arrowhead embedded inside him—and went home to his wife. He told her they were leaving Kiwai. Together they loaded their canoe in preparation for the journey. They departed at sunset, to sail west along the coast of Daudai.

Dubua did not put in at any of the places where people lived, sailing straight past Mawat and Mabudauan and the island of Saibai. When they ran short of water he made a landing at a lonely spot, took the empty coconut shell water-vessels ashore, and went off alone. Out of sight of his wife, he withdrew the arrowhead from the hole made by Ausi's murderous shot, and filled the vessels with the watery fluid which drained from his body. Afterwards he replaced the arrowhead in the wound and went back to the canoe.

The woman was curious to know where they were going and, as they passed village after village without calling or stopping, asked again and again where their journey would end. On and on they sailed—past Boigu and Kawa and Pab—until they reached Milita Kasa.[1]

Dubua made his last landing. This time when he removed the arrowhead from his body to fill the coconut shells, the fluid from his body was putrid and foul. He did not seal up the wound as he had on the previous occasions. Instead, he walked back to the canoe with the arrowhead in his hands and gave it to his wife. He now told her the whole story.

"Leave me," he ordered, "and go to Boigu. There you will be delivered of our son whom you shall name Dubua. Remain at that island until the child has become a man, and then tell him to go to Kiwai and kill Ausi exactly as Ausi killed me."

Dubua stayed at Milita Kasa when his wife set sail for Boigu.

Her crew were ghosts. Some of them left the canoe at Sapural Kawa, others at Tabul Kawa Gizu. There were none aboard when she passed Kawatag and ran in to land at Gerwai.[2]

The Boigu people met her. When they heard her story they took her in to live with them until her son became a man. Then, as her husband had instructed, she told the young Dubua to go to Kiwai and avenge his father's death.

Mother and son departed for Kiwai and reached that island at night. Next morning Dubua sought out an uncle—not Ausi—and asked him to fit a shaft to the arrowhead that his mother had given him. When this was done, Dubua went to Ausi and asked if he would go to his garden and wrap a bunch of bananas the following day. Ausi agreed.

Dubua had concealed himself in a patch of banana suckers before Ausi arrived. He watched his uncle make a ladder, place it against the trunk of a banana tree, climb it, and begin to wrap the bunch of bananas. As Ausi was making the second turn with the dry banana leaves used for wrapping, Dubua shot him in the right side with the arrowhead that had killed his father.

Dubua walked back to the village. "Who wishes to take the part of Ausi?" he asked. The men were silent. No one spoke up. All knew why Ausi had died in his garden that day.

Dubua and his mother settled down in the village at Kiwai.

1. The river just beyond the village called Mari.
2. The new part of the present-day village on Boigu.

235

DUGAMA, MAKER OF DUGONG MAGIC

[Told by Moses Dau at Boigu, 10 October 1968]

At Boigu there are four small stone dugong which are used to call dugong and ensure successful dugong-hunting. This story is an account of the dugong-magic practised by a man named Dugama.

Dugama was expert at making dugong-magic.

When he was approached by a man who wanted to become a successful dugong-hunter, this is what he did:

He went to the stone dugong which is kept in the scrub at Samar[1] and turned it so that its head pointed north. Next he assembled all the bones of a dugong in their correct order on the ground beside the stone dugong. Then he decorated his body with leaves of the yellow-flowering hibiscus.

Now Dugama knelt beside the stone dugong and anointed it first with coconut oil and then with black ash obtained from burnt coconut shells and kernels. Using *parma* (red ochre or clay), he drew a stripe from tail to mouth of the stone dugong. He drove a stake into the ground beside its head, decorated the stake with hibiscus leaves, and hung a *damab*[2] on it. And when all that had been done he sang the song which calls dugong to Boigu.

The following morning he sent a man ("a spy") to examine the reef for signs that dugong had grazed during the night. Should this man find an area where the reef grass had been nipped off, he had to take back some of the grass which grew near it. This grass Dugama placed on the ground at the mouth of the stone dugong. He then whispered into its ear, telling it to call up more dugong.

The next morning the man had to go to the reef again for Dugama. If he reported that dugong had answered the second call, Dugama turned the stone dugong so that its head pointed east of the spot at which the dugong (one or many) had stopped feeding the previous night.

The aspiring hunter presented himself at Samar the morning of the third day. He brought with him his *wap* (heavy spear into which the harpoon, *kuir*, is inserted) and touched it to the stone dugong several times. Afterwards he rubbed the *wap* with coconut oil.

That night Dugama accompanied the hunter to the reef. Dugama took the *damab* and, from a position to the side of the hunter on his *nat*, used it to waft the dugong towards the hunter.

Dugama's magic never failed. That night the hunter speared a female dugong with a baby inside it. When it was cut up, Dugama removed the

1. On the southern side of Boigu.
2. A *damab* is a dugong's windpipe which has been stuffed with flowers of *pog* (a palm which grows in New Guinea) and wrapped round with hibiscus leaves.

grass from the dugong's mouth, with that action ensuring that this hunter would have future success as a hunter of dugong.

Dugama's knowledge of dugong-magic has been handed down from generation to generation among the people at Boigu who have *sam* (cassowary) for *augad*.

The stone dugong at Samar used in making dugong-magic

BABAIA AND SAGEWA

[Told by Moses Dau at Boigu, 10 October 1968]

Ukasar	*mabaig*	*kau*	*Boigulaig,*	*palamun*	*nel*	*ipal*
(Two	people	here	Boigu people,	their	names	here)

keda:	*kuikuig,*	*Babaia;*	*kutaig,*	*Sagewa.*
(thus:	eldest brother,	Babaia;	youngest brother,	Sagewa.)

★

There were two brothers at Boigu named Babaia and Sagewa. Babaia was the elder brother.

The younger brother, Sagewa, was a cripple who could not even walk. He went to Milita Kasa on the Papuan mainland[1] and trained in sorcery. After that he could change into a pig or an eagle or a crocodile whenever he wanted to, and in any one of those animal forms travel much faster than men who had full use of their limbs.

One time when the men of Boigu Village went by canoe to Köwe on the opposite side of the island to hunt dugong, poling their way to that place by way of Köi Kösa,[2] Sagewa, who had been left behind in the village, changed into a pig, ran all the way, and arrived at Köwe before they did.

One morning while they were camped at Köwe, Dugama—the man who made strong dugong-magic—saw freshly grazed grass on the reef. With the help of some of the men who had come to hunt, he erected a dugong platform just beyond the spot at which the dugong had left off feeding at the end of the previous high tide.

At mid-day, when the reef was again covered by the sea, Dugama climbed to the top of the platform to wait for the dugong to come and resume feeding. He tied a *damab* (a dugong-charm)[3] to the platform. His helpers were waiting in a canoe nearby, ready to come to his aid when he called them.

The dugong came in before long. Dugama waved it towards him with the *damab* and harpooned it—a fat, female dugong with a baby inside it. (Dugama was always successful when he hunted. His *damab* enticed dugong away from the platform of other hunters and, as well, ensured that every dugong he caught was a fat one.)

While the cutting-up was in progress, Sagewa put in an appearance and demanded certain bones as his share of the kill. Babaia refused to let him

1. Just beyond the village of Mari.
2. The big channel which divides Boigu in two.
3. See "Dugama, Maker of Dugong-Magic", in this section.

238

have them and, when Sagewa argued with him about it, struck his younger brother.

Sagewa crawled away to his sleeping-place beside the river at Köwe—he slept at some distance from the rest of the men—and used sorcery against Babaia.[4] It took effect when the men went for a swim in the sea after eating some of the dugong that Dugama had killed, causing Babaia to sink like a stone to the bottom of the water.

The men missed Babaia. They searched for him until they found him, and then they carried him ashore and laid him face downwards to let the water run out of him. When nothing they did revived him, they took his body back to their camp.

Presently Sagewa arrived there. At the time, Dugama was sharpening his tomahawk (*aga turik*, a European axe or tomahawk). The moment he saw Sagewa, he told him he would cut off his head with the tomahawk if he did not restore Babaia to life. Sagewa began by denying having used sorcery against his elder brother, but after a while he confessed and told the men to go away and leave him alone with Babaia.

When they were out of sight, a snake came up out of the ground at Babaia's feet and began to crawl along his body, licking every part of him from his feet to his head. When it reached his nose, it inserted its forked tongue in his nostrils, and Babaia stirred to life. Babaia then accused Sagewa of having used sorcery on him.

Sagewa said: "You treated me badly. You would not let me have the part of the dugong I wanted, so I punished you."

Babaia ordered that Sagewa be given the bones he had asked for. When that had been done, the men pushed their canoes into the water and poled back to Boigu Village. They did not take Sagewa with them, but left him behind at Köwe.

Sagewa changed into an eagle and flew to Toga, a place in the middle of the island. At Toga he changed into a pig, and then he ran the rest of the way home to Boigu Village and chased all the people. They were terrified —they knew that the pig was Sagewa.

4. *Nuid senau Babaian tidamair*
(He there Babaia used sorcery
si   muinu.
there inside there.)
The full meaning of this sentence is: "He [Sagewa] drew an outline of Babaia on the ground [or, perhaps, made another kind of likeness of his brother] inside [the place where he camped] and then performed on the figure the details of the evil which he intended should befall Babaia. While miming the calamity, Sagewa talked to the figure, commanded it, and addressed it with magic words as if it were Babaia in the flesh." The transitive verb *tidamair* conveys the exact nature of the kind of sorcery employed (here) by Sagewa. (*Babaian* is objective case of *Babaia*.)

239

GARUGE

[Told by Moses Dau at Boigu, 10 October 1968]

Garuge had a younger brother named Atau. Their *augad* was *kadal* (crocodile).

Their mother came from Top, the original home of the people who now live at Buzi, a Papuan village which can be seen from Boigu with the naked eye. Like his mother, Garuge had *gad* ("second skin"), a fungus-like growth which covered his whole body. He looked crinkled and grey all over.

Garuge and his wife lived at Sere. His wife fell ill. He looked after her for a long time, but eventually he became sick and tired of her. So, after digging a hole, he stood on her chest until she was dead. Then he buried her in the hole. Afterwards he bit his tongue in a fury of remorse.

Garuge's niece was away fishing when he killed his wife. Presently she came back, went to a basket that belonged to him and took something from it. Garuge saw her and asked what she had taken. The girl confessed and then went back to her fishing.

After she had gone, Garuge sharpened a knife and hid it under a mat.

When the girl returned to Sere late in the afternoon she was cold, so she squatted beside the fire and held out her hands to the flames to warm them. Garuge whipped the knife from under the mat and sliced the fingers from one of her hands.

People saw nothing unusual in what Garuge had done. He was a great warrior, and they were accustomed to his rages. He had many heads in the *sibui* (place where bones are heaped) at Kadal Bupur.

stories from the

CENTRAL ISLANDS

stories from

MASIG *Yorke Island*

During my stay at Yorke Island in July 1966, I drew a rough outline of the island to locate the places named for me by "Uncle" Lawrence Mosby and Langley Warria. Some of these names are Mabuiag (the language of the Eastern Islands of Torres Strait). They illustrate Haddon, I, 93: "Maino told me that the speech of the Masig people was half Miriam and half Western."

Some notes on the place names

PEDIG The stone called IKAN, used in "calling up" the wind, was formerly kept near PEDIG. IKAN today is to be seen in the porch of the church.

KANDARAWAL A bull-roarer (*bigu*) used to be hung from a tree here.

APASAU There was once a *zogo* stone at APASAU. The *zogo* was said to make coconuts plentiful. The stone was removed from Masig many years ago.

MUKUNKUP A diamond fish used to come ashore here at sunset. From this fish, a girl and a boy emerged each evening. They used to kick a red ball. They had long flat heads.

GARIBA A man by this name died here before Europeans came to Masig.

SANINLAG The place was named after a man named SANI.

UMI This is the spot, outside the home reef, where the Government supply boat anchors during the S.E. season. It was formerly the home of spirit women, UMI MARKAIL.

MUR At this spot, on the beach itself, dense *mur* bushes grow. (*Mur* is a tall, spreading shrub with small, pointed leaves.) The place, MUR, is mentioned in the story of "IGOWA".

SAU The rocky outcrop on the beach is a landmark on this coral cay. Here, three hero brothers, SAU, KULKA, and MALO are said to have landed —the fourth brother had stayed behind at YAM ISLAND. SAU remained at MASIG, KULKA went to AURID, MALO to MER.
The *markai* of the story of "IGOWA" lived at SAU. (*Markai*, ghost).

RISAU Prior to 1871, the *kod* was at RISAU. It was destroyed by the early missionaries.

MARUS This was once a village (I was told, "the first village").

GUDAMADU This was the site of the village in "Yankee Ned's" time.

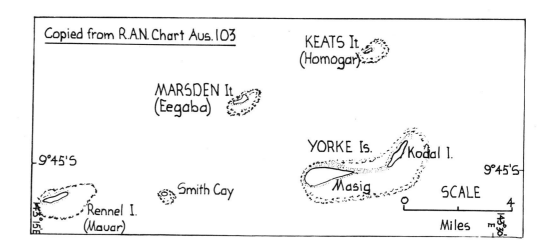

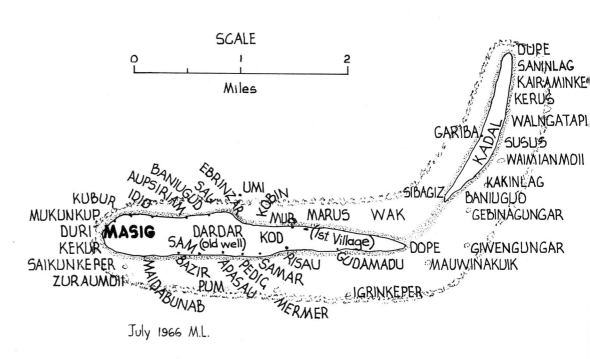

July 1966 M.L.

MASIG (Yorke Island)

IGOWA [Told by Ned Mosby at Yorke Island, 18 July 1966]

Igowa, head man of Masig, lived on the northern side of the island near the thicket of *mur* which grows across the beach almost to the water's edge. He had a fish spear which had four wooden prongs. He loved this spear, and so afraid was he of blunting its sharp tips that he never used it: he took it from its hiding place in the *mur* bushes and carried it when he walked about on the reef at low tide, but he only pretended to throw it.

Sometimes the people of Masig used to walk across to the neighbouring cay, Kadal, to fish, and camp there for several days. Igowa did not accompany them on these visits, remaining instead at Masig to keep an eye on things.

On one occasion when he was alone at Masig, he was disturbed to see canoes plying between the outcrop of rock on the beach at Sau (west of the *mur* bushes) and Umi, the anchorage off the edge of the home reef used during the season of south-east winds. So when he found a drifted log a few days later, he decided to use it as camouflage and go to Sau to discover what was going on. And this he did, pushing the log in to the beach after dark and watching from behind it.

He saw a *markai* camp and, later on, *markai* dancers. In the middle of the night a canoe ran in with turtle on board. Two *markai* who walked down to help unload it saw the log behind which Igowa was hiding and pushed it into the sea. As soon as they returned to their camp, Igowa came in and stole one of the turtles.

He took it to his people at Kadal and helped them place it in an earth-oven to cook. But when, early in the morning, the oven was opened, there was no turtle inside it. "Who gave you this turtle?" the people asked Igowa. And only then did he tell them about the *markai* camp at Sau, and that the turtle that he had given them was one brought back by *markai* hunters. Igowa said that he would go again to Sau and steal another turtle.

So the following evening Igowa crept up to the *markai* camp and hid beneath some dry coconut palm fronds. Presently the *markai* began to dance, but they stopped before long because they felt tired—a sign to them that a human was watching them. The *markai* leader ordered his men to search for this person.

They soon found Igowa and chased him away from Sau, beating him with sticks all the way along the beach to the thicket of *mur* bushes. There Igowa ran and got his spear and fought back against the *markai*. But they were too many for him, and soon he was again being beaten and chased by them. They kept at it until they reached the sandbank between Masig and Kadal, where they were seen by the people who were camped at Kadal. To them Igowa and the *markai* looked like a black cloud.

Igowa was in sorry plight when he reached his people and told them of his treatment by the *markai*. They tried to give him food to eat, but he refused it, saying that all he needed was sleep. In the morning he was dead.

The people wrapped him in a mat and took him by canoe to Sau. They buried him not far from the outcrop of rock on the beach.[1]

1. The reason for taking Igowa's body to Sau was that his sister had been buried there at some time prior to Igowa's discovery of the *markai* camp. One may still see Igowa's grave.

THE DIAMOND
FISH
[Told by Langley Warria at Yorke Island, 20 July 1966]

Once upon a time a diamond fish (*baldang*) lived on the reef at Mukunkup. Every evening at sunset it came ashore, and from it came a boy and girl who played on the beach. They used to kick a red ball.

These children had zebra stripes on their bodies. Each of them had a flat head (*palai sawiu kuikulnga*).

GAIBIDA

[Told by Langley Warria for Lawrence Mosby at Yorke Island, 20 July 1966]

A favourite pastime of the children who lived at Mauar (Rennel Island) was poking the midribs of coconut palm leaves into cracks in the ground.

Now there were *markai* living underneath Mauar, and one day, while a girl named Gaibida was playing this game, she pierced the soft spot of a *markai* baby's head and killed it. This so angered all the *markai* that they caused the ground to open wide and took Gaibida down to them.

Gaibida's parents became very worried when she failed to return as the day wore on and at sunset, when there was still no sign of her, they began to weep. No one had seen her since morning; only one thing could account for her continued absence: she had been stolen by *markai*. So late that night an attempt to frighten them into sending her back was made by blowing *bu* shells, but it was unsuccessful.

Gaibida's father approached the head sorcerer, a man named Zogo. "Will you find my daughter for me?" he asked.

Zogo rubbed his body with the scented root of the plant called *kusi-bagai*[1] and walked to the place where Gaibida had been playing that morning. There he saw a wide cleft in the ground—which told him how she had been taken to the *markai*'s home—and he went down it. He asked some *markai*: "Is Gaibida here?" But they only said, "Ch–ch–ch–ch," so he walked on until he came face to face with the head *markai*. "Will you tell me if Gaibida is here?" Zogo asked him. "Gaibida is here," said the *markai* leader. "Will you permit her to return to her parents?" Zogo requested him. "No," said the *markai* leader, "we will not permit her to return to her parents. She killed one of our babies this morning."

Zogo began to plead for Gaibida's release, and he kept on pleading until the *markai* leader told him to take the girl home.

Gaibida's parents were overjoyed when Zogo brought their daughter to them. They gave him a present of armshells.[2]

1. *Kaempferia* sp.
2. The armshells were made from the cone shell, *Conus leopardus* Röding.

UMI
MARKAIL

[Told by Langley Warria at Yorke Island, 20 July 1966]

Formerly at Masig there was a rule which forbade men to walk on the reef near Umi in the evening. The superstition clings that men should not sleep on deck when their ship anchors overnight at this spot. In addition, those who visit Umi should throw food or drink into the water for the spirit women at Mekei—failure to do so entails bad luck.

Amongst all the tales that I collected in Torres Strait there are only two about spirit women (*markai* [West Torres Strait], *lamar* [East Torres Strait]) who lived under the sea: "Umi Markail", told at Yorke Island (Masig), and "The Two Spirit Women of Daoma Kes", told at Stephens Island (Ugar). There is a reference to a *lamar* who lived under the sea in the story, "Wakai and Kuskus", told at Murray Island.

1. Iawasu was head man at Masig in 1871.

Spirit women used to live underneath a rock called Mekei at Umi, an anchorage at the edge of the reef which surrounds Masig. During the day they could sometimes be seen as seagulls, at others as women walking on the reef looking for bêche-de-mer. At night, however, it was their custom to go ashore as women. They always went to the spot known as Marus.

One of the spirit women of Umi became the wife of Iawasu.[1] She could spend the night with him, but she had always to return to Mekei before daylight.

stories from

IAMA *Turtlebacked Island or Yam Island*

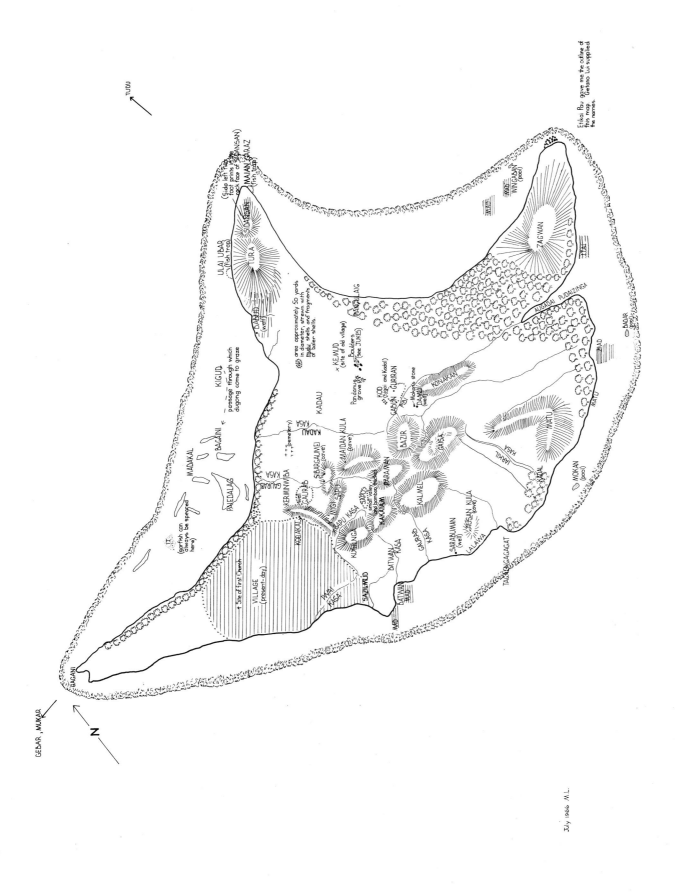

IAMA (Turtlebacked Island or Yam Island)

IAMA (Yam Island, or Turtlebacked Island) is a small island. Haddon gives its size as "about a mile in length and averaging half-a-mile or more in width". It is located at approximately 142° 47' East and 9° 55' South.

Jukes I, 155–57: "On Turtle-backed Island we found a few small groves of coconut trees near a group of huts, with a little thicket of bamboo . . . . [The huts] stood in a picturesque little spot, backed by some huge blocks of sienite, on which some large shells were arranged. About 50 yards from them, under some widely-spreading thick-leaved trees, with gnarled trunks and twisted boughs, were some great blocks of sienite, resting fantastically one upon another."

MOKAN

[Told by Asou Thaiday at Yam Island, 8 July 1966]

Long ago a man named Mokan lived at the foot of Tura, the hill at the northern tip of Yam Island. He had no wife.

Every day at low water, Mokan walked about on the reef shooting fish with his bow and arrows. When he had enough for his needs, he came ashore and cooked them in an earth-oven. After his meal he went to the well called Babud[1] for a drink.

One year *kuki*, the north-west wind, failed to bring rain, and Babud began to dry up. The day came when there was not a single drop of water left in it, as Mokan found after he had eaten a very big meal of fish. He had a raging thirst, so he set out to look for water in other parts of the island.

He walked to many places and had almost resigned himself to dying of thirst when he found a beautiful pool of clear water on a ridge in the centre of the island. He drank from it and wallowed in it and drank again, and then he floated on top of it—he was as fat as a dugong with all the water that he had drunk. And as he lay there, belly down, he sang a song:

> *Mokan wazider buzar köi buzar (e) dangal wazider (e),*
> *Mokanan nguki taraika köi gab.*

> (Here lies Mokan, his belly as big as a dugong's.
> Mokan is filled to overflowing with water,
> With water from Mokan's well.)

At last Mokan dragged himself out of the water-hole and lay down beside it to rest and gloat. After a while he swept the ground clean around it, and then he walked back to his home.

At this time, there also lived near Tura a woman named Geinau and her daughter Wiba, and they, too, were tortured by thirst. The girl begged her mother for water. "Mother," she moaned, "I am dying for want of water." And Geinau, herself parched and weak, yet found strength to sling *kusul* over her shoulders and go in search of it. At length she stumbled upon Mokan's pool. She drank from it, filled the *kusul*, and hurried back to her daughter.

When Mokan arrived at his pool the following morning, he noticed Geinau's footprints. He was furious at the thought of anyone but himself drinking this water and, as soon as he had quenched his thirst, hid behind

1. Babud is a small pool in the rocks on the seaward side of Tura, not very far above sea level.

251

some bushes in order to catch the thief. Presently Geinau appeared, and while she was drinking, he shot an arrow at her and killed her. He hid her body, swept around his pool, and went off singing, happy again because once more he alone knew about the beautiful water.

Wiba was desolate when Geinau failed to return by dark and, as soon as it was light enough to see next morning, found her mother's footprints and followed them. Thus, she in turn discovered Mokan's pool and, seeing the ground swept clean around it, immediately guessed that her mother had been killed and the reason why. Shortly afterwards, she found Geinau's body in some bushes. Wiba determined to avenge her mother, so she swept away all traces of her own visit and hid in nearby undergrowth to wait for the murderer.

Before long, Mokan came striding towards his pool. *"Mokan wazider,"* he was singing, *"buzar köi buzar."* He laid down his bow and arrows and entered the water, drank his fill, and then floated contentedly. He thought of Gelam who had called at Iama on his way to Mer. Was he, Mokan, not like Gelam, the boy who became a dugong? *"Mokanan nguki taraika köi gab,"* he warbled.

Wiba crept from her hiding place, snatched up Mokan's bow and arrows and shot him as he lay face down in his pool. Then she filled her *kusul* and walked home to Tura.

Mokan, mortally wounded, clambered from the water and turned to stone.

The names of the characters in this myth are interesting. *Mokan* is also the name of an inedible fish, a "sea toad", which, when disturbed or hooked on a line, puffs itself up to several times its normal size. *Geinau* is the name of the Torres Strait pigeon, and *Wiba*, I was told, is a "blue dove".

Until recently, it was customary to pour a little water on the stone which once was Mokan every time water was drawn from his pool. If this were not done, it was thought that the pool might go dry: Mokan must not be allowed to go thirsty; otherwise he would cause all the water to disappear.

Mokan's pool is still the principal source of water for the people of Yam Island. But they no longer draw water by hand—there is an engine and pump at the pool, and the water is piped to the village.

SIGAI   [Told by Getano Lui at Yam Island, 5 July 1966]

1. Baidam (shark) was used by Getano Lui as an alternative name for Kulka. See the story, "Malo", in the Eastern Islands section.
2. Utu is a small island off Tidiu reef, south of Iama (Yam Island). There are said to be many snakes on this island.

There were once four brothers, Sigai, Malu, Sau, and Kulka,[1] each of them a powerful man well-versed in magic. They took counsel amongst themselves one day at Utu[2] and reached a decision of great importance.

Hitherto they had worked together wherever they went. They would now part, each going to a different island. In this way they would spread their influence over a far greater domain, for they and the people who followed their rule would be united by the common bond of brotherhood. When Sigai was asked where he intended to go, he pointed his nose towards Yam Island.

At sunset of the same day Sigai took on the form of a canoe and set sail. He arrived off Zagwan[3] during the night, and, the tide being low, remained outside the reef until daybreak.

A woman named Pasia came early round the hill called Tura, searching the reef for octopus. To her wonder and delight she saw a strangely beautiful canoe close to the edge of the reef. She and her husband were in luck, for it must have drifted down from Daudai,[4] and she, having chanced upon it first, could claim it as theirs.

As Pasia ran towards it, it began to sink. By the time she reached the place where she had seen it there was nothing of it left, but she saw instead a pool of murky water where there had been no pool before.[5]

Sadly she turned back towards Tura. She was in a state of bewilderment. It was not to be believed that the canoe should have disappeared completely. She had seen it—there, quite plainly, at the edge of the reef off Zagwan. Pasia looked again at the spot, and stopped dead: the canoe rode there as before.

She ran towards it again. Again, as she did so, the canoe disappeared.

This was beyond her understanding. She ran to tell her husband at once.

Pasia's husband, Garu, called the men together. Here was a matter for weighty discussion at the kod,[6] and thither they went. They would seek the advice of those versed in magic.

The following morning their leader ordered every man to fill his iana[7] with scented leaves and bark, boars' tusks, and oils. They should arm themselves as if for war and go to the pool in the reef at Zagwan.

Pasia would lead the way, for it was she who had made the discovery. Garu, her husband, should go next in line, then he who was their head man, then the sorcerers. The men would take up the rear, equipped as the head man directed. Strict silence should be observed throughout.

As they rounded Tura Pasia could not contain herself, for there it was, the canoe she had seen the day before. "Look, husband!" she cried.

The head man gave the signal: "Kiss the ground!" The men prostrated themselves. Alert now in all their senses, they would give instant obedience from that moment, imitating every movement of their leader exactly. They were one with him.

From his iana the head man took kusibagai,[8] takar,[9] and kerikeri,[10] and placed them in his mouth. He anointed himself with magic oil. Chewing and spraying out scented spit he advanced to the pool off Zagwan. He, too, saw the canoe sink before his eyes.

3. On Yam Island.
4. New Guinea, the northern mainland (*naigai dagam daudai*).
5. This pool, close to the edge of the reef, is called Wingaban.
6. *Kod*, meeting place for men. Some informants said that the *maidalgal* (sorcerers) lived at the *kod*.
7. *Iana*, woven bag worn over the shoulder; it contained a man's magic paraphernalia.
8. *Kusibagai* (*Kaempferia* sp.), a plant which has a scented root. The root was chewed in certain magical practices.
9. *Takar* (*Ocimum basilicum*), valued in magic because of its scented leaves.
10. *Kerikeri* (*Zingiberaceae* sp.), valued in magic because of its scented root.

Arrived at the pool, he signalled to his men to form a circle round it. He chewed and spat[11] into the water.

"Now show yourself, strange *augad*,"[12] he said. "If you are for us we will worship you. If you are against us we will thrust our spears at you until nothing remains of you but fragments which we will cast into Magan, our master current."[13]

The canoe began to emerge, until it revealed itself as the like of which they had never seen. "*Ngalpun augad* (Our protector)!" they cried with one voice. "You are our *augad*."

"Bring mats," the leader ordered the women. This new and powerful *augad* would be taken with honour and reverence to the *kod*.

The women spread coconut leaf mats. The men stood at each side and at the stern and pushed with all their strength. The canoe remained where it was.

"Bring decorated pandanus mats," commanded the head man. The pandanus mats were spread before the *augad*.

Slowly the canoe left the pool and, as the mats were laid before it, glided along on top of them, past Zagwan, and round into the inlet known ever since as *Augadau pudaizinga*. Here the canoe turned itself round and moved of its own volition, stern first, in the direction of the *kod*. The men could not keep pace with it, but they saw a cloud of dust after it had gone inside. When they reached the place they saw nothing but a stone part-buried in the ground.

The head man broke the silence that followed: "Who are you? What are you called?"

They heard a gentle voice. "I am Sigai. I have made Yam Island my home."

The men bowed low. They placed *bu*[14] shells around the sacred stone.

Henceforth Sigai was their most powerful *augad*.

From Sigai they drew the strength that gave them victory against their enemies. They brought their weapons to him before they departed for war. They did homage to him when they returned with the heads, and so great was his power that in the *kod* at Iama there were soon many skulls.

11. "Spat" was given to me in translation. Later, at Murray Island, the action was demonstrated for me, and I then observed that the action was one of spraying, rather than spitting.

12. *Augad*—here meaning strange object or creature, deemed to have mysterious strength, and revered as a protector against enemies.

13. It has its origin in a whirlpool off Tudu (Warrior Island). Magani or (Magan) was "worked" by canoes travelling between Tudu and Iama (Yam Island).

14. *Bu* shells were used to decorate a *kod*, and used also as a trumpet sounded in victory and to summon people together. The *bu* is the Australian Trumpet Shell (*Syrinx aruanus* Linne).

KAWAI

[Told by Simeon Harry and Salu Bann at Yam Island, 6 July 1966]

PART I

At low tide one morning, a man was walking on the reef at Gebar (Two Brothers Island) when he came to grass which had been nipped off short during the night by a dugong. So he hurried home, told his wife about it, and prepared for hunting.

First of all he cut six mangrove poles for a platform, which he erected just beyond the spot at which the dugong had stopped feeding, and then he cut vines for rope. This, together with his harpoon and spear, he placed on the platform.

As soon as it was dark, he lit a small fire on the beach.[1] When the tide rose, he swam straight out to the platform and sat on it, watching for the dugong to come in and resume feeding where it had left off the previous night. From time to time he glanced at the fire—and then, to his horror, he saw Kawai, the wicked, black *dogai* standing beside it. She was turning her head from side to side, peering out at the reef, trying to locate the dugong platform and the hunter—looking for him!

Noiselessly he picked up his harpoon and spear, slid into the water, and swam as fast as he could towards a rocky point. On the other side of it, then out of Kawai's sight, he went ashore and ran home. He woke no one, going straight to his sleeping mat and cowering inside it. For a long time he lay sleepless, trembling at the narrowness of his escape from the wicked, black *dogai*.

Meanwhile, Kawai had discovered the empty platform and guessed that the hunter must have seen her and fled. She had picked up his tracks beyond the rocky point and was already following them when her intended victim reached his house. She stood outside it for a while, until she judged him to be asleep, and then went in to where he lay, his harpoon and spear on the ground beside him. By and by she ate him, leaving only his bones inside the mat.

In the morning, the men in the village went to see what luck he had had during the night. "Where is your husband?" they asked his wife. "Did he spear the dugong?" When she replied that he was still asleep, they said: "Wake him." So she sent her children to rouse their father. From inside the house they called: "Father is dead. He has been eaten." The woman rushed to the mat and saw the bones inside it.

1. There is always a possibility that a hunter may become entangled in the rope as the dugong tries to escape after it has been harpooned. Therefore, when a man hunts alone, he leaves a small fire burning on the shore to indicate the position of the dugong platform. Should he come to harm, men will know where to look for him.

255

After they had made a platform and placed the bones upon it to smoke,[2] the men discussed Kawai. "Something will have to be done about this *dogai*," they said. And they made a plan to trick and kill her.

PART II

For a long while Kawai was never once sighted by the people of Gebar, and the people became careless.

One day, two brothers went fishing on the reef at Walikun, the younger stringing the fish as the elder speared them, and on the way home the younger brother—he was only a small boy—got left behind. Kawai, fearing the mood of the people after she ate the dugong hunter, had stayed well away from everyone on the island, but she had, nevertheless, kept an eye on the movements of each and every person the whole time from her hill-top cave, Bugan Kula, and she now saw a chance to grab a human without anyone being the wiser. So she hurried down to the reef and, assuming the face of the boy's mother, called to him with his mother's voice: "Come, my child." Hearing her, the child ran to her happily. Kawai took him in her arms, raised him to her shoulders, and strode off with him, back to her home on Iem Pad.[3]

She never permitted the boy to leave the cave, keeping him a close prisoner, but she fed him well the whole time until he had grown big and strong. And then she said to him one day: "Not this moon, but the second moon, I will kill you and eat you." So the boy knew that he must very soon find an opportunity to escape. It came when Kawai went off for three days to dig yams. The moment she was out of hearing, he squeezed through the narrow opening at the entrance to the cave and ran all the way to the village.

"All this time," he told the people, "I have been Kawai's prisoner. She pretended to be my mother that day I was stringing fish for my brother at Walikun, and she took me to Bugan Kula. She always fed me very well, but a few days ago she said that next moon she would kill me and eat me. So I ran away."

Now the men knew that Kawai would come looking for the boy as soon as she missed him, so they set to work according to the plan that they had made a long time ago. They made a ladder and stood it against a tree, and then they climbed it and built a platform high up in the branches. The two steps at the top of the ladder looked no different from the rest, but they would, in fact, bear no weight without breaking. The men sat down on the platform, each with his bow and arrows beside him, and the women hid in the grass. The latter had armed themselves with sticks.

Kawai had only dug three or four yams from the ground when her digging stick broke. "Something is wrong at my home," she thought. She was convinced of it when another digging stick broke. When the third stick broke, she said: "Something has happened to that boy. He must have run away." And with that, she ran back to Bugan Kula. Finding him gone, she flew into a rage and stormed: "I'll find that boy and eat him and all the other people besides." She dressed herself in *dogai* fashion, picked up a heavy stick, and charged down the hillside.

The men waiting on the platform could follow her progress, because birds flew up from trees as she reached them. "Everybody ready," the men called, "the *dogai* is coming." They told the boy whom she had stolen to sit at the front of the platform and hold his bow at the ready.

When Kawai reached the bottom of the ladder, she shouted at the boy: "You ran away, but you will die today and so will everyone else." Step by step she climbed the ladder until she put her feet on the two at the top and then she crashed to the ground.

The boy shot an arrow into her heart. The women came out from their hiding places in the grass and beat her with their sticks, and the men came down from the platform and cut off her head with a bamboo knife. Finally, they made a big fire and threw the wicked, black *dogai* into the flames.

UZU, THE WHITE DOGAI

[Told by Asou Thaiday at Yam Island, 6 July 1966]

At the top of Gebin Pad, a hill on the island of Gebar which many people today call Two Brothers Island, there lived inside a stone a *dogai*[1] named Uzu.

Uzu looked like all other *dogai*, tall and skinny, with a face like a flying-fox. She had long teeth and big ears; indeed, her ears were so big that when she lay down to sleep, she could use one as a mat and the other as a cover to keep her warm. But Uzu was a good *dogai*, and she was very kind to anyone in trouble.[2]

1. The people of the Western Islands of Torres Strait formerly believed in witch-like creatures whom they called *dogai*. *Dogai* lived in stones, or trees, or underground. They could impersonate living women. Most *dogai* were evil and all were greatly feared.

2. When Asou Thaiday had finished telling the story of Uzu she said: "That white *dogai*, this one. 'Em no savvy *kaikai* man, this one tame one. Some 'nother one in this part here, this one *kaikai* man, but this one no *kaikai* man."

One day the women and the girls from the village of Gebi went out fishing on the reef, stringing the fish together as they caught them. In the late afternoon they turned back.

Alas, one poor girl, whose name also was Uzu, was stung by a stone-fish. The pain was so bad that she could not walk. She had to sit down and watch her friends disappear from sight around Umai Piti Gizu. The tears streamed from her eyes. There she was, alone, the sun nearly gone down into the sea.

From her home Uzu saw all that had happened, so she made her way towards her namesake.

The girl saw her coming and screamed with fright: "Mother! Mother! The *dogai* is going to kill me!"

But she was quite wrong.

This *dogai*, the white one, the good one, pulled a hair from her head, tied it round Uzu's foot over the wound, put her over her shoulder, and carried her up to her home inside the stone. She made the girl sit down, spread leaves over the sore place on her foot, and told her to sleep. Then she went off to dig *kutai* and *kog* and *bua* (yams).

When the girl woke next morning she was given the best parts of the freshly roasted yams, Uzu the *dogai* contenting herself with the burnt outside crusts.

Every day this white *dogai* rubbed the girl's foot and dressed it with fresh leaves, and every day she fed the girl well.

When the girl's foot was healed, and there was no more pain in it, the good *dogai* took her back to her village, saying, as she left her: "When the men are cutting up dugong and turtle, set aside a portion for me. Go now, and give your family this present of yams."

The girl ran to her mother and told her the whole story.

And ever after, when the canoes returned from hunting, and the men had butchered their kill, the girl Uzu filled a basket and made her way up the hill. Outside the stone where Uzu, the white *dogai* who did not eat people, had her home, she called: "*Aka! Aka!* (Granny! Granny!) I have brought your share of meat and fat."

MAIDA

[Told by Harry Simeon at Yam Island, 10 July 1966]

Maida ino (wa) Maida,
Kaubuka ulaika,
Kaubuka ulaika (wa) (a).
Maida ina (wa),
Maida kaubuka.

(Here is Maida going to war, going to war.
Here is Maida, Maida going to war.)

(Old song)

★

Maida of Yam Island was a great fighter. He lived in a hollow beneath a big boulder.

Whenever turtle or dugong were caught, the people always called Maida to come and allot them their share of the meat and fat from these animals. Maida, however, was very greedy and always kept back for himself the choicest cuts and most of the fat. His behaviour was noted by the sorcerers.

One day he was called to divide three turtles amongst the people. Afterwards the sorcerers said: "He took nearly all the fat. He gave us very little. He always does that." One sorcerer said: "I'll attend to it. I'll kill him by making him choke on a lump of fat."

The next time Maida divided a turtle for the people, he took home most of the fat as usual. Then he cooked a meal and sat down to eat it. His first mouthful was a great lump of fat which, when he tried to swallow it, stuck fast in his throat. Presently he died of it, choking to death.

After a few days, the people in the village began to wonder what had happened to Maida. No one had seen him. So one of the men went to look for him. He found Maida dead in the hollow beneath the boulder which was Maida's home. There was a lump of turtle fat in Maida's throat.

DUGAMA

[Told by Mareko Maino of Yam Island at Thursday Island, 31 August 1966]

Dugama of Dauan set sail for Mer with a party of men and a woman. Off Bourke Island,[1] a strong south-westerly sprang up, and the canoe overturned and sank. All were drowned except Dugama who began to swim with the tide.

Dugama was now a castaway, a *sarup*,[2] and his plight was grave; nevertheless, he determined to try and stay alive and somehow find a way to return to Dauan. So he swam.

He passed between Kebi Keian and Au Keian, two small islands close to Masig (Yorke Island), and reached Aurid at sunset. He could see people at one end of this island, so he crept ashore at the other and went into the scrub, where he spent his first night as a *sarup*.

Dugama was hungry when he woke in the morning, so he moved about quietly in search of food until he came to a *wongai*[3] tree which was laden with ripe, red fruit. As he ate the *wongai*, he threw the seeds on the ground.

They were noticed by a woman who came along soon afterwards to fill her baskets with fruit. "Hullo," she said, "somebody has been here during the night. Can there be a *sarup* on the island?" Presently she was joined by other women, who had also come to pluck *wongai*, and she showed them the seeds of freshly eaten fruit. They discussed what should be done and decided to fill their baskets as quickly as possible and return to the village. They would tell their husbands what they had seen.

Dugama had been hiding at the top of the *wongai* tree, having climbed up at the first sound of the woman's approach, and he now watched them all the way back to their homes from this vantage point. He stayed where he was, from time to time eating a ripe *wongai*, and saw the people go out on the reef to fish. A girl was stung by a stone-fish and her mother and father took her back to their house. But they did not stay with her long, because they had not yet caught any fish, and were soon on their way to the reef again, leaving the girl behind. Seeing that, Dugama came down the tree in a flash and ran for her.

When he reached the round house in which the girl lived, he stood to one side of the small, low door for a while, listening to her crying, and then he bent down and peered in at her. She lay on her back, her sore foot raised because of the pain from the sting. Seeing Dugama's face, she

---

1. Not to be confused with Burke Island (Sauraz), north of Mt. Ernest Island. Bourke Island, for which I could find no memory of the original name, is SSE. of Yorke Island (Masig).
2. See introductory note to "Beug and the Sarup" in the section, "Stories from Badu".
3. The name in popular use today for *ubar* (or *eneo*), the wild plum.

screamed: "*Ama, sarup* (Mother, *sarup*)!" Dugama said: "I am a man, Dugama. I have come to mate with you." "*Ama, sarup!*" the girl screamed a second time. But soon afterwards she went outside to Dugama, and the couple spent the rest of the day together until the tide turned, and the people began to come in from the reef. Before leaving the girl, Dugama told her that he would visit her that night and bring leaves with which to dress her foot. He asked her in which part of the house she slept and, after learning that her parents lay to the right of the fire and she to the left of it, ran back to the *wongai* tree which he had made his home, climbed up, and resumed his watch on the people of Aurid.

At sunset they were grilling the fish which they had caught over open fires. They ate their evening meal, and the fires began to burn low. Soon afterwards they went inside their houses, and all was silent.

Dugama left his tree and walked noiselessly towards the village. He crouched down in the grass not far from the house in which his girl lived. When he was sure that everyone was asleep, he crept towards it and scratched the wall beside the girl with a leaf. Hearing Dugama's signal, she crept out to him. Dugama kissed her and treated her foot, and whispered his intention to come again in the morning after everyone had gone to the reef to fish. The girl said: "Come then. I want you to come." Dugama returned to his *wongai* tree and went to sleep in it, high above the ground.

Dugama spent many days at Aurid, visiting the girl whenever he was sure that everyone else was out fishing on the reef, caring for her foot, making love to her. He never stirred from his hiding place, the *wongai* tree, if there was the least danger that he be seen by those who would kill him because he was a *sarup*. And then, one day when he went to the girl, she said: "I am going to have a baby." To which Dugama replied: "I shall leave this evening. Your father and mother will find out about the baby, and I shall be hunted and killed if I stay." So, that afternoon, Dugama lashed together two drifted logs that were lying on the beach, loaded them with *wongai* and departed from Aurid.

From Aurid Dugama made his way to Iarpar[4] (Pumpkin Island), a small island not far from Poruma (Coconut Island). No one lived at Iarpar, which he reached at daybreak, so he pushed his raft up on to the reef and went ashore. He found some *wongai* trees in fruit and some dry coconuts [lying on the beach]. He had to make up his mind which island to go to next. Poruma was not far away, and he had two friends who lived there, but it lay south of Iarpar and would place him further than ever from Dauan. On the other hand, he could go to Utu (Dove Island): it was un-inhabited and would not take him from the direction he had to follow. There were said to be snakes at Utu, but he was not afraid of snakes. So to

4. *Iarpar* is marked on charts as Roberts Island.

261

Utu he went, leaving Iarpar in the same manner as he had left Aurid—on two drifted logs tied together with vine. He took *wongai* and dry coconuts with him for food and set out after dark.

He spent the following day at Utu and planned the next stage of his journey. He thought again of his friends at Poruma, which he could easily reach from Utu, and then he thought of two brothers whom he knew at Tudu (Warrior Island). Tudu lay to the north, so he chose to go to Tudu. He would have to avoid the big reef, Tidiu (Dungeness Reef), and he would do this by going first to Garboi (Arden Island). When the early morning tide began to flow east, he would leave Garboi and be caught by the strong current, Magani, which would shoot him along to Wipain, the small reef between Zegei (Dungeness Island) and Tudu. When the tide turned and began to flow west, he would be taken by Magani straight to Tudu.

And that is exactly what Dugama did: he made use of tides and currents and fetched Tudu the day after his departure from Utu.

Dugama entered the swampy passage which separates the main part of Tudu, where the people lived, from the smaller part of the island, Magi Tudu, which was uninhabited, and landed at Manmura, where there was a grove of coconuts. There he lay down in the grass to rest, but with no thought of sleeping, for Tudu was an island of fierce, fighting men who never permitted a *sarup* to land and survive.

Presently he heard the sound of boys' voices. Parting the grass, he saw ten big boys and one small boy at target play on the beach. They were tossing something up into the air and throwing their spears at it as it fell. Dugama threw a coconut out to the beach. The small boy saw it first and said: "That's my coconut." He ran to get it, but was quickly overtaken by the others. A big boy named Kuida reached it first and had just bent to pick it up when Dugama left his hiding place in the grass and began to run towards him. The boys who had been left behind in the chase for the coconut saw Dugama and shouted a warning to Kuida: "Kuida, *sarup*!" But Kuida took no notice and squatted down to break the coconut open with a stone. Dugama grabbed him and beat him until he collapsed on the sand.

Kuida's companions ran away as fast as they could, back to their fathers at the village, and told the story of Kuida and the *sarup*. The men of Tudu armed themselves with bows and arrows and *gabagaba* and began to hunt for the castaway.

Dugama knew very well what would happen when the men of Tudu learned of his presence on their island. Showing himself to the boys and beating Kuida had not been reckless stupidity, but part of a calculated plan by which he hoped to establish quick contact with his friends and thus obtain the help which would speed him on his way home to Dauan. By using his wits he intended to elude the men who were hunting him and gain an opportunity to attract the attention of his friends at a time when they were apart from the rest. Right now, however, it was urgent that he find a safe hiding place, for already the men of Tudu would be on the way to Manmura. So he swam out to a rock called Pagaral Urui. There was a hole in it facing seawards, one big enough to hold a man standing upright.

The men of Tudu searched for the *sarup* until dark and could not find him, so they went to the *kod* to talk things over—all, that is, except a man name Musu.

Believing that the hunt for him would not be resumed until morning, Dugama swam in from Pagaral Urui and climbed a pandanus tree, where he settled down to rest in a fork between branch and trunk. And there Musu caught up with him, having picked up the tracks which led from the sea.

At first Musu did not realize that Dugama was in the pandanus tree. Temporarily he lost the trail which he had been following. He did not think to look up and so wasted time trying to find it in the grass and scrub about. Then he decided that there was only one place where the *sarup* could be—in the pandanus tree. He came back, glanced up—and saw the *sarup*.

Dugama glared down at Musu, tensed to meet Musu's reaction. When Musu fitted an arrow to his bow and aimed at him, Dugama yelled: "Stop! I'll come down. Wait till I'm on the ground to kill me." By this ruse, Dugama gained time enough to climb down the pandanus tree, throw himself at Musu, and grab hold of him. He lifted Musu above his head, squeezed the breath from his body and threw him down hard on the ground. Using Musu's bamboo knife, he nicked Musu's face from ear to ear and from forehead to chin and afterwards broke Musu's arrows into many small pieces. Finally, he shoved Musu's body into soft sand, and then he swam back to Pagaral Urui.

Later that night Musu recovered sufficiently to walk to the *kod*, but before he went inside the wall of dry coconut fronds, he rubbed his face with burnt husks of coconuts to cover up the cuts made by Dugama. The men in the *kod* were not deceived for an instant. "What happened to you?" they said. "A crocodile nearly got me," Musu told them. The men were disbelieving and laughed. "It wasn't a small *sarup*, eh?" they joked. So Musu told them the full story of his encounter with Dugama. After lengthy discussion it was decided to wait for daylight and then continue the search for the *sarup*.

In the morning, Dugama's friends—the two brothers—went fishing in their canoe. From his hiding place in Pagaral Urui, Dugama saw them poling their way through the tall reeds of the swampy passage near Manmura and come in his direction. He had recognized his friends, but he did nothing to attract their attention until they were very close to Pagaral Urui, but on the landward side of it. "Pssssssss!" hissed Dugama. The elder brother said to the younger: "Why did you make a noise?" The younger brother denied having done so. Dugama signalled again: "Ch-ch-ch-ch-ch!" Convinced by then that someone was hiding nearby, the elder brother poled round to the seaward side of Pagaral Urui. "Dugama! Dugama, are you the *sarup*?" he cried.

Dugama told his friends all that had happened since his canoe capsized and sank off Bourke Island. "Will you help me?" he asked. "Will you find a way to help me reach my home?" The brothers agreed and told him what they would do.

They would lengthen their anchor rope so that their canoe would drift out from the beach with the tide that night. They would put into the canoe a mat sail, food, and a baler-shell full of live coals. Dugama must stay hidden inside Pagaral Urui until dark and then come in with the tide like a fish, only using his feet to steer him—no movement of his arms or splashing must be seen from the shore. "For," said the elder brother, "they'll all be keeping a sharp lookout tonight. You beat that boy badly—he's still very poorly."

That night the brothers decided that only one of them should go to the canoe and meet Dugama: if both went, it would be said after Dugama's escape became known and their canoe was found to be missing that they had helped the *sarup*. So the elder brother went to the canoe, while the younger stayed behind, pretending to look for the *sarup*.

Dugama was waiting in the canoe when his friend arrived. "Go a long way out before you put up the sail," whispered the friend, "and keep the fire hidden until you are nearly at Zegei (Dungeness Island). I'll go in to the beach now and pull out the anchor." Presently the canoe began to drift away from Tudu.

When the men at Tudu saw fire off Zegei, they immediately understood that the *sarup* had got away. They looked to see which canoe was missing, and then they accused Dugama's friends of aiding and abetting him; but there was no proof, and the brothers lied convincingly.

On fetching Zegei, Dugama ran his canoe into some mangroves, where it was effectively screened, and slept in it until late afternoon. He woke to see a canoe approaching.

On board it were a man and five women who were on their way back to Tudu with a load of water[5] from Damud (Dalrymple Island). It was their intention to rest at Zegei before making the final run home. They drove a mangrove pole into the mud dangerously close to Dugama's retreat. Thus

5. During the dry season of the year, Tudu often ran short of drinking water, which had to be fetched from neighbouring islands. Long, thick lengths of bamboo—obtained from New Guinea—were used for carrying the water.

264

anchored, they prevented Dugama's escape during the night. At sundown the man made a shelter for the women with the mat sail, and presently all on board slept.

Dugama swam to their anchor stick and pulled it out of the mud. The Tudu canoe began to drift. Dugama swam beside it, keeping pace with it.

One of the women stirred—the wind was coming from the wrong quarter. "Wake up!" she shouted. "We're adrift!" The man rubbed the sleep from his eyes, stood up and went to examine the anchor rope. Holding on to the side of the canoe with one hand, Dugama struck the man with the other and pulled him into the water. Each of the women came in turn to find out what was going on. Dugama treated every one of them as he had treated the man. Then he swam back to his own canoe, cleared the mangroves, and ran for Iama (Yam Island).

Meanwhile his victims clambered aboard their canoe. The women said to the man: "Go and find out who tricked us. He must be still there in the mangroves." The man made the excuse that his shoulder was still sore from the blow he had received and urged the women to go. "No," said the women, "you're a man, you should go first." And so they argued, back and forth, until Dugama was well on the way to Iama, and they could see his sail. It was too late then to do anything about their tormentor so they sailed to Tudu.

Dugama was afraid. The encounter at Zegei had delayed his departure from that island; it was nearly daylight; there was no chance of landing at Iama before the people stirred; Ausa of Iama was said to have speared every *sarup* who had ever cast up at his island since he became a man. His only chance lay, Dugama thought, in sinking his canoe some distance from the edge of Iama's home reef and swimming in.

By doing this, Dugama reached the shore without being seen by Ausa and ran across the island to Tura. But there he was seen by women who had been sent by Ausa to pluck *wongai*. "*Sarup!*" they yelled, and they ran away to give the alarm to Ausa. Dugama ran to the beach at the foot of Tura, pushed a log into the water, and headed for Mukar (Cap Island).

He was able to spell at Mukar for a while—no people lived there—but he took to the water again at sunset. He reached Gebar (Two Brothers Island) just before daybreak and landed, but within a very short time he was seen by a woman who was digging up yams. She ran away immediately to tell her husband about the *sarup*, so Dugama had very little time in which to hide. He chose to run out across the reef and shelter inside a rock—similar to Pagaral Urui at Tudu.

In the afternoon a man in a small fishing canoe came close to this rock. "Pssssss!" hissed Dugama. The man started. "Psssssss!" Dugama hissed again. The man poled round the rock to see who was inside it. Dugama said: "Good friend, save me. I am Dugama. Dauan is my home. Will you lend me your canoe?"

Now the man was terrified of Dugama who, by this time, after all the hardships and exposure that he had endured, presented a truly dreadful appearance. So afraid was he of what Dugama would do to him if he refused, that he agreed and told Dugama to come in and get the canoe after dark. Dugama would find it ready for his journey. And as the friendly brothers at Tudu had advised Dugama, so now this man counselled him not to let his fire show until the beach at Gebar could no longer be seen from the canoe.

Late that night, the people on Gebar saw the fire with which Dugama signalled his escape to them.

Nothing now lay between Dugama and his island, Dauan, but he knew he would have to convince his people that he was a man, not a *markai*. How to do it occupied his mind the whole night long.

At Sapul Maza, a small reef not far from Gawa Giz, the northern tip of Dauan, Dugama abandoned the canoe and swam ashore. Then he climbed the hill at Gawa Giz and, keeping to high ground, ran along the island until he reached the well behind the village, Buli. There he climbed a tree and kept himself hidden amongst the leaves until his wife came to fetch water. As she bent down to fill her containers, he showed his face so that it was reflected in the well. "Dugama! Are you a ghost?" the woman gasped. Dugama tried to reassure her that he was not a ghost, that he was not a *markai*, but her flesh-and-blood husband. She did not believe him and ran back to the village. All the people ran to the well and, when Dugama came down the tree, surrounded him.

Dugama talked to his people. He told them everything. "Dugama," they said when he had finished, "we are sad. We are sorry that you suffered so much." But they could not bring themselves to believe that he was a man.

So Dugama ordered his fighting gear to be brought to him. He put on his head-dress and boar's tusks and stood before his people, fully armed. He spoke to them again: "You say I am dead. You say I am a *markai*. Stand up and fight me. I tell you I am a man, Dugama. I swam from Bourke Island to Aurid; from Aurid to Iarpar; from Iarpar to Utu; from Utu to Garboi; from Garboi to Tudu. I outwitted the people of Tudu and Iama and Gebar. Could you do that? I am Dugama, and Dauan is my place."

No one had anything to say. One after the other, every man on Dauan went to Dugama and scraped Dugama's palm with his fingernails.

story from

WARABER *Sue Island*

Bu shells at Waraber arranged around the
spot at which skulls collected in former
times have since been buried

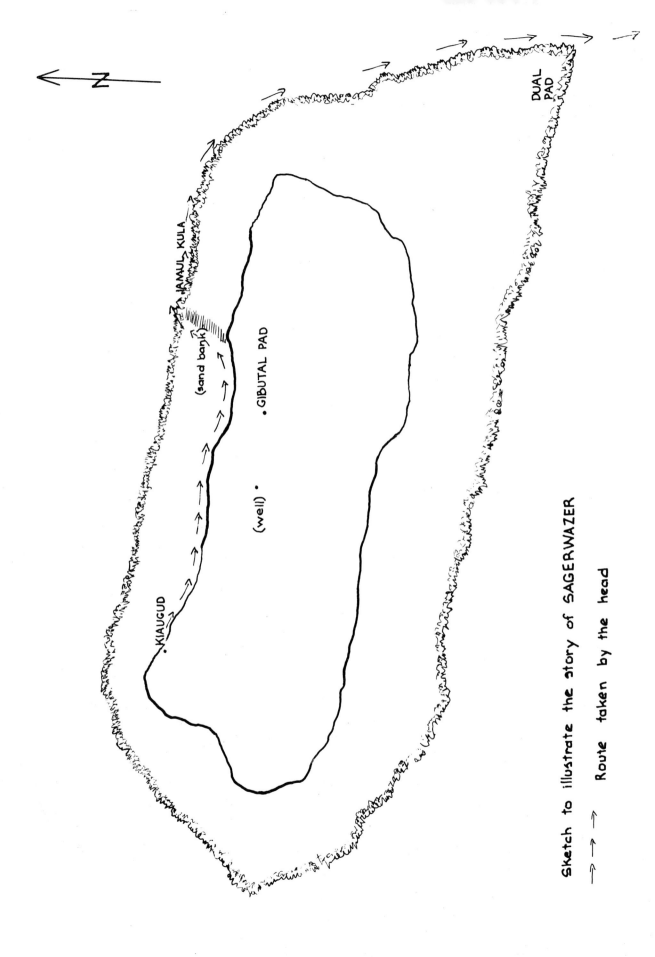

N

KIAUGUD

(sand bank)

JAMUL KULA

.GIBUTAL PAD

(well) .

DUAL
PAD

WARABER (Sue Island)

Sketch to illustrate the story of SAGERWAZER

→→ → Route taken by the head

SAGERWAZER

[Told by Daniel Pearson at Coconut Island, 8 March 1967]

Long ago, when the island of Waraber was much bigger than it is today and the people had their homes at Gibutal Pad,[1] there lived a man named Sagerwazer. He was big and strong and possessed magical powers which he used whenever he had a mind to.

Very early one morning, before sunrise in fact, he decided to go for a walk. So he told his friends about it and then set out alone for Kiaugud at the western end of the island. Try as he might, when he got there he could think of nothing to do.

Suddenly the idea of cutting off his head and magically rejoining it to his body flashed into his mind. At once he walked down to the beach and cut off his head. His body dropped to the sand. His head, however, fell into the sea and began to intone:

> Sagerwazer wazer (o)
> Ngana inu ngana (o)
> Bauana (o) sikana (o)
> Gud malaika gud (o)
> Sagerwazer wazer (o).
>
> (Here am I, Sagerwazer,
> Wave-foam fills my mouth,
> Sagerwazer-wazer. O.)

Then it glided away from the shore.

When it reached the sandbank in front of the village, it skirted along it to the outer edge of the reef and swept east with the flowing tide. It passed Iamul Kula, the rock where fish called *iamul* abound, and was well on the way to Dual Pad as the sun came up out of the sea. But beyond Dual Pad stretched the open sea, and afraid to abandon the protection of the reef that encircled Waraber, at this point, regretfully, the head turned back.

It had rounded the tip of the sandbank and was gliding in to Kiaugud, when it felt the frantic attraction exerted by the body on the beach striving to recapture its head. Faster and faster the head was drawn through the water, until it met its body with a thud.

Sagerwazer got to his feet and strode back to Gibutal Pad a new man. He swelled with pride, for to have cut off his head and successfully rejoined it to his body proved that his magical powers were extraordinarily great.

He was awake at first bird call the following day. For a time he lay

1. East of the present-day village.

269

restless, then he crept from his bed. No one was stirring in the village when he set out for Kiaugud, where he again cut off his head.

> *Sagerwazer wazer (o)*
> *Ngana inu ngana (o)*
> *Bauana (o) sikana (o)*
> *Gud malaika gud (o)*
> *Sagerwazer wazer (o),*

intoned the head, eager to be on its way, for, as before, it had fallen into the sea when its body dropped to the sand.

It travelled faster than it had the previous day. The sandbank, Iamul Kula, and Dual Pad were soon left behind as, without a qualm, it forsook the shelter of the home reef and ventured out into the open sea.

Sagerwazer's absence was noted when the village woke to life, but the people felt no concern, assuming him to be busy about his own affairs. Nevertheless, as the morning wore on and there was still no sign of him, his brother began to worry. Towards mid-day he searched for Sager-wazer's footprints, found them, and followed them west to the beach below Kiaugud.

He was utterly bewildered. There was nothing to indicate the presence of strangers at Waraber; there had been nothing unusual in the behaviour of any of the people at Gibutal Pad; the sand all around was clean and unmarked—yet there lay the headless body of Sagerwazer. He threw himself upon it and wept; then, raising it to his shoulders, he carried it away and buried it.

The head, which had continued all the while to travel further and further from Waraber, began to feel sick and unhappy. When waves smacked angrily at its face, it realized that the tide had turned and was taking it west now instead of east as was the case earlier in the day.

At its last glance backward the island had seemed to it no bigger than a *kusu* (the shell of the dry coconut used to carry water) fast sinking into the sea. From the crest of the next wave only the trees that grew at Waraber remained above the horizon.

When the tide turned, the head raced towards home in a flurry of foam. Arrived at Dual Pad it skimmed along the water at the edge of the reef, passed Iamul Kula, and swept round the point of the sandbank. As it raced in to Kiaugud, expecting each moment to be drawn to the beach, instead, it felt nothing—nothing at all. This way and that it sped, in a frenzy to become one with its body.

Small fish called *daram* began to nibble at the tissues inside the head and it could not dislodge them. It began to sink, water bubbling in and out at its lips. Presently it was swallowed by a big fish.

Landtman in his *Folk-Tales of the Kiwai Papuans* (Helsingfors, 1917), pp. 436–37, gives a tale, "The Man Who Took Off His Head and Played with It in the Sea", which he obtained at Mawata (on the Papuan mainland). The setting of this story is Saibai.

I found no one at Saibai who knew Landtman's tale, but did record the tale, "Kasakuik" (Only-head), of a living head which had no body.

It is of interest, perhaps, that Daniel Pearson, who told the story of Sager-wazer, heard it from an old man of Waraber who had married a woman of Saibai.

stories from the

EASTERN ISLANDS

stories from

UGAR *Stephens Island*

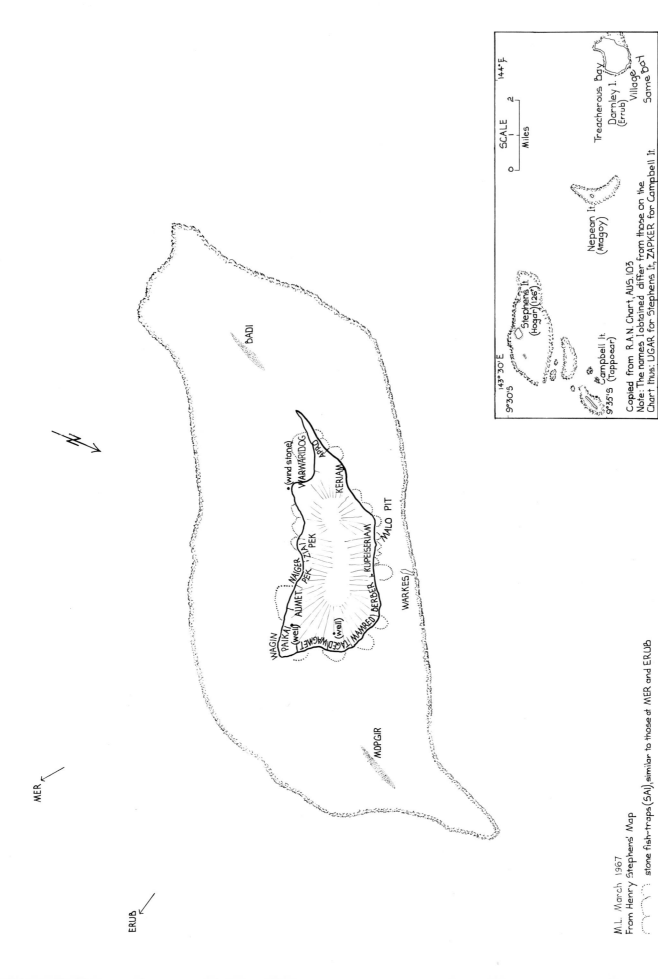

UGAR (Stephens Island)

M.L. March 1967
From Henry Stephens' Map

stone fish-traps (SAI), similar to those at MER and ERUB

Copied from R.A.N. Chart, AUS.103
Note: The names I obtained differ from those on the
Chart thus: UGAR for Stephens It, ZAPKER for Campbell It.

SCALE
0   1   2
Miles

143°30'E   14.4°E
9°30'S
9°35'S

Stephens It.
(Hogar)(126')
Campbell It.
(Tappoear)

Nepean It.
(Attagoy)

Treacherous Bay
Darnley I.
(Erub)   Village
           Same Bay

WAGIN
PAIKAI
(well)
AUMET
NAIGER
PEK ZIAT
PEK
WARWARIDOG
(wind stone)
APRO
KERIAM
KUPEISERIAM
MAMRED
BERBER
TAGEDIWAGMET
(well)
MALO PIT
WARKES

BADI
MDPGIR

MER
ERUB

BADI AND THE SABEI

[Told by Ned Stephen at Stephens Island, 16 June 1966]

One day, Badi walked from his home at Apro along the big sandbank which extends far out across the home reef. He saw a fish called *sabei*[1] and speared it.

This fish was one which was new to Badi, and he did not know if it was edible. So he cut pieces from it and fed them to a black reef heron (*kaubet*) and a white reef heron (*sir*). He watched the birds carefully. They did not die from eating *sabei*; therefore, he thought it safe for him to eat the rest of the fish, and he cooked it and ate it. He found it good.

Badi thought: "I shall go again tomorrow and spear another of these fish." And at low tide the following day he went out on the sandbank and again speared a *sabei*.

Now, in spearing the *sabei*, Badi drove its companions out to deep water. They never returned to the shallow water and pools of the fringing home reef: henceforth, *sabei* lived only in the blue sea outside.

Badi turned into a *bonao*, a big brain coral[2] (which may still be seen). The black reef heron and the white reef heron, to which he fed pieces of the first *sabei* he speared, turned to stone at Apro, close by the stones of the fireplace on which he cooked his portion of the strange new fish with the spike on its head.

Kaubet   *Sir*

1. *Sabei* (or *bologor*), unicorn fish, *Naso unicornis*.
2. *Platygyra lamellina*.

Sabei

275

THE SNAKE OF
APRO [Told by Ned Stephen at Stephens Island, 16 June 1966]

1. There are many stone fish-traps on the fringing reef of Stephens Island. They are similar to those at Mer, Dauar, Waier, and Erub, where their construction is attributed to the brothers, Kos and Abob of Mer.

Long ago there was a big snake which lived inside a cave at Apro. One day it crawled out over the reef. It was so big that when its head arrived at Warwaridog its tail was still at Apro.

When the men of Warwaridog saw the snake's head, they struck it with their stone-headed clubs and severed it from its body.

The snake turned to stone. It became a stone fish-trap (*sai*).[1]

ZUB AND THE
LAMAR [Told by Ned Stephen at Stephens Island, 16 June 1966]

1. *Terminalia catappa*. Its popular name is "the Fiji almond".

Formerly, the people of Ugar used sometimes to load their canoes with food and water and go and stay at the neighbouring island of Zapker for a few days. Once, just before the canoes left for Zapker, one of the men quarrelled with his wife, a woman named Zub. She ran away and hid in the scrub, and the party sailed without her.

Zub, now alone on Ugar, dug in her garden for yams and took them to her home at Wagmet. At mid-afternoon she roasted them and ate them, and then she began to worry about how to get through the night. She was afraid that *lamar* (ghosts) might visit Ugar and find her if she stayed in her house, so she worked out a plan which would deceive the *lamar*—should they come—into thinking that there was no one at all on the island.

Zub dug a hole and buried the ashes of her fire in it, and afterwards built a sleeping platform for herself at the top of a *meker* (the wild almond tree of Torres Strait).[1] She was already seated on the platform at sunset, when she saw a canoe approaching from Maizab Kaur (Bramble Cay). She shook with fear, for the canoe was filled with *lamar*—she recognized them as the ghosts of people whom she had previously known.

The *lamar* carried their belongings ashore at Wagmet, lit a bright fire, and before long began to dance in its glare, singing a *tap*[2] as they danced:

> *Perper turidua perper (ai)*
> *Ki asamare ki asamare.*
>
> (Quick! Be quick!
> We will put out the light.)

From time to time they struck the ground with the *piru*[3] that they held.

During a lull in the dancing, they wafted air to their nostrils with the *piru* and, in so doing, caught the smell of a living person. "There is a human close by," they said.

Immediately, all the *lamar* began to search for the human. They went into Zub's house and even prodded the wall and the roof with their *piru*, but they found no one, so they resumed their dancing.

Later on, still unconvinced that there was not a human on the island, they went to another village, Aumet, and searched it. Laughing, whistling, hitting the ground with their *piru*, the *lamar* visited every village, right round the island. When they arrived back at Wagmet, they loaded their canoes and set sail for Maizab Kaur. By then it was almost dawn.

At daylight, Zub left her platform at the top of the *meker* tree and climbed down to the ground. She went at once to Wagin Paikai and lit a fire in order to attract the attention of the people at Zapker. When her husband reached Naiger Pek later in the day, she swam out to meet him.

Zub told her husband all that had happened during the night, naming the *lamar* who had visited Ugar. Her husband said that he, also, had known some of the *lamar* as men before they became ghosts.

Zub accompanied her husband to Zapker, where she told everyone about the *lamar* who had come to Ugar from Maizab Kaur. At the end of her story, she taught the people the song to which the *lamar* had danced:

> *Perper turidua perper (ai)*
> *Ki asamare ki asamare.*

2. *Tap*, a song which is intoned on a single note.
3. *Piru*, the lower half of the stem of a coconut palm frond.

THE TWO SPIRIT WOMEN OF DAOMA KES [Told by Ned Stephen and Andrew Stephen at Stephens Island, 16 June 1966]

A man who lived at Kupei Seriam on the island of Ugar was visited by two spirit women when he was working in his garden one day. He made love to them. Afterwards, the women returned to their home under the sea in Daoma Kes (Crab Passage).

The man went to his garden again the following day and was again visited by the two spirit women. They invited him to go and live with them at their place which, they said, was much better than his. To this the man agreed. So, the two spirit women leading the way, the three walked out along the sandbank called Mopgir and went down into the deep water at the edge of the reef.

The women took him to an undersea coconut grove, inside which were giant clams which they called *bazgiz*.[1] This was their home in Daoma Kes. It was very beautiful.

When the man of Kupei Seriam failed to return from his garden at the end of the day, the people of Ugar began to search for him. When it grew dark, they lit bundles of dry coconut fronds and carried them to light up their way around the island. They searched for him everywhere and, not finding him, spoke insultingly of the *lamar* (ghost or ghosts) who had spirited him away.

An old *lamar* woman who lived on the reef at Warkes[2] overheard them and went straight to Daoma Kes, where she told the spirit women what was being said by the people of Ugar and counselled that they send the man back to his own home.

And this they did, taking him by the same route as they had come and leaving him at Naiger Pek with a present of food which they had brought with them from their garden under the sea. They then took the form of birds and sat chattering on the branch of a nearby tree.

Within a very short time, the people of Ugar arrived at Naiger Pek and saw the missing man by the light of their flaring torches. He was standing on the path which led round the island to Kupei Seriam, clamshells and coral and *memsus*[3] at his feet. When the people came close to him, they noticed that an evil odour came from him; they asked him where he had been, but he could not speak—his jaws were locked tight. So they took him home, bathed and anointed his body until it was clean and sweet-smelling, and applied heated leaves of *eneo*[4] to each side of his face.

1. *Bazgiz* is the name given to the clusters of tubers which grow as off-shoots from the parent tuber of the perennial yams called *ketai* and *kakidgaba*. The clusters of tubers produced by *ketai* and *kakidgaba* represent wealth. One may take one part at a time throughout the season, and the plant will reproduce a new cluster the following year, and the next, and the next—as the *ketai* and *kakidgaba* were to humans, so the clamshells were to the spirit women who lived under the sea.
2. Not far from the village, Kupei Seriam.
3. *Memsus*, soft coral, of different varieties and colours. Some is as thick as a finger, some is hair-fine. Murray Islanders also give the name *memsus* to the Poisonous Anemone (*Rhodactis howesii*).
4. *Eneo*, the wild plum of Torres Strait.

278

Next morning he could talk, and then he told everyone of his visit to the home of the spirit women of Daoma Kes, and how their present to him of yams and fruit had turned to coral and clamshells and *memsus* at the moment of their leaving him at Naiger Pek and becoming birds.

THE LAMAR WHO BECAME A RAINBOW
[Told by Henry Stephen at Stephens Island, 16 June 1966]

Once there was a man of Ugar who had a spirit wife. For some time the pair met only in his garden, where they worked side by side, but when she gave birth to a son, the man took her to live in his home in the village. There she kept his house clean and tidy and cooked his meals for him. Neither she nor the child, however, was ever seen by the people of the village, even when the child grew old enough to walk.

The village people found it hard to understand how this man who, as they believed, had no wife, yet had a house which always appeared cared-for and himself had the demeanour of a married man.

But as time went by the man began to worry. The spirit woman who was his wife had forbidden him to betray her presence in his home, threatening him with serious trouble if he so much as breathed a word of her existence. And there was his son, daily growing bigger and stronger, who would surely escape from the house one day. When that happened, his marriage would no longer be secret.

The man decided to enlist the help of his friends. "Come to my house and frighten this *lamar* wife of mine into leaving me. Help me to keep my son and to give him freedom to play with the village children," he begged them.

A few days later, the friends armed themselves with bows and arrows and *kusbager*[1] and came and stood outside his house, where they made such a din that the spirit woman ran away. Thereafter, until they judged that there was no danger of the spirit woman returning to steal the child, they kept a daily watch over the house.

In time, the man forgot the threats made by his spirit wife.

Then, one day, a storm with a rainbow inside it approached the village.

1. *Kusbager* is a single-pointed spear (*bager*) made from the wood of the tree called *kus*.

279

Heavy rain fell, and as the children left their play and ran to their homes for shelter, one end of the rainbow alighted on the son of the spirit woman. The watching villagers saw the boy's feet leave the ground and heard his screams as he was taken into the rainbow. They never saw him again. Everyone understood that the rainbow was the spirit wife who had returned and punished her husband for his betrayal of her existence to his friends.

stories from

ERUB *Darnley Island*

N

WATOTO
SERMAD
WARDO
UKEN
MADARUB
BARUADOG EG
SERAR URPI
AWAR
KIARI
KAMKOB
BAZ
LEIWAG
KEIRARI
KES
MEI
ZAUM
GOLEGDLE
WERKES
EWI
PERA
DERE
DERE PAIKAI
KEMUS
GAZIR PIT
WADAIAM
DURU
MAUR
GARSAO
SIRSIR
GID
AIMUR
SEBU
BUMEO
NA BEAI
MOGOR
MOGOR
PAT
GAWAR GIZ
SARPI
BIKAR
KOTOR
AU PASER
TOR
WAUS
BESENGAP
WARGDR
KERIAM
KAREDOG
WARARED
IR.MED
MED
KEB
WAO
AI
DARORMUD
POROI MOGOR
KES
GAB
BADOG
DID
NEUR
ABI
KEREM MOGOR PIT
GEIM
DAROBAN
KAIGIZ
MEKIK PAIKAI
KA PIT
GAO
BAD
TABU AGUD
EGRIU

URZI
KES

SCALE

0   2
Miles

ERUB (Darnley Island)

.·.: stone fish-traps (sai), similar
to those at MER and UGAR

MAIZAB
KAUR [Told by Harry Captain at Thursday Island, 17 March 1967]
(The Origin of Bramble Cay)

Keriba ged i au muris ge irdi.
Ki derserda irdidarda.
Ki nebewe ged im.
Naiger barki, ziai barki,
Kerbi derepda. No bakui.

Wa pe kerbi dikaireta.
Keriba omar wabim.
Nade wa uridli, Paiwer, Rebes,
Madeur-Madeur-Madeurkup?

(Our home is far away. We [have] laid down [the soil] and put it straight [made the sandbank firm and strong]. We set out on [the return journey to our] home. The north-east wind is blowing. [Now] the south-west wind blows. We are caught [by it]. We stand [without moving at that place].

You left us. We sorrow for you. Where are you Paiwer, Rebes, and the men who went with you?)

(Modern Darnley Island song)

★

Paiwer, leader of the Meuram people, sent word to Rebes, leader of the Peidu people at Keriam, asking him to help build a sandbank which would be a safe place for *nam kerem*.

Paiwer and his small son Burwak, and Rebes and the men who are remembered as the Made-urkup, met at Bikar on the northern side of Erub. There they dug soil which they placed in mats, and then they waded out into the sea with it. After they had gone a long way to the north, they called back to the men[1] who were watching them from the hill at Bariadog: "*Aka nade ki andinane? Ge au?*[2] (Where are we going to lay it down? Here?)" "*Mena igandane! Mena igandane! Keniba uzen unken a keniba imut unken!* (Carry it further! Carry it further! [We have the] strength [to reach it with] our paddles and poling-sticks [by canoe]!)" they were told.

From a long way further to the north they called again: "*Aka nade ki andinane? Ge au?*" "*Mena igandane! Mena igandane! Keniba uzen unken a keniba imut unken!*" came the reply from Bariadog.

According to my informant, Harry Captain, the Meuram people of Erub had a sacred stone, *nam kerem* (turtle head), which they kept at Bariadog. They worshipped it, and in return it provided the people of Erub with rich turtle seasons.

Erub was envied by the neighbouring islands, Mer and Ugar, for the great number of turtles which came to its shores. Afraid, on that account, that *nam kerem* might be stolen, the Meuram people of Erub decided to build a sandbank as a hiding-place for their sacred stone. This led to the creation of Maizab Kaur (i.e. Bramble Cay).

[*Maizab* is the name of a reef fish, the diagonal-banded sweetlips, *Plectorhynchus goldmanni* (Bleeker); *kaur,* a small island. Bramble Cay was one of the first places in Torres Strait for which an Island name was collected.]

1. The men who watched from Bariadog are called by most people today "the stone men", the Kobripatri. They identify them with a number of crouching, hunched figures, rudely carved from stone at Erub.
2. The calls from Paiwer and Rebes and from the men at Bariadog are said to be the only examples extant of the original language of Erub, which was a dialect of Meriam. The Erubam appear to have used "n" where the Meriam used "r".

283

Again, still further from Erub, Paiwer and Rebes asked for permission to lay down the soil from Bikar; yet again they were ordered to carry it further.[3] Not until they had journeyed so far from Erub that it looked no bigger than a coconut floating on top of the sea did they receive the command: "*Ge tindinane ge!* (There lay it down. There!)"

Now, at last, they built the sandbank for *nam kerem*. They made it strong and firm.

Rebes and the Made-urkup set out first to return to Erub. For a while, *naiger*, the north-east wind, blew gently. Presently, however, *ziai* blew hard from the south-west, and the way was blocked by high seas. Rebes and the men who were with him could not go on and they turned to stone. The rocks which they became are called *Karem Korsor*.[4]

Paiwer and Burwak remained on the sandbank and they, too, turned to stone. You may see them today. Paiwer still stands with his small son on his shoulders.

The men at Bariadog waited in vain for Paiwer and Rebes and the Made-urkup to return. Finally, they, too, turned to stone.

3. At each of the places from which Paiwer and Rebes called to the men at Bariadog, some soil is said to have fallen from the mats in which it was carried and formed a small reef. The reefs thus formed are in turn: Deur (Brown Reef), Kep (Laxton Reef) and Tot (simply marked "coral" on charts).

4. On the map, this is marked "Black Rocks".

REBES AND ID [Told by Jimmy Idagi at Thursday Island, 20 March 1967]

One day, Id of Mer sent three manned canoes to Erub.

They arrived in the afternoon, but the Meriam did not beach until after nightfall, when they pulled in at Wadaiam, dragged their canoes to a safe hiding place, and then took cover in thick scrub. The tide receded, laying bare the home reef of Erub; the whole time the Meriam neither moved nor spoke in their place of concealment.

Late that night, at dead low water, Koreg of Zaum (an inland village) went to the reef to see if fish had been trapped in the *sai*.[1] Eventually he came to Wadaiam. There he found that many fish had been trapped in the pool at the pocket of the stone fence and he began to spear them.

The Meriam heard the sound of water splashing in the *sai* and said: "There are fish jumping out there. Let us go and spear them." They walked down to the beach and out across the reef, talking as they went.

1. Stone fish-trap.

284

Koreg heard their voices and froze. When he knew that they were coming straight towards him, he jumped over the wall of the *sai* and crouched outside it to find out who the men were. Meriam! Koreg took to his heels.

The Meriam chased him. One of them speared Koreg in the belly; but he did not kill him outright, and Koreg escaped. The Meriam turned back then, took the fish from the pocket of the *sai* at Wadaiam and returned to their hiding place.

Despite his wound, Koreg ran all the way home to Zaum and reported the presence of Meriam on Erub. By this time, however, his bowels had come out through the hole in his belly. No sooner had he given his message than he fell down dead.

Early next morning, the head man of Zaum sent a message to Rebes, telling him what had happened and informing him that the Meriam canoes were still at Wadaiam. Rebes sent word back to the head man of Zaum, telling him to lead his men round by the eastern side of the island; he, Rebes, would lead his men round by the western side; they would join forces at Wadaiam that night and kill all the Meriam except one who would have to be spared to take the news back to Mer.

And so it befell, exactly as Rebes had planned. The Meriam who was permitted to escape ran into the scrub and hid in it until he contrived one day to steal a canoe and make his way back to Mer.

When Id received the news of the massacre, he called together his men and told them to prepare to fight at Erub. As soon as they had armed themselves and loaded the canoes, the war party sailed. Id's plan was to anchor at Seu[2] until the sun went down and complete the journey after dark, when a secret landing could be effected.

While they waited at Seu in the afternoon, the tide was low, so to pass the time the men walked about on the sandbank throwing spears at the husks of dry coconuts. "This is how we will spear the Erubam," they boasted.[3]

They were seen by the people of Erub, who sneered: "What fools those Meriam are! Chasing fish on a dry sandbank!"

The Meriam landed at Mogor in the dark, hid their canoes, and made camp in the scrub. At the end of three days they were still hiding at the same spot, because they did not know where Rebes was living at that time. Rebes, more than any other man at Erub, had incurred Id's anger. Rebes was a warrior and leader of great renown. It was he who had first to be dealt with.

On the fourth day, Id said to his men: "We will move to the western side of Erub and search for Rebes there." So they poled and paddled to Bikar and, after hiding their canoes, made another camp in the scrub.

2. A sandbank between Mer and Erub.
3. One informant said that this sandbank derives its name from the Meriam war-cry ("*Seu! Seu! Seu!*"), which was used while the men practised spearing.

285

Put (decorative armband worn on upper arms)

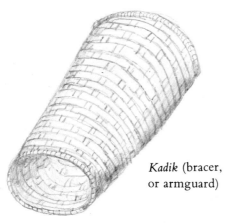

Kadik (bracer, or armguard)

4. Harry Captain said that Rebes had five wives.

5. This point is known as *Kerem Paur* (*kerem*, head; *paur*, skin). It was given this name because the heads taken during the massacre described in this story were skinned there.

Harry Captain said that the reason why Id sent his canoes to Erub was to obtain possession of *nam kerem*, the sacred turtle stone which belonged to the Meuram people of that island. He also said that when Id returned to Mer, after killing Rebes, he took with him *nam kerem*, which has remained at Mer ever since. A few years ago it was cemented to the top of a small cairn in front of the Council office.

For some time, Rebes had been crippled with rheumatism in both legs. He and his two wives[4] were living in a secluded cave at Kotor, close to the summit, on the seaward side, of the hill called Waus, overlooking Bikar.

The night that the Meriam slept at Bikar, Rebes had a premonition of impending disaster. At daylight he ordered one wife to make a fire to warm his aching joints and sent the other to the top of Waus to find out if there were Meriam canoes in the bay below. The woman saw none, so she returned to Kotor and told her husband that his fears were groundless.

Early that morning, two women who had accompanied the warriors of Mer to Erub went for a swim in the sea. Suddenly, they saw smoke go up at the top of Waus. They called out to the men—who had stayed hidden in the scrub—and pointed to it. "Nonsense," said the men, "that's not smoke, that's morning mist."

Presently another puff of smoke went up at the same spot on Waus. Seeing it, the women again called to the men. This time Id recognized it for what it was and immediately ordered his men to arm themselves and follow him in *atei* (three rows, the attacking formation). In that manner, Id and his men advanced up the hill to Kotor.

Boz (a tough-stemmed vine) screened the entrance to the cave in which the crippled Rebes lay helpless on his back. Id signalled to his men to stand back out of sight and, parting the vines, called through them to Rebes: "I thought you were my friend; yet, when I sent men across to Erub, you killed them."

Rebes seized the bundle of spears on the ground beside him and flung it at Id, but the latter warded them off by pulling together the canes of *boz*. Id then entered the cave. Shouting, *"Id opnor beizam!* (Id, shark from the great reef to windward!)," he hurled his *kusbager* at Rebes, killing him, and afterwards removed the warrior's head with his *koir* (bamboo beheading-knife). He and his men killed Rebes's wives and beheaded them, too.

The Meriam returned to Bikar, taking the heads with them. They dragged their canoes down into the sea and paddled round to Mogor, going ashore at many places on the way. When they saw people, they left their canoes to kill them; those whom they killed they beheaded, and the heads they placed in the canoes.

At the stony point[5] at the southern end of the bay of Mogor, Id ordered his men to take all the heads ashore and skin and clean them. When this had been done the Meriam set sail for home, their canoes piled high with Erubam heads.

Meriam *ares le* (fighting man)
Artist Segar Passi

AIB

[Told by Daniel Pau of Darnley Island, 21 June 1966]

This story is a sequel to the Murray Island story "Wakai and Kuskus".

Two Meuram *le* (people) from Erub (descendants of Paiwer who helped build Bramble Cay) were members of the ill-fated hunting expedition led by Wakai and Kuskus of Mer to Kerged. When the party returned from Kerged, it brought back water obtained from a pool which had been revealed by a small *kiriskiris* bird. The two men from Erub took some of it to their home at Keirari and kept it in a *bu* shell which they hung from a tree.

1. To become a spring of brackish water at that place.
2. Today there is an engine beside it, pumping water to many villages on Darnley Island.

While all the people of Keirari were away from their village working in their gardens one day, a man named Aib, whose home was at Bumeo, was out fishing on the reef. Aib happened to glance towards Keirari and see something which glistened in the sunlight at that place. Curious, he went to find out what it was.

From a tree hung a *bu* shell filled to the brim with water which caught the sparkle of the sun as the wind blew. Aib removed the shell from the tree and set out for his home with it. He carried it very carefully; nevertheless, a little water spilled at Ewi.[1] When he reached Bumeo, he drank from the shell until he had drained it dry. Then, his belly swollen from drinking so much, he lay down in the shade of a tree and fell asleep.

Later in the day, the people of Keirari returned from their gardens to find that the sacred water brought back after the trip to Kerged had been stolen. The men followed the tracks of the thief to Bumeo, where they saw Aib asleep on the ground. Beside him lay the *bu* shell from Keirari—empty.

Furious, one of the men drove his *kusbager* into Aib's belly, whereupon all the water that Aib had drunk that day gushed out from him.

It became a spring which never goes dry, not even in drought years.[2]

DIDIPAPA AND GORARASIASI

[Told by Harry Captain at Thursday Island, 26 July 1969]

One day the Samsep and Peidu peoples of Erub went to Wargor for an outing. They roasted *ketai* (a variety of yam) in a fire, and then, after scraping away the charred parts, they grated the crusts and floury meal of the *ketai* into *miskor* (halves of big clam-shells). To this they added shredded coconut[1] and coconut-milk, and, after stirring and beating all together, had a rich and delectable mash (*mabus*), a food which everyone relished.

By that time the sun was low in the sky, and it was time to go home. No one wanted to be abroad after dark.

Two Samsep men, Didipapa and Gorarasiasi,[2] had furthest to walk, so they left first of all. They set out by the bush road for Ina, their village, taking with them their share of the *mabus* in a *miskor* which Gorarasiasi carried on his shoulder, and had not gone very far when they saw a ghost blocking their way. Terrified, the two men stood stockstill. So did the ghost.

Gorarasiasi was a very stupid man, a half-wit, but Didipapa was very clever, and he nudged his friend and whispered: "Do as I do." Didipapa closed his eyes and Gorarasiasi followed suit. When they opened their eyes, the ghost shut his. Didipapa and Gorarasiasi watched the ghost and found that the ghost kept his eyes closed for the same length of time as they had theirs. The moment the ghost opened his eyes, the friends closed theirs, and this time they kept them closed for a long while. The second time the ghost shut his eyes, Didipapa mouthed "Go!" to his friend and gave him a push and Gorarasiasi, silly man, instead of leaving the heavy *miskor* behind, took it with him when he tiptoed past the ghost and continued on the way to Ina.

The sun set about the time that the ghost opened his eyes. He saw that one of the men was missing. Quickly Didipapa shut his eyes. He kept them tight shut for a very long while. Then, no sooner was it the ghost's turn to shut his eyes, than Didipapa made a silent dash for it, past the ghost and along the path towards the safety of his home at Ina. At Tor—on the hill at the back of Ina—he nearly tripped over Gorarasiasi's feet.

Now Gorarasiasi had had plenty of time to reach Ina. He should have been there by the time Didipapa opened his eyes the third time, yet there lay the foolish fellow, his head and body in the grass and *weskepu* (a ground creeper) at the side of the path, his feet in the middle of the path beside the *miskor* of *mabus*. Didipapa kicked him. "Get up! Come on, get up! The

1. Obtained by scraping with shells called *kaip*.
2. *Gorarasi* is a noun compounded from *gorar* (singeing to the point of discoloration) and *asi* (pain). *Gorarasiasi* is the adjective formed from *gorarasi*.

289

ghost is close behind me," he told his friend. Gorarasiasi did not move. He said: "You go. Don't wait for me. I'm still tired. I'll rest a while longer and follow you later." Didipapa ran on alone.

"Where is Gorarasiasi?" he was asked when he reached Ina. "He's probably been taken by a ghost by now," Didipapa told them. "There was one close behind me when I passed him at Tor. I tried to get him to come with me, but he refused."

Gorarasiasi was discovered by the ghost soon after Didipapa left Tor. The ghost stumbled over the *miskor*, looked down, and saw Gorarasiasi's feet. "What's your name?" asked the ghost. "Gorarasiasi." "Where's your friend?" "He passed me. He's home at Ina by now." "Why didn't you go home when you had the chance?" "Oh, I wanted to rest. That *miskor* is very heavy." "Well, you're not going to rest any longer. Get up. Go on, get up. Pick up the *miskor* and carry it. You're coming with me now." Gorarasiasi shouldered the heavy *miskor* and followed the ghost.

The ghost made a bee-line for Zaum. Nor far from his home, he hid Gorarasiasi in some scrub and went on alone to ask his companions if he might bring Gorarasiasi to join them. When they saw him coming they were busy cooking a meal. "Where have you been?" they asked him. "I went for a walk," he replied. "You smell bad. You must have touched a 'ghost' while you were away," the other ghosts said. "I met two," he said. The other ghosts smeared him with substances which made him less offensive to their noses, though he would have disgusted humans.

The ghosts kept Gorarasiasi with them for two full days and then decided to send him home. On the morning of his departure from Zaum, they gave him a present of bananas and yams and asked what he was going to do with the *miskor* he had brought with him. And although the contents of the *miskor* were by this time maggot-ridden and foul-smelling, Gorarasiasi said: "I'll take it with me. It belongs to Didipapa as well as to me. We arranged to share it."

Gorarasiasi and the ghosts set out from Zaum in company and walked together as far as Mimur. There the ghosts turned back, afraid lest they be seen by the people of the villages. They took with them the fruit and vegetables that they had earlier given to Gorarasiasi.

When Gorarasiasi reached the point between Ina and Isem, he was seen by the people of Ina. "Gorarasiasi's coming!" they cried. Gorarasiasi came nearer, and then they said: "Go and wash yourself. Throw your *mabus* to the fish in the sea. Rub your body with sand."

After he had done these things, the people gathered round him and listened to his story. "The ghost took me to Zaum," he said. "There are a lot of ghosts at that place. Many of them I recognized. They're my friends." "That's not surprising," said the people of Ina. "You're silly like them."

IMERMER AND KIKMERMER

[Told by Rachel Pilot at Darnley Island, 18 June 1966]

Beside the little bay of Irmed, there once lived a woman named Tekei and her two daughters, Imermer and Kikmermer.[1] They were pretty girls; only, when Imermer spoke she sounded as if she were crying, and when Kikmermer spoke, her nose ran. They were Peidu[2] people.

On the other side of Erub, where the Meuram lived, there was at this time a young man named Kiari[3] who stayed with his mother at Kaip.

Kiari badly wanted a wife, so one day he walked round to the Peidu side of the island to look for one and, when he reached Irmed, saw Imermer and Kikmermer. He said to himself: "I'll find a way to get them to Kaip, and then I'll keep them both and have two wives."

He pretended to be sick. Tekei, seeing him in that state, took him to her home and looked after him well, bringing him roast yams and fish to eat. Presently, he told her that he must go back to Kaip and asked if her two daughters might accompany him part of the way, because he was still feeling far from well; he promised to send them home from Mekik Paikai. Tekei consented to this arrangement, and Imermer and Kikmermer set out with Kiari.

When they reached Mekik Paikai, however, Kiari said to the girls: "Come a little further with me—as far as Kaiziz—then you may leave me." Imermer and Kikmermer went willingly.

At Kaiziz, Kiari asked them to go on to Sesengab, and at Sesengab he asked them to go on to Bikar. His plan was working. The girls were still with him at Kemus, where he persuaded them that he must have their help if he were to reach the top of the small hill, Serar-urpi. From Serar-urpi it was a very short distance only to Kiari Awak, where the Meuram people were gathered for a feast that day, but, because Kiari was by now leaning on them for support and seemed very ill indeed, Imermer and Kikmermer took him the rest of the way. "Mother," Kiari called, "spread mats for my two wives!"

Imermer and Kikmermer looked at each other in alarm—it was news to them that they were Kiari's wives. Food was brought to them, and people from round about came to stare at them. Kiari was greatly envied by the men for having obtained not one wife, but two, both of them young and pretty. Shortly afterwards, he had to leave for Bariadog to take part in a

1. *Tekei*, the Meriam word for the Groper (*Promicrops lanceolatus* [Bloch]). *I*, tears; *mermer*, filled. *Kikmer*, mucus from the nose.

2. There appear to have been four named patriclans at Erub: Peidu (a special term for the kind of *womer* [man-o'-war-hawk] which frequents the reef outside Peidu territory in large numbers); Meuram (which means, literally, belonging to the tree, *meur* [*Barringtonia calyptrata*]); Saisireb (which derives its name from *sai*, the stone fish-trap of the Eastern Islands); and Samsep (this being the name of the barnacle-like growth seen on logs and bamboo which drift down to the Eastern Islands of Torres Strait during the north-west season). They were exogamous. Each clan had its own territorial division. The Meuram and Peidu divisions accounted for the greater part of the island, the Meuram taking up most of the eastern half, the Peidu most of the western half. Whatever the position in the past, today all Meuram claim putative descent from a man named Paiwer, all Peidu from a man named Rebes. (See the story of "Maizab Kaur", in this section.) The clan totem of the Peidu is the man-o'-war-hawk. It is not an ancestor totem. The *lanog* (dying movements) performed by Peidu people are man-o'-war-hawk movements. Saisireb people are noted for the fact that they eat fish raw.

3. Or Kaiari. The name was pronounced differently at different times, even by the same speaker.

291

ceremony for *nam kerem*. "Take good care of my wives for me," he said to his mother.

Tears streamed from the girls' eyes. They had no wish at all to be Kiari's wives, wanting only to return to their mother at Irmed. Kiari's mother felt so sorry for them that when they said they wanted to go into the bushes to relieve themselves, even though she knew it to be a ruse on their part to enable them to escape, she raised no objection.

When Kiari arrived back from Bariadog and found his wives gone, he ran after them, to catch them and bring them back. From the top of Serar-urpi he could see Imermer and Kikmermer running along the beach at Kemus, so he plucked fruit from a tree called *ubar*[4] and threw them at the girls. But they were too far away, and the fruit fell to the ground well short of them.[5]

Imermer and Kikmermer reached Irmed breathless. As soon as they had gasped out their story, Tekei armed herself with a sharp-pointed stick, which she threw at Kiari the moment he came close enough. It struck him to the ground, at which Imermer and Kikmermer rushed at him and beat his head with clamshells until he was dead. Mother and daughters dragged his body away to a hole in a rock at the edge of the sea.[6]

Tekei's daughters, Imermer and Kikmermer, turned to stone on the beach at Irmed—they are two shiny, black rocks in the sand.

4. *Ubar* bears small, pungent fruit which are soft-fleshed and grey-green when ripe. Not the same fruit as the *ubar* of West Torres Strait.
5. The fruit thrown by Kiari turned to stones which are part red, part black.
6. This rock is at the point of one arm of the bay of Irmed.

stories from

MER *Murray Island*

A Meriam wearing the head-dress, *dari*

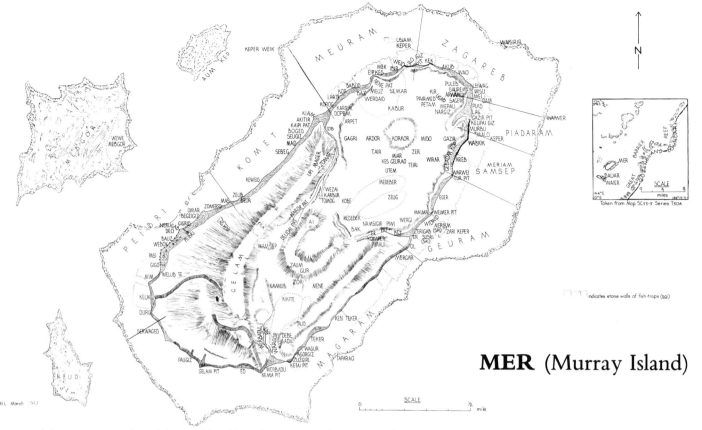

MER (Murray Island)

This is a copy of the map we made at Murray Island in February, March, 1967, to fix the location of the place names mentioned in the stories told to me by the older men.
Dagi Gisu and Segar Passi helped to obtain the first rough outline.
Moses Omey then drew the map as it now appears.
Sam Passi, Dagi, and Moses indicated the correct position of places and clan divisions.
Marou checked our work and helped us with information.

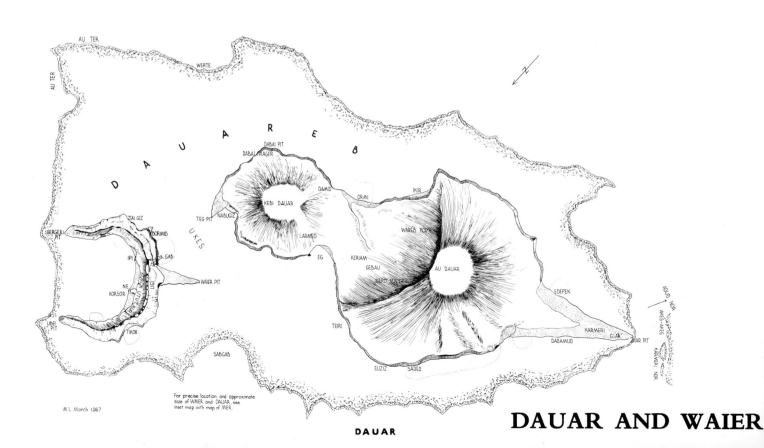

For precise location and approximate size of WAIER and DAUAR, see inset map with map of MER.

M.L. March 1967

DAUAR AND WAIER

DAUAR

The islands of Waier (at left) and Dauar (at right), photographed from Murray Island

Dela Mopwali, one of the story-tellers

GELAM [Told by Dela Mopwali at Murray Island, 21 February 1967]

The boy Gelam lived with his mother, Atwer,[1] at Bulbul on the island of Mua. When he became a youth, his mother bent a bow for him and made him some arrows, and from that time he set out from his home every morning to spend the day shooting birds. Every afternoon, he used to knot the wing-tips of each bird that he had killed during the day, slip the birds on to his bow, and carry them back to Bulbul. He gave the lean birds to his mother and kept the fat birds for himself.

Now although Gelam and Atwer had separate cooking fires, Atwer soon discovered the difference between the birds that she and her son were cooking—Gelam's birds were always fat, hers were always thin—and she determined to punish him by frightening him while he was in the bush.

And this she did. One day, she smeared clay over her face and head, as if she were in mourning, stole to the small shelter in which her son crouched hiding—waiting for unsuspecting birds to come his way—and startled him. Terrified, often stumbling and falling and cutting himself on stones, he ran back to Bulbul.

Atwer, meanwhile, returned home by a faster route than Gelam's and quickly washed herself clean in the sea. When Gelam arrived, he found her sitting down waiting for him. Atwer asked him what he had done with the birds he had shot during the day, to be told that he had left them behind when he ran away from a ghost.

Gelam continued to go to the bush to shoot birds, and, every time he went, his mother frightened him by pretending to be a ghost. Then one evening he noticed traces of clay in his mother's ears. "Mother," he said to himself, "it is you who have been frightening me."

Next morning, he told Atwer that he was going to shoot birds, but he had no intention of doing so. Instead, he cut down a tree called *wapad*, which has very light wood, scraped it into the shape of a dugong,[2] and put it into the sea. He found, however, that it was not the kind of dugong he wanted: it was far too light and floated on top of the water. So he sent it away, saying: "Go, dugong. Go to Mabuiag."

Another day he cut down a *iutarkub* (a wild cotton-tree) and from it made another dugong which, while heavier than the first, was still too light for his needs. "Go, dugong. Go to Badu," he ordered it.

This is the most popular myth of Torres Strait.

Gelam, creator of the dugong, also became the most striking physical feature of Murray Island (Mer)—the hill, *Gelam paser*. As one approaches this island, Gelam emerges from the sea until he is seen clearly as a dugong. From a distance, Murray Island is unforgettably, indelibly, Gelam.

1. Gelam's mother is always called Usar in West Torres Strait. *Atwir* (n.) means "criticism". The cloud and mist which sometimes obscure the top of Gelam hill on Murray Island are called *Atwer ira kemur*, Atwer's smoke.

2. What follows at this point in the story accounts for the origin of dugong. Wees Nawia of Kubin (at the southern tip of Mua) named four different kinds of dugong found in Torres Strait, each belonging to the region named in this story.

   The dugong of East Torres Strait (*malu dangal*) is very big, heavy-bodied, and dark in colour. It comes once to the surface to breathe and then remains underwater for long periods (up to an hour) before coming up to breathe again. It is difficult to harpoon this dugong.

   By contrast, the dugong of West Torres Strait are small-bodied and light in colour. When these dugong breathe, they come to the surface three times in fairly quick succession and remain close to the surface between breaths. The dugong of West Torres Strait are said to be better-flavoured than those of East Torres Strait.

297

On yet another day, he fashioned a dugong from *garagar tulu* (a species of bloodwood). When he tried its performance in the sea, this one proved nearly, but not quite, heavy enough. "Go, dugong. Go to *zei dagam daudai* (south-side mainland, Australia)," he commanded.

That night, his father came to him in a dream and told him what he must do to find the right kind of wood for a heavy dugong. "Tap the trunk of every tree that you see in the bush until you find one that makes the sound, 'Pi-i-i-i!' The top of this tree will be thick with busy, twittering little black birds (*mutil*). They will be a further sign to you that you have found the right tree."

Gelam followed his father's instructions and found the tree which had been described to him in the dream. From the wood of this tree—*baidam tulu* (a bloodwood)—he shaped and hollowed out a dugong which performed as he required of it, submerging itself deep in the water. He got inside it and swam about. It suited his every need. So he took it ashore and placed inside it good soil and fruit and vegetables and the seeds of many trees, and then he went home to his mother.

In the morning he said to her: "Mother, if you should see a very big fish when you go to the reef today, call me. I'll come and spear it."

No sooner had Atwer gone to the reef with her basket and sharp-pointed stick to fish, than Gelam hurried to the dugong that he had made the previous day. Inside his armguard (*kadik*)[3] he placed the seeds and plants and soil which he had collected, and then he got inside the dugong and swam deep to the place where his mother was standing. There he came to the surface and allowed her to see him. "Gelam, come quickly with your spear!" called Atwer.

Gelam swam very close to the edge of the reef and his mother grazed his dugong with her pointed stick. He swam away, wheeled, and came back to her, opening the mouth of the dugong so that she could see inside to her son. "Mother," said Gelam, "you frightened me by pretending to be a ghost. You did that not once, but many times. Now I am going far away to a place where you will never see me." And with that, he closed the mouth of the dugong and swam away. Atwer called him back to her, but he would not come. Weeping, she said: "*Bakiamu Mer ge, au lewer-lewer ged ge, esigemerua* (Go and lie down at Mer, an island rich in food)."

Gelam came to the surface of the water at Nagi and looked back at Mua. He saw Atwer, who still stood at the same spot on the reef as when he had left her. "If I stay here, my mother will be able to see me and may come to visit me," he thought. So he closed up the dugong and swam deep to Iama. But there, also, he felt himself too close to Mua. He swam to many islands,[4] to Sasi, Poruma, Masig, Aurid, Ugar, and Erub, but at none of them had he any wish to stay—all were too close to Mua and his mother.

3. Worn on the left arm to protect it from the bow string.
4. Opinions vary on the islands visited by Gelam. Every informant names Nagi (Mt. Ernest Island), and Iama (Yam Island). Some also include Sasi (Long Island), Poruma (Coconut Island), Masig (Yorke Island), Ugar (Stephens Island), and Erub (Darnley Island).

From Garsao, the big lagoon in the reef of Erub, Gelam saw Mer. "That is where I am going to make my home," he said.

Gelam swam to Mer and lay down beside her, his face to the north-east. *Naiger*, the north-east wind blew hard up his nostrils, so he swung round to face south-west. He spat two *wada* seeds from his mouth, which became the islands of Dauar and Waier, and with his left hand he threw out all the seeds and plants and soil that he had brought with him from Mua.[5] Then he fixed himself firmly in place, before *sager* the south-east wind began to blow, and became a hill.

Later on, when the sharks attacked the small island of Peibri—she lived to the right of Gelam on the small reef called Mebgor—she left her home and came to rest beside Gelam. Mer was a small island once, but Gelam came, and then Peibri, to make her big and strong and rich.

At Mua, Atwer remains at the spot at which she was standing when Gelam swam away. The tide came in, but she did not move. Tears streamed from her eyes until, at last, she was covered by the sea. Then she turned to stone.

That Atwer[6] still weeps for Gelam may be seen at every low tide. Then, fresh water trickles from her "eyes"—two holes close to the top of the rock which she became.

5. The seeds and plants included: *waiwi*, a variety of mango; *sorbi*, a tree which bears edible fruit on its trunk; *wais* and *kud*, trees which bear edible, red fruit; *u*, coconut palms; and different varieties of yams (*lewer kar* [true food]).

The rich, red soil of Mer is said to have been brought from Mua by Gelam. Mua, thus deprived, was left with poor soil only.

6. The rock of course is called Usar, since it is by that name that Atwer is known in West Torres Strait.

Robert Pitt informed me that Gelam's father was a great warrior and a powerful sorcerer at Wabada in the Fly River delta. He was killed by his own people because of his sorcery.

Gelam then kept his father's bones and aids to sorcery in a bag which was always beside him when he slept at night. His father used to appear to him in dreams, foretelling future events and giving advice. Thus forewarned, Gelam was able to escape with his mother from Wabada at a time when there were plans afoot to kill the pair of them.

Gelam and his mother fled across Western Papua by way of Kiwai, Gaima, the Oriomo River, Daru, Mawat, Ture-ture, and Buzi to Boigu and Mabuiag in Torres Strait. Finally, they crossed to the island of Mua and made a home for themselves at Bulbul.

Deger (or *dangal*). *Deger* is the Meriam word for dugong. *Dangal* is the Mabuiag word.

299

APININI AND SIDIPUAR

[Told by Robert Pitt at Murray Island, 19 August 1968]

Dauar is a small volcanic island. The two hills mentioned in this story are part of the rim of the crater.

Two sisters, Apinini and Sidipuar, wove the two hills of the island of Dauar. Apinini was the elder sister, Sidipuar the younger. They sat at opposite ends of the island to do their weaving.

After a while, Sidipuar felt thirsty and she went to visit her sister.

When Sidipuar reached her, Apinini laid down her work and did not take it up again. But because Apinini had worked at her hill longer than Sidipuar had at hers, Apinini's hill was bigger than Sidipuar's.

The two sisters turned to stone and may be seen on Au Dauar, the big hill woven by Apinini. The smaller hill woven by Sidipuar is called Kebi Dauar.

The island of Dauar, showing the two hills woven by the sisters, Sidipuar and Apinini

THE STORY
OF PEIBRI [Told by Marou at Murray Island, 1 February 1967]

Formerly, the district of Peibri on Mer was a little coral island which lived on the small reef called Mebgor, close to the south-west part of the home reef of Mer.

When Peibri was attacked by sharks one day, it fled for protection to the foot of Gelam hill. Where it had been, it left behind a patch of sand, nowadays called Wewe Mebgor.

The sharks pursued Peibri as far as they could and were stranded. There they turned to patches of sandstone rock, as can be seen at low tide between Gigred and Gigo.

For Peibri never left the haven it found, but remained where it had come to rest and became part of the island of Mer.

Very often when one stands on the beach in the district of Peibri, one sees sharks pursuing stingrays almost to the water's edge. These stingrays are of a particular kind: *Aetobatus narinari* (Euphrasen). The Meriam call them *Peibri sor*.

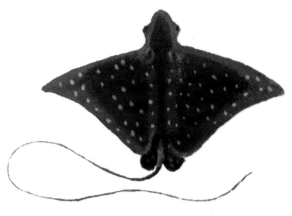

Peibri sor

Marou, one of the story-tellers. He is wearing a *dibidibi* round his neck. In his right hand he holds a *gabagaba* (club with round stone head) and under his left arm a *seuriseuri* (club with rayed head). Marou died in 1968.

Pilauar

MUKEIS

This myth belongs to the island of Dauar and is said to be very old. Two reasons were advanced in support of the great age of the story: "the men were really animals; the men had no clan."

Given here are an edited and a re-translated version of the story recorded in Meriam in the Pasi MS (*Reports*, III, 242–43). A detail which Pasi omitted is that the men who escaped from Mukeis while he was a whale turned to stone after they landed at Zuzgiri. Mukeis abandoned the whale *nog* (form, or shape), left it behind as a lifeless whale, and stepped ashore as a man. Then the whale *nog* turned to stone.

It would be in keeping with other myths of Torres Strait for the spirit of each of the five characters in this story either to adopt the *nog* of another living creature, or to take a previously non-existent shape or form and become the first ancestor of a new species of living animal creature. At any rate, there are sea-birds called *serar*, *pilauar*, *gob*, and *bi*, and the Meriam word for rat is *mukeis*.

Serar

1. The Meriam includes the word *kepol*, i.e. "separately", indicating that the water was for his own use, and would not be shared with anyone else.

Mukeis ira mer pe ike. Able Mukeis au weserweser le. Wi abi detuaklare: "Ki nole mari lagkak. Ma au weserweser, ma no naoa."

Mukeis ide tabara ni kepol eper tag u. E ge Bi kikem damos kega: "Ma kari nakaueret?" Bi de abi detager: "Ma no naoa. Ki mari tonar umele."

E ge bakiamulu Serar i damos kega: "Mi nabakiamulei?" Serar ide abi detager kega: "Ma no naoa. Ki mari tonar umele."

E ko bakiamulu Gob i damos: "Meriba mi nabakiamulei?" Gob ide abi kega: "Ma no naoa." E ga Pilauar i damos kega: "Meriba mi nabakiamulei?" Pilauar ide abi detager: "Ma no naoa. Ki mari tonar umele."

E ge no akailu we ge ekueilu. E oka batager, able mer e etkalu kega: "Mi Bi ra nar darapei, le mi argei asemulei. Mi Serar ira nar darapei, le mi argei asemulei. Mi Pilauar ira nar darapei, le mi argei asemulei. Mi Gob ira nar darapei, le mi argei asemulei." Able Mukeis ira mer pe ike.

Keubu e bakiamulu galbol nog ge balu, nar erap, le ereg esemulu, ga bakiamulu nerut nar erap, le ereg esemulu. Able neis nar nab darager darakair. Wi eirsilei Zuzgiri ge. E ko eirsilu. Sina esemuda able mer Mukeis ira.

This is the story of Mukeis.

Mukeis was a very greedy man whom others would not have as a companion. They said: "We don't want you. You are a glutton. You may not come with us."

Carrying his water in one hand,[1] Mukeis went first to Bi and said to him: "May I go with you [in your canoe]?" But Bi refused to have him aboard, saying: "You stay behind. We know your greedy ways."

So Mukeis went to Serar, and then he went to Gob, and after that to Pilauar, but each of these men also refused to take Mukeis with him. "We know your habits," said Serar and Gob and Pilauar.

Mukeis stood on the beach and thought for a while, and then he said: "We'll wreck Bi's canoe and eat everyone in it. We'll wreck Serar's canoe and eat everyone in it. We'll wreck Pilauar's canoe and eat everyone in it.

302

We'll wreck Gob's canoe and eat everyone in it. There will be nothing left of canoes and people." That is what Mukeis said.

After he had finished speaking, Mukeis went and entered the form[2] of a living whale, wrecked two canoes, one after the other, and ate everyone who had been on board each. He then chased the other two canoes, but these he could not overtake, and they ran ashore at Zuzgiri. Mukeis also landed at Zuzgiri.

So ends the story of Mukeis.

2. *Nog ge balu: nog*, form; *ge*, into, at; *balu*, entered. Here Mukeis, as a man, entered inside a whale. While he was inside the whale, he retained his own human appearance, mind, and personality, and the actions and thoughts of the whale were those of Mukeis. The whale was possessed by him.

Nog also means "mask". Thus, the donning of an animal mask by a man was a dramatized presentation of the belief in the transformation of human to animal or animal to human.

POP AND KOD

[Told by George Passi at Murray Island, 20 August 1968]

Adarmei adarmo adarmei adarmo
Wabi kaied ei, wabi kaied ei.

Adarmei adarmo adarmei adarmo
Wabi nap ei, wabi nap ei.

(You and your grandchild are crawling.)

("*Samela Wed*", ancient Meriam song, sung by Pop when he climbed the *in* tree)

Samaito samaito
Samela samela samaito.

(*Kamut* [string figure] song)

★

Pop and Kod lived at Er. Every day Pop climbed to the top of an *in*[1] tree and sang. Kod sat on the ground at the foot of the tree and wove mats.[2]

At first they did not know that they were male and female. Later they came together as man and woman.

Kod gave birth to a male child whom she and Pop named Au Teter (big legs).

The population (*nosik*) grew from Au Teter and spread out over Mer, Dauar, and Waier.

Abou Noah told this story in much greater detail than George Passi did. He named Bez as Pop's home. He also said that Kod lived alone at Kes until such time as Pop was led to that place one day by the smoke from her cooking fire. Until then neither Pop nor Kod knew of the other's presence on Mer.

At the end of his story, Abou gave an account of a visit to Mer by men of Erub. They landed at Beur, only to be told by Pop that Mer belonged to him and Kod and he would kill them if they did not return at once to their own island.

Marou sang the *samela wed* for me in 1967. He gave Bez as the site of the *in* tree which Pop climbed: "Every morning Pop and Kod went up to a place called Bez, where Pop climbed the *in* tree and sang the *samela wed*." (Marou was twelve years old at the time of the Cambridge Anthropological Expedition to Torres Strait in 1898. He had vivid memories of every member of the Expedition. Marou died at the beginning of 1968.)

1. *Cordia subcordata.* Some say Pop climbed a *pinar* tree.
2. These were *pot moder*, very strong mats woven from pandanus leaves from which the outer edges have been stripped.

TAGAI

This story of the origin of certain constellations is widespread in Torres Strait. It is told in great detail at Mabuiag and Saibai.

Landtman records it in *The Folk-Tales of the Kiwai Papuans* (Helsingfors, 1917), 482–84. He obtained several variants as well. All were told to him at Mawat, on the Papuan mainland. It is of interest that the story and the variants obtained by Landtman assign Tagai's origin either to Mabuiag or to Saibai, islands in Torres Strait.

There are stone relics of Tagai and Kareg at Dauar and Murray Island. Marou told me that Tagai landed at Ormi on Dauar and went to Warebkop where he turned to stone, and that there are two stones on the reef at Las which are Tagai's canoe and Tagai's friend, Kareg.

Ownership of the constellation Tagai is claimed by the Giar-Dauareb, that is, by those people who are descended from Koit of Las who went to live at Giar on the island of Dauar. A family belonging to Gigred on Murray Island claims ownership of the name, Tagai.

Tagai is seen by the Meriam as a large constellation in the sky to the south of them. They see it as a man standing aboard a canoe, spear in hand. Tagai's left hand is the Southern Cross.

The story told to me in 1967 and 1968 by members of the Passi family (who are Giar-Dauareb) did not differ from that told by their grandfather and Arei to Ray in 1898. Given here are an edited and a retranslated version of the story dictated to Ray (*Reports*, III, 250).

1. The *Usiam* are the Seven Sisters.
2. The *Seg* are the stars in alignment in Orion.

Tagai abra dikereder nar. Kareg e kaimeg Tagai ra. Tagai ekueilu tarim ge, Kareg ekueilu kor ge. E imut etaiuer. Tagai baur erpeirer, e dasmerer lar em.

Abra gair pazar emreder eipu, Seg a Usiam, neis, neis, neis, neis, neis, neis. Wi lewer eroare a ni iriare nole damosa Tagai.

Kareg e egremalu, e detager Tagai. Tagai, e keub em egremalu, tabakiamulu eip em, e tais gogob, isisir Usiam kikem, batdaueredlu gur ge, keubu Seg isisir, kepu batdaueredlu gur ge. Abra au urker.

E detager Kareg kega: "Ma netat le namidaua nar ge."

Tagai was the owner of the canoe; his friend Kareg was with him. Tagai stood at the bow, Kareg stood at the stern and poled. Tagai held a spear in his hand and looked for fish.

The crew sat in the middle of the canoe. They were the Usiam[1] and the Seg,[2] twelve men altogether. They ate the food and drank the water [which was stored on board for the journey] without asking Tagai.

Kareg saw them do it and told Tagai, who came to the middle of the canoe with a loop of rope. With it he strung the Usiam together, and [then] he threw them into the sea. He afterwards strung the Seg and threw them into the sea. He was very angry.

Tagai said to Kareg: "You are the only man who may stay in the canoe."

304

Dau Tom standing behind Tagai's canoe (the long black stone) and Kareg (the red stone) at the edge of the reef at Las

Tup (the kind known as *Kos tup*)

NAGEG AND GEIGI

Given here are an edited and a retranslated version of the story in the Pasi MS (*Reports*, III, 229–33).

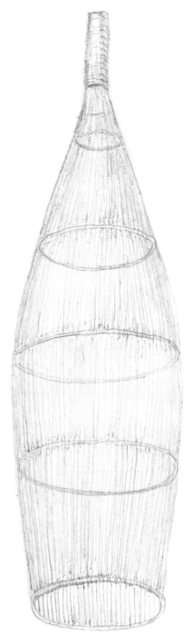

Weres (sardine scoop)

Able Nageg ira mer pe ike. Nageg dauer Ne ge. Keubu e werem esemelu abra nei Geigi. E batai au le bailu. Nageg ide abra sarik digiameilu abi ikuar. Geigi e bakiamulu keper em, kikem itimed bozar. E dabgeri tabara apu: "Ama, na lar?" "Bozar areg lar." Keubu e itimed gas. E dabgeri tabara apu: "Ama, na lar?" "Gas areg lar." A e itimed wirwir. E dabgeri tabara apu: "Ama, na lar?" "Wirwir areg lar." Keubu e baur eter abi ikuar. E bakiamulu, paris erem. E dasmeri netat au le abra nei Iriamuris. Geigi ikedilu tabara baur. E erapeilu u kupi, larerkep itkub, kerem ge dimrilu, a neis teter ge daramrilu, pako neis tag ge daramrilu. E baraigilu gur ge, e bakiamulu karem ge, batimedlu. Keubu ikariklu, tup dikiam. Iriamuris e tabara weres tikalu, tup akemelu. Geigi e ko tabara apu em akomelu. E adem dergeir able larerkep. E bakiamulu erdar tabara apu a nerut nole atager kak. Apu lam bagem. Nerut gerger e ko bakiamulu ko okaderdar mokakalam kikem. Able korep e tup dikiam. Iriamuris e weres tikalu e tup akemelu. E erdar Geigi ra neis teter gab kakake. Iriamuris e mer detager kega: "Ao? Mama le nali. Kaka dikepuali lar. Neis gerger ma kari okanardari. Ma mabu baseseredua." Nerut gerger, able au le e barkak detaut a Geigi de dikepuar bes. Nerut gerger e ko bakiamulu, Iriamuris emetu dirsirer Geigim. Iriamuris ide weres kikem akmeilu, Geigi bakiamulu muige abra weres. E tikalu, epaiteredlu pao ge. Iriamuris erertekri kega: "Sogi werem kem, wa tabatuer a wa taisare sop a irmad a ur." Sogi werem kem wi taisare sop, irmad, ur, tawer ge bamer okasise. Gair omasker bakiauare Geigi ra poni depomedlare. Iriamuris ide daraisumdarare. Wi ge tabakiauare apu detagrare kega: "Kerbi daisumdarda Iriamuris ide." Wi bog tabara uteb. Iriamuris ide ditimedlu kikem esak Geigi, e dikasir a igor, wader ga dikasir igor, wader ga dikasir a igor, pako tup able korep esemulu. E Geigi ereg, keubu e tup ereg. E weres erap irim, irmad irim, tibi alu, irim, wirwir alu irmilu. Sina no ga amdalare. Nageg e nab dekair tabara werem. Neis gerger barkiei, e tabakiamulu tikalu tabara kusbager. E ditimedlu erertekri kega: "Geigi, kara werem, ma neti kem ge nazirkedi? Ma kem em tekep, a bub em tekep, a sor em tekep." A ko tekri able netat mer. E tabakiamulu Waier Pit ge, ko erertekri kega: "Geigi, kara werem, ma neti kem ge nazirkedi? Aka Iriamuris i kem ge?" Akarikda Dauar ge. "Iriamuris, Geigi nade?" Iriamuris ide detaut kega: "Nole. Karim e Eg ge dali. Neis a neis kebi le kem." Nageg bakiamulu wiabi nautmerare kega: "Geigi nade?" Wi detautare kega: "Wa! E nade dali. Ki nole abi asmerkak." A Nageg takomelu,

dasmer Geigi ra kerem mus. E dikepuar: "Iriamuris ide emetu abi irgi." E abi
kusbager u ikos ke ko deketilu a keubu abra ib deparsilu. E eumilu. Nageg
bakiamulu, soni meta tidikemulu, tabakiamulu, disur abra kerem, eupamalu
teter ge ekueilu. E ekueilu, disur, ko eupamalu kerem ge ekueilu. Geigi eded
akailu. Apu et abi itmer kega: "Ma na ged lam?" Geigi de detaut kega: "Iriamuris ide kari nakemeda weres u." Nageg ide abi detager kega: "Mi nabakiamulei merbi ged im." Wi akomelei taba ged im. Wi ekueilei Ukes ge. Nageg ide
detager kikem tabara werem kega: "Ma bakiamu. Karem ge batimed. Ese gair
le mari mekik u wanaoguatmurauem, ma mekik ikeua, a baur u wanaskauem,
ma baur erapua." E ko apu detager kega: "Mari nab wanaosmerauem, mari o
seker ide wanariua." Geigi karem ge batimedlu. Nageg e no kur ge balu. Sina.
Nageg ira mer esemuda.

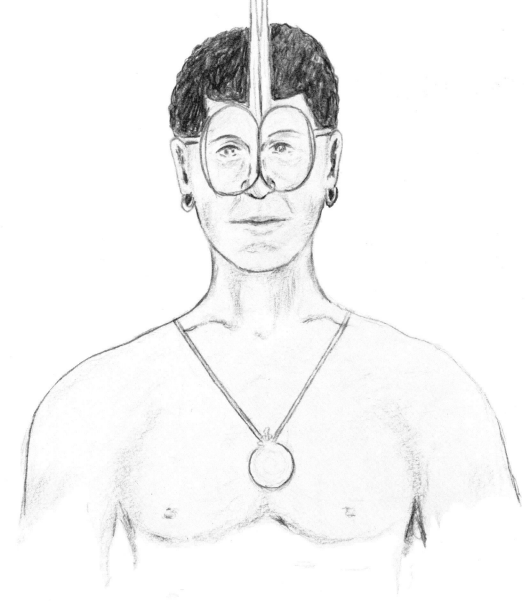

Head of a man wearing *larerkep* (ornamental "fish-eyes") in such a manner as
to illustrate the significance of the
adornment. In actual practice, the string
is tied so that the "eyes" are on the
forehead.

This is one of the best-known stories at Murray Island. To the word-for-word translation recorded here I have added a few explanatory details which were given to me by Robert Pitt. These additions are everywhere enclosed in square brackets.

The story of Nageg and Geigi includes the origin of the triggerfish (in Meriam, *nageg*) and the Great trevally (in Meriam, *geigi*).

Bozar

Wirwir

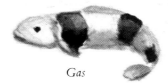

Gas

1. *Bozar*, a crested mud goby.
2. *Gas*, a mudskipper.
3. *Wirwir*, a mud-hopper.
4. In Meriam, *paris*.

This is the story of Nageg.

Nageg lived at Ne. She gave birth to a male child whom she named Geigi. When he became a youth, Nageg bent a bow and gave it to him.

Geigi went to a lagoon on the reef and shot a fish called *bozar*.[1] He called to his mother: "Mother, what fish is this?" "That is *bozar*, an edible fish," said Nageg. He shot a fish called *gas*.[2] "Mother, what fish is this," he asked. "That is *gas*, an edible fish," his mother told him. He shot a fish called *wirwir*.[3] "Mother," he said, "what kind of fish is this?" Nageg told him that it was *wirwir* and was good to eat.

Later on, Nageg made a fish spear and gave it to her son.

Geigi now went further from home and speared a Long Tom.[4]

He saw at Teg a man whose name was Iriamuris. Laying aside his spear, Geigi broke off young coconut leaves, from which he made fish-eyes (*larerkep*). These he tied over his eyes and to his legs and to his hands, and then he swam underwater, going far down when he came to deep water. When he came up, he broke the surface of the water in the middle of the shoal of sardines at which Iriamuris was scooping with his *weres*.

Geigi then returned to his mother at Ne, but he tore off the fish-eyes before she saw him. He told her nothing, keeping secret from her what he had done that day.

He played the same trick the following day, breaking up the shoal of sardines where Iriamuris was scooping with his *weres*. But this time the white soles of his feet were seen by Iriamuris.

"Aha!" said Iriamuris, "so you are a human, are you? I thought you were a fish disturbing the shoal. You have fooled me twice. Young man, you had better be very careful!"

Geigi went to Teg again. Iriamuris was ready for him and scooped him up before he reached the surface of the water in the middle of the shoal of sardines. Iriamuris emptied his *weres* into one half of a canoe which had split lengthwise, and then he called to the *sogi neur* [the grass-skirted girls who lived at Damid on Kebi Dauar, the smaller of the two hills on the island of Dauar]: "Come down, with your children, *sogi neur*! Come down and bring leaves [to be used as mats upon which to place food], stones for a fireplace, and firewood!"

The *sogi neur* and their children came at Iriamuris's bidding, bringing with them all that he had asked them to bring, and sat down on the beach.

Paris

308

Their children went to the half-canoe in which Geigi lay and poked his eyes with their fingers; and when Iriamuris forbade them to do it, they ran to their mothers and said: "Iriamuris stopped our play." Straightaway the *sogi neur* stood up and returned to their home, taking their children with them.

Iriamuris cut up Geigi and boiled him bit by bit; after he had boiled all of Geigi, he boiled some sardines. He then ate Geigi [after cutting off his hair] and the sardines. After that, he broke his *weres* and swallowed it; he swallowed the stones of the fireplace; he scooped up the ashes of his fire and swallowed them; finally, he swallowed the red-hot coals. And then he drowsed off from over-eating.

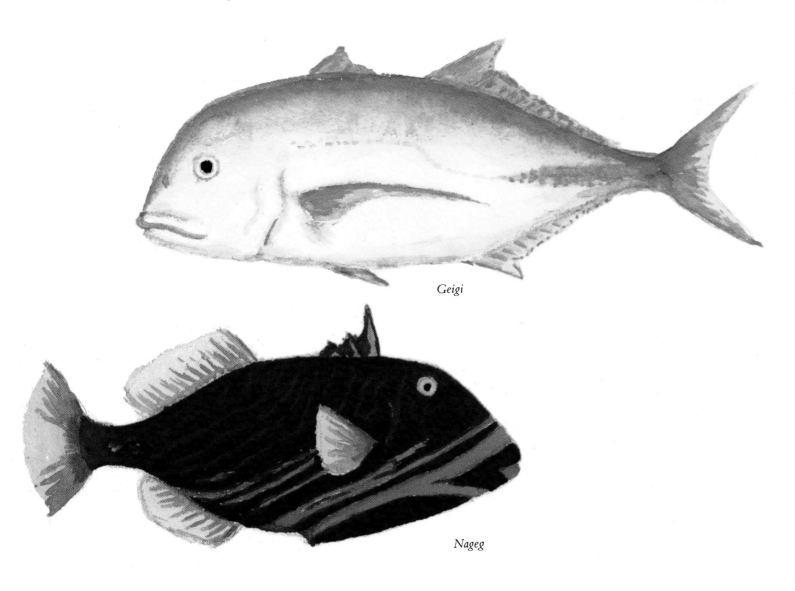

Geigi

Nageg

After two days of waiting in vain for her son to return, Nageg set out to look for him. She took her *kusbager* with her and, as she walked round the island, called repeatedly: "Geigi, my child, in whose belly are you? Attach yourself to the belly and chest and back of the one who has eaten you." From the sandspit called Waier Pit she called across to the sandspit called Teg on Dauar: "Geigi, my child, are you in Iriamuris's belly?"

She walked and swam to Dauar and, seeing Iriamuris, asked him if he had seen Geigi. Iriamuris replied: "I do not know where your son is. Is he, perhaps, at Eg, with the four young men [Ab, Wid, Monan, and Zirar]?"

So Nageg went to Eg and asked these young men [who had been wrapping bunches of bananas[5] and were now throwing spears at a banana trunk for target play] if they had seen her son. "We do not know where he is. We have not seen him," they told her.

She returned to Teg, where she found Geigi's hair [lying on the sand]. "Iriamuris ate him," she said. She drove her *kusbager* right through his body and afterwards struck his jaw. Iriamuris died.

[Now she cut Iriamuris open and took out of him every part of Geigi's body, which she pieced together in correct order.] Nageg went to a tree and plucked from it a green ants' nest. She placed the nest on Geigi's head; whereupon the ants bit him, and the "fire" from the bites went into his bones. She jumped to his feet and "burnt" them next. She "burnt" his head once more, and then Geigi came to life. Nageg said to him: "How did you come to be there [in Iriamuris's belly]?" "Iriamuris scooped me up with his *weres*," Geigi told her. Nageg said: "You and I are going home."

They began the journey back. At Ukes [the narrow channel between Teg Pit and Waier Pit] they halted. Nageg said to her son: "Go. Go down into deep water [and become a fish]. You will snap the line of every man who catches you on his line; you will break the spear of every man who spears you." Geigi said to his mother: "[Go and become a fish which lives in holes inside coral and stone. No one] will be able to pull you out, because the spike on your breast will hold you firmly in place."

Geigi went down into the deep water. Nageg entered a hole inside the coral reef.

Thus ends the story of Nageg.

[The following detail was given by George Passi, who obtained it from Robert Pitt]:

When the *sogi neur* had gone part of the way back to their home, after leaving Iriamuris, they built a shelter for themselves and their children facing the north-east; then they pulled it down. They built another shelter at the same spot, this one facing the south-east; then they pulled it down. They built a shelter facing the south-west and pulled it down, and one facing the north-west. This also they pulled down, and then they went the rest of the way home.

5. Young bunches of bananas were wrapped ("parcelled") to improve the size, colour, and flavour of the fruit.

Wrapped bananas. The parcel, *sop*, is made by wrapping a young bunch of bananas with the leaves of *iger*, *wasao*, and *arerarer* and tying it with coconut fibre string. Wrapped bananas turn red in colour and acquire additional flavour.

311

MARKEP AND
SARKEP

Given here are an edited and a retranslated version of the story told to Ray by Pasi in 1898 (*Reports*, III, 244–46).

Able neis le ra mer pe ike. Markep a abra keimer Sarkep. Wi kikem oka baskiei.

Markep abu, bakiamulu tawer em, e dasmer gair neur wi gur bagrer, tag ditilare Dauar ge, a pako Waier ge.

Markep e tais able tonar mokakalam maek kosker, e nesur esolu atperiklu, tibi u tabara gem desao, pako tabara kerem desao. E koket ikalu, abu tawer em.

E darabgerare gair neur kega: "Karim neur watabaker neis a neis kari wanagardare a ged ge kari wanamarkare." A wi neur neis a neis baker Markep i tigardare, able kebi paser ge, detagrare kega: "Nako mari ge ki namarkare?" Markep wiabim detaut kega: "Larmed ge mari namarkare."

Wi bakiauare Larmed ge, Markep i detagrare kega: "Nako mari ge ki namarkare?"

Markep ide wiabi daratagrare kega: "Maik'e kara uteb, debele wa kari nagardare uteb ge taramridare."

Able neur wi abi detagerda kega: "Wao." Wi uteb em bakiauare a uteb ge Markep ide wiabi daratagrare kega: "Wa keriba kosker bamer ge niai-karem."

Sarkep e bakiamulu, baur ikalu, bakiamulu lar em, able lar nei bologor. Gair bologor kes bazigualare, a e dasmer netat, e tekimelu deg em. Sarkep ikos, erpeilu, a tikalu able lar uteb em. Tabara narbet etomelu, "Pe ike meriba lar." Markep ide abi detager kega: "Mara neis kosker kara neis kosker, wi obamer niai-karem."

Nerut gerger wi ko bamariklei ad ge.

Sarkep e bakiamulu neur darabgerare kega: "Wa kari nagardare ge namarkare neis a neis a neis a neis neur." Able neur asrare abra mer, wi tabakiauare abi igardare, abi detagrare kega: "Ge ki mari namarkare."

Sarkep e wiabi daratagrare kega: "Ge kari namarkare." Wi bakiauare Larmed ge. Abra nesur adem deuselu. Wi gair neur abi dasmerare, tabara batagrare kega: "Kimiar dali," a wi korider adem gur im batirik.

Sarkep bakiamulu taba uteb ge, emrilu.

Markep e tais baur lar em. E dasmer bologor.

Emetu Sarkep ide tabara narbet detager kega: "Ma nole eip u ikos, ma deg ge ikos." Markep e eip u ikos, e eupamalu, erpeilu bologor, abi asare gem ge au asiasi.

Markep takomelu uteb em, emrilu taba uteb ge, dasmer tabara keimer Sarkep. Wi batapertei: "Nole mokakalam kikem gerger mi irpiei neis a neis neur a pako lar, a pe irdi mi nole kar."

Sina. Esemuda able neis le ra mer.

This is the story of two brothers. Markep was the elder brother, Sarkep the younger. The two made a plan.

Markep went down to the beach and saw many girls swimming in the sea at Dauar and Waier. Afterwards they played in the sand [at Teg], inserting their hands in the sand and rubbing them backwards and forwards in it to see if spirits would scratch a message on their palms.

Markep went back and dressed himself as a widow, tying on a petticoat which he fastened between his legs and smearing his head and his body with ashes. He then took a walking stick and returned to the beach where the girls were playing.

He called to them, saying: "Will four of you walk part of the way home with me?" Four girls agreed to do this and accompanied him to the small hill, Kebi Dauar, where they said: "Supposing we send you on alone from here."

But Markep said: "Go with me to Larmed and then send me on my way."

So the girls went with him to Larmed, where they said again: "Supposing you go on alone now."

Markep replied: "My home is not far away. It would be better if you took me to it."

The girls agreed to go all the way with Markep, but when they reached his home Markep said: "You are wives for my brother and myself. You do not leave this place."

Meantime, Sarkep had taken his spear and gone to fish for *bologor*.[1] He saw many at one spot, fighting for space. He moved to one edge of the shoal, speared one, caught it, and took it home, where he showed it to Markep, saying: "Here is a fish for us."

Markep said to Sarkep: "Here are two wives for you and two wives for me. They stay here for ever."

Another day, Markep and Sarkep went down to the beach together. There they separated.

This time Sarkep went to [where] the girls [of Dauar and Waier were playing on the sand at Teg]. He said to them: "Eight of you take me part of the way home." Eight girls agreed to accompany him and, after they had gone part way, said: "We will go back now. You go on alone."

But Sarkep said: "Take me further." So they agreed and went as far as Larmed with him. There his grass skirt came off. "This is a man!" the girls cried, and they ran away, down into the sea.

Sarkep went home and sat down.

Markep had gone fishing with his spear after he and his brother separated. He saw some *bologor*, as Sarkep had.

Now Sarkep had told his elder brother: "Don't use your spear in the

1. *Bologor* (*Naso unicornis*) has an alternative name in Meriam—*sabei*. This fish has a spike on its head.

313

middle of a shoal of *bologor*. Go to the side of the shoal and spear a fish there." Markep, however, stood at the middle of the shoal and threw his spear. The *bologor* leaped up at Markep and scratched his body very painfully.

Markep went home and sat with his brother. The two complained bitterly: "This is not like the first day when we caught four girls and a fish. This time we caught nothing."

That is the end of the story of the two men.

THE STORY OF MEIDU

Meidu became the first nipa palm. During the north-west season, nipa trunks and nuts drift down from New Guinea and cast up on island beaches and reefs in Torres Strait.

Given here are an edited and a re-translated version of the story in the Pasi MS (*Reports*, III, 239–40).

1. A cove at the foot of the northern slope of Au Dauar.
2. *Karmeri Nor*, a reef off the western tip of the island, Dauar.
3. *Dibadiba*, a small, green bird which has an orange breast and a patch of red on its head. It is found throughout the year at Murray Island. It is a land-bird.
4. Meidu's words "where *dibadiba* flock at sunrise and feed until sunset" are metaphorical: "Mer and Dauar, though your people eat from sunrise till sunset, they cannot eat all the food you provide." These words (*a dibadiba te ge, lem weieudua ki waiasameiua*) have the same significance for the Meriam as "*Urpi Gigu poiad ras*" for the people of Mabuiag. Each expression praises an island for its wealth, which is measured in terms of the food it provides. Each of these islands

Meidu dauer Teiri ge. Abra neis a neis kimiar werem wi kaba eterlare. Wiaba nei Ab a Wid Turper, Monan a Zirar. Able neur, wiaba nei Baiso, Eupe, Izeiraged. Wi urder op ge. Meidu erertekri kega: "Nako wabi mam ide dimueda?" Meidu gur im baraigilu a tabaruk we ge ut eidilu. Able meg toger, kikem abi teter ge igilu, e ge teter narapeilu, a meg ga toger abi igilu esemulu. Meg ide abi ikalu. Meidu e mena ut ipereder. Karmeri nor ge e ekiamlu a darasmer able neis ged op em. Meidu etkalu kega: "Mer, Dauar, dirdidauam; a dibadiba te ge, lem weieudua, ki waiasameiua." E ko ut eidilu, able karem ge ikalu, Deudai ge iper wekes ge. Tabara sip namarkare. Sina. Able Meidu ra mer esemuda.

This is the story of Meidu.

Meidu lived at Teiri.[1] Her four sons wrapped bunches of bananas. Their names were Ab, Wid Turper, Monan, and Zirar.

There were girls whose names were Baiso, Eupe, and Izeiraged. They lived on the slope [of Au Dauar].

Meidu called [to the girls, and when they did not answer her, said]: "Why do you behave like this? Is it because of something in your blood? Are you driven to it by your blood?"

Meidu bathed in the sea and then came and lay on the sand. The tide came in and the water covered her legs. She moved her legs out of the water. The tide rose up to her waist. Again she withdrew her legs from the water. The tide rose still higher and covered her whole body; then it carried her away. Meidu still slept.

She woke at Karmeri Nor,[2] to find the two islands to windward of her. She said: "*Mer, Dauar, dirdidauam; a dibadiba te ge, lem weieudua, ki waiasameiua* (Mer and Dauar, where *dibadiba*[3] flock at sunrise and feed until sunset,[4] you stay where you are, but I go)."

314

Meidu slept again, on top of the water. She drifted until she cast up on the beach at Deudai. There she took root.

So ends the story of Meidu.

4. (*continued*)

is rich in food—though different in kind—and the people of each are (on that account) proud of their home. The true Meriam was a gardener, rather than a fisher or hunter. He worked the rich, volcanic soil of Mer and Dauar in garden land which he himself owned. His pride, and the collective pride of the Meriam, was centred in the food which was grown in the gardens. At Mabuiag, on the other hand, where the soil is, for the most part, poor, a man's pride lay in his success as a hunter of dugong and turtle. And, whatever the position in the past, today the waters of West Torres Strait appear to be richer in these animals than those of East Torres Strait.

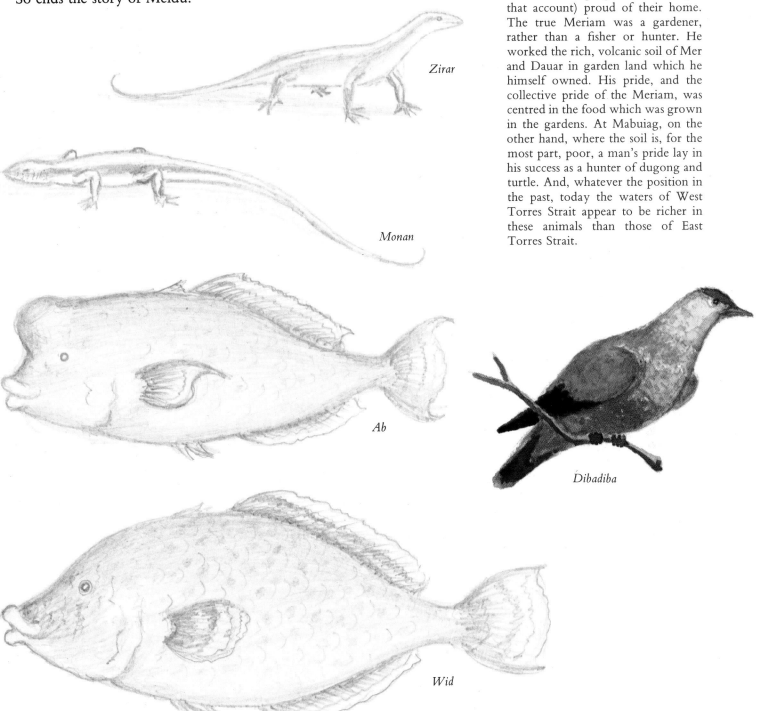

Zirar

Monan

Ab

Dibadiba

Wid

315

KAPERKAPER THE CANNIBAL

[Told by Caroline Modee at Murray Island, 19 August 1968]

Kiar[1] and his five daughters, Ai, Bak, Arpet, Kabur, and Seskip, lived on the hill called Korkor.

One day, at the time of year when the wild cotton-trees (*kob*) were in full red flower, Kiar and the girls were walking together in their garden when Kiar noticed that the whole reef lay bare and dry.[2] So he said: "Daughters, go and collect *deirdeir* (an edible shell-fish)."[3]

Ai, Bak, Arpet, Kabur, and Seskip went down to Las and, after removing their grass skirts, walked along the beach to Er. They then went out on to the reef and began to collect *deirdeir*, working their way as far as Ibir. There they came in to the beach and sent Seskip, the youngest sister, to fetch their skirts from Las.

After Seskip returned, the girls dressed themselves and were about to set out for Korkor when an old man named Kaperkaper came up to them and said: "Girls, where are you going? Spend the night with me here at my place and go home in the morning." To this the girls replied: "We may not stay. Our father is waiting for us."

But Kaperkaper was insistent. "Stay here," he urged. "If you try to return now, you cannot reach your home before dark. You will slip and fall; trees may poke at your eyes." In the end the girls agreed to spend the night at Ibir.

Kaperkaper hurried on ahead of them to make everything ready and, after he had lit a big fire inside his house, called to the five sisters: "Come in! But crawl in backwards, don't come in head first."

The eldest sister led the way, and, as soon as she was inside the house, Kaperkaper grabbed her and put her in the fire. The second sister followed the first and was also grabbed by Kaperkaper and put in the fire. And so with each of the other girls—as each crawled backwards through the low doorway, she was grabbed and put in the fire. Seskip, the youngest, was the last to enter Kaperkaper's house.

Now of all the girls, only Seskip could speak—the rest, Ai, Bak, Arpet, and Kabur were dumb. From the flames Seskip cried out: "Alas, Kiar's daughters! Alas, father's daughters! (*Kilikili Kiar ira neur e! Bab ira neur e!*) That was why you made us stay with you. We told you we wanted to go home, but you would not let us. You insisted that we stay, because you planned to kill us."

1. Others said it was a woman named Gad, not the man Kiar, who lived at Korkor with a number of daughters.
2. The very low tide which occurs during the flowering of the cotton-tree (*kob*) is referred to as *kob ira meskep* (*kob*'s dry reef).
3. *Lunella chrysostoma* Linne.

316

Kaperkaper cooked Kiar's five daughters and ate them. He threw their hair outside his house.

That night, Kiar waited in vain for his daughters to return to Korkor. He had a premonition that all was not well with them, so he cut pointed sticks from the wood of a *kus* tree and, as soon as it was daylight, threw them. They fell to the ground at Kabur, so he walked to Kabur. He picked up the *kus* sticks (*kusbager*) and again threw them. This time they landed at Semar, so he walked to Semar. When he threw the *kusbager* at Semar, they landed at Baur Pit, not far from Ibir. He threw them once more, and they fell to the ground beside the wall of Kaperkaper's house.

Kiar crawled through the doorway and said to Kaperkaper: "Have you seen five young girls?"

Kaperkaper replied: "I saw them come in from the reef yesterday, and as it was nearly dark, I told them to spend the night with me. They refused."

"Oh," said Kiar, "I'll be off, then, and look for them at Weid." But Kiar knew very well that Kaperkaper had lied to him, because, before he entered Kaperkaper's house, he had seen his daughters' hair, with blowflies settling on it, on the ground outside the house, and he had no intention of going to Weid.

After leaving the house, he took a few steps round it and thrust his *kusbager* through the wall. He withdrew the *kusbager*, took a few more steps, and again pierced the wall of the house with the *kusbager*. Kiar did this several times, and then he hurled a *kusbager* which struck Kaperkaper.

He now went in to the cannibal, hit him with a stick, and killed him, afterwards slitting open his belly and removing the bones of the five girls. These he put in one heap and on top of it placed a green ants' nest which he plucked from a tree.

The ants crawled over the bones and bit them, whereupon the "fire" from the bites permeated the bones. Kiar "fired" the bones a second time and a third time, jumping to different places beside the heap between each application of the green ants' nest. After that the bones separated and then assembled, fully fleshed, as Kiar's five daughters, each alive and well.

"How did you come to Kaperkaper's place?" asked Kiar. Seskip told him.

Kiar took his daughters home to Korkor, and then he said to them: "Ai, you go to Ai. Bak, you go to Bak. Arpet, you go to Arpet. Kabur, you go to Kabur. Seskip, my youngest daughter, stay with me."

Ai, Bak, Arpet, and Kabur became garden places. Kiar and Seskip turned to stone on Korkor, where they may be seen to this day. Kiar is a big stone; Seskip, a smaller stone, stays not far from her father.

An old man named Benny Mabo gave a different version of this story:

A woman named Gad lived at Korkor. She had many daughters, of whom the youngest was Seskip, a chatterbox.

One day the girls walked down to the reef to catch fish. They went as far as Ibir, by which time it was late afternoon. Kaperkaper, an old woman who lived nearby in the cave which bears her name —Kaperkaper Kur—persuaded them to spend the night with her. She said: "Crawl into my cave backwards." And, as each girl came in, Kaperkaper grabbed her and threw her into her fire. Seskip, last to enter, said from the flames: *"Kilikili! Ma ablegem kerbi tadaisi, ma peno kerbi deresa. (You only invited us to stay because you wanted to kill us.)"*

Gad, frantic with worry for her daughters, set out to look for them next morning. A blowfly (*abob*) told her that her daughters were in Kaperkaper's cave and led her to it. As she climbed up from the beach, she saw her daughters' hair and bones lying on the ground outside the cave, so she went inside and killed Kaperkaper with a *kusbager*.

She then lit a fire outside the cave and threw her daughters' hair and bones into it. When the fire died away to red coals, the girls jumped out live and whole. Seskip emerged last and told her mother the whole story.

Gad sent each of her daughters except Seskip to a different place on Mer: to Bak, Mene, Ai, Arpet, Maur, Werge, Pairgir, Semar, Saurem, Pairmed, Tair, and Zibir. Seskip she sent down into the sea to become the shellfish known by her name: *seskip* (*Vasum turbinellus* Linne). Then Gad returned to Korkor and turned to stone.

And ever since mothers have fed *seskip* to any of their children who are slow to speak. When they throw the shell into the fire to cook, the flesh bubbles and boils and says: "Kilikili!"

Artist Segar Passi

KULTUT [Told by Marou at Murray Island, 1 February 1967]

Long ago a man named Kultut lived at Widwid. He had a very long right arm.[1]

One day when he was sitting outside his house, he looked towards Er and saw some girls place food in an earth-oven. After they had covered it with leaves of trees and banana leaves and soil, they went to the reef to gather shell-fish. Kultut made up his mind to steal the girls' food.

He did this very easily from where he sat: he simply reached out to the earth-oven with his long right arm.

When the tide turned and the reef began to cover with water, the girls came in and went straight to their earth-oven, expecting to find their meal cooked and ready to eat. They were puzzled and angry when they discovered the theft of their food.

Kultut tricked the girls again and again, robbing their earth-oven while they were fishing on the reef.

At last the girls determined to catch the thief in the act: one of them would stay behind and watch while the rest were out on the reef.

Kultut saw nothing unusual in the girls' behaviour the following day: as always, after preparing their earth-oven, they went to the reef to gather shell-fish. Therefore, the moment he judged their food to be cooked, he stretched out his long right arm, plunged it into the earth-oven, removed the food, and brought it back to himself at Widwid.

The girls came in from the reef. "Who is the thief?" they immediately asked their companion who had stayed behind.

1. Landtman in *The Folk-Tales of the Kiwai Papuans* (Helsingfors, 1917), pp. 419–22, records a story about a man with a very long right arm, which he obtained at Mawata on the Papuan mainland.

318

"I did not see him," she replied. "What happened was this: a hand at the end of a long arm went inside our oven, reappeared holding our food, and withdrew in the direction of Widwid."

"Kultut!" cried the girls, "Kultut is the thief. He watched us from Widwid and stole our food while we fished."

The next day several girls stayed at home, each armed with a sharp-edged clamshell, and when Kultut's arm appeared, they used these shells to cut it off. It was still quivering on the ground when their friends returned from the reef.

All the girls then walked to Widwid and stoned Kultut to death. After-wards they threw his body into the sea.

THE MUIAR

[Told by Benny Mabo at Murray Island, 22 August 1968]

Four men, known as the Muiar, felled a cotton-tree (*kob*) and made a canoe[1] from it by hollowing out its trunk. They dragged it down towards Las, blazing a trail of cleared ground which can still be seen.

The Muiar did not put their canoe into the water, however, be-cause branches of *sem*,[2] the yellow-flowering hibiscus, had been hung at the boundary of Las. These were recognized and respected as a sign of *gelar* (taboo), the people of Las having shown in that manner that "outside people"—people who did not belong to Las—must not set foot in Las territory until the branches of *sem* had been removed. The Muiar turned back: they were men who belonged to Piad. On the way, all four turned to stone, one at Sager, one at Zeum, one at Pairmed, and the fourth at Korkor.

The story of the Muiar has great signi-ficance for the Meriam. It is an old story, cited as the perfect manner of behaviour towards others' property and the rights which those people have over the use of their property. Trespass is abhorrent to the true Meriam.

The highly refined system of owner-ship which pervaded the Meriam world, a system which included individual and/or group ownership of stars and winds and reefs and sea and names as well as land, was reinforced by the prac-tice of erecting signs of *gelar* (taboo), and by verbal injunctions.

"*Ad le mimikak Muiar* (Outside people, people who do not belong to or own a place, must not trespass in it—as the Muiar did not)" was, in the first place, a rule of conduct for the *Piadaram le*. Later it was adopted into the Malo cult and taught as a sacred and fundamental principle of behaviour:

Malo Muiar kemerkemer Muiar,
Ad le mimikak Muiar,
Ad le ged lukep atarukak Muiar.

(Malo is exactly like the Muiar. Do not tres-pass—as the Muiar did not. Do not enter another man's garden. Do not pluck the fruit in his garden. Turn back from it, in the man-ner of the Muiar.)

Another rule of Malo which stemmed from the Muiar (and thus, from the *Piadaram le*) was:

Lis lam a wam lam ka nakekrer.

(I will not enter a place while a small branch of *sem* bars my way to it.)

1. The place at which the cotton-tree was felled was afterwards called Nargiz (from *nar*, a canoe; and *giz*, a beginning). The tree is said to have stood on land owned today by Moses Sagigi. When it fell, the top came to rest on land owned by Jimmy Wailu.
2. *Sem* was used as a sign of *gelar* (taboo) in this instance, but *sem* is not the only plant used to denote taboo on property at Murray Island. The custom is still practised.

Paimi a Nawanawa
Artist Segar Passi

PAIMI A
NAWANAWA

[Told by Henry Kabiri at Murray Island,
17 February 1967]

Two men, Paimi and Nawanawa,[1] failed to put in an appearance at Ebau at a feast to which all the Dauareb had been bidden. "Where are Paimi and Nawanawa?" the people began to ask.

As the day wore on and there was still no sign of the two, resentment against them mounted. At last, all the men took up their *kusbager* (spears) and set out to look for them on Au Dauar, the big hill which forms one half of the island of Dauar.

"Paimi! Nawanawa!" the men called. "Where are you?"

The reply came from a distance: "We're here! We're here in this tree!"

1. During the middle of the year, a bird called *nawanawa* visits Murray Island, Dauar, and Waier. It is a grey land-bird, bigger than the Torres Strait pigeon.

320

The Dauareb climbed higher, so angry that they determined to kill the two men when they found them.

Paimi and Nawanawa saw the men coming towards them and flew from the branch on which they were sitting to a smaller one near the top of the tree. There they sang:

> *Paimi Nawanawa (e) Paimi Nawanawa (e) iki digiredi (o)*
> *iki eupreiei (o).*

(Here we are, Paimi and Nawanawa,
Sitting up here on the branch of a tree.
Here we are, Paimi and Nawanawa,
Hopping higher and higher, from branch to branch.)

"Come down! Come down!" shouted the Dauareb. *"Paimi Nawanawa (e) Paimi Nawanawa (e) iki digiredi (o) iki eupreiei (o),"* sang the two birds, as they hopped higher and higher, from branch to branch.

Before the Dauareb could throw their spears at the maddening pair, Paimi and Nawanawa climbed down to the ground and turned to stone.[2]

2. The two stones which were once Paimi and Nawanawa are at Igero Mager, on the side of the big hill, Au Dauar.

BEIZAM [Told by Marou at Murray Island, 1 February 1967]

> *Able neur gise beizam i eweda (a) (e)*
> *Sab neur kem dug neur abi eweda.*

(The girls are wading on the reef dragging a shark.
The girls of the North and the girls of the swelling waves
Are hauling as they wade through the water.)

(Meriam song composed by Tapim Bennyfather)

★

One day, four girls—Waigi, Sigi, Kiami, and Dugi—caught a shark on the reef in front of Sebeg[1] and killed it. Waigi and Sigi lifted the front of the shark, Kiami and Dugi, the tail; together they took it to the edge of the reef and threw it into the sea.

The shark and the girls went up to the sky, where they became the constellation, Beizam.[2]

1. Sebeg is a village in the district of Komet.
2. This constellation is called Baidam in the Western Islands. Aniba Asa of Saibai told me that Baidam is seen to the north of Torres Strait during the hard, dry months of the year, September and October.

TERER

[Told by Meb Salee at Murray Island, 2 September 1968, and Uni Passi at Thursday Island, 28 October 1968]

"Terer, kara werem!
Terer, kara werem!"

"Ama, nalugem?"

"Mara lid Beig em."

("Terer, my son!
Terer, my son!"

"Mother, why do you call me?"

"Your bones will go to Beig.")

(Modern Meriam dance song)

★

The youth, Terer, and his mother, Aukem, belonged to Kes and Geurao, places on Mer. They lived at Kes. They were *Geuram le*.[1]

One day, when young Meriam[2] men were performing the *melpal*[3] dance at Utem (not far from Kes and Geurao), Terer was walking home by himself after watching them, when he was caught by Meriam *maid le*[4] in the scrub at Geurao. These men skinned him and then sent him back to Kes.

He went to his mother who, at the time, was sitting on the ground in the shade of a fig tree weaving a *pot moder*.[5] When she looked up from her work and saw him, she cried out in horror: "Terer, my son, what have you

1. *Geuram le*, people who belonged to the territorial division of Geuram.
2. "Meriam" here refers to either or both of the territorial divisions, Piadaram and Meriam Samsep—possibly the latter.
3. *Melpal*, a big eel.
4. *Maid le*, sorcerers. (*Maid*, sorcery—described by one informant as a "kind of secret warfare".) The belief that "poisonous substances" were used by sorcerers seems to be widespread at Murray Island. One of the plants named was identified as *Tacca leontopetaloides* (L.) O. Ktze. A water-extract killed mice by subcutaneous injection, but not when fed to them (J. Watt and R. Ladd, University of Queensland). For an account of the history of this plant and its use as a source of edible starch, see Hayward, "The Cultivated Taccas", in *Baileya* (1957), V, 89–96.
5. *Pot moder* is a very strong mat woven from pandanus leaves from which the outer edges have been stripped.

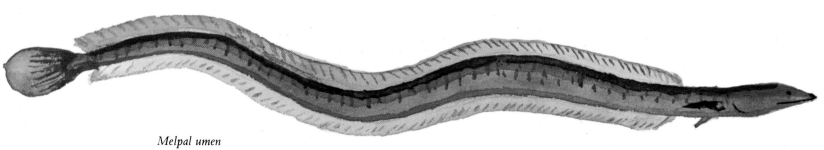

Melpal umen

322

done at Kes and Geurao! You are only a *zer* (a person from whom the life essence, *agud*, has departed)! Your bones will go to Beig!"[6]

Terer jerked a few steps sideways[7] in the direction of Geurao, a few steps back to Kes, and then a few skips to the same foot in one spot,[8] accompanying his convulsive movements with a *tap*:[9]

> *Terer a we! we!*
> *Markai a we! we!*
> *We! We! We!*

(Alas! Alas! Terer is a ghost!)

And then he left Kes and began to run across the island.

He sang and danced on Zaum Paser; on the other side of Zaum Paser at Zor; in Wargor, the region beyond Zor; and again when he came down to the beach at Werbadu. At each of these places he performed in the same manner as he had before his mother at Kes. And now at Werbadu, having skipped towards the *lokot*[10] and back towards the sea, and then in one spot, he entered the water and crossed to the island, Dauar.

Terer danced and sang at Saded. He went round the rocks at the base of the high hill, Au Dauar, and danced and sang at Giz, and so came to the white sandbeach which stretches unbroken to the tip of the island at Giar Pit. Running, halting at Dadamud to dance the *kuir*, running, the youth who was a *zer* reached the edge of the sea.

There Aukem, who had followed him since he left Kes, caught up with him.

Terer danced for the last time, to the words:

> *Terer a we! we!*
> *Markai a we! we!*
> *We! We! We!*

and went into the water where he changed into *bonao* (brain coral). His mother followed him.

Terer's ghost took the form of a whirlwind. It returns to Mer and Dauar every year during the season of *sager*, the south-east wind, to dance at all those places at which Terer danced as a *zer* after being flayed by the *maid le*. On Dauar, the whirlwind which is Terer's ghost begins to gather intensity when it reaches the beach at Giar, twisting higher and higher, faster and faster, as it races along the white sand to the sea off Giar Pit.

6. *Beig* was believed to be the land to which the spirits of dead people went. It lay somewhere to the west. Very few spirits returned from Beig. Those who did were called *lamar*. *Lamar* had pale skins.
7. The verb used for Terer's jerky movements sideways is *esakeida*: "*Terer esakeida*".
8. The jerked skips in one spot are called the *kuir*.
9. *Tap*, a song intoned on one note.
10. *Lokot*, the area of scrub immediately behind *tawer*. The people built their houses on *tawer*, which is the sandy ground immediately behind, and adjacent to, the beach.

KOL

[Told by Joe Jib at Murray Island, 14 August 1968]

Joe Jib is the present owner of the stone, Kol, which is similar to the black stones at Er. Kol is still at Zeub. It is said to have once been a man.

Ray, the linguist who accompanied the Cambridge Expedition to Torres Strait in 1898, obtained a version of the story of Kol in South Seas Mission-influenced Meriam (*Reports*, VI, 11). In pure Meriam this reads:

Wi erpariklare batuerer Er ge. Wi terpariklare Zeub ge batuerer. Wi erpariklare Er ge batuerer. Wi erpariklare Zeub ge batuerer. Wi erpariklare Zeub ge. E emrilu niaiem.

(They rolled him [from Zeub] down to Er, and from Er back to Zeub. They rolled him from Zeub down to Er, and from Er back to Zeub. They rolled him from Zeub down to Er, and from Er back to Zeub. They rolled him at Zeub. He stayed there for ever.)

People rolled Kol from Er to Zeub. They put him there.

GEDOR OF LEIWAG

[Told by Marou at Murray Island, 20 June 1966]

The south-west wind blew hard during a cyclone, stripping a coconut palm which grew at Leiwag. A coconut fell on the beach and was taken by the outgoing tide to Waisirir at the edge of Mer's fringing reef. It lay there throughout low water and came in with the next tide.

Gedor of Leiwag, who had been fishing with his three-pronged spear outside the wall of a stone fish-trap, saw what he took to be a fish coming towards him and speared it, the prongs of his spear piercing the "eyes" and "mouth" of the coconut. He took it ashore, removed the stringy husk, and broke the hard shell to expose the flesh inside. "I wonder if it is good to eat," he thought to himself. He determined to find out.

So he called to all the dogs about the place: "*Se, se, se, pokara, se, se, se!*" They ran to him, and he fed them with shredded coconut. They ate it readily and afterwards lay down satisfied. "It can't be poisonous and it must taste nice," Gedor decided.

Next, he fed some coconut to ants. He watched them carefully. None of the ants died. "I've found something good to eat," said Gedor.

Now he scraped coconut for himself and tasted it. He waited anxiously, wondering if he would die. Nothing happened—indeed, he felt very well. He tasted a little more, again waiting to see what effect it would have on him. Then, as he still felt well, he knew that he had discovered an excellent food. Gedor was very happy and ate the rest of the coconut.

KORSEIM   [Told by Marou at Murray Island, 1 February 1967]

One day, Korseim decided to leave his home at Bumeo on Erub (Darnley Island), because it was no longer congenial to him, and go and live at Mer. So he set out in a canoe with two men, Neiu and Sager, as crew, and their two sisters, Pip and Zabaker, as cooks for the party.

On the way across to Mer, Korseim changed into a large moth (*paimpaim kap*) and flew back and forth between bow and stern. And the whole time he did this his companions sang this song:

> *Orbei orbei orbei*
> *Kaur em (a) pas em (a) sosoi em (a).*
>
> (Row! Row! Row!
> To an island, to a shore, to a beach.)

When they reached Mer, they went round the island by way of Gigo and Keuk and Werbadu to Warwei, where they landed.

All then walked inland, looking for a suitable place for Korseim. They went as far as Zer, a thickly-forested area, and had still not found what they were looking for, so they turned back. Wirar proved suitable, and there Korseim stayed under a *kozo*[1] tree. Pip remained in the bush close by.

Zabaker walked on with Sager and Neiu, but the two brothers left her at Warwei[2] and went down to the highwater mark on the beach by themselves.

All may be seen as stones: Korseim at Wirar, Pip in the bush close to Korseim, Zabaker at Warwei, and Sager and Neiu at highwater mark on the beach at Warwei.

Nothing more is known about the brothers and sisters who accompanied Korseim from Erub to Mer. Korseim, however, lived on as a very big *paimpaim kap*, the form into which he changed on the way to his new home.

Korseim, *paimpaim kap*, the stone at Wirar, and the area in the immediate vicinity of Wirar are associated with madness. Indeed, *paimpaim* means mad or foolish; *paimpaim kap* is, literally, mad moth; and there was a firm belief in the past that if a person were dusted by the wings of a *paimpaim kap*—a large, grey-brown moth which is sometimes seen inside houses at Murray Island—he or she would go mad. An eighty-seven-year-old informant told me: "That place where they been acting there (i.e. Wirar) some people go mad about in that place. Make 'em garden there, they lose their head." Nor is that tradition by any means forgotten today.

Marou, who told the story of Korseim —and for whom it had very great personal significance—sang another song which Korseim is said to have taught his people (*boai*):

Lumai (e)

Kazi lumai (e) lumai (e)

Kazi lumai (e) lumai (e)

A ega (e) wa besi kupainu

Ga inagi.

The words are Mabuiag. They are strongly reminiscent (in a mutilated form) of a song which occurs in a story called "Wawa" which is told at two of the Western Islands of Torres Strait, Badu and Boigu, and is recorded in those sections of this book.

1. *Kozo*, a tree which grows to a height of about thirty feet. The wood is light purple and has a very pleasant smell. The bark is very smooth and is grey in colour.
2. The stone, Zabaker, is on top of a cairn of stones at the old village site of Warwei.

MALO

The story of Malo is more important by far than any other told at Murray Island, for the reason that Malo became the central figure of a religion which embraced everyone at Mer, Dauar, and Waier, except those who were *nog le* (*no* [g], only; *le*, people), that is, those few who were not Meriam through the male line of descent. Worship of Malo also spread to the other Eastern Islands, Erub and Ugar.

Mention is made in the story of Malo's brothers (called Sigar, Siu, and Kolka by the Meriam; Sigai, Sau, and Kulka by those who speak the Mabuiag tongue), each of whom chose to settle at islands south of Mer: Sigar at Iama (Yam Island), Siu at Masig (Yorke Island), and Kolka at Aurid. The religion which developed at these places after the coming of the brothers created a bond with Mer. It was known at Waraber and Nagi. Murray Island informants said that aboriginals from the Cowal Creek and Lockhart River areas of Cape York Peninsula supplied turtle oil and red ochre for Malo. Sigai's story is given in the Yam Island section of the stories from the Central Islands. Sau has been forgotten at Yorke Island, except for the detail: "Sigai and Kulka visited Masig. Sigai told Kulka and Sau that they must take a present of shells and coral to their brother Malu at Mer." Aurid was abandoned by its people many years ago. In Torres Strait, Kulka is only a name from the past.

Malo cannot be dissociated from the shadowy, terrifying Bomai. No one but fully initiated members of the cult knew that worship of Malo meant worship of Malo-Bomai. The uninitiated did not know the secret name, Bomai. They did

Malu ged au abimedabimed, kaur au abimedabimed, kab pur au abimedabimed.

(Malo smoothes the way, overcoming treachery and resistance on land and sea, both at home and abroad.

Malu terpar, kiaurkiaur terpar.

(Malo is exactly like the oyster growing on the reef. He cannot be moved. He is fixed in his ways, inflexible.)

(Instructions given to Malo initiates)

★

Gair Malo ra mer pe ike.

Malo, nerut le abra nei Sigar, pako Siu nerut le, pako Kolka nerut le. Neis a neis gair le. Wi neis a neis nar wiaba nagriueretlare, a wi nar par darakrida. Nar ge Sigar ira par derparki, e ekueilu nar tam ge erertekri kega: "Wa ko tabakiaudare." Wi nole lagkak wemridare Am ge.

Wi neis a netat le mena nor ge emridare, keubu kepu bamarkidare. Siu emrilu Masig 'e. Kolka emrilu Aurid ge. Malo, e kei tabakiamulu Mer em.

E waka akariklu karem nor ge, able au zeuber tedao abra nar diter desemulu. E gur ge baraigilu, keubu nar ira maumer dikiam. E baskomedlu able lager ge. E emarik. E tikalu iper kikem Begeigiz ge.

Wi gair le, Dauer, Malo i detagerda kega: "Keriba agud, ged seker em." Wi berber kar dirkare, abi detagerda kega: "Mese emri. Ki nabakiauare lewer em dasmerare." Wi bakiauare lewer em dasmerare. Malo 'de erap able kar, baraigilu gur ge, ikalu Giar ge iper.

Gair Giar-Dauar le abi erpeirare, detagrare kega: "Ma keriba agud, ged seker em, emri." Wi abra kar dirkare dairumertare. Wi bakiauare lewer em dasmele, e kar erap, baraigilu gur im, a ikalu Ormi ge iper.

Gair Ormi le abi erpeirare a imrirare, abi detagrare kega: "Ma keriba agud, ged seker em." Wi bakiauare lewer em dasmele, e erap able kar, e gur im baraigilu, e ikalu Ne ge iper.

Netat le abi erpeilu detager kega: "Ma keriba agud, ged seker em." E abi detager: "Ma emri. Ki nabakiauare lewer em dasmerare." Wi bakiauare dasmerare lewer em. E erap able kar, e baraigilu gur ge, ikalu adem, iper Teker ge.

Netat kosker mekik em ikueireder. Malo de tabara gem dipigemelu mokakalam nar. Able kosker et dikepuar nar. Keubu e dipigemelu mokakalam lu. E dikepuar able lu. E maik 'e abi doge mokakalam arti. E abra neis teter narpeilu.

Kabur ikos abi malili u, epei em alu, e akariklu. Malo i kebi keper ge emariklu, Kabur tabara nesur igmesilu, keubu Malo i ikailu epei em alu.

E op em akariklu, tabara kimiar detager kega: "Dog, mara o dali." Wi abi ikailei meta mui ge emreredlei, a tabara batagriei kega: "Mi ki ge abi dedlei."

Wi balei meta em able ki ge batkapriklei netat sik 'e. Wi nole utkak. Able ki ge, Malo, e erkep bi nagilu, keubu ib kep napit, e teosmelu adem.

E deraueilu narbit pek 'e. E bakiamulu Peibri ge, bakiamulu meta ge balu.

Able le wi ekiamlei gerger ge, able kimiar, e tabara mair tikalu, gem etkopar, pako peris u baoderedlu, a sam dimrilu kerem ge. E deraueilu narbit pek 'e. Abra kosker Kabur esolu debe nesur, pako ner mair bagrameilu, papek isigemelu, emrilu maik 'e abra kimiar.

E bakiamulu Las ge deketilu; gair le Las ge urder abi dasmerare. Wi mer batagerda kega: "Auim ira nalu nako dike?" Dog, e akomelu tabara kosker erdalu.

A nerut gerger ge gair le wi oka ipuare, neis le namarkare. Wi Kabur ira tup dikalei, tabakiamulei abi ikuarei. Kabur ide wiabi nautmer kega: "Nako ia ko bakiamulam?" Wi Kabur i detagrei kega: "Mi ut naididare." Wi neis le oka baskiei kega: "Mi nole utkak." Wi ki ge bartidare ut em. Wi batkapriklei netat sik 'e. Wi nole utkak. Wi erkep nakereder.

Dog, e abkorep ko deraueilu mokakalam kikem gerger ge. Kabur ide wiaba lewer ais wiabi naisuer. Wi bes bakiamulei, Kabur i detagrei kega: "Ma naoa." Wi bakiamulei lu ispiei, wi ko takomelei, meta luneb erapei, balei, a Malo i titrumlei; wi tabara ikalei.

Able Sarkep, e Zagareb le. Dam, e Beizam le.

Wi maik 'e barmei Aud ge. Dam, e kab le. Sarkep, e warup le. Ga bakiamulei Keugiz ge barmei, ege Sarkep nab Dam i etkelu, abi kega: "Kaimeg, ma ko karim tikao." Ege Dam ide Sarkep i detager kega: "Kaimeg, ma no warup le naoa. No kari tararemoa."

Wi Keugiz ge barmei, ga bakiamulei Gebadar Kop ge barmei, a ga bakiamulei paser ge, Gazir ge barmei, a ga bakiamulei Dam ge barmei, ikailei emreredlei, wi ge bakiamulei tawer ge etrumlei.

Gair le wiabi nardarare. Gair le wiabi nautmerare kega: "Nade pa ike?" Ege neis le wiabi daratagrare: "Inoko op ge teme."

Dog e deraueilu; abra sir dormeilu. E akomelu Kabur i detager: "Mese bakiamu, naluglam kara sir ormeida."

Kabur bakiamuda meta mui ge, dasmer able luneb, erertekri Dog im kega: "Neis le wi Malo i itrumdariei. Nako tabara ikadariei."

Dog ide ditimedlu au mer igar, igar, keubu detager tabara kosker kega: "Mi nabakiamulei Las em."

not know the whole nature of the *agud* (god) which had come to Mer in the form of an octopus, only believing that obedience to Malo guaranteed peace and protection. "*Ma nole Maloi disrir.* (Do not bare your teeth at Malo.)" "*Ma nole op mer detager.* (You must not speak against Malo.)" "*Ma nole Maloi teter u itur.* (Do not kick—oppose or offend—Malo.)" They did not know that behind these commands lay the threat: "or Bomai will strike." Bomai's men, "the sharks of the forests", the *Beizam boai* (shark kin, men whose original *agud* was the shark, descendants in the male line of the seven brothers of Las who obtained possession of the sacred octopus from its first owners, Dog and Kabur), were as swift to strike those who disobeyed Malo as the sharks which hide in the deep lagoons in the reef. Penetration of cult mysteries by the uninitiated earned death, which was accomplished by a secret method in the name of Malo-Bomai.

When the *Beizam le* acquired the precious *agud* (the octopus), they developed rites for its worship. Later, men from the high islands like Nagi, and men from the low coral cays, came in search of the brother of Sigai, Kulka, and Sau, whom they called Malu. (The Meriam word for the deep sea which lies beyond an island's fringing reef is *malo*; the Mabuiag word is *malu*.) They brought with them ceremonial dances for worship of Malu, and another concept of his nature. This was grafted on to the original concept— hence Malo-Bomai.

Aet Passi (or Pasi—see footnote 13 of Introduction), one of the *Beizam boai*, who had risen to a high rank in the Malo-Bomai religion before the coming of members of the London Missionary Society to Mer, wrote the story of Malo in Meriam for Ray in 1898. Given here are an edited and a retranslated version of the story in the Pasi MS (*Reports*, III, 233–39). Aet's grandson, George, spent many hours helping me with the retranslation.

Wi bakiamulei Las em. Gair le urder Las ge, wi mer batagrare. Dog pako abra kosker wiabi nautmerare kega: "Netide Malo i tikada?"

Wi abi sogob emerare a detagrare: "Ma no dikaer. Meriba agud ge wadauer." Wi takomelei ged im Teker em.

Wi ge oka batagrare. Keubu, u kupi erapeirare, larerkep itkubare, wi kerem ge demrare, pako neis teter ge, a tag ge. Wi kab barier.

Wi tabaragare Nagiram le pako Sikaram le, Malo i tidiraimrare. Mi puleb pako asor puleb tikadarare ga ikadarare. Werbadu ge nar namarare, Gep i itmerare kega: "Nade Malo?" "Penoko!" Wi Gep ira nam ditimdare, warup u dermare. Gep ide natomertare.

Nar nataiuare Er em, Er ge namarare, wi Barat i itmerare kega: "Malo nade?" Barat ide wiabi daratagrare kega: "Tedali nade lu mairmair deskedi."

Wi Barat ira nam ditimdare a warup u dermare. Wi nar nataiuare Las em, Las ge namarare. Wi baupamaret gesep em, gesep ge bamer. Gair le wiabi lewer u darasisiare. Ga urder, utbaider.

Gair nar: Beizam le ra tabara nar, a Zagareb le ra tabara nar, a Omai le ra tabara nar, a Deumer le ra tabara nar, a Geregere le ra tabara nar.

Wi demarerdare ati em. Netat le, e mer aosos kem lewer tais. Wi ge asrare able le ra mer. Wi bako a batir nar ge, tarakerare kor we ge daramarare. Wi ge nar ge mud demare.

Omai le kikem moder dikriare, tabaupamaret, pigir bagrare, baker baid. Deumer le tabara moder adem dikriare, tabaupamaret, bauper, baker bamer; a Geregere le tabaupamaret, bauper, bauper, baker bamer.

Zagareb le tabaupamaret; wi atug a bamer. Beizam le keubu tabaupamaret. Keubu wi baker nar em batir, Malo i sor dikriare, akmeirare gur ge.

Gair Nagiram le pako Sikaram le, wi nar darakrare, bakiauare tabara ged. Sina esemuda able Malo ra mer.

Beizam

This is the whole story of Malo.

Malo, Sigar, Siu, and Kolka, each of these four men in his own canoe, dropped anchor on the reef. Sigar's anchor dragged, and as he drifted away he stood on the platform of his canoe and called to the others: "Come, too!" But they did not want to stay at Yam Island where Sigar was going.

The three who remained together parted company in the end. Siu stayed at Masig. Kolka stayed at Aurid. Malo came to Mer.

Soon after Malo reached the edge of the reef, a big wave sank his canoe. He jumped overboard and broke off the gunwale of the canoe. There was a rope tied to the gunwale; he clung to the rope for a while, and then he let go. He drifted and cast up at Begeigiz.

The people of this village saw him and said: "You are our god, our protector." They penned him in with *berber* vine and told him to wait

328

while they went to fetch food for him. Malo broke the fence, entered the water, drifted, and cast up at Giar.

The people received him, saying: "You are our god, our protector. Stay here." They built an enclosure around him. They went to their gardens for food for him, and during their absence Malo broke the fence, re-entered the sea, and drifted again with the tide. The tide took him to Ormi.

There the people received him and bade him sit down. "You are our god, our protector," they said. But after they went to gather food from their gardens, he escaped from the fence that they had built around him, again went down into the sea, and once more drifted with the tide.

At Ne on the island of Waier where he cast up next, the man who received him also hailed him as god and protector and penned him; and then the man went off with his people for food. He departed from the place with the tide.

Off Teker he assumed different forms.

That day, Kabur stood on the reef line-fishing. When she saw a canoe approaching, she did not know that it was Malo; to her, what she saw was merely a canoe. When she saw something in place of the canoe, she thought it was that thing. Close to her Malo became an octopus and he entwined himself about her legs.

Kabur speared the octopus with a pointed stick, put it in the basket which she carried, and walked back towards the shore. She released the octopus in a pool while she wrung out her skirt; then she returned it to her basket and climbed the hill to her home at Aud.

"Dog," she said, showing her husband the sacred thing she had found, "here is courage for you." The two carried the basket inside the house; both agreed that they would watch it throughout the night.

Sleepless, husband and wife lay close together on one bed in the dark, their eyes on the basket. Suddenly Malo's eyes lit up. They heard him slap the sound of *ibkep* and afterwards leave the house.

Malo walked to Peibri, on the other side of the island, and went into a house.

In the morning Dog painted himself, stuck feathers all over his body and tied on a head-dress of cassowary feathers. Kabur put on a good skirt and painted her temple. Then she laid a mat and sat on it beside her husband.

Dog went for a walk round the island. The men of Las saw him go by and said: "What can our brother-in-law have acquired that he flaunts himself in this fashion?" Dog returned home to Kabur.

Arti

The men of Las thought up a plan. They sent two men, Sarkep and Dam, with a present of sardines for Kabur. "How can you return to your home [before dark]?" she asked [for it was late when they rose to go]. "We will sleep here," they said. That night, the two men lay close to-

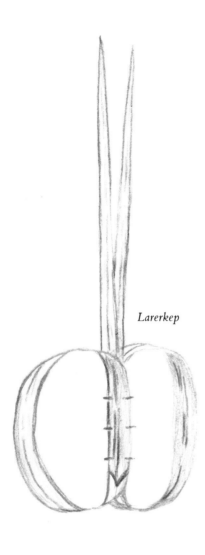

Larerkep

gether inside the house, but they did not sleep: they kept their eyes wide open.

In the morning, after Dog had departed to walk round the island again, Kabur brought food to the men. They took their leave, but they did not go far before hiding their belongings and returning. They made a hole in the wall of the house, went inside, took Malo and left.

Sarkep was a Zagareb man; Dam was a Beizam man.

Not far from Aud, Sarkep beat a drum and sang while Dam performed a dance. They walked a little further, to Keugiz. There, also, Sarkep beat the drum while Dam danced. Then Sarkep wanted to dance with the basket [containing Malo], but Dam refused to part with it. "You beat the drum and sing for me, that is your part," Dam told his friend.

They sang and danced at Gebadar Kop; they went to the hill at Gazir and sang and danced. At Dam they sang and danced, and then they hung up the basket and went down to the beach at Las.

The men saw them coming. "Where is it?" they asked. "Hanging in the bush," Dam and Sarkep replied.

As he walked that morning, Dog's happiness left him. All was not well at his home, he knew it. He returned at once to Kabur and said: "Go inside our house. Find out why my happiness went from me."

Kabur went inside the house, saw the hole in the wall and called: "The two men took Malo down. They stole it."

Dog spoke many angry words. Afterwards he said: "Come! We are going to Las!"

At Las, Dog and Kabur said: "Who took Malo?"

The men of Las gave Dog and Kabur a pipe of tobacco to smoke and said: "Let Malo remain here to be *agud* for all of us." Dog returned with Kabur to Teker.

At Las, the men broke a young, green leaf from a coconut palm and used it to make *larerkep* (ornamental "fish eyes") to tie on their heads and their legs and their hands. Then they danced.

Men from the high islands like Nagir and men from the low coral cays (the *Nagiram le* and the *Sikaram le*) crossed the sea, searching for Malo. They brought with them clamshells and spidershells which had special significance. When they reached Mer, they anchored at Werbadu and asked the man, Gep: "Where is Malo?" "There!" pointed Gep. They threw him a turtle and beat drums for him.

They rowed to Er, anchored, and asked Barat: "Where is Malo?" "He stays where the trees with red paint on them grow," Barat told them.

They threw a turtle to Barat and beat drums for him, and then they rowed to Las. There they anchored, went ashore and sat down. The people of Las brought them food. Later they slept.

330

Many canoes had come to Las: Beizam men in their canoe, Zagareb men in their canoe, Omai men in their canoe, Deumer men in their canoe, and Geregere men in their canoe.

When the men from the islands across the sea announced their return to their homes, food was brought to them for their journey. One of the Meriam grumbled about the amount of food which had been carried for the visitors; he was heard and understood. As one man, the *Nagiram le* and the *Sikaram le* stood up and went straight to their canoes. They dragged them round stern first on the beach and erected mat screens on board.

The Omai men threw aside their mat sail, jumped down, performed like dogs, then went and sat down. The Deumer men threw down their sail, jumped down, performed like Torres Strait pigeons, then went and sat down. The Geregere men threw down their mat sail, jumped down, performed like parrots, then went and sat down.

The Zagareb men jumped down, performed, then went and sat down. The Beizam men jumped down.

All then returned to their canoes. They took Malo with them, broke his back, and sank him in the sea.

The Nagiram men and Sikaram men hoisted their sails and sailed back to their homes.

Thus ends the story of Malo.

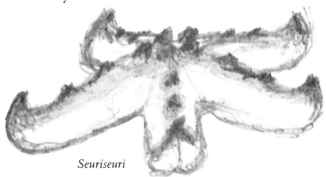

Seuriseuri

[The following added detail came from Tat Mabo, Tapim Benny-father, Benny Mabo, Abou Noah, and, in particular, Marou]:

Four brothers, Sigar, Kolka, Siu, and Malo, of whom Sigar was the eldest, came to Torres Strait from the Tuger country in New Guinea.[1] Each travelled in his own canoe.

While they were sailing from Nagir to Sasi late one afternoon in early summer, a strong south-east wind sprang up, so they dropped their anchors on the reef called Tediu. The wind continued to blow hard during the night; Sigar's anchor dragged, and his canoe began to drift. He called to his brothers: "I am going to Am, an island where there is plenty of water."

Deumer le

It was felt at Murray Island that some points of Aet Passi's story needed clarification if they were to be understood by future generations of Murray Island people. An annotated version of Aet's story is recorded below left.

1. The Tuger (or Tugeri) were the east Marind people. Haddon gives a map after Wirz in the *Reports* (I, 252), which places the Marind territory south of the Digul River, just west of the border between Papua and what is now West Irian; and, in the Introduction he wrote for Williams (*Papuans of the Trans-Fly* [Oxford, 1935]), says that Wirz ("Head-hunting expeditions of the Tugeri

331

1. (*continued*)

into the Western Division of British New Guinea", *Tijdschrift voor Indische Taal-Land-en Volkenkunde*, lxxiii [1933], 105–22 and map) "informs us that the now uninhabited coastal area east of the Bensbach [in Papua], as far as the Wassi-Kussa . . . is considered by the Marind as the dwelling place of their ancestors . . . and they claim it as their own territory . . . It was here their ancestors created all things and held the earliest *mayo* ceremonies, which gradually were carried westward as far as the Kumbe river [in West Irian]".

The Tuger raided the coastal areas of western Papua as far east as Mawata and the islands of the northern part of West Torres Strait, Saibai and Boigu. They were head-hunters, for whom the lower jaws had the same properties as the whole skull. (See *Reports*, I, 251–54, where Haddon gives abstracts of certain sections of Wirz, *Die Marind-anim von Holländisch-Süd-Neu-Guinea* [Hamburg, 1922, 1925].)

While I was recording in Torres Strait, informants at Dauan told a story which, they said, was also known on the Papuan mainland "in the Tuger country from Jerai to Gamar-Mai (just east of Buzi—opposite Boigu)". (See the story "Kogia" in the section, "Stories from Dauan".) When speaking of Malo, a Saibai informant said: "We call him Wasi Malu, because he came from the Wasi country (in west Papua)." A Murray Island informant also associated Malo with the region of the Wasi Kösa.

The *zogo mer* (sacred words), "*Ib abra lewer, kerem abra lewer* (Jawbones his food, heads his food)", were given as religious instruction to all who were initiated into the Malo-Bomai cult at Mer.

2. *Ka moder*, stitched, waterproof, mat sails of New Guinea origin.

3. Malo's canoe is said to have turned to stone where it sank off the edge of the reef.

4. "*Keriba agud, ged seker em*": *Keriba*,

In the morning, Kolka, Siu, and Malo sailed for Aurid, at which island they were received by the people. Kolka and Siu sat down amongst the people of Aurid on the *ka moder*[2] which they had brought ashore with them from their canoes, but Malo refused to keep company with them. Instead, he broke off the end of a coconut palm leaf and sat on it aloof from everyone else. He ate and slept in isolation from his brothers and the people of Aurid.

Kolka did not leave Aurid. It became his place.

Siu and Malo went to Masig where they landed on the rocky part of the beach on the eastern side of the island. Siu joined with the people of Masig; Malo behaved in the same manner as he had at Aurid, thus indicating his intention of establishing his rule at an island far removed from his brothers.

Siu stayed at Masig. Malo sailed alone to Mer.

Soon after he reached the edge of the small reef called Mebgor, close to the edge of Mer's fringing reef, a big wave sank his canoe.[3] He jumped overboard and broke off a part of the gunwale. For a while he clung to the rope which was tied to the gunwale, but he afterwards let go of it and drifted, to cast up on the beach at Begeigiz in the district of Peibri.

The people of the village of Begeigiz hailed him with the words: "*Keriba agud, ged seker em*[4] (Our god, our protector)." They enclosed him with sandstone and told him to wait while they went and fetched food for him. But after they went, he broke out and swam away, drifting with the tide to Edepek on the island of Dauar.

Malo was called protector and god by the people of that place, who penned him with *berber*[5] vine before going to their gardens for fruit and vegetables for him. When they returned, they found him gone: Malo had escaped and was drifting away with the tide.

He next cast up at Ormi, on Dauar. The sandstone enclosure built round him by the people of that place did not prevent him from escaping, and as soon as they went to their gardens for food for him whom they had received as their *agud* and protector from their enemies he swam away.

The tide took him to Ne on the neighbouring island of Waier, where a man fenced him in with branches of *zi*.[6] When the people of Ne went to fetch food for him, he broke out and departed with the tide.

our; *agud*, god, sacred, precious thing; *ged*, home, place, island; *seker*, thorn; *em*, for. The notion of Malo as protector is conveyed by the idiomatic expression, "*ged seker em*". He was to be like the thorn in the ground outside a person's home: an enemy (who would approach in bare feet) would tread upon such a thorn; therefore the thorn was a protection for that home and the people who lived in it.

5. The stem of *berber* (*Malaisia scandens*, the fire-vine) is a vicious rasp.

6. *Zi*, a tree which grows (like the mangrove) at the edge of the sea.

At Aud, on the hillside above Teker on the island of Mer, there lived a husband and wife, Dog and Kabur, and the day that Malo escaped from Ne, Kabur announced to her husband that she was going down to the reef to catch fish. Dog stayed behind to work in his garden.

Kabur went down at Teker, walked along the beach to Kebi Teker and waded out to the edge of the reef—to the spot called Taparao—where she began to fish with a line. Presently she saw a canoe at Saper Kes, the passage between the reefs of Waier, Dauar and Mer, but thought no more about it, believing it to be bringing Waier-Dauareb on a visit to Mer, and continued to fish. When, however, she happened to glance in that direction again, there was no sign of the canoe: where she had expected to see a canoe she saw, instead, a drifting log. She kept on fishing, having no idea that both canoe and log had been Malo in different forms.

Malo came closer to Taparao and began to gather speed, at the same time undergoing a series of rapid transformations: from log to *zaibu*, from *zaibu* to *tauap*, from *tauap* to *gor*. Just before he reached Taparao he changed from *gor* to *mipud*.[7] Waves carried him swiftly towards Kabur.

The woman had seen none of the transformations at the moment they were effected—each occurred when she took her eyes off the object which was approaching. Now, the sea rose with a surge, buoying her grass skirt, and Malo as an octopus entwined himself about her thighs and had connection with her. Only after he left her did Kabur discover what it was that had penetrated her, and then she speared the octopus with a pointed stick, lifted it up, and said: "*Dog ira o!*[8] (Dog's strength and courage!)" She put the octopus and the stick upon which it was still impaled into her basket and, after closing the opening, carried it in over the reef to the shore. There she placed her basket on a stone,[9] removed the octopus and, after pulling out the stick, put the octopus into a pool of water. As she stood watching it, the octopus turned red in colour and made slapping, sucking sounds.[10] "*Dog ira o!*" said Kabur. After wringing out her skirt, she transfixed the octopus with the pointed stick and replaced both in her basket. She climbed up the hill to Aud and hung up the basket.

Kabur now gave expression to her great joy at having obtained a treasure by putting on a wig and marking her right temple with red clay,[11] and then she sat down to wait for Dog. When he returned, he immediately asked what it was she was celebrating. "Come and see our *agud*—your strength and courage," she said. Afterwards the two carried the basket inside the house and hung it there. Both were agreed that they should watch it throughout the night.

Sleepless, husband and wife lay close together, their eyes on the basket. In the middle of the night they heard slapping, sucking sounds coming from it and presently saw the octopus appear on its rim, light beaming

7. *Zaibu, tauap,* and *gor* are seeds and pods of plants which grow in New Guinea. *Mipud (Phragmites karka)* is a tall, cane-like grass, which bears a seed-head like that of sugarcane. During the north-west monsoon, many seeds, plants, and logs are washed into Torres Strait, there to drift and cast up at islands and sandbanks.

8. *Dog ira o!* literally, "Dog's liver (*o,* liver)." The liver was considered to be the seat of courage and strength. There is a crevice at the edge of the reef at Taparao where Kabur stood. The sea enters it with a sound like that of the spoken words, "*Dog ira o!*"

9. Outside Au Teker.

10. Later, the reproduction of this sound by Malo initiates became a *zogo* ritual practice. They called the sound *ibkep*.

11. This marking was known as *kali mair*.

333

from its eyes. They saw the door of the house open, heard again the slapping, sucking sounds which had come from inside the basket a short time before—and then there was silence.

Malo walked round the island[12] to Peibri[13] where he went into a house.[14]

Just before dawn, Dog and Kabur heard slapping, sucking sounds at the door of their house and soon afterwards saw the octopus sitting on the rim of the basket, eyes lit up. When it disappeared, slapping, sucking sounds came from the basket. And after—no sound at all.

In the morning, Kabur tied on a fresh grass skirt and marked her right temple with red clay before laying a mat and seating herself upon it. Her husband painted himself, stuck feathers all over his body, and tied on a head-dress of cassowary feathers.

Dog went for a walk round the island, exactly following the route taken by Malo the night before. The men of Las saw him walk by and said: "What can our brother-in-law have acquired that he shows himself in this fashion?"

That night there was a lengthy discussion at Las of Dog's extraordinary conduct. At Aud, the husband and wife again lay sleepless, their eyes on the basket. Malo behaved in the same manner as he had the previous night and again visited the opposite side of the island.

When the men of Las saw Dog go by next morning, decorated as he had been the day before, they held a meeting at which they worked out a plan to discover the reason for Dog's proud bearing. They called Sarkep, a *Zagareb le*,[15] and Dam, a *Beizam le*[16] of Piad, and told them to go and find out what had come into Dog's possession at Aud. Sarkep was Kabur's younger brother; Dam, her cousin-brother. Sarkep had yaws on one foot.

These two men set off for Teker. They had with them *weres*, with which they scooped up sardines on the way. From Teker they climbed up to Aud, gave the sardines to Kabur and stayed talking until late in the afternoon. Kabur asked them if they were going home. "It is now too late for us to be able to arrive before dark because of Sarkep's yaws," Dam said. "Stay here tonight and return in the morning," Kabur told them.

That night, Dam and Sarkep lay close together inside the house, but they did not sleep: they had noticed the basket as they crawled through the doorway. When, in the middle of the night, the octopus left the basket in the same manner as on the preceding nights, the two men pinched each other and whispered: "That is the reason for Dog's display."

Next morning, Kabur brought food for Sarkep and Dam after Dog left to go walking. After they had eaten, they took their leave of her, but they did not go far before hiding their belongings and sneaking back. Silently stealing to the opposite side of the house to where Kabur was now sitting outside on a mat, they removed a thatch from the wall. Sarkep

12. Malo walked round the island on three consecutive nights. On each of the three successive mornings that Dog walked round the island, he was following the exact route taken by Malo the previous night. Amongst the ritual practices associated with the worship of Malo was the re-enactment of Malo's walks (and Dog's).

Tami le (initiates who carried out work for the *zogo le*) walked along the beach at the edge of the sand from Las to Gigo (in the district of Peibri). Behind them walked the *zogo le* (in a supervisory capacity). Only one set of footprints was left in the sand by the whole procession, each man treading in the prints made by the leader. The participants in the procession were known as *we serer le* (*we*, sand; *serer*, edge; *le*, men).

The *we serer le* called in and stayed at Kiam first, and Begeigiz second, and then walked on to Gigo where they immediately turned back. Stays were made at Begeigiz and Kiam, and then the procession continued without a halt until it arrived back at Las.

13. On the opposite side of the island to Aud and Teker.

14. The tradition is that Malo visited a woman in this house.

15. *Zagareb le*, a man born to the Zagareb territorial division of Mer.

16. *Beizam le*, "shark man". Dam belonged to the district of Piad, and was therefore a *Piadaram le*. As the shark was *agud* for the *Piadaram le*, the *Piadaram le* were on that account called *Beizam le*.

334

crawled inside the house, took down the basket, and handed it out to Dam.

A short distance from Aud, Dam, the basket held in one hand, danced while Sarkep sang and kept time for him by beating the ground with a *piru*,[17] as if he were beating a drum. Further on, at Keugiz, Sarkep again sang and kept time with the *piru* for Dam's dancing. Sarkep wanted to dance with the basket, but Dam refused to part with it. "You beat the drum and sing for me—that is your role. It suits you," Dam said.

They sang and danced at Gebadar Kop and at Gazir hill. They sang and danced at Dam, and then they hung the basket in the bushes and went to Las. The men of Las said: "Where is it?" "Hanging in the bush," replied Sarkep and Dam.

Meantime, Dog's happiness left him while he was walking; his body did not perspire as it should; therefore, he knew that something was wrong at Aud. He turned back at Begeigiz and hurried home to Kabur. In reply to his anxious questions, she assured him that all was well. So Dog looked round outside and, still unconvinced, said to her: "Go inside the house. Find out why my happiness left me." And when Kabur went into the house she saw the hole in the wall. "The two men took Malo down," she called. "They stole it." Dog spoke angrily for a long time.

The next day, Dog and Kabur decorated themselves, Dog armed himself, and then they went to fight the men of Las for the *agud*.

The husband and wife came down at Teker and took the beach road to Las. At Mergar, Dog fired arrows which fell at Er. At Er, he fired arrows which fell at Eger. At Eger, he fired arrows which fell at Areb. At Areb, he fired arrows which fell at Gazir Pit. The arrows fired by Dog at Gazir Pit landed at Las. Kabur growled from the beach in front of Las: "Who took Malo?"

The men of Las stood up and said: "Let there be no fighting between you and us." And they called Dog and Kabur to them. They made the husband and wife sit down and brought them a pipe of tobacco to smoke. "Let Malo remain here to be *agud* for all. You are only two; we are many," said the *zogo le*. Dog and Kabur returned to Aud.

At Las, the men broke a young, green leaf from a coconut palm and used it to make *larerkep* (ornamental fish eyes) to tie on their heads and their legs and their arms. They danced.

Later, men from the high islands like Nagir (the *Nagiram le*) and men from the low coral islands (the *Sikaram le*) crossed the sea, searching for Malo. They brought with them presents for Malo—clamshells and spider-shells having special significance[18] and two drums, Nimau and Wasikor.[19]

When they reached Mer, they anchored at Werbadu and asked the man, Gep: "Where is Malo?" "There!" pointed Gep. They threw him a turtle and beat drums by way of thanking him.

An impression of one of the two masks exhibited at Malo-Bomai initiation ceremonies, the last of which was performed less than one hundred years ago.

Attached by string to the back of the mask was the shell of *olai*, the hawksbill turtle. It symbolized the peaceful nature of Malo: "*Olai taba daike etkobei* (*Olai* is peacefully in its nest [when laying its eggs])."

"Mr. Ray was informed that 'Olai' was the *zogo nei* (sacred name) of this mask, even the name Bomai was withheld from the uninitiated." (*Reports*, VI, 307, fn. 1)

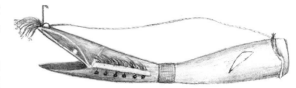

Wasikor

17. *Piru*, the lower half of the stem of a coconut frond.
18. These shells were placed at Dam, one of the important sites in Malo worship.
19. Nimau and Wasikor were used in the sacred Malo ceremonies. The open end of these drums represented an open mouth with gaping jaws. Nimau was destroyed by the crew of the "Woodlark" more than a hundred years ago. Wasikor is still at Murray Island.

Keparem le

They rowed to Er, anchored, and asked Barat: "Where is Malo?" "He stays where the trees with red paint on them grow," Barat told them. They threw a turtle to Barat, beat drums, and rowed to Las.

There they anchored, went ashore and sat down. They were made welcome, and food was brought for them. Each family at Las chose a friend from among the visitors and took him into its home. (Friendships made at that time have endured through succeeding generations and are recognized today.)

Many canoes had come to Las: the Omai men in their canoe, the Deumer men in their canoe, the Geregere men in their canoe, Zagareb men[20] in their canoe, and Beizam[21] men in their canoe.

These men stayed at Las for some time without revealing the full purpose of their visit. The *Zagareb le* and the *Beizam le* of Mer continued to feed them well, but at last one of the *zogo le* said one day while food was being heaped for the guests: "Why do we bring food for the *Gam le*?[22] Our shoulders are sore from the quantity of food we have carried for them." A visitor understood Meriam and passed word to those who had come with him. As one man the *Nagiram le* and the *Sikaram le* stood up and walked straight to their canoes. They dragged them round, stern first to the beach, and erected mat sails on board them.

The Omai men threw down their sail, jumped down, performed like dogs, then went and sat down.

The Deumer men threw down their sail, jumped down, performed like Torres Strait pigeons, then went and sat down.

The Geregere men threw down their mat sail, jumped down, performed like parrots, and then went and sat down.

The men who beat the drums for the performers and the men who directed the ceremonies had come ashore from their canoes.

All now returned to their canoes. On the reef outside Las, they drove a pole through the back of Malo: "*Malo i sor dikriare*[23] ([They] broke Malo's back)." Then the *Nagiram le* and the *Sikaram le* hoisted their sails and departed from Mer.

20. Zagareb men, so identified by the Meriam because, like their own *Zagareb le*, they beat drums and sang for the ritual dancing.

21. Beizam men (shark men), thus identified by the Meriam because, like the *Piadaram le* (the *Beizam le*) who had obtained possession of Malo as octopus, they directed the ceremonies and rites.

22. *Gam le* (= *Gem le* [*Gem*, body; *le*, people]), Island people of Torres Strait other than those belonging to the Eastern Islands. The Meriam called them "body people" (that is, big-bodied people) because they were heavily built by comparison with the slim-bodied Meriam.

23. I was told that *sor dikriare* is used only for breaking the back of a turtle.

336

MALO RA GELAR

[Given by Marou at Murray Island, 15 February 1967]

(Malo's Law)

Malo tag mauki mauki,
Teter mauki mauki.
Malo tag aorir aorir,
Teter aorir aorir.
Malo tag tupamait tupamait,
Teter tupamait tupamait.

(Malo keeps his hands to himself; he does not touch what
   is not his.
He does not permit his feet to carry him towards another
   man's property.
His hands are not grasping, he holds them back.
He does not wander from his path. He walks on tiptoe,
   silent, careful,
Leaving no sign to tell that this is the way he took.)

Arokak arokak lug-ise waipedawa.
Deregkak deregkak lug-ise waipedawa.

(You would not pluck fruit which was not fit to be eaten.
What does not belong to you is as unattractive as the fruit
   you would shun.)

Malo Muiar kemerkemer Muiar.
Ad le ged mimikak Muiar.
Ad le ged lukep atarukak Muiar.

(Malo is exactly like the Muiar. People who do not own,
   or belong to, a place, must behave towards it in the
   manner of the Muiar. Treat another man's fruit that
   grows on his land as the Muiar would have done—as
   Malo does.)

Abi mi doasmelei ne arborem a pes arkem!

(Look at him—plucking green bananas and fruit before
   they are ready!)

It is known that the *Zagareb le* recited one part of "Malo ra Gelar" during the ceremony at which the sacred masks were exhibited to members of the Malo-Bomai cult. (See *Reports,* VI, 298.) It is also known that another part of "Malo ra Gelar" was recited at the time when a taboo was being placed on a garden. (See *Reports*, I, 147.)

337

[This insult to Malo was spoken only by *Zagareb le*, because of the part a *Zagareb le* played in singing and beating time for the *Piadaram le* when he danced with Malo after having obtained possession of Malo from Dog and Kabur. Having said these words, the Zagareb immediately afterwards spoke in praise of Malo]:

Bezar

Malo bezar kemerkemer bezar.
Malo irkes bezar sep bezar.
Wali aritarit, sem aritarit,
Lug aritarit, sumes aritarit.

(Malo is exactly like *bezar*, the lonely, secretive fish.
Where Malo walks, he keeps to a narrow path, which is hardly to be seen or recognized by those who do not know him.
Malo planted everywhere—under *wali*[1] and *sem*, the yellow-flowering hibiscus,
Under trees, and in forests. Do likewise.)

Daikem eburlem esmaolem.
Malo pupkem eburlem esmaolem,
Lerokem eburlem esmaolem.
Malo urbuzikem eburlem esmaolem,
Pirukem eburlem esmaolem.
Malo beikem eburlem esmaolem,
Pesurkem eburlem esmaolem,
Malo irpurpurkem eburlem esmaolem.

(Malo says:
"Let mounds of yams, *ketai* and *kakidgaba*, remain undisturbed.
Let vines rot till no trace remains,
The bamboo poles that support them vanish;
Tree-trunks and branches, dry coconut leaves and stalks,
Faded, fallen flowers—let them go back to the soil.
You have enough and to spare without them.")

Gaka nakariklu Usiami gab ge a Segi gab ge.[2]

(Stars travel their own paths across the sky.
I cannot walk the path that is Usiam's, nor can I walk the path that is Seg's.)

1. *Wali, Pipturus argenteus.*
2. Those Giar-Dauareb who are descendants of Koit of Las (who went to live at Giar Pit on the island of Dauar) claim that this instruction belongs to Tagai, not Malo. (See the story of "Tagai", in this section.) They say that the Malo instruction is: "*Wer taba gab ge baupamaretli* (Stars travel their own path [across the sky])."

338

SAID

[Told by Marou at Murray Island, 1 February 1967]

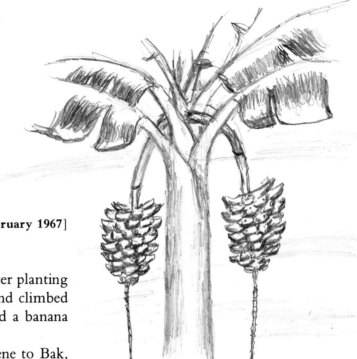

Neis kerem-kerem kaba

Said travelled from Deudai[1] to Mer. He landed at Gigo and, after planting a tree called *kaplewer,* walked round the island to Werbadu and climbed up to Aud. From Aud he walked to Kikite, where he planted a banana sucker of the variety called *idid kaba.*[2]

Said continued to walk about the island, going through Mene to Bak, and from Bak to Zeug and Namsigir and Mido. He planted the kind of banana sucker known as *iwir kaba*[3] at Mido. When he came to Petam he planted yet another variety of banana sucker: *neis kerem-kerem kaba.*[4]

At Arpet Said found flourishing coconut palms, so he praised that place with these words:

> *Arpet iai, Arpet iai, uraba niba uraba kuikui gamuriba.*[5]

At Gagri, he scratched the soil with his toe and finding it good, said:

> *Gagri ai Gagri ai naba mataiba siai ba*
> *Iadi nuba iadi Saidi sagadi.*[6]

Said turned back at Gagri and retraced his steps as far as Arpet. Going by way of Ardor, Tair, Kes, Utem, and Medeber, he came again to Namsigir and then went down the path called Zirugab to Er. At Er, he looked towards Teker and Mergar, but he did not go to those places; instead, he went to Warwei where a man named Gobai lived.

Gobai greeted Said and asked where he was going. When Said replied that he was merely walking about the island, Gobai asked him if he were by himself and, on learning that he was, told Said about a girl at Wao for whom a number of young men who had painted their bodies with the markings of *beizam, lewerem,* and *kamosar*[7] were dancing. This girl, Pekari,[8] had so far accepted no young man.

1. *Deudai*, here, the northern mainland, New Guinea.
2. *Idid kaba*: *kaba* is the Meriam word for banana. The three varieties named in this story are said to have been introduced to Murray Island by Said. *Idid* means oily or greasy.
3. *Iwir kaba* is a very long, U-shaped banana, dark green in colour until it ripens, when it turns yellow-green.
4. *Neis kerem-kerem kaba* is a variety which bears two heads of bananas simultaneously.
5. These words are not Meriam.
6. See previous footnote.
7. *Beizam*, hammerhead shark (*Sphyrna lewini* [Griffith]); *lewerem*, black-tip shark (*Carcharhinus spallanzani* [Le Sueur]); *kamosar,* epaulette shark (*Hemiscyllium ocellatum*).
8. *Pekari* is a corruption of *pakarar*, a virgin. The use of Pekari as the girl's name was deliberately adopted to conceal the fact that the girl was a virgin.

Kamosar

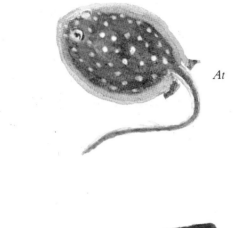

At

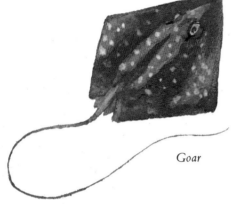

Goar

Said asked Gobai to accompany him to Wao. So the two men groomed themselves and put on wigs, and then they went out to a pool on the reef to examine their appearance. They gazed at themselves in two other pools a little further along the reef, one at Gazir, and Malo Keper. And then, as they walked round the island towards Wao, each in turn sang a love charm, vying with one another.

Said sang first, at Las:

> *(E) deumer (i) ezonei (i) ezoli.*
> *(E) dibadiba (i) ezonei (i) ezoli.*

> (*Deumer* [the Torres Strait pigeon] is calling. *Dibadiba* [a small green bird with an orange breast and a patch of red on top of its head] is calling.)

At the end of each verse he breathed: "Pekari!" This was a song which never failed.

Gobai stood still and watched Said while he sang, for Gobai, too, knew how to woo a woman. So, when Said had done, Gobai matched him:

> *Orbei orbei orbei kaur em (a) pasi em (a) sosoia (a).*
> (Row, row, row. To an island, to a shore, to a beach.)

At Orbid, Said sang another song:

> *At (e) goar at (e).*[9]

Gobai countered with the song that he had sung earlier at Las:

> *Orbei orbei orbei kaur em (a) pasi em (a) sosoia (a).*

> *E deumer (i) ezonei (i) ezoli,*

sang Said. "Pekari!" he called in a whisper.

And so they continued until they reached Leiwag, where their approach was observed by the people at Wao. Said now directed very powerful magic at Pekari, waving a magic feather, *rabaraba*,[10] towards her and saying: *"Pekari, Pekari, ngau ipi, aidi aidi waleika, Saidi Saidi waleika.*[11] Then he stuck *rabaraba* in his hair and walked with Gobai straight to Wao.

On their arrival they were greeted by Pekari, who took them to her place, spread a mat for them, and invited them to sit down. At this, the young men who had been courting Pekari departed, and, later in the afternoon, Gobai also left Wao, for Said pleased Pekari. These two, Said and Pekari, remained together throughout the night.

In the morning, Said woke to the sound of palm fronds[12] stirred by wind: overnight, coconut palms had sprung up where he had lain with Pekari. He took his leave of the girl and walked away in the direction of Ero Giz.

9. *At*, blue-spotted stingaree (*Dasyatis kuhlii*); *goar*, cowtail or fantail ray (*Pastinachus sephen*). The song does no more than mention these two fish.
10. *Rabaraba*, a feather of *womer*, the man-o'-war hawk.
11. These Mabuiag words address Pekari as the girl whom Said will soon possess.
12. The sound made by palm fronds stirred and scraped together by the wind is *garagara* in Meriam.

At Ero Giz, he met Kudar, mother of Kos and Abob. He speared her with his *kusbager* and put her in the basket[13] which he wore over his shoulder.

Kos and Abob, who had returned to Mer after their fight with the Warib at Waier, found their mother's footprints leading away from their home at Akub and followed them. Thus, they came upon Said's footprints also and, realizing that their mother had been abducted, set out across the reef in pursuit of her captor.

Kudar saw them approaching, for there was a hole in Said's basket through which she could see out. "You took me as if I were a woman who had no sons," she told Said, "but my sons are already close at hand and overtaking you fast. See! Foam like *dari*[14] is flung up by the speed of their coming."

Kos and Abob raised their *nagnag*[15] to strike Said. He, however, had inserted a tail feather of the man–o'–war hawk in his anus the instant he saw Kudar's sons, and he now changed into a man–o'–war hawk and flew up into the air at Mad. Too late the brothers struck at him—they only succeeded in removing two of his tail feathers.[16] Said rose higher and then, removing Kudar from his basket, he dropped her into the sea where she became the reef, Aum Kep.

Higher and higher into the sky flew Said, so high that he could see far-off Deudai (New Guinea). He landed at Garsao at Erub (Darnley Island), went round to the eastern side of the island to Irmed, and there drank brackish water. Afterwards, he went to Deudai.

Kos and Abob followed Said to Erub. They, too, went from Garsao to Irmed and drank brackish water. Then they swam to Deudai.

13. This basket is called *buzil epei*. It is a New Guinea basket, worn over the shoulder. In it a man kept his aids to magic. The Mabuiag equivalent for *buzil epei* is *topi iana*.

14. *Dari*, the head-dress made from the feathers of *sir*, the white reef heron

15. *Nagnag*, a length of bamboo 10–12 feet in length with a V-shaped notch cut at one end. It is used by men crouching in the sea to cripple man–o'–war hawks by breaking their wings. The hawk is retrieved with the notched end of the *nagnag*, and its feathers used to stuff sardines so that they will float on top of the water and attract other birds.

16. This accounts for the wedge-tail of *womer*, the man–o'–war hawk. The man–o'–war hawk which has white at its throat is called *said* in Meriam.

Womer

Said

341

Kos

Abob

KOS AND ABOB

[**Told by Robert Pitt at Murray Island, 19 August 1968**]

1. Akub is in the territorial division of Mer called Zagareb.
2. Stone fish-traps (*sai*) are a noticeable feature of the home reef surrounding each of the Eastern Islands, Mer (Murray Island), Dauar, Waier, Erub (Darnley Island), and Ugar (Stephens Island). While many fish-traps have fallen into disuse, some are still regularly repaired during the season of the north-west monsoon. I assisted at the repair of a fish-trap at Murray Island in February 1967.
3. A variety of garfish is called *warib* by the Meriam. One informant thought it possible that the Warib people changed into garfish.

Two brothers, Kos and Abob, lived at Akub[1] with their mother, Kudar.

They quarrelled at Paugiz one day, and when, as a result of the quarrel, Kos refused to accompany Abob to the island of Dauar, Abob set out alone.

But before long, Kos had a change of heart and, with the aid of a tuft of grass which he put on top of his head, flew to the bow of Abob's canoe. There he alighted and the two brothers made friends again. They landed at Saded on Dauar and began to build stone fish-traps[2] on the reef around that island.

That day, people called the Warib[3] had come from their home on the adjacent island, Waier, to fish at Dabai Mager on Dauar. They caught *neud* (a green fish) and, after eating all the flesh, threw the guts to an old woman named Gawer.

When Kos and Abob reached Ormi—on the opposite side of Dauar to Saded—they saw Gawer and would have killed her; only, she called to

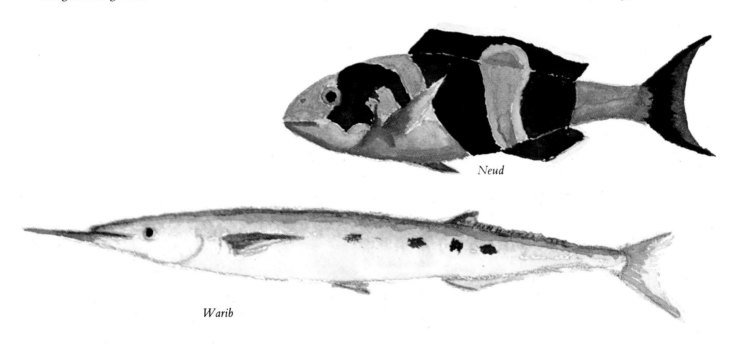

Neud

Warib

342

them: "Come here, good boys! Those people, the Warib, have ill-treated me and mocked me." Whereupon they accompanied Gawer to her home at Keriam, cut sticks with which to kill the Warib from the wood of a *kus* tree and, after being decorated by Gawer, left for Waier. Gawer sat down and turned to stone.

From Keriam, Kos and Abob went to Werte and from Werte to Auter (a big reef). From Auter they skimmed across the surface of the water to Waier, where they set about killing the Warib. As they went from one end of the island to the other and then back, they struck the Warib down with such force that their *kus* sticks cracked the rock wall of Waier into fissures and clefts. They killed many Warib, but they could not kill all. "However many of us you kill," said those who survived, "there are as many, or more, of us to take their place."

Kos and Abob returned to Mer. They landed at Mergar and began to work their way round the island, building fish-traps as they went. When they reached their home at Akub, they found that their mother, Kudar, had walked away in the direction of Ero Giz, and they began to track her . . .

The story of Kos and Abob is inextricable from that of Said, yet each is always told as a separate story. As the conclusion of the story of Kos and Abob has already been given in the story of Said, it seems unnecessary to repeat it here.

Robert Pitt said that he had always understood the story of Kos and Abob ended with the two brothers following Said to Erub and Deudai. His nephew, however, had told him the detail which follows:

Kos and Abob followed Said all the way to Goodenough Island (in the D'Entrecasteaux Islands).

Not far from Goodenough Island there is a small island on which, at that time, there lived an old woman and some girls. There were no men at all on the island.

One of the brothers—which of the two is not known—left his brother in deep water while he went ashore to inspect this island. When he returned to tell him what he had found, his brother had turned to stone. After looking back at the island, he, too, turned to stone.

Repair of a stone fish-trap (*sai*) at Murray Island, February 1967. There are many *sai* at this island, and some at the neighbouring islets, Dauar and Waier. They are said to have been built by the brothers Kos and Abob.

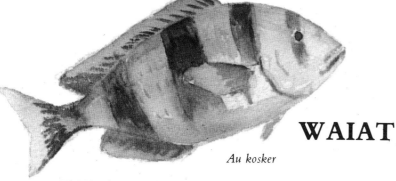

Au kosker

WAIAT

[Told at Murray Island by Dela Mopwali, 16 February 1967, and Robert Pitt, 20 August 1968]

This is the sequel to the story told at Mabuiag about Waiat, head sorcerer of Widul. The night after men killed his wife and daughter in obedience to his commands, Waiat suffered from remorse. He beat his drum all night long and then murdered his nephews for a trifling offence. By that time he could hear the sound of a drum a long way off and he set out to find it. The elusive drum-beat led him from island to island in West Torres Strait, but he never caught up with it there. So he sailed east.

1. Actually, "he pulled out his navel (*kopor*) and put it" at each of the places mentioned. The *kopor* are seen as stones. The particular spot at Areb where he left his *kopor* is called Kapiab.

2. Waier is a small, black, volcanic island of riven rock and battlemented crags. It is horseshoe-shaped. The name of the semi-circular area within the arms of the horseshoe is Ne.

3. The language of this song is corrupt Mabuiag. At the island of Mabuiag it was suggested that the words were:

Wa gub pudema [repeated]
Ngalmun lag ia
Wa kapu lag ia kapu lag ia
Wa gub pudema.

(The wind blows, the wind blows.
Our island,
Good island,
The wind blows.)

It was also suggested that the wind was the north-west wind, which reminded Waiat of his home and his wife and daughter.

4. Nothing is known about the *Au Kosker* (old women) except the details included in the story of Waiat. The *Au Kosker* were *lamar* (spirits).

Waiat came to Mer from Mabuiag.

After his arrival, he went to Werbadu on the other side of the island—as Malo had done. He walked on, past Teker, and Areb, and Kaipi Pat, to a spot between Boged and Akitir, looking for the kind of place he wanted for a home. He placed a stone[1] at the places he visited, a sign that he laid claim to them, but none of them suited his purpose, so he left Mer and sailed to Dauar.

His canoe broke on the reef called Akesakes. Clinging to the *sal* (the platform of a canoe, used as a seat), he swam ashore at Giar, the western end of the island of Dauar, and began to search for somewhere to live. But he only left stones at Giar and Euziz and Eg and Teg, for they were no more pleasing to him than the places he had visited at Mer, and then he crossed to the island of Waier.[2]

He left a stone on the sandspit opposite Teg and, after walking round the island by way of Gergeri Pit, came to Ne. There he watched the leaves of the trees moving in the wind and beat his drum for them and sang:

(Wa) dumiaba,
(Wa) dumiaba,
Galmun lagia,
(Wa) kapu lagia lagia
(Wa) dumiaba.[3]

Two women, the *Au Kosker*,[4] came out of their home—the hole inside the big rock, Korsor, at the edge of the sea—when they heard Waiat's drum. Half-running, half-dancing, they made their way along the beach, passed Waiat, and returned in the same manner as they had come to their home in Korsor.

Waiat heard the sound of another drum close at hand. It answered his beats from the cliffs behind him. So he climbed the rocks to look for a place in which he could settle at last. High up he found a cave for a home, and to it he took the *sal* of his canoe and his drum.

Later, the people from those places at which he had left stones became his followers.[5]

5. Waiat became the head of a cult of evil repute (see *Reports*, VI, 277–80).

Both Dela Mopwali and Robert Pitt spoke of Waiat as a "proper bad man".

DEUMER

[Told by Robert Pitt at Murray Island, 17 August 1968]

Tole

A man[1] and his daughter, Deumer,[2] were out fishing one day at Mabuiag during the north-west season when the north-west wind sprang up and blew hard. They could not go up against it in their canoe and drifted away from their island.

Eventually they reached Adud Nor, a small reef off the island of Dauar, where their canoe sank. The two castaways (*sarup*) swam until they reached Ne on the neighbouring island of Waier and landed without being seen.

They made their way to a *meker*[3] tree which grew beside the beach. There the father stood his bow and arrows against the trunk of the tree and sat down beside them in the shade to rest. Deumer climbed up and began to eat the fruit of the *meker* tree, at the same time throwing some down to her father.

From time to time, small brown birds called *tole* rose up into the air and flew about whistling—as is the habit of *tole* when someone comes near them—and whenever they did this, the father got up and went to see if there was anyone in sight.

That day, a man named Bame—of Sebeg, a village in the district of Komet, Mer—had made his way ashore at Waier Pit after his canoe sank. Daugiri of Waier saw him land and went towards him with the intention of killing him. Bame, however, was accepted by people who lived at Waier Pit before Daugiri could reach him.

In a rage because he had been thwarted, Daugiri left Waier Pit, climbed the rocky precipices of the island by the route called Korok Gab, and came down on the other side of Waier to Ne at Utut Kur. *Tole* flew up into the air and whistled when they caught sight of Daugiri, and it was then that he discovered the presence of a *sarup* on Waier, for he saw the father who had left the shelter of the *meker* tree to find out what had disturbed the birds.

Daugiri hurried back to Waier Pit by the same route as he had come and told his brothers, Waida and Pitari, about the *sarup*.

At once the three set off for Ne along Korok Gab, discussing as they climbed who should kill the *sarup*. Pitari, the youngest brother, was appointed to do it, "because," said the other two brothers, "you are the best man with a spear—you always spear fish which have thick scales".[4] When they came down at Utut Kur, they startled a curlew[5] which flew up and called. The *sarup* went to see who or what had flushed it, and

Aet Pasi included "Deumer" in the MS stories which he gave to Ray of the Cambridge Expedition in 1898, but it is not included in the *Reports*. It is listed, however, in the *Reports* (III, 228), and an outline of the story is given in English (*Reports* I, 349). There the man is called Dagapur, and the girl Meket. The story is, I think, between one hundred and seventy and two hundred years old.

Karor

1. Robert Pitt did not know his name.
2. Deumer is remembered as a girl who had a pale skin.
3. *Meker* is the almond tree of Torres Strait (*Terminalia catappa*).
4. *You always spear fish which have thick scales:* your aim is deadly.
5. The Meriam word for these birds is *karor*. The people of Murray Island call them "curlews" when they speak English. I did not see the birds for myself at Murray Island.

345

while he was walking about, the brothers crawled towards the *meker* tree—towards the *sarup*'s bow and arrows.

Deumer, who was still in the tree, saw the men and shouted a warning to her father. He ran for his bow and arrows, and as he did so, Pitari hurled his *kusbager* at him, the pointed end of the lance going right through the *sarup*'s body, entering at the back and coming out in the region of the heart. Daugiri and Waida ran to the stricken man and clubbed him. The girl jumped down from the tree and wept over her father's dead body.

Daugiri, Waida, and Pitari took Deumer with them when they set out for Waier Pit. On the way, each of them used her. Then they killed her.

Stem and leaves of the yam called *ketai* in Meriam, and *kutai* in Mabuiag

1. Descendants of Paiwer who, with Rebes, had helped to build Maizab Kaur for *nam kerem* (see the Darnley Island story of "Maizab Kaur").
2. From Giar on the island of Dauar.
3. The spot at which Irado found the root is called Ketai Pit.
4. I think *Eudam Meuram* here means: "Meuram wives of men thought to be dead."

WAKAI AND KUSKUS

[Told by Tarau Giaz at Murray Island, 2 September 1968]

It was the season of mating turtle, so Wakai and Kuskus—two brothers who were at that time the head men of the Meuram on Mer—decided to go to Kerged (East Cay) on a hunting expedition. They invited Meuram of Mer, Boged-Komet men (of Mer), two visiting Meuram from Erub,[1] and a Giar-Dauareb[2] to accompany them. The party was so long in returning from Kerged that its members were given up for dead.

One day, Irado of Werbadu saw the root of a wild yam called *ketai* at the foot of cliffs[3] not far from her home. She followed the root right across the island to Werdaid before she found the yam and dug it up. Then, on looking out to sea, she saw canoes returning to Mer from Kerged. "*Eudam Meuram*,"[4] she called to the wives who were mourning for their husbands, "your husbands' canoes are in sight." The women bathed themselves and began to prepare food.

Wakai and Kuskus were the first to arrive. The others followed soon afterwards, Urgop being the last to run in. They made their landing at Baz and stood their paddles against a stone at the foot of a rocky headland between Mek and Babud. Every member of the hunting party to Kerged had returned safely except one—Marwer, a Boged-Komet man.

346

The wives ran to meet their husbands. Marwer's wife, not seeing her husband, asked where he was. One of the men told her.

"On the way to Kerged, we all threw food into the sea for the *lamar* at Gaidan Kes—all, that is, but Marwer, who abused the *lamar* and neglected to make his offering.

The morning after we arrived at Kerged, we saw a pair of mating turtles, and a canoe was immediately put into the water. But we found it impossible to jump for the turtles: no sooner did a man go to the bow and tie the rope to his arm than the turtles disappeared into the water below. At last, when only Marwer had not taken his turn at the bow, we urged him to try his luck. He went to the bow, made ready—the turtles continued to float on top of the water, and he jumped.[5]

Marwer elbowed the male turtle aside, caught the female, and went down with her. Presently we saw a *kamad*[6] at the surface—Marwer was between the pair, the male turtle having joined on top of him underwater while Marwer was clinging to the female. The *kamad* sank, reappeared, several times. Each time we saw it, another male turtle had added itself to the *kamad*. Marwer's body was crushed and raw from the weight of the turtles on top of him. That was the last we saw of our friend."[7]

5. Moses Sagigi gave a different reason from that of Tarau Giaz for the behaviour of the turtle and the death of Marwer. Moses said that Marwer's friend remembered the *zogo mer*, certain sacred words, at the instant Marwer jumped. To think these words while a person was at sea, or in the sea, was believed to be disastrous.

6. A *kamad* is a pair of mating turtles which have been joined on top by one or more additional male turtles.

7. Tarau Giaz differed from Moses Sagigi on the detail of the finding of Marwer's bones. In Tarau's account there is no mention of the visit to Omeome Kaur. Tarau said that Marwer's bones were found at Garboi on a subsequent hunting trip to Kerged.

Leaf of *ketai*

Old-style canoe

Roots and tuber of *ketai*

Turtle of the kind known as *nam*. This kind of turtle was associated with the clan to which the story of Wakai and Kuskus belongs. This clan, Meuram, owned "knowledge" which enabled them to catch *nam*, the green turtle.

347

Kiriskiris ti

Beuger

8. The flat, sandy ground immediately adjacent to the beach.
9. The high ground where most of the gardens are made.
10. The bird called *beuger* is the booby. It is the sacred bird of the Meuram.
11. *Sesareb* has a meaning similar to *nosik*, population.

Tarau Giaz and Moses Sagigi claim direct descent from men who accompanied Wakai and Kuskus to Kerged. Moses is descended from Urgop.

The garden lands on *op*, which were given by the Meuram to Boged-Komet families, include Newar, Eror, Semar, Meuz, and Budau.

Wakai and Kuskus, head men of the Meuram, owned Kerged (East Cay) and the strip of sea between Kerged and the land, beach, and reef owned by them on Mer.

Marwer's companions continued to search for him. They had been following the *kamad*, heading towards it whenever it came up to the top of the water. It had been taking them further and further away from Kerged, and now they went on until they reached Omeome Wesor, a very small island on which grew a single fig-tree. The men landed and looked for their friend's body. They found his bones; they spoke to them in sorrow.

The men had no water. They were a long way from Kerged. The wind dropped. It was *naiger* time (when the south-east wind begins to swing to the north-east, *naiger*), and for days on end the sea remained dead, flat calm. There was food to be had—turtle and fish—but there was no water to drink, so the men could not eat. They lay on the sand, parched.

One night, Marwer's friend had a dream: Marwer came to him and said: "There is water here. It is covered by pumice." In the morning after he woke up, he saw a *kiriskiris ti* near him. When it flew away, he followed it. Suddenly, the *kiriskiris ti* swooped down low over some pumice and came to rest just beyond it. Marwer's friend, his eyes on the bird the whole time, trod on the pumice, which yielded beneath his foot with a splash. He lay beside the pool and drank till he could hold no more. He thought his fingernails and his toenails must be thirsty, so he filled them with water, too. Then he hurried back to the other men and said: "Wake up! Wake up! Eat food and drink water! Eat food and drink water!" These men replied dully: "You should not have said that while we are so very thirsty."

Marwer's friend decorated his body in imitation of the *kiriskiris ti* and, calling the men to follow him, led them to the pumice and hopped to the other side of it. As he had done, they stumbled unknowing into the pool and immediately afterwards were drinking. Like him, they, too, filled their fingernails and toenails as well. And afterwards they ate.

A fair breeze sprang up. The men loaded their canoe, taking water from the pool for their journey, and were soon on their way to Kerged, which place they reached the same day. Next morning, the whole party set sail for Mer.

The second day after the return of the hunting party to Kerged, Wakai and Kuskus summoned the Meuram and Boged-Komet families to a meeting. The Meuram then gave a part of their land, both *tawer*[8] and *op*,[9] to the people of Boged-Komet. This land, in the heart of the Meuram division of Mer, was called *beuger*[10] *ira marmot* (*beuger's* breast). The Meuram also named the Boged-Komet people "*Meuram sesareb.*"[11]

The gift of land and the bestowal of the term "*Meuram sesareb*" permanently linked the Boged-Komet families with the Meuram people of Mer.

348

THE ORIGIN OF MOSQUITOES

[Told by Sam Passi at Murray Island, 5 March 1967]

Noreb ti

Long ago there were some girls living at Zomered whose daily custom it was to go fishing on the reef in canoes which were the sheaths of the flower-heads of coconut palms. Before they set out, they placed food in an earth-oven to cook. When they came back, they uncovered the earth-oven, removed the food and ate it.

One day, however, they found upon their return from the reef that their oven had been robbed. They had no idea who the culprit was, but they determined to find out. So they made a plan.

The following day they prepared their meal and placed it in the earth-oven as usual, but instead of every girl going off to fish, one stayed behind to watch for the thief. This girl adopted the form of a small bird, *noreb ti*,[1] and perched on the branch of a tree which overlooked the earth-oven.

Presently she saw a man named Dopem creep to the earth-oven, uncover it, remove the food from it, and steal away. All this she told her companions when they returned from the reef. Many angry words were spoken.

Next day none of the girls went fishing. After covering the earth-oven they all went and hid behind nearby bushes.

Before long Dopem approached in stealthy fashion, and, at the moment of his beginning to uncover the earth-oven, the girls rushed out from their hiding places and beat him with sticks. They beat him until he fell down dead, and then they dragged his body down to the beach and threw it into the sea.

Dopem's body was washed up at Beur by the next high tide, so the girls threw it back into the sea. But it was returned by the tide to the beach at Zeub. Again the girls threw it into the sea.

This happened many times: it was useless trying to get rid of Dopem's body by throwing it into the sea, for it was always brought back by the tide. Finally, after the body washed ashore at Korog, the girls decided to take it up to the high ground behind that place and bury it. There it turned to stone.

After the girls had buried Dopem, they went back to Zomered. They decided to change into mosquitoes and go and live in a shady, damp nook close by. Their new home was afterwards called Lag Kop.[2]

1. Haddon (*Reports*, VI, 8) identifies *noreb ti* as the female *Nectarinia australis* (the Sun bird).
2. *Lag*, mosquito; *kop*, secluded place. There was formerly a ritual for the control of mosquitoes, conducted at and belonging to Lag Kop.

Deo

IRUAM

VERSION 1

[Edited version, and translation, of story told by Aet Pasi in 1898]

Iruam ira mer pe ike. Iruam nipat ge dauer. Wi ge gair tabakiauare Las lam ni atatkoem. Wi ager iglare. Gair neur wiaba nei Te pipi a Te sabersaber. Pako nerut neur abra nei Deo. Wi kikem gair neur Deo i nab ikairare kega: "Mi naba ni agrem." E ge Deo ide bes darardare kega: "Kara nisor mermer ike." Wi ga tabakiauare Gazir Pit ge tedeketrare i ko tederaueirare. E ge Deo ide tabara nisor tais keubu tabakiamulu, gair neur ge bager, Tur Pit ge abi dasmerare. Gair neur tabara mer batagrare: "Deo ide merbi bes tidirida." E keubu ikasereder. Wi ge Er ge bog, ge bamer maik'e. E ko keubu og, wiabi nardarare, daratagrare kega: "Waba adud ni iriauem. Kai noge Eu Pat ge debe ni tarie." Wi ge gair neur sopkak iriare kei ko kikem bakiauare. E ge Deo og. E Eu Pat ge nisor edag. E ge neis nisor naiter. E ge Iruam bamareredlu nerner okaderdar. Emetu okaderdar. E eosmelu Deo i itmer kega: "Ma nete?" Deo ide abi detager kega: "Kaka Deo nali." E ko abi itmer kega: "Ma nete?" E ge Iruam ide abi detager: "Taba a mi adud akailei." Deo nole lagkak. E tabara nisor tais, tabakiamulu kikem, Iruam keubu tabakiamulu, tawer ge etrumlu. Deo e baraigilu Au Narte ge. E Mubagab em bakiamulu. Iruam keubu bakiamulu, Deo, nerner, tabara arborker nisor oker. E ge euprer ga ko aiser. Wi ge gair neur tabager abi tadasmerare a wi bagrerdare kega: "Deo i Iruam ide digeli." Wi ge au dudum ge bakiauare Las ge, ni idagare, iko u em bakarik. Able pesur dikeuare, oker didbarare, Deo ira kikem batauerdare. Deo ide tabara ni edag, e ge pesur etaruklu, wi abi damrikare. E ge usi ditpulu kikem maber etatko a keubu ditpulu Au Keper etatko, eupamalu keret sor ge balu. Wi ge keret dipitare. E ge eosmelu asor sor ge balu. Wi ge asor dipitare. E ge eupamalu nazir sor ge balu. Wi ge nazir dipitare. E ge eupamalu semep sor ge balu. Wi ge semep dipitare. E ge waiwer ge balu niaiem niaikarem. Sina. Esemuda able Deo ira mer.

Three versions of this tale are recorded here. The first is an edited version of the story as told in 1898 in the Pasi MS by a Meriam (Aet Pasi) in the Meriam language (*Reports*, III, 229–33). It is followed by a translation of this edited version. The second is a story-song composed in Meriam in 1935 (or thereabouts). It is so similar to Aet Pasi's story that it is unnecessary to provide a translation. The only details which have been omitted in the ballad are names of places and Iruam's demand of Deo. The order of the shells into which Iruam jumped differs slightly. Version 3 was told in Meriam in 1967 (and afterwards translated into English) by a man who was nearly eighty years old. The translation only is given here. A comparison of the three versions illustrates the accuracy with which the story has been preserved during the past seventy years.

In modern times, a number of myths of Torres Strait have been, and are being, transmitted through the medium of the story-song or sung ballad. These are very popular with young and old alike. While detail which was formerly included in the tale is sometimes absent from the story-song, I think it true that the myth as sung today is known by every person at its island of origin, whereas it would formerly have been known only by a limited number of people at that island.

Here is the story of Iruam.

Iruam lived in a waterhole. People came there from Las to fill their water-containers.

Te pipi and Te sabersaber[1] roasted *ager*.[2]

There was another girl whose name was Deo. They asked her to go with them and fill her *nisor*[3] at the same time as they went to fill theirs. Deo told them a lie: "Mine are full."

Te pipi and Te sabersaber went without her. They had walked round Gazir Pit, when Deo put on her *nisor* and came after them. The other girls looked back when they reached Tur Pit and saw her coming. They said to each other: "Deo did not tell us the truth."

At Er, Te pipi and Te sabersaber climbed up and sat down close by [a well]. Deo also climbed up at Er. She saw the girls and said: "You are filling your *nisor* with bad water. I shall climb up further to Eu Pat and fill my *nisor* with good water." Te pipi and Te sabersaber quickly filled their *nisor* and set out for their home.

Deo went higher up and put down her *nisor* at Eu Pat. She dipped them into the waterhole. At that, Iruam moved and blew out his breath to make a bubbling sound in order to fool Deo.

After he had fooled her, he came up out of the waterhole and said to her: "Who are you?" Deo told him and asked who he was. Iruam said: "We are going to do a bad thing together." Deo was unwilling. She picked up her *nisor* and ran away down to the beach. Iruam chased her.

Deo went down to the reef at Au Narte and then went to Mubagab. Iruam continued to chase Deo [who was] breathless. Her *nisor* bumped and clattered [as she ran]. She hopped [like a *deo* bird] and then picked up [her *nisor* and ran on].

The other girls looked back and saw her. They pointed to her and said: "Iruam is chasing Deo." Very quickly, they went and laid down their *nisor* at Las and climbed a coconut palm. They pulled off *pesur*[4] and tied the end of each. They threw a *pesur* to Deo. She put down her *nisor* and picked it up. They flogged Iruam.

Iruam urinated and filled a *bu* shell. He urinated a second time and filled Au Keper.[5] Afterwards, he jumped inside a strombus [shell].[6]

The girls beat the strombus. He left it and went inside a spider shell.[7] The girls beat the spider shell, and he went inside a trochus shell. The girls beat the trochus shell, and he jumped out and went inside a *semep*[8] shell. They then beat the *semep*. He then went into a cleft at the edge of the reef and stayed there for ever.

That is the end of Deo's story.

1. *Te pipi and Te sabersaber:* the girls were both named "*Dusty-mouth*" (*te*, mouth; *pipi* and *sabersaber*, dusty—from the dust which settles around a person's mouth when he or she drinks from a dry coconut).
2. *Ager* (a kind of *Amorphophallus*), a tuber which is rendered edible by correct preparation (charring and removal of the charred outer skin) and cooking.
3. *Nisor* (or *basor*), the shell of the dry coconut when used as a vessel for carrying and storing water. *Nisor* are always carried in pairs, the connecting string between the two shells being worn over the shoulder. Called *kusul* in the Western Islands.
4. *Pesur*, the dry, branched stalk from which coconuts depend.
5. A lagoon on the reef.
6. *Strombus (Conomurex) luhuanus* Linne.
7. *Asor*, a spider shell (*Lambis [Lambis] lambis* Linne).
8. *Semep* (?). The oldest men on Murray Island had never heard of a shell by this name in their language.

351

Te pipi, Te sabersaber, neur, ge urder.
Wi tabara ager iglare.
Meb dauer, wez u barmer,
Iabim toger. Wi ge erdarlare.
"Ama! Babi dasmerare
Ibiibi, tagimtagim, pe merbim ogli."

Te pipi, Te sabersaber, neur, ge urder.
Wi ge tabara ager amei deurlare ge.
Ager iglare ge igorlare ge able mer kem:
"Kara nene kat tetitili,
Muimui kat tetitili."
O ikrislare ge.

Esaprare ge.
Niap iaba barukda,
Batueri, ged im batueri.
Lu tabara dirsirda, basor aisa, basor aisa,
Basor aisa, bakirki Er em bakiauda,
Pat ge tabarti, Piripiri Pat ge tabamri.

Deo ide tabara basor keubu aisi,
Baka-bakamuda, keubu tabada,
Iabi sor ge iabi nakerda,
"Waba lili usiusi ni iriauem.
Kai nabakiamulu kabara Kokaper ge debe ni tarie."

Wi tabara ni etatkolare,
Basor iaba bosi. Wi bakui,
Bakirki, ged im bakiauda.
E ge ogi.
Kokaper ge tegimulu, temrilu,
Basor tabara titer.

Iruam ide tasor,
E ge eudi teosmelu.

Deo ide tabara basor terep, korider temrilu.
E ge abi tidiskemelu.
Deo ide tabara basor terep, korider temrilu.
E ge abi tidiskemelu.
Bakir u terborker, bakir u terborker.
E ge tabara basor tipiter.

Wi ge abi erdarare korider bamer,
Lokot ge pesur tetakrare ge,
O tabakiauare basib.

Deo ira pesur kikem ditimdare ge,
Wi ge batkamrik terpeirare ge,
Damrikare ge, damrikare ge,
Eupamalu keret[9] ge balu.

Keret deraimrare ge,
Nab keret deraimrare ge
Nab ge, darareg.

Keret dipitare ge,
Keret dipitare ge,
Eupamalu asor[10] ge balu.

Asor deraimrare ge,
Nab asor deraimrare ge
Nab ge, darareg.

Asor dipitare ge,
Asor dipitare ge,
Eupamalu nazir[11] ge balu.

Nazir deraimrare ge,
Nab nazir deraimrare ge
Nab ge, darareg.

Nazir dipitare ge,
Nazir dipitare ge,
Eupamalu as[12] ge balu.

As deraimrare ge,
Nab as deraimrare ge
Nab ge, darareg.

9. *Keret*, a shell (*Strombus* [*Conomurex*] *luhuanus* Linne).
10. A spider shell (*Lambis* [*Lambis*] *lambis* Linne).
11. *Nazir*, trochus shell.
12. *As*, the large Horned Helmet (*Cassis cornuta* Linne).

353

As dipitare ge,
As dipitare ge,
Eupamalu maber[13] ge balu.

Maber deraimrare ge,
Nab maber deraimrare ge
Nab ge, darareg.

Maber dipitare ge,
Maber dipitare ge,
Eupamalu waiwer ge balu.

Waiwer deraimrare ge,
Nab waiwer deraimrare ge
Nab ge, darareg.

Waiwer dipitare ge,
Waiwer dipitare ge,
Wi waiwer nab dipitlare ge.

Meg togri wiabi nagida; wi ge waiwer nab dipitlare ge.
Meg togri nagida narimda.
Wi bakui, ged im tebeui.

13. *Maber*, either the Pacific Triton (*Charonia tritonis* Linne) or the Australian Trumpet Shell (*Syrinx aruanus* Linne), the *bu* shell of West Torres Strait. *Bu* shell was always given as an alternative name for *maber* during the translation of this story, so possibly *Syrinx aruanus* is to be understood.

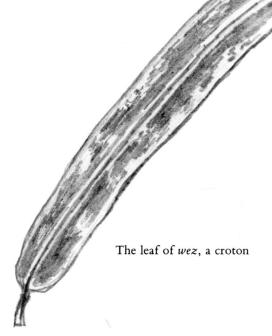

The leaf of *wez*, a croton

VERSION 3
[Told by Dela Mopwali at Murray Island, 16 February 1967]

A woman named Deo lived at Mei. At Wisu, not far from Mei, there lived two girls whose names were Te pipi and Te sabersaber.

Te pipi and Te sabersaber went up into the scrub behind Wisu one day and made an earth-oven at Mepau. Close beside it they lit a fire into which they threw *ager* to char. While they waited, they stood and watched the *ager*, pointing to them and saying: "*Kara nene kat tetitili! Muimui kat tetitili!* (Look! the hollow part at the top of my *ager* is burning!)"

The moon rose, and, seeing it, the girls were afraid. "*Ibi-ibi tagimtagim. Wez u barmer* (The moon is sick with rheumatism. He is dressed with croton leaves)," they said. As the moon rose higher, it looked at the

354

girls, and to them it appeared to be so close, that they snatched their *ager* from the fire and ran deeper into the scrub to escape from it.

They prepared another earth-oven and, after scraping away the charred skin of their *ager*, put them in it to cook.

Te pipi and Te sabersaber now felt thirsty, so they walked down to Wisu, slung their *nisor* over their shoulders and set out to fetch water from Er Pat. They saw Deo, who was sweeping the ground clear of pumice at her place at Mei—some of the pumice she swept towards Gazir, some in the opposite direction towards Leiwag—and asked her to go with them and fill her *nisor*. Deo, however, refused to accompany them, saying that she had plenty of water; so they went by themselves.

Te pipi and Te sabersaber roasting *ager* in their earth-oven

Artist Segar Passi

As they disappeared from Deo's sight around Gazir Pit, Deo changed her mind about going to Er Pat and, snatching up her *nisor*, hurried after Te pipi and Te sabersaber. But by the time she reached Gazir Pit, the two girls were already at Wabkik. When she reached Wabkik, they were at Eger, at which place they looked back and saw Deo. "There's Deo coming with her *nisor*—she lied to us," they said. They walked on without her, continuing along the beach until they arrived at the mouth of Er Pat. From there they walked upstream to the waterhole.

Deo caught up with them as they were filling their *nisor*. "That water is dirty, not fit to be drunk," she told them. "I am going further up to get water."

She climbed up to Kokaper, sat down beside the waterhole and lowered her *nisor* into the water. They began to fill with a gurgling sound: "Bu-bu-bu-bu-bu."

Now a man named Iruam lived at the bottom of the well at Kokaper and he heard Deo's *nisor* filling. He echoed, "Bu-bu-bu-bu," and came up to see who was taking his water. "Who are you?" he asked Deo. "Who are you?" Deo asked Iruam. Iruam then made advances to Deo, but she would have nothing to do with him and, snatching up her *nisor*, ran away. Iruam chased her.

Deo stumbled down the hillside, *nisor* clattering as they bumped against each other. She fell, and they broke. When she reached the beach at Er, she ran straight out across the reef to the wall of the stone fish-trap. Iruam threw a stone at her from the foot of the trap.[14] Deo jumped over the wall of the fish-trap and, skirting its outside edge, ran towards her home. When she came to the end of the fish-trap outside Er, she followed round the next fish-trap, and the next, and the next, until she reached Leiwag. Sometimes she had to halt to draw breath, but Iruam was always close behind her, throwing stones at her, to drive her on. From Leiwag she ran back to Mei, when she was seen by Te pipi and Te sabersaber.

Te pipi and Te sabersaber ran and got three *pesur*, one each for themselves, and one for Deo, which they threw to the beach for her. While Deo was running to pick it up, they ran straight to Iruam and began to beat him with their *pesur*. Deo joined them, and then the three of them beat him until he lay on his back, half-dead.

Iruam urinated twice—the first time towards the reef outside Las where, as a result, the big lagoon, Au Keper, formed; the second time into the scrub behind Las, where a waterhole came into existence.

Presently Iruam managed to escape from the girls. He ran out across the reef and jumped into a shell (*keret*) to try and hide from them. But the girls found him and cracked the shell with stones. He ran away and jumped into a spider shell (*asor*). When the girls cracked the spider shell,

14. Close to the beach.

356

he jumped into a trochus shell (*nazir*). When they cracked the trochus shell, he jumped into a helmet shell (*as*). From the helmet shell he fled to a *bu*[15] shell (*maber*) and at last escaped from the girls and Deo by crawling away, with the shell still on his back, into a narrow opening (*waiwer*) in the sandstone at the edge of the reef. There he could not be reached.

Deo and Te pipi and Te sabersaber tried in vain to smash the coral and sandstone which protected him. They kept at it until they stood waist-deep in the water of the incoming tide and were forced to go back to the shore.

Eventually, Iruam's body became a *bu* shell which was discovered by a man named Adba.

15. The Australian Trumpet Shell (*Syrinx aruanus* Linne).

ADBA

PART I

[Told by Bai Day at Murray Island, 14 June 1968]

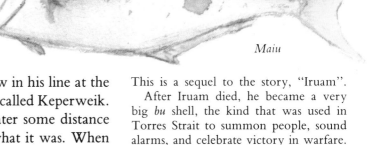

Maiu

Adba lived at Korog.

One day he went fishing for *maiu*,[1] but before he threw in his line at the edge of the reef, he drove an *elukaz*[2] into the reef at a spot called Keperweik.

Presently he saw something white floating on the water some distance out from where he stood, but he could not make out what it was. When it came closer, however, he saw that it was a *bu* shell. He coiled his fishing line into the palm of his hand, took it to the *elukaz* and hung it on one of the arms, and then he went back and swam to the *bu* shell. He caught it, returned to the *elukaz*, which he pulled up, and walked in to his home on the beach above the high-water mark. There he drove the *elukaz* into the sand and hung the *bu* shell on it.

The next morning he removed the *bu* shell from the *elukaz* and took it with him when he walked up to Karem. There he blew it; but no one answered his call. He walked further, to higher ground at Arpet, and blew again. This time there were answering calls from *bu* shells at Mene, Bak, Zer, and Kabur.

Adba thought: "This *bu* is a good thing to own." So he placed it on a small mound of stones at Arpet and afterwards returned to his home on the beach at Korog.

Thereafter, whenever he went up to garden, he always went to Arpet as well, picked up the *bu* and blew it. And every time he did this, *bu* shells replied from Mene, Bak, Zer, and Kabur.

This is a sequel to the story, "Iruam".

After Iruam died, he became a very big *bu* shell, the kind that was used in Torres Strait to summon people, sound alarms, and celebrate victory in warfare. This shell is still carefully preserved at Arpet, on land which is owned by a member of the Day family.

1. *Maiu*, golden trevally. This fish is said to be caught by Komet people. Adba was a Komet man.
2. *Elukaz*, the branch of a tree, stripped of its leaves and small twigs, which is driven into the reef and used as a hanger for the fish which a man catches.

PART II

[**Told by Bai Day at Murray Island, 15 August 1968**]

Adba had two wives. They were sisters.

One day he said to them: "You stay here. I am going to Las to attend a *zogo*[3] ceremony.

After he had gone, the younger sister said to the elder: "I am going up to the garden at Meuz to get some food." And she took up her knife and went off. Her real reason for going to Meuz, however, was different from what she had told her sister: she went there to keep an appointment with a man.

The two met as planned. When the man was about to leave Meuz, he plucked a *miwar*[4] leaf and tied it round his neck. Then he went down to Las to attend the same ceremony as Adba. The moment he entered the *zogo* place, the leaf at his neck was noticed by Adba, who thought: "*Miwar* grows at Meuz. Can you have been there with one of my wives?"

The ceremony at Las at an end, Adba returned to Korog. He asked the elder of the two sisters who were his wives: "Has either of you been up to the garden at Meuz?" And when she replied that her sister had been there to get food, Adba knew that his suspicions were well-founded.

He told the younger wife to clean their place.

She went into the house[5] to clean there first. Outside, Adba made a loud noise in order to startle her. Hearing it, she jumped and uttered her sweetheart's name. So Adba had proof that what he had previously believed to be the case was, indeed, fact.

He took his *seuriseuri*[6] and went to the house, where he straddled the entrance, standing with his back against the wall.

The woman finished cleaning inside the house, her last job being to put the ashes from the fireplace in a basket. This done, she pushed the basket through the doorway and began to crawl out after it. Adba struck the back of her head with his club. The older wife burst into tears.

Adba picked up the body and carried it into the scrub behind. There he prepared an earth-oven, butchered his dead wife, and set her flesh to cooking.

Now Adba had a cousin who lived at Begeigiz, and about the time that Adba began to be busy in the bushes at the back of his house, the thought of Adba came into this man's mind. So, spear in hand, he set out for Korog. Adba's wife saw him approaching, stopped crying, and wiped her eyes. She greeted him and asked what brought him there. "I was sitting alone at my place, when the thought of Adba came into my head. I came to see his face," the man told her.

3. The Malo *zogo*.
4. *Miwar, Acalypha wilkesiana.*
5. It was a round, bee-hive type house. It had one small door through which one entered or left by crawling on all fours.
6. *Seuriseuri*, club with rayed stone head. It takes its name from its resemblance to the starfish, which also bears the name *seuriseuri*.

The woman said: "Adba speared a *Peibri sor*.[7] He took it into the scrub behind to bake in an *amei*. I don't know how he is getting on. Go and see him."

When Adba saw his cousin coming towards him, he stood up, walked to him, took his hand, and said: "Come! I caught a big fish. We'll eat it." The two men sat down and began to eat.

The cousin noticed some hair on the meat. "I think we are eating human flesh," he thought to himself. "You must have killed someone—your younger wife, perhaps." He felt sick.

He stood up and said to Adba: "*Negwam*,[8] I'm going home now."

Adba told him to take some of the meat with him for his evening meal, but the cousin replied, "You can have it," picked up his spear, and went back to Begeigiz.

Adba ate for a while longer before returning to his house.

7. *Peibri sor*, Spotted Eagle-ray (*Aetobatus narinari* [Euphrasen]).
8. *Negwam*, cousin. A brother's children and his sister's children address each other by the term *negwam*.

BILA [Told by Harry Captain at Thursday Island, 26 July 1969]

One *naiger* season,[1] Bila, a bow-legged man who lived at Teg on the island of Dauar, was visited every day while he was planting in his garden by five small brown birds.[2] They used to perch on the branch of a tree, cock their heads to one side, and coo to him.

After a while Bila began to think the birds must be spirits, though he did not grasp the full truth, that they were spirit girls who had changed their form to that of *koko* because they had fallen in love with him and wanted to be able to see him and watch him at close quarters.

One night the five girls visited Bila at his house. "What do you want?" he asked them. And when the eldest girl said that she wished to be his wife, he accepted the proposal and told her she might stay with him. The other girls then left.

Bila's wife became pregnant. He then took her to Tikor on Waier, and the pair set up house amongst the people of that place.

A male child was born to Bila and his wife. When the boy was able to talk and run about, he played with the other children at Tikor.

Harry Captain of Darnley Island (Erub) had this story from Poi Passi of Murray Island (Mer). Dolly Passi, Poi Passi's daughter, knew the precise location of the setting—Teg, a sandspit on Dauar, and Tikor, a small beach on Waier, the island adjacent to Dauar. These details have been added to Harry Captain's story, which should be compared with the story, "The Lamar Who Became a Rainbow", told at Stephens Island (Ugar).

Bila is the Meriam name for the blue tusk-fish, *Choerodon albigena* (De Vis).

1. *Naiger*, north-east wind. There are really only two prevailing winds in Torres Strait—*koki*, the north-west wind, and *sager*, the south-east wind. At the time of year when *naiger* blows, the south-east wind has begun to abate, there are periods of calm, and the wind sometimes veers to the north-east. Planting begins in the gardens at the onset of *naiger*.
2. *Koko*, a little smaller than *deumer*, the Torres Strait pigeon. See also footnote 5 of "Nilar Makrem", in this section.

It was nor'-west time,[3] and one day while Bila's wife was fishing on the reef along with the other women of Tikor, a heavy black rain-cloud came towards Waier. Seeing it, some of the women called out: "Come on! We'd better go home." Bila's wife continued to fish. "You go," she said. "I'll stay a little longer."

At Tikor, Bila was calling to his son: "Come home. Run!" The boy took no notice of his father. The other children left him and ran to their homes for shelter. Bila became angry. "Come on, you spirit-child (*lamar-werem*)! Hurry up!" he ordered.

Although Bila's wife was a long way off, she knew that her husband had addressed their child as *"lamar werem"*. Immediately she coiled her fishing line. The rain-squall was almost upon her by that time, and she went inside it to Tikor.

A fierce wind came with the rain and blew Bila's house away, leaving Bila lying on the ground at the spot where it had previously stood.

And at the same time, the spirit-child, who had refused to return at his father's bidding, was swallowed by the "rain-black"[4] and snatched by his mother. Together, spirit-woman and spirit-child were taken by the cloud to the spirit-land. Bila never saw either of them again.

3. The season of the north-west monsoon.
4. "Rain-black" is Torres Strait pidgin for a visibly moving cloud from which rain is seen to be falling.

GANOMI AND PALAI   [Told by Tat Mabo at Murray Island, 3 March 1967]

Ganomi and his younger brother, Palai, were warriors who lived at Umar in Peibri, a district of Mer. They were visited one day by Badwei of Zeub, a village in the neighbouring district, Komet, who came without sending word beforehand.[1]

When Badwei arrived, the brothers knocked down a coconut for him, opened it with a *wisker* (the rib of a coconut palm leaf), and gave it to him to drink from. As he drank with distended throat, Ganomi and Palai signalled to each other with their eyes to decide which of them should kill him. Ganomi, as the elder brother, wanted to do it, but Palai did not wait. He picked up his *gabagaba* and struck at Badwei's throat. In his haste he missed his aim but knocked the coconut from Badwei's mouth to the ground.

1. A man from another clan would visit only his connections by blood or by marriage. If he set foot outside his relative's place, he would be killed.

360

Badwei took to his heels, with Ganomi and Palai in hot pursuit. They caught up with him at Umar Pit, where they struck at the base of his skull from behind. The Komet men, who were holding a drive (*gir*) to catch sardines with their scoops, saw Ganomi and Palai kneeling on the beach, face to face, one on either side of Badwei, with their *gabagaba* raised. They knew the sign—their kinsman lay eating sand: Badwei was dead.

The brothers ran home, armed themselves, and made for the cliff above Serwaged, where they sat down and rolled the stone edges of their *gabagaba* crabwise, from side to side, across the ledge at the top of the wall of rock.

When the Komet men arrived to avenge Badwei, they shot arrows up at Ganomi and Palai from the bottom of the cliff. But the brothers were in a commanding position and could not be reached, so the Komet men at length returned to their homes.

Ganomi and Palai waited at Serwaged until it grew dark. Then they came down to the beach, made a raft by tying together drifted logs, and paddled across to Dadamud, on the island of Dauar, where an old man, Gazim, a kinsman of theirs, was line-fishing on the shore.

Gazim rolled up his line and walked backwards from the approaching raft until he and Ganomi and Palai had recognized each other and exchanged greetings. The brothers beached their raft, after which Gazim took them to his home.

News of the brothers' visit to Dauar spread to the villages of Ormi and Teg, and to the neighbouring islet of Waier, where Dauareb also lived. These people told Gazim that they wished to kill his guests. Gazim replied that Ganomi and Palai were his kinsmen and that they stayed with him as long as they wished.

At Mer, meanwhile, the Komet men had visited the Malo *zogo* at Gazir, and a course of action had been plotted which would be fitting recompense for the murder of Badwei.

They sent Paradi to visit Ai Tibei, father of Ganomi and Palai, who lived in the cave, Nawaiub, a short distance from the summit of Gelam hill.

Paradi was welcomed by Ai Tibei who spread a mat for him and brought out a roll of tobacco for them to smoke. Ai Tibei climbed a coconut palm and knocked down a coconut. He opened it with a *wisker* and gave it to his guest for drink.

At length Paradi spoke: "Let us go to Kabur where the men are roasting and eating *iger*[2] (a nut)."

To this Ai Tibei agreed, asking only that Paradi wait until he made ready. He went inside his cave, put on his *bisiwam*[3] and head-dress of cassowary feathers, and took up a bundle of arrows and a bow, and then the two men set out.

At the hill called Ai Paser, Ai Tibei looked back towards Nawaiub.

2. *Iger* (*Semecarpus australiensis*), the tar-tree, closely related to the cashew nut tree.
3. *Bisiwam*, fringed skirt of sago leaf obtained from New Guinea.

When he saw that the shadow of Gelam covered the entrance to the cave which was his home, and the *ketai* and *kakidgaba* (yams) which grew outside, tears fell from his eyes, for he knew he looked at it for the last time.

At Mair, Paradi and Ai Tibei called to the men waiting at Kabur. Hearing this, they hid Gado, who had been chosen to kill Ai Tibei because he never missed in his aim. They sat down, placing themselves in such a manner that when Ai Tibei should join them, he would have his back to the bushes behind which Gado was concealed.

Paradi and Ai Tibei called again as they climbed the hill called Korkor. Soon afterwards they reached Kabur, where mats were spread for them.

A *zub* (bamboo pipe) was prepared, and when Ai Tibei had smoked, he was given a coconut to drink from.

As he raised it to his lips, Gado sprang out from the bushes. He shouted, "*Gado beizam* (I am Gado the shark)", implying that he never missed his prey, and thrust his *kusbager* into Ai Tibei's back, the tip coming out near his heart.

Ai Tibei struggled to pick up his bow and arrows, but the men at Kabur fell upon him and pinioned him. At this Ai Tibei tapped his forehead with his right hand to signify that not one of them would have beaten him in fair fight. Then he struggled no more.

The men at Kabur broke Ai Tibei's neck. When he was dead, they removed his jawbone, then covered his body with leaves. They took the jawbone to the Malo *zogo* at Gazir, then returned to their homes.

News of the killing of their father reached Ganomi and Palai at Dauar a few days later. The brothers passed word of it to Giar, Ormi, Teg, and Waier-Dauareb.

All these men gathered at Dadamud, to be told that Ganomi and Palai needed their help at Mer. Seven canoes set out, some landing at Serwaged, some at Gigo. After beaching the canoes, the men followed Ganomi and Palai to Seugiz, where Genamai, head man of the Komet people lived. The brothers thrust their *kusbager* through the walls of his house.

When Genamai asked who attacked him in the manner of women digging up *keupai* (a fish which buries itself in the sand),[4] the brothers gave their names.

Genamai spoke: "I have stayed here alone, being old and sick. I did not visit the Malo *zogo*. I had no part in the plot to kill Ai Tibei. There is no quarrel between you and me."

Ganomi and Palai withdrew their *kusbager*, and went on to Nane Pat with the Dauareb following behind. From there they went to Kabur, where they saw blowflies swarming around a spot that was covered with leaves. They uncovered the body of Ai Tibei and wept.

The men made a *paier* (a stretcher made from poles of bamboo or wood),

4. *Keupai*, bar-checked Wrasse (*Novaculichthys taeniourus*).

placed Ai Tibei's body on it, and carried it back to Begeigiz. There they laid the old warrior in scrub on his own land, and when they had made all decent and orderly, they came away.

Ganomi and Palai then escorted the Dauareb to their canoes and sent them home. They themselves returned to Umar, and there they lived until they died.

NILAR MAKREM

[Told by Moses Sagigi at Murray Island, 22 August 1968]

The *Zagareb le*[1] who lived at Wao[2] also had homes on the high ground at Kabur where they sometimes stayed. One of these people was a man named Gir,[3] a sorcerer. He did not fear ghosts.

At low tide one night when the people of Wao were at Kabur, Gir lit a torch of pandanus wood and went down to look for fish in his stone trap. He left the torch standing outside his house when he walked out to the reef.

After he had speared some fish, he ran them through from gill to mouth on one of the prongs of his spear, raised the spear to his shoulder, and walked in to the beach. On reaching his house he heard snores coming from it. He stood very still and listened for a while, and then he leaned his spear against the wall of the house, picked up the torch, and crawled through the doorway—to find *nilar makrem* asleep on the sand floor.

No one had ever before seen the *nilar makrem*, and Gir now observed that they were very handsome, young men: they had beautifully-shaped,

Nilar makrem were the spirits (*lamar*) associated with *puleb zogo*, *puleb* being small figures of men and fish and animals, rudely carved from pumice and lava. The *puleb* are the *nog* (form) of the *nilar makrem*, the form taken by the *nilar makrem*. I could find no one who knew the significance of *puleb zogo*, and no one who had any memory of ritual associated with this *zogo*. Nor could anyone tell me the exact meaning of *nilar makrem*. *Makrem* are bachelors; *nilar* is the name given to a pointed object—a nail would be called *nilar*, for example. *Puleb zogo* was at Leiwag.

The *nilar makrem* were once seen by a man named Gir. They were never seen by anyone else.

1. *Zagareb le*, people who belonged to the territorial division of Zagareb.
2. Wao is more generally known today as Ulag, which is a corruption of "Woodlark", a three-masted bêche-de-mer fishing vessel which operated from Mer and Dauar, probably during the mid 1860's. Some Murray Islanders one day "made a rough model of a ship in the sand beach at Wao and stuck three sticks in it for masts, and since then that place has been called Ulag ("Woodlark")." (*Reports*, VI, 190.)
3. Gir had two other names—Madi and Sek.

Baur (fish-spear)

long, straight noses, and their bodies shone as if they had been rubbed with oil. They had slung their *basor*[4] over the ends of the rafters.

Gir took one of the *basor* and buried it in a hole in the sand. After that, he lay down between two of his strange visitors and slept.

In the middle of the night the scent of the human in their midst woke the *nilar makrem*. They would have left the house at once; only, one of them could not find his *basor*. He searched for it for a long time, but in the end gave up, and the *nilar makrem* then departed. By that time it was almost dawn.

Gir woke soon afterwards and saw no trace of his visitors. The *nilar makrem* might never have slept at his place—cobwebs stretched unbroken; the sand floor was marked only by tracks made by hermit crabs. He dug up the *basor*, put his spear with the fish on it over his shoulder, and set off for Kabur.

He had not gone far when two cuckoos[5] flew to his spear, removed two fish from the prong on which they had been threaded, then let them fall from their beaks. Gir picked up the fish, put them back on his spear, and continued on his way. But the cuckoos returned again and again, each time snatching two fish. Immediately after they did this, Gir picked up the fish, returned them to the prong of his spear, and walked on.

4. *Basor*, the shells of dry coconuts when used to carry and store water. They are always carried in pairs, the connecting string between two shells being worn over the shoulder.
5. The Meriam word for these birds is *koko*. The people of Murray Island call them cuckoos when they speak English. I did not see the birds for myself at Murray Island.

Two of the many *puleb* at Leiwag, Murray Island, rudely worked pumice figures which are said to be the *nog* adopted by the *nilar makrem*
(Left), a fish; (right), a man

Back at Kabur, he gave the fish to the people and showed them the *basor* that he had stolen from his visitors of the night before. He described the appearance of the *nilar makrem* and gave the *basor* to a little girl named Pasi for a plaything.

Without warning, a small stormcloud burst overhead, and rain poured down. The people ran to their houses for shelter. Pasi left her new toy behind on the ground. When the shower ended and the people came outside, the *basor* had vanished.

PASLAG

[Told by Mrs. Jessie Sagigi at Murray Island, 22 August 1968]

Madi[1]—the man who saw the *nilar makrem*—was sitting at his place at Ulag a few days after the woman Paslag died when he was visited by her *lamar*.[2] He recognized her as Paslag, even though she had taken the face of a woman whom he knew to be alive. Paslag asked him for some of his fire, saying that her own had gone out.

He stared at her and said: "You're not a real woman. You're a *lamar*." To which Paslag replied: "You are wrong. I am a flesh-and-blood woman. I came here to ask you for fire."

Madi said: "You are a *lamar*. Your feet are not touching the ground. Your eyes are like *materkurup*."[3]

Paslag repeated what she had said before, that she was a living woman and had come for fire. Madi lit the husk of a dry coconut and gave it to her, and she then left him.

He watched her as she walked away and, when she glanced back at him, said: "You are Paslag. Your feet are not touching the ground. Your eyes are like *materkurup*."

Paslag walked along the beach and went up at Leiwag (not far from Wao).

Soon afterwards, Madi heard the laughter of many voices in the scrub behind Leiwag. It was the sound that was always heard after a *lamar* had failed in an attempt to hoax a human. Paslag's *lamar* companions were laughing at her.

1. This man had three names: Madi, Sek, and Gir.
2. *Lamar*, a ghost. From *le ra mar*, person's shadow, or reflection.
3. *Materkurup*, the periwinkle-blue flowers of the plant, *mater* (Wandering Jew).

Ib was believed by those who had not been initiated into the cult of Malo-Bomai to be a kind of male ghost who went from village to village on Murray Island making the sound called *ibkep*.

Ibkep consists of slapping sounds—in imitation of the sound made by Malo as octopus. Thus: "making *ib* (*ib ikimri*)" was a sacred ritual of the cult, to be hidden from the uninitiated. The secrecy required for the performance of the ritual was obtained through the notion of Ib, the ghost.

Initiates spread word during the daytime that Ib would be abroad in certain villages that night. This had the effect of keeping indoors all who were uninitiated, and of ensuring privacy for the ritual, sacred re-enactment of the sounds made by Malo as octopus.

Recorded here is the story of a woman who spied on Ib.

1. The *Zogo le* were those men who had advanced through the cult of Malo-Bomai to the final degree, that of wearing the sacred masks. To Bai, the *zogo le* were Malo *zogo le*. To her, as to all the uninitiated, Malo stood for protection and peace. No one who was uninitiated knew that behind Malo lurked Bomai who was always ready to strike secretly, savagely, and ruthlessly at anyone who either penetrated the sacred mysteries, or broke the rules, of the cult.
2. *Tami le* were the fully initiated members of the Malo-Bomai cult who gave effect to instructions issued by the *zogo le*.
3. *Maid*, sorcery. Here, the form of sorcery used by members of the

One day, when word got round that Ib would walk that night, a woman named Bai who lived at Warwei was so afraid that she went to stay with relatives at the village of Las. There she would be safe, she thought, for she would have the protection of the *zogo le*[1] whose headquarters it was.

When Ib was heard at Las that night, Bai, who was hiding inside a house with other women and a boy named Mabo, poked her finger through the thatch of the wall and peeped through the hole she had made. She recognized Ib as men she knew!

"There's Baton, and Guiai, and Wano!" she whispered to the women—and she named others, too. "The men have been fooling us. Men have been making *ib*, pretending to be ghosts."

In the morning, Bai said to the men at Las: "You've been frightening us all this time by making us believe you were ghosts. But I saw you last night. It was you, Mamai, you, Wano, Baton, Guiai." And she went on to name every man whom she had seen. The men flashed glances at each other.

Afterwards they talked and made a plan: as the first move, Wano was to take Bai—she was a close relative of his—to his garden at Teiri.

So presently Wano, his wife, Kak, and Bai left for Teiri, and there the three of them began to clean the land of weeds. After a while they felt thirsty, so Wano suggested that they go to Tar, which was not far away, where he told Bai to climb a coconut palm and knock down some coconuts for drink. Bai refused. At this, Kak ran away into the scrub, leaving Bai alone with Wano: Kak had been told by her husband that Bai was to be punished for betraying the secret of Ib.

The *tami le*[2] who were in hiding at Tar looked at each other. It was time to act.

They ran out from the bushes and grabbed hold of Bai, demanding that she give herself to them; when she would not, they commenced the process of *maid*[3] on her, squeezing her windpipe until she dropped to the ground unconscious. They were, however, unable to complete every stage of *maid* before Bai regained consciousness, and had only just forced "poison" down her throat when Bai struggled free and ran away.

The *tami le* chased her, but they could not catch her; they threw stones at her, but they missed in their aim. One man, Gasu, left the path and took a shortcut through the bushes to get in front of her and block her. At Nargiz he came back to the path ahead of Bai and stood waiting for her. She tried to dodge round a *sem* tree. Gasu threw a stone at the back of her head, killing her instantly.[4]

The *tami le* took Bai back to Tar and placed her body at the foot of a coconut palm. One of them climbed it, stripped off leaves and coconuts and threw them to the ground. These the *tami le* arranged over and around Bai to make it appear that she had died of a fall while knocking down coconuts. They returned to Las.

After Wano and Kak had drunk from coconuts at Tar, they, too, returned to Las.

The day Bai was killed she was missed by her people at Warwei, who, when they could not find her in the village, went to Las to inquire if she was there. Wano and Kak told them that Bai had gone with them to their garden at Teiri and had run away from them.

The people of Warwei searched for Bai until they found her. They carried her body home; and, as soon as the men had armed, they set off to avenge her. At Gazir Pit they began to fire arrows at the men of Las.

Koit of Las stepped out to meet the men of Warwei. "The woman spoiled our *zogo*,"[5] he called to them. "She told its secret to some of the women."

Immediately, the men of Warwei stopped firing arrows and walked to Las, where they sat down and smoked and talked.

The women and the boy, Mabo, who had been with Bai the night that she learned about Ib, kept still tongues in their heads until after the missionaries arrived in 1871. Bai talked, so she died.

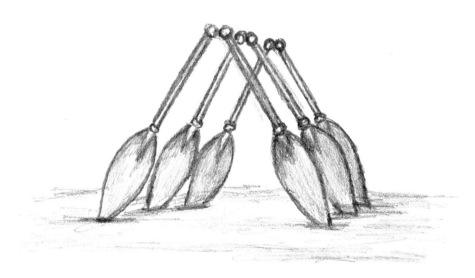

3. (*continued*)

Malo-Bomai cult to kill outsiders who penetrated sacred rites. It is said to have proceeded by stages. Briefly, these were: startling the intended victim, overpowering him, throttling him unconscious, administering "poison", erasing from his mind all memory of the attack—this, to the accompaniment of a chanted formula which began with the words, "Malo-Bomai"—and finally, after the victim had regained consciousness and was on his way home, again startling him. The victim invariably died some days later; nothing could prevent him from dying. Before death he manifested physical symptoms characteristic of all people who died by this type of *maid*; after death his body showed signs which were always found on people who had been *maided* in the name of Malo-Bomai.

It is also said that *maid le* needed to concentrate to the degree of excluding everything else from their minds when they were performing *maid*, and they must have observed sexual continence for a certain period beforehand. A pregnant wife precluded the successful performance of *maid*.

For an early account of this type of *maid*, see *Reports*, VI, 222–25, 300.

4. Since Bai recovered consciousness before the details of the attack had been erased from her mind, and since, had she reached home, she could have identified her attackers as the men who had been masquerading as Ib the previous night, she had to be killed at all costs. *Maid* had failed, so another means was used.

5. The practice of *ib*.

APPENDIX

The myth that follows belongs to Badu, I understand, but it appears to have been forgotten at that island. I heard it by accident, several months after I had handed my MS to the publishers, when I revisited Murray Island.

NORINORI [Told by Sarou Billy at Murray Island, 30 July 1970]

One evening an old man, Sarou Billy, came and sang old songs for me, and one of them, an *ikok*—a traditional dance-song, sung with tears in the voice—was of haunting beauty. Sarou said that the words had been sung originally by Norinori, the sacred snake ancestor (*tabo augad*), and he then went on to tell me the story of this mythical being. Tom Dau of Murray Island had heard it about seventy years ago as a young man when he was working on a lugger. Before he died he told it to Sarou Billy who had heard Norinori's song at Kubin (on Mua) nearly fifty years ago from an old man who died soon afterwards.

Haddon obtained a version of this story (see *Reports*, V, pp. 62-64) which is somewhat different from that told at Murray Island, 30 July 1970. Sarou told his story in Meriam. Sam Passi helped with the translation.

For many years Norinori, a big snake, lived at Paira (Cape York).

Norinori did not obtain his food on land. Instead, he used to lie watching the sea and, when he saw a canoe, swim out to it, sink it, and swallow all the people who had been aboard it. And then he used to sing:

> *Tabo ngai ad (ia),*
> *(A) kai ad (ia).*
> *Wa, tabo ngai ad (ia),*
> *(E) (a) kai ad (ia) O!*
> (I am the sacred ancestor snake. Yes, I am *tabo* [snake], great ancestor, sacred ancestor.)

The day came when Norinori decided to leave Paira and go to Tuined (Possession Island). There, too, he obtained his food from the sea, sinking every canoe that came near and swallowing its people, afterwards singing:

> *Tabo ngai ad (ia),*
> *(A) kai ad (ia).*
> *Wa, tabo ngai ad (ia),*
> *(E) (a) kai ad (ia) O!*

From Tuined he went to Zuna (Entrance Island), from Zuna to Muralag (Prince of Wales Island), from Muralag to Nurupai (Horn Island), from Nurupai to Waiben (Thursday Island), from Waiben to Kiriri (Hammond Island), from island to island in the chain that extends northward from the southern mainland, and at each he left offspring.

At last Norinori reached Badu and, finding at Argan on the north-west side of the island a spot that pleased him, decided to settle. Now he made a large home for himself in the ground and came out only when he wanted food, which he caught either at Badu or at the neighbouring island, Mua. He could enter or leave his underground home by any one of many openings.

A party of women arrived at Argan from Mabuiag one day to cut pandanus leaves for weaving into mats. One, a woman named Staurab, chose to work by herself at some distance from the rest and, at the end of the day, was much later than they in returning to the beach. She did not know that Norinori had scented her.

After spending the night on the beach, the women set out again to cut pandanus leaves, Staurab, as on the previous day, going off by herself. Late in the afternoon when all the other women had long since shouldered their bundles and gone back to the beach, Staurab was still cutting leaves.

It was nearly dark when she stopped. She stooped to pick up her bundle—and saw Norinori's head and staring eyes.

Staurab screamed and took to her heels. Norinori withdrew into the ground and easily followed her pounding feet. And as she approached one of the entrances to his home he pushed his head through it and blocked her. Staurab turned and ran in another direction. Again Norinori followed her below ground, and again he prevented her from escaping him. She ran this way and that way, calling her husband's name: "Aburab! Aburab!"—but Norinori's head always popped up to cut off her retreat. Crazed with fear, breathless, exhausted, she at last collapsed. Then Norinori took her in his mouth and drew her into his home. There he set her down and watched her.

In the morning he left her. The woman needed food. He soon caught a small, speckled, brown ground-bird (*kor*), which he swallowed, and then he went to Mua to search for more food for himself and the woman.

Alone, Staurab explored Norinori's home. Presently she found a *kaip*.[1] Shell in hand, she began to scrape away the soil above her head, singing as she worked:

> *Aburab (a) Staurab (ia),*
> *Norinori (e) Norinori (ia).*

When Norinori returned in the evening he cooked the food he had caught during the day and gave Staurab the choicest parts.

Such was the pattern of the days that followed: in the morning the snake set out for Mua for food for himself and the woman; while he was gone the woman scraped away at the soil above her; in the evening the snake fed the woman well.

★

The Mabuiag women sailed home in their canoes, to be greeted on the beach by their husbands. Aburab said: "Where is Staurab?" The women told him that Staurab had cut pandanus leaves out of sight of them and had not rejoined them on the evening of the second day at Argan. They knew only that.

News of Staurab's disappearance spread to the other villages of Mabuiag. The men made ready their fighting gear and sailed to Badu. At Argan they formed into three columns with Aburab at the head of the tongue (*werut*), the shorter column in the middle of the formation (*atei*), and marched inland to Norinori's home.

They heard Staurab singing. Aburab stood above the sound of her voice. "Staurab!" he called. "Stamp your feet hard," his wife told him. And when Aburab stamped his feet the ground gave way beneath them, and he found himself standing beside Staurab. "There's no time to be lost,"

1. One half of the bivalve shell which was—and still is—used for grating and scraping coconut and roots of plants, and for cleaning the cloth-like fibre found at the base of coconut fronds.

said Staurab. "Norinori, the snake who caught me and kept me here, will soon be back from Mua." All set out for Argan at a run.

"Norinori will come swiftly through the air to take me from you," Staurab told her husband. "He will look like a big black cloud in the sky. Is he already coming?" Aburab glanced behind, but he could not see Norinori. Husband and wife ran on.

Norinori returning from Mua with food found his home spoiled and Staurab gone. He drew a red line from the middle of his forehead to the tip of his nose and another from the base of his right nostril diagonally down across his face to the point of his right jaw, and put on a small head-dress of feathers of the white reef heron.[2] Then he went up into the sky and set out in pursuit of the woman.

By that time Staurab and Aburab and the Mabuiag men were close to the beach at Argan. Eagles sitting in a tree nearby said: "Run your canoes into the water and sail home. Forget Norinori. We'll attend to him."

Two eagles flew to Norinori and grabbed him. One seized his head, the other his tail. They soared high in the air and winged north. And when Badu and Mabuiag had disappeared from sight and the coast of the northern mainland was plain to be seen, they dropped the great ancestor snake into the sea.

Norinori's body broke in three. His head became Dauan; his body, Saibai; his tail, Boigu.

2. The lines drawn by Norinori on his face were the *beizam* (shark) marking. The head-dress was a small *dari*.